Religion
Explained

Religion Explained

The human instincts that fashion gods, spirits and ancestors

Pascal Boyer

WILLIAM HEINNEMANN: LONDON

First published by William Heinemann in 2001

1 3 5 7 9 10 8 6 4 2

William Heinemann
The Random House Group Limited
20 Vauxhall Bridge Road, London SW1V 2SA

Random House Australia (Pty) Limited
20 Alfred Street, Milsons Point, Sydney,
New South Wales 2061, Australia

Random House New Zealand Limited
18 Poland Road, Glenfield,
Auckland 10, New Zealand

Random House South Africa (Pty) Limited
Endulini, 5A Jubilee Road,
Parktown 2193, South Africa

Random House Group Ltd Reg. No. 954009
www.randomhouse.co.uk

A CIP record for this book is available from the British Library

Papers used by Random House are natural, recyclable products made from wood grown in sustainable forests. The manufacturing processes conform to the environmental regulations of the country of origin

ISBN 0 434 00843 5

Typeset by SX Composing DTP, Rayleigh, Essex
Printed and bound in Great Britain by Biddles Ltd, Guildford and King's Lynn

Contents

Acknowledgements

That I should write this book was clear in the minds of my editors, Abel Gerschenfeld and Ravi Mirchandani, long before I had even started. I am grateful for their gentle prodding. Abel in particular showed great persuasive power, was patient enough to read many different versions, and always trusted me to produce something readable, a real triumph of hope over experience. I must also express my deep gratitude to a number of people whom I coaxed or coerced into imparting their knowledge and intuitions, perfecting or rejecting many versions of each argument, reading and correcting parts or even the whole of the original manuscript, and generally helping me better understand all these complicated issues: Anne de Sales, Brian Malley, Carlo Severi, Charles Ramble, Dan Sperber, E. Thomas Lawson, Harvey Whitehouse, Ilkka Pyssiäinen, John Tooby, Justin Barrett, Leda Cosmides, Michael Houseman, Paolo Sousa, Pascale Michelon, Robert McCauley and Ruth Lawson.

Chapter One

What is the origin?

A neighbour in the village tells me that I should protect myself against witches. Otherwise they could hit me with invisible darts that will get inside my veins and poison my blood.

A shaman burns tobacco leaves in front of a row of statuettes and starts talking to them. He says he must send them on a journey to distant villages in the sky. The point of all this is to cure someone whose mind is held hostage by invisible spirits.

A group of believers goes around warning everyone that the end is nigh. Judgement Day is scheduled for October the second. This day passes and nothing happens. People carry on telling everyone the end is nigh (the date has been changed).

Some villagers organise a ceremony to tell a goddess she is not wanted in their village any more. She failed to protect them from epidemics so they decided to 'drop' her and find a more efficient replacement.

An assembly of priests finds offensive what some people say about something which happened several centuries ago in a distant place, where a virgin is said to have given birth to a child. So these people must be massacred.

Members of a cult on an island decide to slaughter all their livestock and burn their crops. All these will be useless now, they say, because a ship full of goods and money will reach their shores very shortly, in recognition of their good deeds.

My friends are told to go to church or some other quiet place and talk to an invisible person who is everywhere in the world. That invisible listener already knows what they will say, because He knows everything.

I am told that if I want to please powerful dead people – people who could help me in times of need – I should pour the blood of a live white goat on the right-hand side of a particular rock. But if I use a goat of a different colour or another rock it will not work at all.

You may be tempted to dismiss these vignettes as just so many examples of the rich tapestry of human folly and to leave it at that. Or you perhaps think that these illustrations, however succinct – one could fill volumes with such accounts – bear witness to an admirable human capacity to comprehend life and the universe. Both reactions leave some questions unanswered. Why do people have such thoughts? What prompts them to do such things? Why do they have such different beliefs? Why are they so strongly committed to them? These questions used to be *mysteries* (we did not even know how to proceed) and are now becoming *problems* (we have some idea of a possible solution), to use Noam Chomsky's distinction. Indeed, we actually have the first elements of that solution. In case this sounds hubristic or self-aggrandising, let me add immediately that this 'we' really refers to a community of people. It is not an insidious way of suggesting that *I* have a new theory and find it of universal significance. In the rest of this book I mention a number of findings and models in cognitive psychology, anthropology, linguistics and evolutionary biology. All these were discovered by other people, most of whom did not work on religion and had no idea that their findings could help explain religion. This is why, although bookshelves may be overflowing with treatises on religion, histories of religion, religious people's accounts of their ideas, and so on, it makes sense to add to this and show how the intractable mystery that was religion is now just another set of difficult but manageable problems.

Giving airy nothing a local habitation

The explanation for religious beliefs and behaviours is to be found in the way all human minds work. I really mean *all* human minds, not just the minds of religious people or of some of them. I am talking about *human* minds because what matters here are properties of minds that are found in all members of our species with normal brains. The discoveries I will mention here are about the ways minds in general (men's or women's, British or Brazilian, young or old) function.

This may seem a rather strange point of departure if we want to explain something as diverse as religion. Beliefs are different in different people; some are religious and some are not. Also, obviously, beliefs are different in different places. Japanese Buddhists do not seem to share much, in terms of religious notions, with Amazonian shamans or American Southern Baptists. How could we explain a phenomenon (religion) that is so *variable* in terms of something (the brain) that is *the same* everywhere? This is what I shall describe in this book. The diversity of religion, far from being an obstacle to general explanations, in fact gives us some keys. But to understand why this is so, we need a precise description of how brains receive and organise information.

For a long time people used to think that the brain was a rather simple organ. Apart from the bits that control the body machinery, there seemed to be a vast empty space in the young child's mind destined to be filled with whatever education, culture and personal experience provided. This view of the mind was never too plausible, since even humble organs like the liver and the gut have a much more complex structure. We did not know much about the way minds develop, so there were no facts to get in the way of this fantasy of a 'blank slate' where experience could leave its imprint. The mind was like those vast expanses of unexplored Africa that old maps used to fill with palm-trees and crocodiles. Now we know more about minds. We do not know everything, but one fact is clear: The more we discover about how minds work, the less we believe in this notion of a blank slate. Every single discovery in cognitive science makes it less plausible as an explanation.

In particular, it is clear that our minds are not really prepared to acquire just about any kind of notion provided it is 'in the culture'. We do not *just* 'learn what is in the environment' as people sometimes say. That is not the case, because no mind in the world – this is true all the way from the cockroach to the giraffe to you or me – could ever learn anything without having a very sophisticated mental equipment that is prepared to identify relevant information in the environment and to treat that information in a special way. Our minds are prepared because natural selection gave us a very special kind of mind, with particular predispositions. Being prepared for some concepts, human beings are also prepared for certain kinds of variations around these concepts. As I will show, this means, among other things, that all human beings can easily acquire a certain range of religious notions and communicate them to others.

Does this mean religion is 'innate' and 'in the genes'? I – and most people interested in the evolution of the human mind – think that the question is in fact meaningless and that it is important to understand why. Consider other examples of human capacities. All human beings can catch colds and remember different melodies. We can catch colds because we have respiratory organs and these provide a hospitable site for all sorts of pathogens, including those of the common cold. We can remember tunes because a part of our brain can easily store a series of sounds with their relative pitch and duration. There are no common colds in our genes and no melodies either. What is in the genes is a tremendously complex set of chemical recipes for the building of normal organisms with respiratory organs and a complex set of connections between brain areas. Normal genes in a normal milieu will give you a pair of lungs and an organised auditory cortex, and with these the dispositions to acquire both colds and tunes. Obviously, if we were all brought up in a sterile and non-musical environment, we would catch neither. We would still have the disposition to catch them but no opportunity to do so.

Having a normal human brain does not imply that you have religion. All it implies is that you can acquire it, which is very different. The reason why psychologists and anthropologists are so concerned with *acquisition* and *transmission* is that evolution by natural selection gave us a particular kind of mind so that only particular kinds of religious notions can be acquired. Not all possible concepts are equally good. The ones we acquire easily are the ones we find widespread the world over; indeed, that is *why* we find them widespread the world over. It is said of poetry, that it gives to 'airy nothing' a local habitation and a name. The remark applies in fact much better to the supernatural imagination. But, as we will see, not all kinds of airy nothing will find a local habitation in the minds of people.

Origin scenarios

What is the origin of religious ideas? Why is it that we can find it wherever we go and, it would seem, as far back in the past as we can see? The best place to start is with our spontaneous, common-sense answers to the question of origins. Everybody seems to have some intuition about the origins of religion. Indeed, psychologists and anthropologists who like me study how mental processes create religion have to face this minor occupational hazard, that we constantly run into people who think that they already have a perfectly adequate solution to the problem. They are often quite willing to impart their wisdom and sometimes imply that further work on this question is, if not altogether futile, at least certainly undemanding. If you say 'I use genetic algorithms to produce computationally efficient cellular automata', people see quite clearly that doing that kind of thing probably requires some effort. But if you tell them that you are in the business of 'explaining religion', they often do not see what is so complicated or difficult about it. Most people have some idea of why there is religion, what religion gives people, why they are sometimes so strongly attached to their religious beliefs, and so on. These common intuitions offer a real challenge. Obviously, if they are sufficient there is no point in having a complex theory of religion. If, as I am afraid is more likely, they are less than perfect – then our new account should be at least as good as the intuitions it is supposed to replace.

Most accounts of the origins of religion amount to one of the following suggestions: human minds demand explanations, human hearts seek comfort, human society requires order, human intellect is illusion-prone. To express this in more detail, here are some possible scenarios:

Religion provides explanations:
> [1] People created religion to explain puzzling natural phenomena.
> [2] Religion explains puzzling experience: dreams, prescience, etc.
> [3] Religion explains the origins of things.
> [4] Religion explains why there is evil and suffering.

Religion provides comfort:
> [5] Religious explanations make mortality less unbearable.
> [6] Religion allays anxiety and makes for a comfortable world.

Religion provides social order:
> [7] Religion holds society together.
> [8] Religion perpetuates a particular social order.
> [9] Religion supports morality.

Religion is a cognitive illusion:
[10] People are superstitious, they will believe anything.
[11] Religious concepts are irrefutable.
[12] Refutation is more difficult than belief.

Though probably not exhaustive, the list is fairly representative. Discussing each of these common intuitions in more detail, we will see that they all fail to tell us why we have religion and why it is the way it is. So why bother with them? I am not trying here to ridicule other people's ideas or show that anthropologists and cognitive scientists are more clever than common folk. I discuss these spontaneous explanations because they are widespread, because they are often rediscovered by people when they reflect on religion, and more importantly because they are *not that bad*. Each of these 'scenarios' for the origin of religion points to a real and important phenomenon that any theory worth its salt should explain. Also, taking these scenarios seriously opens up new perspectives on how religious notions and beliefs appear in human minds.

Unfamiliar diversity

Let it not be said that anthropology is not useful. Religion is found the world over but it is found in very different forms. It is an unfortunate and all too frequent mistake to explain all religion by one of its characteristics, one that is in fact special to the religion we are familiar with. Anthropologists are professionally interested in cultural differences and they generally study a milieu other than their own to avoid this mistake. In the past century or so, they have documented extremely diverse kinds of religious notions, beliefs and practices. To illustrate why this knowledge is useful, consider the information you can find in an atlas. In the same way as it tells you that the Arctic is all ice and the Sahara mostly sand and rock, it often provides information about religious affiliation. You will read for instance that Ulster has a Protestant majority and the rest is Catholic, that Italy is overwhelmingly Catholic and Saudi Arabia Muslim. So far, so good. Some other countries are more difficult to describe in these terms. Take for instance India or Indonesia. Most of the population belongs to one of the familiar 'great religions' (Hindu, Muslim) but in both countries there are large so-called 'tribal' groups that will have no truck with these established denominations. These people are often described as having animistic or tribal religion, two terms which (anthropologists will tell you) mean virtually nothing. They just stand for 'stuff we cannot put in any other category', so that you might as well call these people's religions 'miscellaneous'. Also, what about Congo or Angola? The atlas says that most people in these places are mainly Christian and this is true in the sense that many are baptised and go to church. However, people in Congo and Angola constantly talk about ancestors and witches and perform rituals to placate the former and restrain the latter. This does not happen in Christian Northern Ireland. If the atlas says anything about religion it is using a very confusing notion of religion.

The diversity of religion is not just the fact that some people are called or call themselves Buddhist and others Baptist. It goes deeper: in how people conceive supernatural agents, what they think these agents are like or what they can do, in the morality that is derived from religious beliefs, in the rituals performed and in many other ways. Consider the following findings of anthropology:

Supernatural agents can be very different. Religion is about the existence and causal powers of non-observable entities and agencies. These may be one unique God or many different ones or spirits or ancestors or any combination of these different kinds. Some people have one 'supreme' god, but this does not always mean that he or she is terribly important. In many places in Africa there are two supreme gods. One is a very abstract supreme deity and the other is more down-to-earth, as it were, since he created all things cultural: tools and domesticated animals, villages and society. But neither of them is really involved in people's everyday affairs, where ancestors, spirits and witches are much more important.

Some gods die. It may seem obvious that gods are always thought to be eternal. We might even think that this must be part of the definition of 'god'. However, many Buddhists think that gods, just like humans, are caught in a never-ending cycle of births and reincarnations. So gods will die like all other creatures. This, however, takes a long time and that is why humans since time immemorial pray to the same gods. If anything, gods are disadvantaged in comparison with humans. Contrary to gods, we could, at least in principle, escape from the cycle of life and suffering. Gods must first be reincarnated as humans to do that.

Many spirits are really stupid. To a Christian it seems quite obvious that you cannot fool God. But in many places fooling superhuman agents is possible and in fact necessary. In Siberia for instance people are careful to use metaphorical language when talking about important matters. This is because nasty spirits often eavesdrop on humans and try to foil their plans. Spirits, despite their superhuman powers, just cannot understand metaphors. They are powerful but stupid. In many places in Africa it is quite polite when visiting friends or relatives to express one's sympathy with them for having such 'ugly' or 'unpleasant' children. The idea is that witches, always on the lookout for nice children to 'eat', will be fooled by this naïve stratagem. It is also common to give children names that suggest disgrace or misfortune, for the same reason. In Haiti one of the worries of people who had just lost a relative was that the corpse might be stolen by a witch. To avoid this people sometimes buried their dead with a length of thread and an eyeless needle. The idea was that witches would find the needle and try to thread it, which would keep them busy for centuries so they would forget all about the corpse. People can think that supernatural agents have extraordinary powers and yet are rather easily fooled.

Salvation is not always a central preoccupation. To people familiar with Christianity or Islam or Buddhism, it seems clear that the main point of religion is the salvation or deliverance of the soul. Different religions are thought to offer different perspectives on why souls need to be saved and different routes to salvation. Now in many parts of the world, religion does not really promise that the 'soul' will be saved or liberated and in fact does not have much to say about its destiny. In such places, people just do not assume that moral reckoning determines the fate of the soul. Dead people become ghosts or ancestors. This is general and does not involve a special moral judgement.

Official religion is not the whole of religion. Wherever we go, we will find that religious concepts are much more numerous and diverse than 'official' religion would admit. In many places in Europe people suspect that there are witches around trying to attack them. In official Islam there is no God but God, but many people are very much scared by *jinn* and *afreet*, spirits, ghosts and witches. In the United States religion is officially a matter of denomination: Christians of various shades, Jews, Hindus, etc. But many people are seriously engaged in interaction with aliens or ghosts. This must also be put among the religious concepts to consider and explain.

You can have religion without having 'a' religion. For Christians, Jews or Muslims it is quite clear that one belongs to *a* religion and that there is a choice, as it were, between alternative views on the creation of the universe, the destiny of the soul or the kind of morality one should adhere too. This results from a very special kind of situation, where people live in large states with competing Churches and doctrines. Many people, throughout history and today, live in rather different circumstances, where their religious activity is the only one that is conceivable. Also, many religious notions are tied to specific places and people. People for instance pray to their ancestors and offer sacrifices to the forest to catch lots of game. It would not make sense for you to pray to other people's ancestors or to be grateful for food that you will not receive. The idea of a universal religion that anyone could adopt (and that everyone should adopt) is not a universal idea.

You can also have religion without having 'religion'. We have a word for religion. This is a convenient label that we use to put together all the ideas, actions, rules and objects that have to do with the existence and properties of superhuman agents like God. Not everyone has this explicit concept or the idea that religious stuff is different from the profane or everyday domain. In general, you will find that people begin to have an explicit concept of 'religion' when they live in places with several 'religions'; but that is a special kind of place, as I said above. That people do not have a special term for religion does not mean they actually have no religion. In many places people have no word for 'syntax' but their language has a syntax all the same. You do not need the special term in order to have the thing.

You can have religion without 'faith'. Many people in the world would find it strange if you told them that they 'believe in' witches and ghosts or that they have 'faith' in their ancestors. Indeed, it would be very difficult in most languages to translate these sentences. It takes us Westerners some effort to realise that this notion of 'believing in something' is a rather peculiar one. Imagine a Martian told you how interesting it is that you 'believe' in mountains and rivers and cars and telephones. You would think the alien had got it wrong. We don't 'believe in' these things, we just notice and accept that they are around. Many people in the world would say the same about witches and ghosts. They are around like trees and animals – though they are far more difficult to understand and control – so it does not require a particular commitment or faith to notice their existence and act accordingly. In the course of my anthropological fieldwork in Africa I lived and worked with Fang people of Cameroon, who say that nasty spirits roam the bush and the villages, attack people, make them fall ill and ruin their crops. My Fang acquaintances also knew that I was not too worried about this and that most Europeans were remarkably indifferent to the powers of spirits and witches. This, for me, could be expressed as the difference between believing in spirits and not believing. But that was not the way people saw it over there. For them, the spirits were indeed around but white people were immune to their influence, perhaps because God cast them from a different mould or because Western people could avail themselves of efficient anti-witchcraft medicine. So what we often call 'faith', others may well call knowledge.[1]

The conclusion from all this is straightforward. If people tell you that 'religion is faith in a doctrine that teaches us how to save our souls by obeying a wise and eternal Creator of the universe', these people probably have not travelled or read enough. In many cultures people think that the dead come back to haunt the living but this is not universal. In some places people believe that certain special individuals can communicate with gods or dead people, but this idea is not found everywhere. In some places people assume that humans have a soul which survives after death, but this idea is not universal. When we put forward general explanations of religion, we had better make sure that they apply outside our parish.

Intellectual scenarios: the mind demands an explanation

Explanations of religion are scenarios. They describe a sequence of events in people's minds or in human societies, possibly over an immense span of historical time, that led to religion as we know it. But narratives are also misleading. In a good story one thing leads to another with such obvious logic that we may forget to check that each episode really occurred as described. So a good scenario may put us on the right track but also leave us stuck in a rut, oblivious of an easier or more interesting path that was just a few steps aside. This, as we will see, is precisely what happens with each general explanation of religion, which is why I will first describe their valuable points before suggesting that we step back a little and take a different path.

The most familiar scenario assumes that humans in general have certain general intellectual concerns. People want to understand events and processes, that is, to explain, predict and perhaps control them. These very general, indeed universal, intellectual needs gave rise to religious concepts at some point during human cultural evolution. This was not necessarily a single event, a sudden invention that took place once and for all. It might be a constant re-creation as the need to explain phenomena periodically suggests concepts that could work as good explanations. Here are some variations on this theme:

[1] *People created religion to explain puzzling natural phenomena.* People are surrounded by all sorts of phenomena that seem to challenge their everyday concepts. That a windowpane breaks if you throw a brick at it poses no problem. But what about the causes of storms, thunder, massive drought, floods? What 'pushes' the sun across the sky and moves the stars and planets? Gods and spirits fulfil this explanatory function. In many places the planets *are* gods; in Roman mythology thunder was the sound of Vulcan's hammer striking the anvil. More generally, gods and spirits make rains fall and fields yield good crops. They explain what is beyond the ken of ordinary notions.

[2] *Religion was created to explain puzzling mental phenomena.* Dreams, precognition, as well as the feeling that dead persons are still around in some form (and frequently 'appear' to the living), are all phenomena that receive no satisfactory explanation in our everyday concepts. The notion of a spirit seems to correspond to such phenomena. Spirits are disembodied persons and their characteristics make them very similar to persons seen in dreams or hallucinations. Gods and a unique God are further versions of this projection of mental phenomena.

[3] *Religion explains the origins of things.* We all know that plants come from seeds, animals and humans reproduce, etc. But where did the whole lot come from? That is, we all have common-sense explanations for the origin of each particular aspect of our environment but all these explanations do is 'pass the buck' to some other process or agent, and so on. However, people feel that the buck has to stop somewhere, and uncreated creators, like God or the first ancestors or some cultural heroes, fulfil this function.

[4] *Religion explains evil and suffering.* It is a common human characteristic that misfortune cries out for explanation. Why is there misfortune or evil in general? This is where the concepts of

Fate, God, devils, ancestors are handy. They tell you why and how evil originated in the world (and sometimes provide recipes for a better world).

What is wrong with these accounts? There are in fact several problems. We say that the origin of religious concepts is the urge to provide certain general aspects of human experience with a satisfactory explanation. Anthropologists have shown that (1) explaining such general facts is not equally pressing in all cultures and (2) the explanations provided by religion are not at all like ordinary 'explanations'.

Consider the idea that everybody wants to identify the general cause of evil and misfortune. This is not as straightforward as we may think. The world over, people are concerned with the causes of *particular* evils and calamities. These are considered in great detail but the existence of evil *in general* is not the object of much reflection. Let me use an example that is familiar to all anthropologists from their Introductory courses. The British anthropologist Evans-Pritchard is famous for his classic account of the religious notions and beliefs of the Zande people of Sudan. His book became a model for all anthropologists because it did not stop at cataloguing strange beliefs. It showed you, with the help of innumerable details, how *sensible* these beliefs were once you understood the particular standpoint of the people who expressed them and the particular questions those beliefs were supposed to answer. For instance, one day the roof of a mud-house collapsed in the village where Evans-Pritchard was working. People promptly explained the incident in terms of witchcraft. The people who were under that roof at the time must have powerful enemies. With typical English good sense, Evans-Pritchard points out to his interlocutors that termites had undermined the mud-house so there was nothing particularly mysterious in its eventual collapse. But people are not interested in this aspect of the situation. As they point out to the anthropologist, they know perfectly well that termites gnaw through the pillars of mud-houses and that decrepit structures are bound to cave in at some point. What they want to find out is why the roof collapsed *at the precise time* So-and-so was sitting underneath rather than before or after that. This is where witchcraft provides a good explanation. But what explains the existence of witchcraft? No one seems to find that a pertinent or interesting question. This is in fact a common situation in places where people have beliefs about spirits or witches. These agents' behaviour is an explanation of particular cases but no one bothers to explain the existence of misfortune in general.

More generally, the origin of things *in general* is not always the obvious source of puzzlement that we may imagine. As anthropologist Roger Keesing points out, describing myths of the Kwaio people in the Solomon Islands, 'ultimate human origins are not viewed as problematic. [The myths] assume a world where humans gave feasts, raised pigs, grew taro, and fought blood feuds', as happens now. What matters to people are *particular* cases in which these activities are disrupted, often by the ancestors or by witchcraft.[2]

But how does religion account for these particular occurrences? The explanations one finds in religion are often more puzzling than illuminating. Consider the explanation of thunderstorms as the booming voice of ancestors venting their anger at some human misdemeanour. To explain a limited aspect of the natural world (loud, rolling, thumping sounds during storms) we have to assume a whole imaginary world with superhuman agents (Where did they come from? Where are they?) that cannot be seen (Why not?) in a distant place that cannot be reached (How does the noise come through all the way?), whose voices produce thunder (How is that possible? Do they have special mouths? Are they gigantic?). Obviously, if you live in a place where this kind of belief is widespread, people may have an answer to all these questions. But then each answer requires a specific narrative which more often than not presents us with yet more superhuman agents or extraordinary occurrences, that is, with more questions to answer.

As another illustration, here is a short account of shamanistic ritual among the Cuna of Panama, by anthropologist Carlo Severi:

> The [shaman's] song is chanted in front of two rows of statuettes facing each other, beside the hammock where the patient is lying. These auxiliary spirits drink up the smoke whose intoxicating effect opens their minds to the invisible aspect of reality and gives them the power to heal. In this way [the statues] are believed to become themselves diviners.[3]

The patient in this ritual has been identified by the community as mentally disturbed, which is explained in religious terms. The soul of the person was taken away by evil spirits and it is now held hostage. A shaman is a specialist who can enlist auxiliary spirits to help him deliver the imprisoned soul and thereby restore the patient's health. Note how all this goes well beyond a straightforward explanation for aberrant behaviour. True, there is direct evidence of the patient's condition; but the evil spirits, the auxiliary spirits, the shaman's ability to journey through the spirits' world, the efficacy of the shaman's songs in his negotiation with the evil spirits, all this has to be postulated. To add to these far-fetched complications, the auxiliary spirits are in fact wood statuettes; these objects not only hear and understand the shaman, but they actually become diviners for the time of the ritual, perceiving what ordinary people cannot see.

An 'explanation' like that does not work in the same way as our ordinary accounts of events in our environment. We routinely produce explanations that (1) use the information available and (2) rearrange it in a way that yields a more satisfactory view of what happened. Explaining something does not consist in producing one thought after another in a free-wheeling sort of way. The point of an explanation is to provide a context that makes a phenomenon less surprising than before and in better agreement with the general order of things. Religious explanations often seem to work the other way around, producing more complication instead of less. As anthropologist Dan Sperber points out, religion creates 'relevant mysteries' rather than simple accounts of events. This leads to a paradox familiar to all anthropologists. If we say that people use religious notions to explain the world, this seems to suggest that they do not know what a proper explanation is. But that is absurd. We have ample evidence that they do know. People use the ordinary 'getting most of the relevant facts under a simpler heading' strategy all the time. So what people do with their religious concepts is not so much explain the universe as . . . well, this is where we need to step back and consider in more general terms what makes mysteries relevant.[4]

The mind as a bundle of explanation machines

Is it really true that human ideas are spurred by a general urge to understand the universe? Philosopher Immanuel Kant opened his *Critique of Pure Reason* (1781) – an examination of what we can know beyond experience – with the statement that human reason is forever troubled by questions it can neither solve nor disregard. Later, the theme of religion-as-an-explanation was developed by a school of anthropology called 'intellectualism', initiated by nineteenth-century scholars such as E. B. Tylor and James Frazer, and quite influential to this day. A central assumption of intellectualism was this: If a phenomenon is common in human experience and people do not have the conceptual means to understand it, then they will try and find some speculative explanation.[5]

Now, expressed in this blunt and general manner, the statement is plainly false. Many phenomena are both familiar to all of us from the youngest age and difficult to comprehend using our everyday concepts, yet nobody tries to find an explanation for them. For instance, we all know that our bodily movements are caused, not by external forces that push or pull us, but by our *thoughts*. That is, if I extend my arm and open my hand to shake hands with you, it's precisely because I want to do that. Also, we all assume that thoughts have no weight or size or other such material qualities (the idea of an apple is not the size of the apple, the idea of water does not flow, the idea of a rock is not more solid than the idea of butter). If I have the intention to lift my arm, to take a classic example, this intention itself has no weight or solidity. Yet it manages to move parts of my body. How can this occur? How could things without substance have effects in the material world? Or, to put it in less metaphysical terms, how on earth do these mental words and images pull my muscles? This is a difficult problem for philosophers and cognitive scientists – and surprisingly enough it is not a problem for anybody else in the entire world. Wherever you go, you will find that people are satisfied with the idea that thoughts and desires have effects on bodies and that's that. (Having raised such questions in English pubs and Fang villages in Cameroon I have good evidence that in both places people see nothing mysterious in the way their minds control their bodies. Why should they? It requires very long training in a special tradition to find the question interesting or puzzling.)

The mistake of intellectualism was to assume that a human mind is driven by a *general* urge to explain. That is not really plausible, no more than the idea that animals, as opposed to plants, feel a general 'urge to move around'. Animals never move about for the sake of changing places. They are in search of food or safety or sex; their movements in these different situations are caused by different processes. The same goes for explanations. From a distance, as it were, you may think that the general point of having a mind is to explain and understand. But if you look closer, you see that what happens in a mind is far more complex; this is crucial to understanding religion.

Our minds are not general explanation machines. Rather, minds consist in many different, specialised explanatory engines. Consider this: It is almost impossible to see a scene and not see it in three dimensions, because our brains cannot help explaining the flat images projected on to the retina as the effect of real volumes out there. If you are brought up among English speakers you just cannot help understanding what people say in that language, that is, explaining complex patterns of sound frequencies as strings of words. People spontaneously explain the properties of animals in terms of some inner properties that are common to their species; if tigers are aggressive predators and yaks quiet grazers, this must be because of their essential nature. We spontaneously assume that the shape of particular tools is explained by their designers' intentions rather than as an accidental combination of parts; the hammer has a sturdy handle and a heavy head because that is the best way to drive nails into hard materials. We find that it is impossible to see a tennis-ball flying about without spontaneously explaining its trajectory as a result of a force originally imposed on it. If we see someone's facial expression suddenly change we immediately speculate on what may have upset or surprised them, which would be the explanation of the change we observed. When we see an animal suddenly freeze and leap up we assume it must have detected a predator, which would explain why it stopped and ran away. If our house-plants wither away and die we suspect the neighbours did not water them as promised – that is the explanation. It seems that our minds constantly produce such spontaneous explanations.

Note that all these explanation-producing processes are 'choosy', for want of a better term. The mind does not go around trying to explain everything and it does not use just any information available to explain something. We don't try to decipher emotional states on the tennis-ball's surface. We do not spontaneously assume that the plants died because they were distressed. We don't think that the animal leapt up because it was pushed by a gust of wind. We reserve our physical causes for mechanical events, biological causes for growth and decay and psychological causes for emotions and behaviour.

So the mind does not work like one general 'let's-review-the-facts-and-get-an-explanation' device. Rather, it comprises lots of specialised explanation-devices, more properly called *inference systems*, each of which is adapted to particular kinds of events, and automatically suggests explanations for these events. Whenever we produce an explanation of any event ('the window broke because the tennis-ball hit it'; 'Mrs Jones is angry that the kids broke her window'; etc.) we make use of these special inference systems, although they run so smoothly in the mind that we are not aware of their operation. Indeed, spelling out how they contribute to our everyday explanations would be tedious (e.g. 'Mrs Jones is angry *and* anger is caused by unpleasant events caused by other people *and* anger is directed at those people *and* Mrs Jones knows the children were playing next to her house *and* she suspects the children knew that tennis-balls could break a window *and* . . .'). This is tedious because our minds run all these chains of inferences automatically, and only their results are spelled out for conscious inspection.

By discussing and taking seriously the 'religion-as-explanation' scenario, we open up a new perspective on how religious notions work in human minds. Religious concepts may seem out of the ordinary, but they too make use of the inference systems I just described. Indeed, all I just said about Mrs Jones and the tennis-ball would apply to the ancestors or witches. Returning to Evans-Pritchard's anecdote of the collapsed roof, note how some aspects of the situation were so obvious that no one, neither the anthropologist nor his interlocutors, bothered to make them explicit: for instance, that the witches, if they were involved, probably had a reason to make the roof collapse, that they expected some revenge or profit from it, that they were angry with the persons sitting underneath, that they directed the attack to hurt *those* people, not others, that the witches could see their victims sitting there, that they will attack again if their reasons for striking in the first place are still relevant or if their attack failed, and so on. No one need say all this – no one even *thinks* about it in a conscious, deliberate manner – because it is all self-evident.

Which leads me to two major themes I will expand in the following chapters. The way our banal inference systems work explains a great deal about human thinking, including religious thoughts. But – and this is the most important point – the workings of inference systems are not something we can observe by introspection. Philosopher Daniel Dennett uses the term 'Cartesian theatre' to describe this inevitable illusion, that all that happens in our minds consists in conscious, deliberate thoughts and reasoning about these thoughts. But a lot happens beneath that Cartesian stage, in a mental basement that we can describe only with the tools of cognitive science. This point is obvious when we think about such processes as motor control: the fact that my arm indeed goes up when I consciously try to lift it shows that a complicated system in the brain monitors what various muscles are doing. It is far more difficult to realise that similarly complicated systems are doing a lot of underground work to produce such deceptively simple thoughts as 'Mrs Jones is angry because the kids broke her window' or 'the ancestors will punish you if you defile their shrine'. But the systems are there. Their undetected work explains a lot about religion. It explains why some concepts, like that of invisible persons with a great interest in our behaviour, are widespread the world over, and other possible religious concepts are very rare. It also explains why the concepts are so persuasive, as we will see presently.[6]

Progress-box 1: Religion as explanation

- The urge to explain the universe is not the origin of religion.
- The need to explain particular occurrences seems to lead to far-fetched constructions.
- You cannot explain religious concepts if you do not describe how they are used by individual minds.
- A different angle: Religious concepts are probably influenced by the way the brain's inference systems produce explanations without our being aware of it.

Emotive scenarios: Religion provides comfort

Many people think there is a simple explanation for religion: we need it for emotional reasons. The human psyche is so built that it longs for the reassurance or comfort which supernatural ideas seem to provide. Here are two versions of this widespread account:

[5] *Religious explanations make mortality less unbearable.* All humans are aware that they are destined to die. Like most animals they have developed various ways of reacting to life-threatening situations: fleeing, freezing, fighting. However, they may be unique in being able to reflect on the fact that, come what may, they will die. This is one concern for which most religious systems seem to propose some palliative, however feeble. People's notions of gods and ancestors and ghosts stem from this need to explain mortality and make it more palatable.

[6] *Religion allays anxiety and makes for a comfortable world.* It is in the nature of things that life is for most people nasty, brutish and short, especially in those Dark Ages when religious concepts were first created by human beings. Religious concepts allay anxiety by providing a context in which these conditions are either explained or offset by the promise of a better life or of salvation.

Like the intellectualist scenarios, these suggestions may well seem plausible enough as they stand, but we must go a bit further. Do they do the intended job? That is, do they explain why we have religious concepts and why we have the ones we have?

There are several serious problems with accounts based on emotions. First, as anthropologists have pointed out for quite a time, some facts of life are mysterious or awe-inspiring only in places where a local theory provides a solution to the mystery or a cure for the angst. For instance, there are places in Melanesia where people perform an extraordinary number of rituals to protect themselves from witchcraft. Indeed, people think they live under a permanent threat from these invisible enemies. So we might think that in such societies magical rituals, prescriptions and precautions are essentially comforting devices, giving people some imaginary control over these processes. However, in other places people have no such rituals and feel no such threats to their existence. From the anthropologist's viewpoint it seems plausible that the rituals create the need they are supposed to fulfil, and probable that each reinforces the other.

Also, religious concepts, if they are solutions to particular emotional needs, are not doing a very good job. A religious world is often far more terrifying than a world without supernatural presence, and many religious create not so much reassurance as a thick pall of gloom. The Christian philosopher Kierkegaard wrote books with titles like *The Concept of Anguish* or *Fear and Trembling,* which for him described the true psychological tenor of the Christian revelation. Also, consider the widespread beliefs about witches, ghouls, ghosts and evil spirits allegedly responsible for illness and misfortune. For the Fang people the world is full of witches, that is, nasty individuals whose mysterious powers allow them to 'eat' other people, which in most cases means depriving them of health or good fortune. Fang people also have concepts of anti-witchcraft powers. Some people are said to be good at detecting and counteracting the witches' ploys; one can take protective measures against witches. All this, however, is rather pitiful in the face of the witches' power and most Fang people admit that the balance of power is certainly tipped the wrong way. Indeed, they see evidence of this all the time, in crops that fail, cars that crash and people who die unexpectedly. If religion allays anxiety, it only cures a small part of the disease it creates.

Reassuring religion, in so far as it exists, is not found in places where life is significantly dangerous or unpleasant, quite the opposite. One of the few religious systems obviously designed to provide a comforting world-view is New Age mysticism. It says that people, *all* people, have enormous 'power', that all sorts of intellectual and physical feats are within their reach. It claims that we are all connected to mysterious but basically benevolent forces in the universe. Good health can be conquered by inner spiritual strength. Our nature is really fundamentally good. Most of us lived very interesting lives before this one. Note that these reassuring, ego-boosting notions appeared and spread in one of the most secure and affluent societies in history. People who hold these beliefs are not faced with war, famine, infant mortality, incurable endemic diseases and arbitrary oppression to the same extent as Europeans of the Middle Ages or present-day Third-World peasants.

So much for religion as comfort. But what about mortality? Religion the world over has something to say about what happens after death, and what it says is crucial to belief and behaviour. To understand this, however, we must first discard the parochial notion that religion everywhere promises salvation, for that is clearly not the case. Second, we must also remember that in most places people are not really motivated by a metaphysical urge to explain or mitigate the *general* fact of mortality. That this fact is unbearable or makes human existence intrinsically pointless are speculations of some particular human cultures, far from universal motivations. But the prospect of one's own death and the thoughts triggered are certainly more to the point. How do they participate in building people's religious thoughts? How do they make such thoughts plausible and intensely emotional?

The common shoot-from-the-hip explanation – 'people fear death and religion makes them believe that it is not the end' – is certainly insufficient because the human mind does not produce adequate comforting delusions against all situations of stress or fear. Indeed, any organism that was prone to such delusions would not survive for long. Also, inasmuch as some religious thoughts do allay anxiety, our problem is to explain how they become plausible enough that they can play this role. To entertain a comforting fantasy seems simple enough, but to act on it requires that it is taken as more than a fantasy, which the emotion itself cannot explain.

Before we believe too much in our emotional scenarios, we should ask simple questions, like this: Human minds may well have death-related anxiety, but what is it about? The question may seem strange as the prospect of death seems simple and clear enough to focus the mind, as Dr Johnson pointed out. But human emotions are not that simple. They happen because the mind is a bundle of complicated systems working in the mental basement and solving very complex problems. Consider a simple emotion like the fear induced by the lurking presence of a predator. In many animals, including humans, this results in dramatic somatic events. The quickened heartbeat and increased perspiration are the signals we are aware of. But other systems are doing complex work. For instance, we have to choose between several behaviours in such situations, for example, freeze or flee or fight, a choice that is made by *computation*, that is, by a mental system going through a variety of aspects of the situation and evaluating the least dangerous option. So fear is not just what we experience about it, it is also a *programme,* in some ways comparable to a computer programme. It governs the resources of the brain in a special way, quite different from what happens in other circumstances. Fear increases the sensitivity of some perceptual mechanisms and leads reasoning through complicated sets of possible outcomes. So Dr Johnson was right after all.[7]

This leads to another important question: Why do we have such programmes and why do they work in this way? In the case of fear triggered by predators, it seems quite clear that natural selection fashioned our brains in such a way that they comprise this specific programme. We and other animals would not be around if we did not have fairly efficient predator-avoidance mechanisms. But this also suggests that the mental programmes are sensitive to the relevant context. You do not survive long if your brain fails to start this programme when wolves surround you, or if you activate it every time you run into a sheep. Mortality anxiety may not be as simple as we thought. It is probably true that religious concepts gain their great salience and emotional load in the human psyche because they are connected to thoughts about various life-threatening circumstances. So we will not understand religion if we do not understand the various emotional programmes in the mind, which are more complex than a diffuse angst.

Progress-box 2: Emotion in religion

- Religious concepts do not always provide reassurance or comfort.
- Deliverance from mortality is not quite the universal longing we often assume.
- Religious concepts are indeed connected to human emotional systems and these are connected to life-threatening circumstances.
- A different angle: Our emotional programmes are an aspect of our evolutionary heritage, which may explain how they affect religious concepts.

Social scenarios: religion as a Good Thing for society

Scenarios that focus on social needs all start from a common-sense (true) observation. Religion is not just something that is added to social life, it very often organises social life. People's behaviour towards each other, in most places, is strongly influenced by their notions about the existence and powers of ancestors, gods or spirits. So there must be some connection between living in society and having religious concepts. Here are some examples of the connections we may think of:

[7] *Religion holds society together.* In Voltaire's cynical formulation, 'If God did not exist someone ought to invent Him.' That is, society would not hold together if people did not have some central set of beliefs that binds them together and makes social groups work as organic wholes rather than aggregates of self-interested individuals.

[8] *Religion was invented to perpetuate a particular social order.* Churches and other such religious institutions are notorious for their active participation in and support for political authority. This is particularly the case in oppressive regimes that so often try to find some support in religious justifications. Religious beliefs are there to convince oppressed people that they can do nothing to better their lot except wait for promised retribution in another world.

[9] *Religion supports morality.* No society could work without moral prescriptions that bind people together and thwart crime, theft, treachery, etc. Moral rules cannot be enforced merely by fear of immediate punishment which all know to be uncertain. The fear of God is a better incentive to moral behaviour since it assumes that the monitoring is constant and the sanctions eternal. In the same way in most societies some other religious agency (spirits, ancestors, etc.) is there to guarantee that people behave.

Again, these scenarios point to real issues and a good account of religion should have something to say about them. For instance, whatever we want to say about religious concepts we must take into account that they are deeply associated with moral beliefs. Indeed, we cannot ignore the point because that is precisely what many schools of religion insist on. In the same way, the connection between religious concepts and political systems is impossible to ignore simply because it is loudly proclaimed by many religious believers and religious doctrines.

However, here too we find some difficult problems. Consider this: in no human society is it considered all right or morally defensible to kill your siblings in order to have exclusive access to your parents' attention and resources. In no society is it all right to see other members of the group in great danger without offering some help. Yet the societies in question may have vastly different religious concepts. So there is some suspicion that perhaps the link between religion and morality is what psychologists and anthropologists call a rationalisation, an *ad hoc* explanation of moral imperatives which we would have for other reasons anyway. The same goes for connections between social order and religion. All societies have some prescriptive rules that underpin social organisation but their religious concepts are very diverse. So the connection may not be quite as obvious as it seems. Naturally, we could brush these doubts aside and say that what matters is that social groups have *some* religion in order to have morality and social order.

What matters then is a set of common premises that we find in most religious notions and that support social life and morality. But then, what are those common premises?

The connection between religion and oppression may be more familiar to Europeans than to other people because the history of Europe is also the history of long and intense struggles between Churches and civil societies. But we must be wary of ethnocentric bias. It is simply not the case that every place on earth has an oppressive social order sanctioned by an official Church. (Indeed, even in Europe at some points people have found no other resort than the Church against some oppressive regimes.) More generally, the connection between religious concepts, Church and State cannot account for concepts that are found in strikingly similar forms in places where there are neither States nor Churches. Such concepts have a long antiquity, dating from periods when such institutions were simply not there. So, again, we have important suggestions that we must integrate into a proper account of religion. But we do not have the easy solution we may have anticipated.

Religion and the social mind

Social accounts are examples of what anthropologists call 'functionalism'. A functionalist explanation starts with the idea that certain beliefs or practices or concepts make it possible for certain social relations to operate. Imagine for instance a group of hunters who have to plan and co-ordinate their next expedition. This depends on all sorts of variables, so that different people have different views on where to go and when, leading to intractable disputes. In some groups people perform a divination ritual to decide where to go. For instance they kill a chicken and the hunters must follow the direction given by the headless body running away. The functionalist move is to say that since such beliefs and practices contribute to the solution of a problem, this is probably why they were invented or why people reinvent and accept them. More generally: Social institutions are around and people comply with them because they serve some *function*. Concepts too have functions and that is why we have them. If you can identify the function you therefore have the explanation. Societies have religion because social cohesion requires something like religion. Social groups would fall apart if ritual did not periodically reestablish that all members are part of a greater whole.

Functionalism of this kind went out of favour with anthropologists some time in the 1960s. One criticism was that functionalism seemed to ignore many counter-examples of social institutions with no clear function at all. It is all very well to say that having central authority is a good way of managing conflict-resolution but what about these many places where chiefs are war-mongers who constantly provoke new conflicts? Naturally, functionalist anthro-pologists could think of clever explanations for that too but then were vulnerable to a different attack. Functionalism was accused of peddling *ad hoc* stories. Anyone with enough ingenuity could find some sort of social function for any cultural institution. A third criticism was that functionalism tended to depict societies as harmonious organic wholes where every part plays some useful function. But we know that most human societies are rife with factions, feuds, diverging interests and so on.[8]

As a student, I always found these criticisms less than perfectly convincing. True, extant functionalist explanations were not very good but that was not sufficient to reject the general logic. Functionalism is a tried and tested method of explanation in evolutionary biology. Consider this: When faced with a newly discovered organ or behaviour, the first questions biologists will ask are, What does it do for the organism? How does the organ or behaviour confer an advantage in terms of spreading whatever genes are responsible for its appearance? How did it gradually evolve from other organs and behaviours? This strategy is now commonly called 'reverse engineering'. Imagine you are given a complicated con-traption you have never seen before. The only way to make sense of how the parts are assembled is to try and guess what they are for, what function they are supposed to fulfil. Obviously, this may sometimes lead you down a garden path. The little statue on the bonnet of some luxury cars serves no function as far as locomotion is concerned. The point is not that reverse engineering is always *sufficient* to deliver the right solution but that it is always *necessary*. So there may be some benefit in a functionalist strategy at least as a starting point in the explanation of religion. If people the world over hold religious concepts and perform religious rituals, if so many social groups are organised around common beliefs, it makes sense to ask, How does the belief contribute to the group's functioning? How does it create or change or disrupt social relations?

These questions highlight the great weakness of classical functionalism and the real reason why it did not survive in anthropology. It assumed that institutions were around so that society can function, but did not explain how or why individuals would participate in making society function. For instance, imagine that performing communal religious rituals really provided a glue that kept the social group together. Why would that lead people to perform rituals? They may have better things to do. Naturally, one is tempted to think that other members of the group would coerce the reluctant ones into participating. But this only pushes the problem one step further. Why would these others be inclined to enforce conformity? Accepting that conformity is advantageous to the group, they too might guess that 'free-riding' — accepting the benefits without doing anything in return — would be even more advantageous to themselves. Classical functionalist accounts had no way of explaining how or why people would adopt representations that were good for social cohesion.

There were no solutions to these puzzles until anthropologists started taking more seriously the fact that humans are by nature a social species. What this means is that we are not just individuals thrown together in social groups, trying to cope with the problems this creates. We have sophisticated mental equipment, in the form of special emotions and special ways of thinking, that is designed for social life. And not just for social life in general, but for the particular kind of social interaction that humans create. Many animal species have complex social arrangements but each has the specific dispositions that make such arrangements possible. You will not make gregarious chimpanzees out of naturally solitary orang-utans, or turn philandering chimpanzees into monogamous gibbons. Obviously, the social life of humans is more complex than the apes', but that is because human social dispositions are more complex too. A human brain is so designed that it includes what evolutionary biologists call a particular form of 'social intelligence' or a 'social mind'.

The study of the social mind, by anthropologists, evolutionary biologists and psychologists, gives us a new perspective on the connections between religion and social life. Consider morality. In some places people say that the gods laid down the rules people live by. In other places the gods or ancestors simply watch people and sanction their misdemeanours. In both cases people make a connection between moral understandings (intuitions, feelings and reasoning about what is ethical and what is not) and supernatural agents (gods, ancestors, spirits). Why is the connection so natural? Without anticipating the substance of another chapter, it now seems clear that Voltaire's account – a god is convenient: people will fear him and behave – got things diametrically wrong. Having concepts of gods and spirits does not really make moral rules more compelling but it sometimes makes them more intelligible. So we do not have gods because that makes society function. We have gods in part because we have the mental equipment that makes society possible, but we cannot always understand how society functions.

Progress-box 3: Religion, morality and society

- Religion cannot be explained by the need to keep society together or to preserve morality, because these needs do not create institutions.
- Social interaction and morality are indeed crucial to how we

acquire religion and how it influences people's behaviour.
• A different angle: The study of the social mind can show us why people have particular expectations about social life and morality and how this is connected to their supernatural concepts.

The sleep of reason: religion as an illusion

Turning to the last kind of scenario, there is a long and respectable tradition of explaining religion as the consequence of a flaw in mental functioning. Because people do not think much or not very well, the argument goes, they let all sorts of unwarranted beliefs clutter their mental furniture. In other words, there is religion around because people fail to take prophylactic measures against beliefs:

[10] *People are superstitious, they will believe anything.* People are naturally prepared to believe all sorts of accounts of strange or counter-intuitive phenomena. Witness their enthusiasm for UFOs as opposed to scientific cosmology, for alchemy instead of chemistry, for urban legends instead of hard news. Religious concepts are both cheap and sensational; they are easy to understand and rather exciting to entertain.

[11] *Religious concepts are irrefutable.* Most incorrect or incoherent claims are easily refuted by experience or logic but religious concepts are different. They invariably describe processes and agents whose existence could never be verified and are consequently never refuted. As there is no evidence against most religious claims people have no obvious reason to stop believing them.

[12] *Refutation is more difficult than belief.* It takes greater effort to challenge and rethink established notions than just accept them. Besides, in most domains of culture we just absorb other people's notions. Religion is no exception. If everyone round about you says that there are invisible dead people around, and everyone acts accordingly, it would take a much greater effort to try and verify such claims than it takes to accept them, if only provisionally.

I find all these arguments unsatisfactory. Not that they are false: religious claims are indeed beyond verification. People do like sensational supernatural tales better than banal stories and they generally spend little time rethinking every bit of cultural information they acquire. But this cannot be a sufficient explanation for why people have the concepts they have, the beliefs they have, the emotions they have. The idea that we are often gullible or superstitious is certainly true; but we are not gullible in just every possible way. People do not generally manage to believe six impossible things before breakfast, as the White Queen in Lewis Carroll's *Through the Looking-Glass*. Religious claims are irrefutable, but so are all sorts of other far-fetched notions that we do not find in religion. Take for instance the claim that my right hand is made of green cheese except when people examine it, that God ceases to exist every Wednesday afternoon, that cars feel thirsty when their tanks run low or that cats think in German. We can make up hundreds of such interesting and irrefutable beliefs. There is no limit to imagination in this domain. The credulity arguments would explain not just actual religious beliefs but also a whole variety of beliefs that no one ever had.

Religion is *not* a domain where anything goes, where any strange belief could appear and get transmitted from generation to generation. On the contrary, there is only a limited catalogue of possible supernatural beliefs, which I will present in chapter 2. Even without knowing the details of religious systems in other cultures, we all know that some notions are far more widespread than others. The idea that there are invisible souls of dead people lurking around is a very common one; the notion that people's organs change position during the night is very rare. But both are equally irrefutable. So the problem, surely, is not just to explain how people can accept supernatural claims for which there is no strong evidence but also why they tend to represent and accept these supernatural claims rather than other possible ones. We should explain why they are so selective in the claims they adhere to.

Indeed, we should go even further and abandon the credulity-scenario altogether. Here is why: In this scenario, people relax ordinary standards of evidence for some reason. If you are against religion, you will say that this is because they are naturally credulous, or respectful of received authority, or too lazy to think for themselves, etc. If you are more sympathetic to religious beliefs, you will say that they open up their minds to wondrous truths beyond the reach of reason. But the point is that if you accept this account, you assume that people *first* open up their minds, as it were; and *then* let it be filled by whatever religious beliefs are held by the people who influence them at that particular time. This is often the way we think of religious adhesion. There is a gate-keeper in the mind that either allows or rejects visitors, that is, other people's concepts and beliefs. When the gate-keeper allows them in, these concepts and beliefs find a home in the mind and become the person's own beliefs and concepts.

Our present knowledge of mental processes suggests that this scenario is highly misleading. People receive all sorts of information from all sorts of sources. *All* this information has some effect on the mind. Whatever you hear and whatever you see is perceived, interpreted, explained and recorded by the various inference systems I described above. Every bit of information is fodder for the mental machinery. But then some pieces of information produce the effects that we identify as 'belief'. That is, the person starts to recall them and use them to explain or interpret particular events; they may trigger specific emotions; they may strongly influence the person's behaviour. Note that I said *some* pieces of information, not all. This is where the selection occurs. In ways that a good psychology of religion should describe, it so happens that only some pieces of information trigger these effects, and not others; it also happens that the same piece of information will have these effects in some people but not others. So people do not have beliefs because they somehow made their minds receptive to belief and then acquired the material for belief. They have some beliefs because, among all the material they acquired, some of it triggered these particular effects.

This is important because it changes the whole perspective on explaining religion. As long as you think that people first open up the gates and then let visitors in, as it were, you cannot understand why religion invariably returns to the same recurrent themes. If the process of transmission only consists of acceptance, why do we find only a handful of recurrent themes? But if you see things the other way around, you can start describing the effects of concepts in the mind and understand why some of them may well become persuasive enough that people 'believe' them. I do not think that people have religion because they relax their usually strict criteria for evidence and accept extraordinary claims; I think they are led to relax these criteria because some extraordinary claims have become quite plausible to them.

Progress-box 4: Religion and reasoning

- The sleep of reason is no explanation for religion as it is. There are many possible unsupported claims and only a few religious themes.
- Belief is not just passive acceptance of what others say. People relax their standards because some thoughts become plausible, not the other way around.
- A different angle: We should understand what makes human minds so selective in what supernatural claims they find plausible.

Turning the question upside down
At this point we should perhaps close this survey. We could in principle carry on for quite some time, as philosophers, historians and psychologists have come up with many more suggestions. However, there is a diminishing return for this kind of discussion, as most origin scenarios suffer from similar flaws. If religion is reassuring, why does it create much of the anxiety it cures? If it explains the world, why does it do it with such elaborate complication? Why does it have these common, recurrent themes rather than a great variety

of irrefutable ideas? Why is it so closely connected to morality, whereas it cannot really create morality? As I have said several times, we cannot hope to explain religion if we just fantasise about the way human minds work. We cannot just decide that religion fulfils some particular intellectual or emotional needs, when there is no real evidence for these needs. We cannot just decide that religion is around because it promises this or that, when there are many human groups where religion makes no such promise. We cannot just ignore the anthropological evidence about different religions and the psychological evidence about mental processes. (Or rather, we *should* not; we actually do it quite often.) So the prospect may seem rather dim for a general explanation of religion. However, this survey of possible scenarios also suggests that there is another way to proceed, which I posted in the progress-boxes as we went along.

The main problem with our spontaneous explanations of religion lies in the very assumption, that we can explain the origin of religion by selecting one particular problem or idea or feeling and deriving the variety of things we now call religion from that unique point. Our spontaneous explanations are meant to lead us from the *One* (the origin) to the *Many* (the current diversity of religious ideas). This may seem natural in that this is the usual way we think of origins. The origin of geometry lies in land-tenure and surveying problems. The origin of arithmetic and number theory is in accounting problems encountered by centralised agricultural states. So it seems sensible to assume that a 'one thing led to many things' scenario is apposite for cultural phenomena.

But we can approach the question from another angle. Indeed, we can and should turn the whole 'origin' explanation upside down, as it were, and realise that the many forms of religion we know are the outcome not of a historical diversification but of a constant reduction. The religious concepts we observe are relatively successful ones selected among many other variants. Anthropologists explain the origins of many cultural phenomena, including religion, not by going from the *One* to the *Many* but by going from the *Very Many* to the *Much*

Fewer, the many variants that our minds constantly produce and the much fewer variants that can be actually transmitted to other people and become stable in a human group. To explain religion we must explain how human minds, constantly faced with lots of potential 'religious stuff', constantly reduce it to much less stuff.

Concepts in the mind are constructed as a result of being exposed to other people's behaviour and utterances. But this acquisition process is not a simple process of 'downloading' notions from one brain to another. People's minds are constantly busy reconstructing, distorting, changing and developing the information communicated by others. This process naturally creates all sorts of variants of religious concepts, as it creates variants of all other concepts. But then not all of these variants have the same fate. Most of them are not entertained by the mind for more than an instant. A small number have more staying power but are not easily formulated or com-municated to others. An even smaller number of variants remain in memory and are communicated to other people, but then these people do not recall them very well. An extremely small number remain in memory, are communicated to other people, are recalled by these people and communicated to others in a way that more or less preserves the original concepts. These are the ones we can observe in human cultures.

So we should abandon the search for a historical origin of religion in the sense of a point in time (however long ago) when people created religion where there was none. All scenarios that describe people sitting around and inventing religion are dubious. Even the ones that see religion as slowly emerging out of confused thoughts have this problem. In the following chapters I will show how religion emerges (has its origins, if you want) in the selection of concepts and the selection of memories. Does this mean that at some point in history people had lots of possible versions of religion and that somehow one of them proved more successful? Not at all. What it means is that, *at all times and all the time*, innumerable variants of religious notions were and are created inside individual minds. Not all these variants are equally successful in cultural transmission. What we call a cultural phenomenon is the result of a selection that is taking place all the time and everywhere.

This may seem a bit counter-intuitive. After all, if you are a Protestant and you went to Sunday school, that was your main source of formal religious education. Similarly, the teachings of the *madrasa* for Muslims and *Talmud-Torah* for Jews seem to provide people with *one* version of religion. It does not seem to us that we are shopping in a religious supermarket where the shelves are bursting with alternative religious concepts. But the selection I am talking about happens mostly inside each individual mind. In the following chapters I will describe how variants of religious concepts are created and constantly eliminated. This process goes on, completely unnoticed, in parts of our mind that conscious introspection will not reach. This cannot be observed or explained without the experimental resources of cognitive science.

Anthropological tool-kit 1: Culture as memes

The notion that what we find in cultures is a residue or a precipitate of many episodes of individual transmission is not new. But it became very powerful with the development of formal mathematical tools to describe cultural transmission. This happened because anthropologists were faced with a difficult problem. They often described human cultures in terms of 'big' objects, like 'American fundamentalism', 'Jewish religion', 'Chinese morality', and so on. Anthropology and history could make all sorts of meaningful statements about these big objects, for example, 'In the eighteenth century, the progress of science and technology in Europe challenged Christian religion as a source of authority.' However, this is a very remote description of what happens on the ground, in the actual lives of individuals. After all, people do not interact with such abstract objects as scientific progress or Christian authority. They only interact with individual people and material objects. The difficulty was to connect these two levels and to describe how what happened at the bottom, as it were, produced stability and change at the level of populations.

A number of anthropologists and biologists (including C. Lumsden and E. O. Wilson, R. Boyd and P. Richerson, L. L. Cavalli-Sforza and M. Feldman, W. Durham) more or less at the same time proposed that cultural transmission could be to some extent described in the same way as genetic inheritance. Evolutionary biology has put together an impressive set of mathematical tools to describe the way a certain gene can spread in a population, under what conditions it is likely to be 'crowded out' by other versions, to what extent genes that are detrimental to one organism can still be transmitted in a population, and so forth. The idea was to adapt these tools to the transmission of cultural notions or behaviours.[9]

Tool-kit 1: Culture as memes

The equations of population genetics are abstract tools that can be applied to genes but also to any other domain where you have (1) a set of units, (2) changes that produce different variants of those units and (3) a mechanism of transmission that chooses between variants. In cultural transmission we find a certain set of notions and values (these would be the analogue of the genes). They come in different versions. These variants are communicated to people who grow up in a particular group (this is the analogue of reproduction). These internal states have external effects because people act on the basis of their notions and values (in the same way as genes produce phenotypic effects). Over many cycles of communication, certain trends can appear because of accumulated distortions: people do not transmit exactly what they received, and biased transmission: people may acquire or store some material better than the rest.

Biologist Richard Dawkins summarised all this by describing culture as a population of *memes* which, like genes, are just 'copy-me programmes'. Genes produce organisms that behave in such a way that the genes are replicated – otherwise the genes in question would not be around. Memes are units of culture: notions, values, stories, etc. that get people to speak or act in certain ways that make other people store a replicated version of these mental units. A joke or a popular tune are simple illustrations of such copy-me programmes. You hear them once, they get stored in memory, they lead to behaviours (telling the joke, humming the tune) that will implant copies of the joke or tune in other people's memories, and so on. Describing most cultural phenomena in terms of memes and meme-transmission may seem rather straightforward and innocuous. But it has important consequences that I must mention here because they go against some deeply entrenched ideas about culture.

First, meme-models undermine the idea of culture as some abstract object, independent from individual concepts and norms, that we somehow 'share'. A comparison with genes shows why this is misguided. I have blue eyes, like other people. But I do not have their genes and they do not have mine. Our genes are all safely packed inside our individual cells. It would be a misleading metaphor to say that we 'share' anything. All we can say is that the genes I inherited are similar to theirs from the point of view of their effects on eye-colour. In the same way, *culture is the name of a similarity*. What we mean when we say that something is 'cultural' is that it is roughly similar to what we find in other members of the particular group we are considering, and unlike what we would find in members of a contrast group. This is why it is confusing to say that people share a culture as if it was common property. We may have strictly identical amounts of money in our respective wallets without sharing any of it!

Second, since culture is a similarity between people's ideas, it is very confusing to say things like 'American culture places great emphasis on individual achievement' or 'Chinese culture is more concerned with harmony within a group'. Saying this, we conclude that, for instance, 'Many Americans would like to relax but their culture tells them to be competitive' or 'Many Chinese people would enjoy competition but their culture incites them to be more group-oriented'. So we describe culture as some kind of external force that pushes people one way or another. But this is rather mysterious. How could a similarity *cause* anything? There is no external force here. If people feel a conflict between their inclinations and a norm that is followed by everybody else, it is a conflict *within their heads*. If American children have a hard time coping with the requirement that 'American children should be competitive', it is because the requirement has been implanted in their minds, maybe to their chagrin. But all this is happening inside a mind.

Third, knowing that culture is a similarity between people is helpful because it forces you to remember that two objects are similar only *from a certain point of view*. My blue eyes may make me similar to some other people, but then my short-sightedness makes me similar to others. Apply this to culture. We routinely talk about whole cultures as distinct units, as in 'Chinese culture', 'Yoruba culture', 'British culture' and so forth. What is wrong here? The term 'cultural' labels a certain similarity between the representations we find in members of a group. So, it would seem, we can do anthropological field-work and surveys among different human groups, say the Americans and the Yoruba, and then describe those representations that we find in only one of them, as being the American and Yoruba cultures respectively. But why do we assume that 'the Americans' or 'the Yoruba' constitute a group? Compare this with natural species. We feel justified, to some extent, in comparing the aubergine with the courgette or the donkey with the zebra. These labels correspond to natural groupings of plants and animals. The problem is that *there are no natural groupings for human beings*. We may think that it makes sense to compare the Americans and the Yoruba because there is a Yoruba polity and an American nation. But note that these are historical, purposeful constructions. They are not the effect of some natural similarity. Indeed, if we look at people's actual behaviour and representations in either group, we will find that quite a lot of what they do and think can be observed outside these groups. Many norms and ideas of American farmers are more common to farmers than to Americans; many norms and ideas of Yoruba businessmen are more common among business people than among the Yoruba. This confirms what anthropologists long suspected: that the choice of human groupings for cultural comparisons is not a natural or scientific choice, but a political one.

Finally, quantitative models of cultural transmission replaced mythical notions like 'absorbing what's in the air' with a concrete, measurable process of transmission. People communicate with other people, they meet individuals with similar or different notions or values, they change or maintain or discard their ways of thinking because of these encounters, and so forth. What we call their 'culture' is the outcome of all these particular encounters. If you find that a particular concept is very stable in a human group (you can come back later and find it more or less unchanged) it is because it has a particular advantage inside individual minds. If you want to explain cultural trends, this is far more important than tracing the actual historical origin of this or that particular notion. A few pages back, I described the way a Cuna shaman talks to statuettes. This seems a stable concept among the Cuna. If we want to explain that, we have to explain how this concept is represented in individual minds, in such a way that they can recall it and transmit it better than other concepts. If we want to explain why the Cuna maintain this notion of intelligent statuettes, it does not matter if what happened was that one creative Cuna thought of it a century ago, or that someone had a dream about it, or that someone told a story with intelligent statuettes. What matters is what happened afterwards in the many cycles of acquisition, memory and communication.[10]

In this account, familiar religious concepts and associated beliefs, norms and emotions are just better-replicating memes than other types of concepts, norms, etc., in the sense that their copy-me instructions work better. This would be why so many people in different cultures think that invisible spirits lurk around and so few imagine that their internal organs change location during the night, why the notion of moralistic ancestors watching your behaviour is more frequent than that of immoral ghosts who want you to steal from your neighbours. Human minds exposed to these concepts end up replicating them and passing them on to other people. On the whole, this seems to be the right way to understand diffusion and transmission. However . . .

Distortion is of the essence

The notion of human culture as a huge set of 'copy-me programmes' is very seductive and it is certainly on the right track, but it is only a starting point. Why are some memes better than others? Why is singing 'Land of Hope and Glory' after hearing it once much easier than humming a tune from Schoenberg's 'Pierrot Lunaire'? What exactly makes moralistic ancestors better for transmission than immoral ghosts? This is not the only problem. A much more difficult one is that, if we look a bit more closely at cultural transmission between human beings, what we see does not look at all like replication of identical memes. On the contrary, the process of transmission seems guaranteed to create an extraordinary profusion of fanciful variations. This is where the analogy with genes is more hindrance than help. Consider this: You (and I) carry genes that come from a unique source (a meiotic combination of our parents' genes) and we will transmit them unchanged (though combined with a partner's set) to our offspring. In the meantime, nothing happens; however much you may work out at the gym, you will not have more muscular children. But in mental representations the opposite is true. The denizens of our minds have many parents (in those thousands of renditions of 'Land of Hope and Glory', which one is being replicated when I whistle the tune?) and we constantly modify them.[11]

As we all know, some memes may be faithfully transmitted while others are hugely distorted in the process. Consider for instance the contrasted fortunes of two cultural memes created by Richard Dawkins himself, one of which replicated very well while the other one underwent a bizarre mutation. The idea of 'meme' itself is an example of a meme that replicated rather well. A few years after Dawkins had introduced the notion, virtually everybody in the social sciences, evolutionary biology or psychology knew about it and they mostly had an essentially correct notion of the original meaning. Now compare this with another of Dawkins's ideas, that of 'selfish genes'. What this meant was that genes are DNA strings whose sole achievement is to replicate. The explanation for this is simply that the ones that do not have this functionality (the ones that build organisms that cannot pass on the genes) just disappear from the gene pool. So far, so simple. However, once the phrase 'selfish gene' was diffused out into the wide world its meaning changed beyond recognition, to become in many people's usage 'a gene that makes us selfish'. An editorial in the British *Spectator* once urged the Conservative Party to acquire more of that selfish gene described by Professor Dawkins. But one does not 'acquire' a gene, it makes little sense to say that someone has 'more' of a gene than someone else, there is probably no such thing as a gene that makes people selfish, and Dawkins never meant that anyway. This distortion is not too surprising. It confirms the popular perception that biology is all about the struggle for survival, Nature red in tooth and claw, the Hobbesian fight of all against all, etc. (that this is in fact largely false is neither here nor there). So the distortion happened, in this case, because people had a prior notion that the phrase 'selfish gene' seemed to match. The original explanation (the original 'meme') was completely ignored, better to fit that prior conception.

Cultural memes undergo mutation, recombination and selection *inside* the individual mind every bit as much and as often (in fact probably more and more often) than during transmission between minds. We do not just transmit the information we received. We process it and use it to create new information, some of which we do communicate to other people. To some anthropologists this seemed to spell the doom of meme-explanations of culture. What we call culture is the similarity between some people's mental representations in some domains. But how come there is similarity at all, if representations come from so many sources and undergo so many changes?

It is tempting to think that there is an obvious solution: some memes are so infectious and hardy that our minds just swallow them whole, as it were, and then regurgitate them in pristine form for others to acquire. They would be transmitted between minds in the way an email message is routed via a network of different computers. Each machine stores it for a while and passes it on to another machine via reliable channels. For instance, the idea of a moralistic ancestor, communicated by your elders, might be so 'good' that you just store it in your memory and then deliver it intact to your children. But that is not the solution.

For the following reason: When an idea gets distorted beyond recognition, as happened to the selfish gene, it seems obvious that this occurs because the minds that received the original information added to it, in other words *worked* on it. So far, so good. But this leads us to think that, when an idea gets transmitted in a roughly faithful way, this occurs because the receiving minds did *not* rework it, as it were. Now that is a great mistake. The main difference between minds that communicate and computers that route email is this: Minds never swallow raw information to serve it to others in the same raw state. Minds invariably do a lot of work on available information, especially so when transmission is faithful. For instance, I can sing 'Land of Hope and Glory' in (roughly) the same way as others before me. This is because hugely complex mental processes shaped my memories of the different versions I heard. In human communication, *good transmission requires as much work as distortion*.

This is why the notion of 'memes', while a good starting-point, is only that. The idea of 'replication' is very misleading. People's ideas are sometimes roughly similar to those of other people around them, not because ideas can be downloaded from mind to mind, but because they are reconstructed in a similar way.

How to catch concepts with templates
People have religious notions and beliefs because they acquired them from other people. Naturally, nothing in principle prevents an ingenious Sicilian Catholic from reinventing the Hindu pantheon or an imaginative Chinese from re-creating Amazonian mythology. On the whole, however, people get their religion from other members of their social group. But how does that occur? Our spontaneous explanation of transmission is quite simple. People behave in certain ways around a child and the child assimilates what is around until it becomes second nature. In this picture, acquiring culture is a passive process. The developing mind is gradually filled with information provided by cultural elders and peers. This is why Hindus have many gods and Jews only one; this is why the Japanese like raw fish and the Americans roast marshmallows. This picture of transmission has one great advantage – it is simple – and a major flaw – it is clearly false. It is mistaken on two counts. First, children do not assimilate the information around them; they actively filter it and use it to go well beyond what is provided. Second, they do not acquire all information in the same way.

To get a feel for the complexity of transmission, compare the ways in which you acquired different bits of your cultural equipment. How did you learn the syntax of your native tongue? It is a very complex system as any foreigner struggling with the rules will tell you. But the learning process all happened unconsciously, or so it seems, and certainly without any effort, just by virtue of being around native speakers. Compare this with etiquette and politeness. These are different from one culture to another and they have to be learnt at some point. Again, this seems to be done rather easily, but there is a difference. In this case you learnt by being told what to do and not do and by observing examples of people interacting. You were aware, to a certain extent, that you were acquiring ways of behaving in order to have certain effects on other people. Now consider mathematics. In this case you were certainly aware that you were learning something. You had to put some effort into it.

Understanding the truth of $(a+b)^2 = a^2+b^2+2ab$ does not come very easily. Most people never acquire this kind of knowledge unless they are guided step by step by competent adults. I could multiply the examples but the point is really simple. There is no single way of acquiring the stuff that makes you a competent member of a culture.

There are different ways of acquiring cultural information because a human brain has dispositions for learning and they are not the same in all domains. For instance, acquiring the right syntax and pro-nunciation for a natural language is trivially easy for all normal brains at the right age, between about one and six. The dispositions for social interaction develop at a different rhythm. But in all these domains learning is possible because there is a disposition to learn, which means, a disposition to go *beyond* the information that is available. This is quite clear in language. Children gradually build their syntax on the basis of what they hear because their brains have definite biases about how language works. But the same is true also in many conceptual domains. Consider our everyday knowledge of animals. Children learn that different animal species reproduce in different ways. Cats deliver live kittens and hens lay eggs. A child can learn this by observing actual animals or by being given explicit information. But there are things you do not have to tell children because they know them already. For example, it is not necessary to tell them that if one hen lays eggs then it is probably true that hens *in general* lay eggs. In the same way, a five-year-old will guess that if one walrus gives birth to live cubs then all other walruses probably reproduce in that way too. This illustrates another simple point: Minds that acquire knowledge are not empty containers into which experience and teaching pour predigested information. A mind needs and generally has some way of organising information to make sense of what is observed and learnt. This allows the mind to go beyond the information given, or in the jargon to produce *inferences* on the basis of information given.

Complex inferences allow children and adults to build concepts out of fragmentary information, but inferences are not random.

They are governed by special principles in the mind, so that their result is in fact predictable. Even though cultural material is constantly distorted and reshuffled inside the head, the mind is not a free-for-all of random associations. One major reason is the presence of mental dispositions for arranging conceptual material in certain ways rather than others. Crucial to this explanation is the distinction between *concepts* and *templates*.

To illustrate this: A child is shown a new animal, say a walrus, and told the name for the species. What the child does – unconsciously of course – is add a new entry to her mental 'encyclopaedia', an entry marked 'walrus' that probably includes a description of a shape. Over the years this entry may become richer as new facts and experiences provide more information about walruses. As I said above, we also know that the child spontaneously adds some information to that entry, whether we tell her or not. For instance, if she sees a walrus give birth to live cubs, she will conclude that this is the way all walruses have babies. You do not need to tell her that 'all walruses reproduce that way'. Why is that so? The child has created a 'walrus' *concept* by using the ANIMAL template.

Think of the ANIMAL template as one of those official forms that provide boxes to fill in. You can fill in the same form in different ways. What stays the same are the boxes and the rules on what should be put in them. The child has identified that the thing you called 'walrus' was an animal, not a heap of minerals or a machine or a person. To put it metaphorically, all she had to do then was to take a new sheet of the form called 'animal' and fill in the relevant boxes. These include a box for the name of the new kind of animal, a box for its appearance: shape, size, colour, etc., a box for where it lives, a box for how it gets a progeny, and so on. In the figure below I give a very simplified illustration of this idea of filling in templates for new animals.

The information in each of these boxes has to be filled in according to certain principles. You are not allowed to specify that an animal has sometimes four legs and sometimes two wings and two legs. You have to decide which is true or leave the box empty. In the same way, the box for 'mode of reproduction' will be filled in with either one

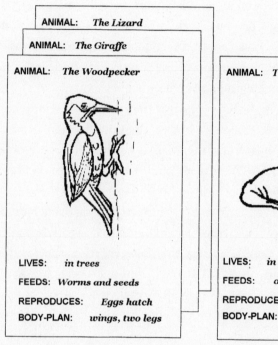

answer or none. This is why I compared templates to official forms. These ask you to give your one given name, not a choice of nicknames your friends call you. This is very important because it means that some generalisations are produced automatically when you learn a new concept. The move from 'this one has live cubs' (a particular fact) to 'they all have live cubs' (a generalisation) is made automatically because the animal template does not allow several different values in the 'reproduction' box. So the child does not have to learn how an animal reproduces more than once for each animal kind. The child is told: 'This is a walrus. See how big her belly is! She'll probably give birth to cubs very soon.' A few days later this child may well tell a friend that walruses do not lay eggs; they get pregnant and deliver live babies. This is not a *replication* of information she received but an *inference* from that information. Even very young children can produce such inferences because they connect the information received about a particular animal to an abstract template ANIMAL. This template works like a recipe and could be called 'recipe for producing new animal-concepts'.

There are, obviously, fewer templates than concepts. Templates are more abstract than concepts, and they organise them. You need only one ANIMAL template for the many, many different animal concepts you will acquire. You need one TOOL template although you may have concepts for many different tools. Concepts depend on your experience – your environment – but templates are much more stable. For instance, people from Greenland and Congo share very few animal concepts, simply because there are very few species that you encounter in both places. Also, a fishmonger certainly has a richer repertoire of fish concepts than an insurance salesman. But the ANIMAL template does not vary much with differences in culture or expertise. For instance, everyone from Congo to Greenland and from fishmongers to insurance salesmen expects all members of a species to reproduce in the same one way. Everyone expects that an animal belongs to one species and only one. Everyone expects that if an animal of a particular species breathes in a particular way this is true of all other members of the species.

The distinction between templates and concepts applies to many other domains. Here is a familiar example: In every place in the world there are very precise notions about which substances are disgusting and which are not. But the concepts are really different. To many in the West the idea of eating cockroaches is rather off-putting, but they would not find anything especially disgusting in having dinner with a blacksmith. The opposite would be true in other places. So we might conclude that there is nothing in common between human cultures in this domain. However, there is a general template of *polluting substance* that seems to work in the same way in most places. For example, whenever people think that a particular substance is disgusting, they also think that it remains so however much you dilute it: Who (in the West) would want to drink a glass of water if they are told it contains only a tiny drop of cow urine? In the same way, some people in West Africa would think that the mere presence of a blacksmith in their home is enough to spoil the food. Take another example, from the domain of politeness. We know etiquette really differs from place to place. In the West it would be rude to sit in your host's lap; in Cameroon, where I did field-work, it shows great respect on some occasions. Concepts are different, but there is a general template of 'face' and actions that can make people lose or save it. You have to learn the local rules, but note how easy it is to produce inferences once you are given the rules. For instance, once told that sitting in a person's lap is a mark of respect, you can infer that it cannot be done all the time, that it is probably absurd to do it with small children, that you will offend people if you fail to do it when it is expected, and so forth. Such inferences are easy because you already have a template for such concepts.

Anthropological background 2: Epidemics of culture
Having templates is one of the devices that allow minds to reach similar representations without having a perfect channel to 'download' information from one mind to another. The child now thinks that walruses deliver live cubs. I happen to think so too, and you probably have the same idea and so does, say, Mrs Jones. But it is very unlikely that we all received precisely the same information about walruses in the same way. What is far more likely is that we extracted this similar information by inference from very different situations and from different statements made by people in different ways. None the less, we converged on similar inferences because the

animal template is the same in the child, you, me and Mrs Jones. (I will show in another chapter how we know this to be the case.) In fact we might all converge on this same notion even if the information the child, you, I and Mrs Jones had received was totally different.

As I said above, the fact that individual minds constantly recombine and modify information would suggest that people's concepts are in constant flux and change. But then why do we find similar representations among members of a particular social group? The mystery is not so difficult to solve once we realise not just that all mental representations are the product of complex inferences – so there is indeed a vast flux and a myriad modifications – but also that some changes and inferences tend to go in particular directions, no matter where you start from. Inferences in the mind are in many cases a centrifugal force, as it were, that makes different people's representation diverge in unpredictable ways. If I spend a whole day with my friends, going through the same experiences for hours on end, our memories of that day will probably diverge in a million subtle ways. But in some domains inferences do the opposite. Acting as a centripetal force, inferences and memories lead to roughly similar constructions even though the input may be quite different. This is why we can observe similarities between concepts both within a group – my notions about animals are quite similar to those of my relatives – and also between groups – there are important similarities in animal concepts from Congo to Greenland, because of a similar template.

At about the same time as meme-models were devised to describe cultural transmission, Dan Sperber and some colleagues put together an *epidemiological* framework to describe the mechanisms of cultural transmission. The substance of this framework is what I have just explained in terms of information and inference. An epidemic occurs when a group of individuals display similar symptoms, for instance when people in a whole region of Africa get high fevers. This is explained as an epidemic of malaria, caused by the presence of mosquitoes carrying the *Plasmodium* pathogen. But note that what we call the epidemic is the occurrence of fevers and assorted symptoms, not the presence of mosquitoes or even *Plasmodium*. That is, to explain what happened you must understand the particular ways in which the human body reacts to the presence of this particular agent. If you do not know any physiology, you will have a hard time explaining why only some animals catch malaria, why people with adequate preventive treatment catch it less than the others, or indeed how the disease spreads at all. We may well study the structure of *Plasmodium* forever; this will tell us nothing about its effects unless we also learn a lot about human physiology. Mental representations are the effect of external vectors, mostly communication with other people. But then the structure of the messages exchanged does not by itself tell us how the mind will react to them. To understand this, we must know a lot about human psychology, about the way minds produce inferences that modify and complete the information exchanged.[12]

Tool-kit 2: Cultural epidemics

Human minds are inhabited by a large population of mental representations. Most of them are found only in one individual, but some are present in roughly similar forms in various members of a group. To account for this is to explain the statistical fact that a similar condition affects a number of organisms, as in epidemics. Different people have inferred similar representations from publicly accessible representations: other people's behaviour, gestures, utterances, man-made objects, etc. The diffusion of particular representations in a group, as well as similarities across groups, can be predicted if we have a good description of which mental resources people bring to understanding what others offer as cultural material, in particular which inferential processes they apply to that material.

To explain religion is to explain a particular kind of mental epidemic, whereby people develop (on the basis of variable information) rather similar forms of religious concepts and norms. I used the example of animal concepts to show how our minds build inferences in such a way that concepts within a group can be very similar and the concepts of different groups, despite differences, can be shaped by the same templates. This applies to religious notions too. There are templates for religious concepts. That is, there are some 'recipes' contained in my mind, and yours, and that of any other normal human being, that build religious concepts by producing inferences on the basis of some information provided by other people and by experience. In the same way as for animal concepts, religious concepts may converge (i.e. be roughly similar) even though the particular information from which an individual built it is in fact very different from one to another.

Religion is cultural. People get it from other people, as they get food preferences, musical tastes, politeness and a dress sense. We often tend to think that if something is cultural then it is hugely variable. But it then turns out that food preferences and other such cultural things are not so variable after all. Food preferences revolve around certain recurrent flavours, musical taste in various cultures varies within strict constraints, and so do politeness codes and standards of elegance.

For anthropologists, the fact that something is cultural is the very reason why it does not vary that much. Not everything is equally likely to be transmitted, because the templates in the mind filter information from other people and build predictable structures out of that information.

A puzzlement of questions

When I started studying anthropology, theories of religion were thoroughly confusing. People in my discipline used to think that the very question Why is religion the way it is? was naïve, ill-formulated or perhaps just intractable. Most people thought this kind of speculation was better left to theologians or retired scientists. What we needed was a good description of those aspects of human nature that lead people to adopt certain ideas or beliefs rather than others. Convergent developments in evolutionary biology and cognitive psychology helped us understand why human cultures display similarities and differences too.

When I say that we now have a better account of religion, I of course mean a better one compared to previous scientific accounts. In this kind of theory, we describe phenomena that can be observed and even measured. We explain them in terms of other phenomena that are also detectable. When we say that *a* implies *b*, our account is vulnerable to counter-examples where *a* occurs without *b*. I do not know if this is enough to define scientific explanations but I am sure it excludes quite a few theories of religion. Some people say that the origin of religion is a long-forgotten visit from wise, extra-terrestrial aliens who were compassionate enough to leave us with fragments of their knowledge. These people will not be interested in the kind of discoveries I discuss here. In a less flamboyant way, people who think that we have religion because religion is *true* (or their version of it is, or perhaps another, yet-to-be-discovered version is) will find little here to support their views and in fact no discussion of these views.

But we can do much better. We can now address as problems rather than mysteries a collection of questions that used to be intractable, such as the following:

Why do people have religion, more or less everywhere?
Why does it come in different forms? Are there any common features?
Why does religion matter so much to people's lives?
Why are there several religions rather than just one?
Why does religion prescribe rituals? Why are rituals the way they are?
Why do most religions have religious specialists?
Why does religion seem to provide 'truth'?
Why are there Churches and religious institutions?
Why does religion trigger strong emotions? Why do people kill for religion?
Why does religion persist in the face of apparently more efficient ways of thinking about the world?

Why does it lead to so much intolerance and so many atrocities? Or, if you prefer, Why is it sometimes conducive to heroism and self-sacrifice?

There remains one big question which most people would think is the crucial one: *Why do some people believe?* The question is often the first one people ask when they consider scientific accounts of religion, yet it will be treated in the last chapter of this book. This is not for the sake of creating a spurious suspense. It turns out that you cannot deal with this question unless you have a very precise description of *what* it is that people actually believe. And that is far from obvious.

This may seem a strange thing to say as religious people are in general all too eager to let us know what they believe. They tell us that an unseen presence is watching our every step, or that the souls of dead people are still around, or that we will reincarnate in some form commensurate with our moral achievements. So all we have to do, or so it seems, is consider these diverse notions and ask ourselves, again: Why do people believe in all this?

But this does not really work. What makes anthropology difficult – and fascinating – is that religious representations are not all transparent to the mind. When people have thoughts about gods or spirits or ancestors, a whole machinery of complex mental devices is engaged, most of which is completely outside conscious access. This, obviously, is not special to religion. Speaking a natural language or playing tennis or understanding a joke also engages this complex machinery (though in different ways). If you want to explain how human minds acquire religious concepts, why these concepts become plausible and why they trigger such strong emotions, you will have to describe all the invisible processes that create such thoughts, make it possible to communicate them and trigger all sorts of associated mental effects like emotion and commitment.

Explaining airy nothing: magic bullets versus aggregate relevance
All scenarios for the origin of religion assume that there must be a

single factor that will explain why there is religion in all human groups and why it triggers such important social, cognitive, emotional effects. This belief in a 'magic bullet' is, unfortunately, exceedingly stubborn. It has hampered our understanding of the phenomenon for a long time. Progress in anthropology and psychology tells us why the belief was naïve. Some concepts happen to connect with inference systems in the brain in a way that makes recall and communication very easy. Some concepts happen to trigger our emotional programmes in particular ways. Some happen to connect to our social mind. Some of them are represented in such a way that they soon become plausible and direct behaviour. The ones that do *all* this are the religious ones we actually observe in human societies. They are most successful because they combine features relevant to a variety of mental systems.

This is precisely why religion cannot be explained by a single magic bullet. Since cultural concepts are the object of constant selection in minds, through acquisition and communication, the ones that we find widespread in many different cultures and at different times probably have some transmission advantage, relative to several different mental dispositions. They are relevant to different systems in the mind. This is why it takes several chapters to approach a question that many people, in my experience, can solve to their entire satisfaction in a few seconds of dinner-table conversation.

Chapter Two

What supernatural concepts are like

Are there any common features in religious concepts? A good way to start is with a little mock-experiment, listing all sorts of concepts and judging whether they could or could not possibly be part of a religious system. This is not the most scientific or indeed rigorous way to proceed but it will provide a first step. Consider the following list of sentences. Each of them describes a particular supernatural notion, in the form of some exotic article of faith, the main theme of some new or unknown religion. It is very likely that you have never heard of places where these propositions are central tenets of religious belief. That is unimportant. This is not a quiz but a question of intuition. The experiment consists in guessing whether it is likely that some people have built a religion around these propositions:

[1] Some people get old and then one day they stop breathing and die and that's that.

[2] If you drop this special ritual object it will fall downwards until it hits the ground.

[3] The souls of dead people cannot go through walls because walls are solid.

[4] Dead men do not talk (nor walk).

[5] There is only one God! He is omniscient but powerless. He cannot do anything or have any effect on what goes on in the world.

[6] The gods are watching us and they notice everything we do! But they forget everything instantaneously.

[7] Some people can see the future but they then forget it immediately.

[8] Some people can predict future events, though only about thirty seconds in advance.

[9] There is only one God! However, he has no way of finding out what goes on in the world.

[10] This statue is special because it vanishes whenever someone thinks about it.

[11] There is only one God! He is omnipotent. But He exists only on Wednesdays.

[12] The spirits will punish you if you do what they want.

[13] This statue is special because you see it here but actually it is everywhere in the world.

Obviously, it is always difficult to predict intuitions. However, it seems to me and to various people with whom I tried this uncontrolled experiment that the above sentences do not sound very promising. It seems unlikely that such ideas could serve as the main tenet of some new faith or that they would attract followers and inspire strong emotions. These are *bad candidates* for a possible religion. They may be bad in different ways, which we will consider below. What matters, for the time being, is that we have some intuition that there is something defective about these ideas as religious ideas.

Perhaps you do not find that terribly obvious and think that, after all, there may be some distant places where these strange ideas are the main source of religious belief. To make the difference more salient consider a list of clearly better candidates:

[21] There is one God! He knows everything we do.

[22] Dead people's souls wander about and sometimes visit people.

[23] When people die their souls sometimes come back in another body.

[24] Some people are dead but they keep walking around. They cannot talk any more, they are not aware of what they are doing.

[25] Some people sometimes faint and start talking in a funny way. That's because God is talking 'through' them.

[26] We worship this woman because she was the only one ever to conceive a child without having sex.

[27] We pray to this statue because it listens to our prayers and helps us get what we want.

Compare this list with the first one. The new propositions sound much better. We can easily imagine some prophet attracting followers or a sect recruiting converts on the basis of these ideas. But I cheated here, as you must have noticed. I listed familiar notions either from Western traditions or from religions most people in the West are familiar with. We all have at least some acquaintance with Buddhist reincarnation [23], Haitian zombies [24] or people who pray in front of statues [27]. So it seems that our little experiment so far only shows one thing: we find that a concept is a possible religious concept when we already know it is a religious concept. That is true but not terribly impressive.

However, I think our intuition is more powerful than that. Familiarity is not really what makes the difference between good and bad concepts. Indeed, we can judge that some concepts are 'promising candidates' for religion even if we have not ever heard of them. Consider these:

[31] Some people suddenly disappear when they are really thirsty.

[32] There are invisible people around who only drink cologne. If someone suddenly goes into a fit and screams for cologne, it is because their body is being controlled by one of these invisible people.

[33] Some people have an invisible organ in their stomachs. That organ flies away at night when they are asleep. It attacks people and drinks their blood.

[34] This wristwatch is special and will chime when it detects that your enemies are plotting against you.

[35] Some ebony trees can recall conversations people hold in their shade.

[36] This mountain over there (*this* one, not that one) eats food and digests it. We give it food sacrifices every now and then, to make sure it stays in good health.

[37] The river over there is our guardian. It will flow upstream if it finds out that people have committed incest.

[38] The forest protects us. It gives us game if we sing to it.

These sound like possible foundations of a religion even though you are probably not aware of any society where they are taken seriously. Indeed, for some of them that is not too surprising since I made them up. The others are taken from actual religious systems. (You may want to try and guess which. The solution will be given below.) I chose to make up some of these examples to emphasise the point that the difference is not just between what is actually found in religion and what is not. Here we have a difference between what we guess *could* be in some exotic religion and what could not.

However clear our intuitions, they leave many questions unanswered. We feel that one list is 'bad' and another 'better' but how do we know? After all, intuitions are not always reliable. Perhaps there are places where items from the first list are part of the local religion? Also, intuitions do not give us precise limits for the set of 'good' candidates and certainly not an explanation for why some ideas seem better than others.

So why use intuitions at all? The point of this rather unscientific experiment is that when we have relatively stable intuitions about what is 'all right' and what is not, it is often because we are using rules without necessarily being aware of them. English speakers may have the intuition that a sentence is wrong without being able to explain why (compare for instance 'He's the man I saw John with' and 'He's the man I saw John and'). So intuitions are valuable as a starting-point in a more serious investigation. This is what we can do with religious concepts too. We have intuitions about which ones are good because they are built according to particular mental *recipes*. If we understand what these recipes are, what ingredients are put together and how they are processed, we will understand why some types of concepts are found in so many religious traditions and others are not.

Is religion just strangeness?

At first sight, it should not be difficult to understand which features are common in religion and which are not. All we would have to do, or so it seems, is collect lots of examples from around the world and tabulate which features come up more frequently than others. In George Eliot's *Middlemarch* (1871–2), the dour religious scholar Casaubon is engaged in precisely this kind of exercise. His goal is to find the 'key to all mythologies' by collecting thousands of myths from thousands of places. In real life, the Victorian scholar James Frazer did exactly that and published twelve volumes of *The Golden Bough* (1890–1915), an interminable journey through world religion and myth.

This is not the way I proceed here. First, even if I and other anthropologists really did research this way, and even if this worked, there would be no reason to inflict such penitential fact-gathering journeys on our readers. But more importantly, this mindless collecting just does not work. It comes as no surprise that Casaubon's search is futile and the *magnum opus* never sees the light of day. It is not terribly surprising either that *The Golden Bough* remained a sterile compilation. Catalogues are not explanations.

To see why this matters, let me pursue our mock-experiment further. What explains the difference between the first list and the other two? One possible answer is that religious concepts invariably include some *strange* properties of imagined entities or agents. Religious ontologies, in this view, surprise people by describing things and events they could not possibly encounter in actual experience. This is a very common view of religion. In a way, this account is nothing more than a dignified version of the familiar notion that 'man bites dog' is news but 'dog bites man' is not. Religious concepts are an *extreme* form of that phenomenon. We sometimes encounter people who bite dogs (well, some of us must have seen that happen). But invisible persons who go through walls, infinite persons who created everything . . .

Take for instance some items out of our first list:

[1] Some people get old and then one day they stop breathing and die and that's that.

[2] If you drop this special ritual object it will fall downwards till it hits the ground.

[4] Dead men do not talk (nor walk).

and compare with a couple of propositions from our second list:

[23] When people die their souls sometimes come back in another body.

[27] We pray to this statue because it listens to our prayers and helps us get what we want

Obviously, the main problem with [1], [2] and [4] is that they express something we all know. They are just too 'banal' to start a religion. Religious concepts are not usually so trite. By contrast, [23] and [27] are surprising in the minimal sense that they describe processes and agencies that are not part of everyday experience.

But this cannot be the solution. There are two obvious, incurable problems with this 'strangeness' theory. First, it says that religious concepts are about objects and events we cannot actually experience. But this flies in the face of the facts. Mystics the world over can recount their many encounters with divine beings. Also, in many cultures we find cases of possession. Someone falls into a trance or some other strange state and starts to talk gibberish or says sensible things in a very strange voice. Everyone around says that this strange behaviour is caused by some god or spirit who is 'possessing' the person. All these people seem to have a *direct experience* of what happens when a god or spirit is around. Even without considering such exceptional circumstances, many people in the world have seen ghosts or dreamed of their ancestors. Many religious concepts are about things and persons that people encounter, or at least think they encounter, so it is perverse to call these 'strange'. Second, if this account was true, religious concepts would be indefinitely variable. This is because the domain of what is *not* part of everyday experience is in principle infinite. But as we saw above, some concepts, however strange, sound like non-starters for religious belief, like this:

[11] There is only one God! He is omnipotent. But He exists only on Wednesdays.

This is certainly 'strange' or 'surprising' and departs from everyday experience. Lectures and concerts and farmers' markets may well happen only on Wednesdays. But gods and people are continuous. They cannot exist at some point and again some time later and not exist in the meantime. So the concept is indeed strange, remote from everyday experience. However, this kind of extraordinary belief is not widespread – indeed I would be surprised if it was taken as a literal description of a god anywhere. Mere strangeness is not really a good criterion for inclusion in a list of possible religious concepts.

The 'strangeness' account has yet another serious flaw. It is blatantly circular. How do we establish that some notion is or is not part of 'ordinary' experience? It is not always clear whether our idea of the 'ordinary' is the same as other people's. It is tempting to say that the idea of invisible people drinking cologne *must* be outside of the ordinary, otherwise people would not find the notion fascinating enough to include it in their supernatural concepts. But here we are assuming precisely what we have set out to demonstrate.

Why badger this half-baked theory? Because it shows what happens when you compare religious phenomena in this mindless way. Many people in the past tried to describe common 'themes' or 'ideas' or 'archetypes' that would be common to all religion. On the whole, this did not prove terribly successful. People thought that religion everywhere must have something to do with the 'sacred' or 'divinity' or 'ultimate reality', or in more fanciful ways, that all religions were about the sun, or the planets, or blood, or fear of one's father, or worship of nature. But human cultures are not that simple. For each of these themes that seemed very general, anthropologists soon found many counter-examples. For instance, people used to think that a religious artefact was, by necessity, a 'sacred' object, treated with awe and respect. In many places in Africa people wear elaborate masks during ceremonies. The person wearing the mask is said to have become the spirit or ancestor represented. The mask is about as 'religious' an object as could be. Yet after the ceremony people throw the mask away or let children play with it. The only way to fit this into a description of religion as 'sacred' is to say that these people either have no religion or else have a special conception of 'the sacred'.[1]

Such contortions are in fact inevitable if we limit ourselves to the surface of religious concepts. Suppose you were a Martian anthropologist and observed that all human beings sustain themselves by eating food. You could compare the different tastes of food the world over and try and find common features. That would take lots of effort without any very clear results. It would seem that there are many, many different foods on earth and no simple way of finding the common elements. But now imagine you were a *good* Martian anthropologist. You would study the chemistry of cooking, which would reveal that there are only a few ways to process food (marinating, salting, roasting, smoking, boiling, grilling, etc.) and a large but limited number of ingredients. You would soon be able to report that the apparently unlimited variety of human cuisine is explained by combinations of a limited set of techniques and a limited set of materials. This is precisely what we can do with religious concepts, moving from the table to the kitchens and observing how the concepts are concocted in human minds.

Acquiring new concepts

In the last chapter I gave a hugely simplified account of what happens when a child receives some new information, for instance when she sees a walrus, a rather unfamiliar animal, give birth to live cubs. Using the ANIMAL template rather like an official form with boxes to fill in, the child can represent for instance that all walruses, not just this one, beget live cubs. If the child sees the animal feed on fish she will think that all walruses can eat fish. What I said of the child so far applies to adults as well, when they include new information in their mental encyclopaedia.

To demonstrate how this occurs, let me take the liberty of introducing new concepts into your encyclopaedia, starting with this:

Zygoons are the only predators of hyenas.

Before reading the sentence above, you knew that cats were born of other cats, elephants of elephants, and so on. Now you will probably agree that zygoons are born of other zygoons. What happened then was that:

1. You were given a new label: 'zygoon'.
2. You created a new entry ZYGOON in your mental encyclopaedia.
3. You placed it in the ANIMAL section of the encyclopaedia.
4. This immediately 'activated' the ANIMAL template, which transferred some information to the ZYGOON entry, like: 'zygoons cannot be made, they are born of other zygoons', 'if you cut a zygoon in two it will probably die', 'zygoons need to feed in order to survive', etc. This process is summed up in the following diagram:

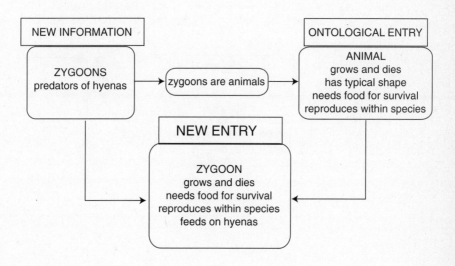

The new information (left-hand box) activates old information (right-hand box) to produce a new entry in the encyclopaedia (bottom box). This is not limited to the animal domain. Consider this:

Thricklers are expensive but cabinet-makers need them to work wood.

You already knew that telephones cannot grow or eat or sleep, nor can screwdrivers or motorbikes. Now you will assume that thricklers cannot grow or eat or sleep either, which we can summarise with a similar diagram:

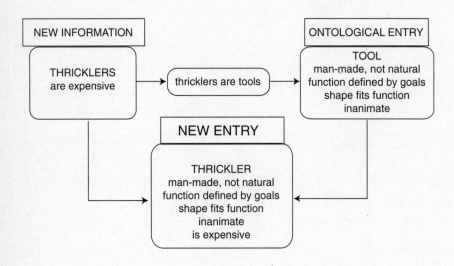

Some necessary jargon. At this point I must introduce several terms that will be useful for the next steps of the argument:

Inference. Some of these ideas you now have about zygoons are called inferences, which means that it is not me who gave you that information (for instance, that thricklers are probably made by people rather than found in nature). You *inferred* that from what I said. What goes on in your mind when you create a new concept is not entirely driven by the input but by a combination of that input with previous representations.

Default inference. Note how easy it was to agree that zygoons must be born of other zygoons, or that zygoons are not made in factories. All you had to do was to 'read' what your mental encyclopaedia says about animals in general. That was the right thing to do. I did not specify that zygoons were exceptional in any way. So you just assumed that, at least as a first approximation, all you know about animals in general applies to zygoons too. This creates a certain representation of the new object that is considered true as long as there is no explicit information to the contrary. An inference produced in this way is called a default inference. This is an analogy with computers: they function in the way the manufacturers decided (their 'default settings') unless you modify various parameters.

Expectations. Note that your opinions on zygoons and thricklers are conjectural. It is after all just possible that zygoons are really exceptional animals that survive dissection, never feed or never grow. This is not important for the time being. We are describing what you now expect of zygoons and thricklers. We are not discussing whether you are right to have these expectations. Smart brains consider not just what happened, but why it happened, what might follow and so on. If you have a brain that produces inferences, you constantly entertain *expectations*.

Ontological categories. This is the most important term here. Not all concepts are the same. Some very abstract concepts, like ANIMAL but also TOOL or PERSON or NUMBER are called ontological categories to distinguish them from the more concrete ones like CAT or TELEPHONE or ZYGOON. Ontological categories are special because they include all sorts of default inferences that help us acquire new kind-concepts like THRICKLER without having to re-acquire information such as: Thricklers do not sleep, nor do they eat or breed, etc.

Having rich ontological categories like ANIMAL or TOOL amounts to having 'mini-theories' of certain kinds of things in the world. Our expectations about animals are not just the outcome of repeated encounters with animals. They differ from such mindless accumulation of facts in two very important ways. First, we speculate about many aspects of animals beyond what we know. For instance, we all assume that if we opened up a tiger and inspected its innards what we would find could be found in other tigers too. We do not need to cut up a huge number of tigers, produce a statistic of what we found and conclude that organs are probably similar in all members of the TIGER category. We just assume that; it is part of our expectations. Second, we establish all sorts of causal links between the facts available. We assume that tigers eat goats because they are hungry, they are hungry because they need food to survive, they attack goats rather than elephants because they could not kill very large animals, they eat goats rather than grass because their digestive system could not cope with grass, and so on. This is why psychologists call such concepts 'theoretical'.

Templates in religious concepts: Step 1

It is quite easy to have precise expectations about imaginary objects. (As you may have suspected, there are no such things as thricklers or zygoons.) On the basis of very little information we spontaneously use ontological categories and the inferences they support to create particular expectations. This confirms a general psychological finding, that human imagination generally does not consist in a loosening of constraints, an intellectual free-for-all where all conceptual combinations are equally possible and equally good, once the mind breaks free of its conceptual shackles. Imagination is in fact strongly constrained by mental structures like the animal and tool templates. Psychologist Tom Ward used simple experiments to illustrate this point, asking people to draw and describe imaginary animals. He allowed them to make up any odd features they wanted. The results are indeed strange but it is remarkable how most subjects' creations abide by implicit principles about animal body-plans. For instance, they all preserve bilateral symmetry; people invent ten-legged animals but they are sure to put five legs on each side. Also, the animals move in the direction of their sense organs; if they have ten eyes, they have at least two in the front. So apparently unconstrained fantasy cannot easily break free of intuitive expectations. The general point is not new. Indeed, philosophers like Immanuel Kant argued that the structure of ordinary concepts provides the backbone for apparently unconstrained flights of imagination. What is new, on the other hand, is that we now have a much better description of how ordinary concepts give structure to fanciful ones.[2]

This applies to religious concepts as well. Religious representations are particular combinations of mental representations that satisfy two conditions. First, the religious concepts *violate* certain expectations from ontological categories. Second, they *preserve* other expectations. All this will become quite clear if we return to some examples of possible though unfamiliar religious notions:

[35]   Some ebony trees can recall conversations people hold in their shade.

[32]   There are invisible people around who only drink cologne. If someone suddenly goes into a fit and screams for cologne, it is because their body is being controlled by one of these invisible people.

Note that the sentences above describe *particular kinds* of more *general* categories. That is, [35] is not just about ebony trees, it is also a description of a PLANT with special characteristics. [32] is about persons with special characteristics. The plants described in [35] differ from other kinds of plants and the persons in [32] are distinct from other kinds of persons. This is generally true of religious concepts. They (more or less clearly) describe a new object by giving (i) its ontological category and (ii) its special features, different from other objects in the same ontological category. To use the same kind of diagram as before, this is how one can build a minimal representation of the special ebony trees:

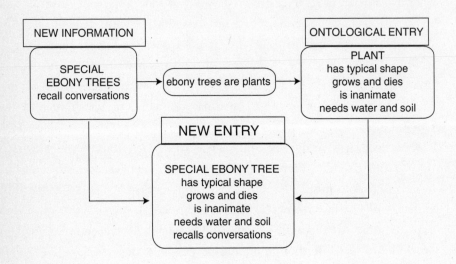

This process can be extended to all our examples but it would be tedious to use a separate diagram for each of them, so we can summarise the process using a formula:

[35] Special ebony tree → {all PLANT features} + recalls conversations

This just means: to build your representation of the new object (special ebony trees), just get your PLANT template, copy all the information that is true of plants (your default expectations about plants) and add a special 'tag' that says what is special about these particular plants. This works in the same way for the other examples of religious concepts. Here are the familiar ones:

[21] Omniscient God → {PERSON} + special cognitive powers

[22] Visiting ghosts → {PERSON} + no material body
[23] Reincarnation → {PERSON} + no death + extra body available
[24] Zombies → {PERSON} + no cognitive functioning
[25] Possessed people → {person} + no control of own utterances
[26] Virgin Birth → {PERSON} + special biological feature
[27] Listening statue → {TOOL} + cognitive functions

The principle is similar for the other, less familiar concepts. Even though we know nothing about the particular cultural context of these descriptions we can see how each of them combines a particular ontological category and a special characteristic:

[31] Thirsty people disappear → {PERSON} + special biology, physics
[32] Cologne spirits → {PERSON} + invisible + drinks perfume
[33] People with flying organ → {PERSON} + extra organ
[34] Counter-intelligence wristwatch → {TOOL} + detects enemies
[36] Gourmet mountain → {NATURAL OBJECT} + digestion
[37] Guardian river → {NATURAL OBJECT} + incest abhorrence
[38] Guardian forest → {NATURAL OBJECT} + likes a good tune

This, obviously, is a terribly simplified description of people's actual representations. But that is an advantage. Summarising concepts in this way highlights a very important property of religious concepts. Each of these entries in the mental encyclopaedia includes an ontological entry between brackets and a 'tag' for special features of the new entry. These tags added to the default category seem very diverse, but they have one property in common:

The information contained by the tags contradicts information provided by the ontological category.

Since this is a rather important property, allow me to labour the point a bit. When you activate an ontological category like ANIMAL, this delivers all sorts of expectations about the object identified as a member of the ANIMAL category. Now the concepts listed above seem to (1) activate those categories and (2) produce something that goes against what the category stipulates. Our category PERSON (or mini-theory of persons) specifies that they are living things and living things are born of other living things of the same species, they grow if they feed. Our entry for PLANTS specifies that they are inanimate (they move fast only if they are pushed), that they grow, that they need nutrients, and so on. Our entry for NATURAL OBJECTS specifies that they are inanimate like plants but that they are not living things. And so on and so forth. But religious concepts seem to go against some of that information. They describe PERSONS (therefore with a body) without a body, NATURAL OBJECTS (therefore without physiology) with a physiology, PLANTS (therefore inanimate) with animacy, and TOOLS (therefore without biology or cognition) with biology or cognition. To sum up: *Religious concepts invariably include counter-intuitive information*, relative to the category activated.

'Counter-intuitive' is a technical term here. It does not mean strange, inexplicable, funny, exceptional or extraordinary. What is counter-intuitive here is not even necessarily surprising. That is, if you have the concept of cologne-drinking-invisible-persons, if everyone around you talks about these visitors, you cannot really register puzzlement or astonishment every single time it is mentioned. It becomes part of your familiar world that there are invisible persons around that drink cologne. In the same way, Christians and Muslims are not surprised every time someone mentions the possibility that an omnipotent agent is watching them. This is completely familiar. But these concepts are still counter-intuitive in the precise sense used here, namely 'including information contradicting some information provided by ontological categories'. I will show in another chapter how we know what information is provided by these categories. For the time being, we must just remember that the ordinary sense of the term 'counter-intuitive' may be misleading. (A neologism such as 'counter-ontological' might have been a better choice.)

Counter-intuitive biology

To illustrate how these rather dry formulae correspond to actual concepts, let me start with counter-intuitive biological features. Our mental encyclopaedia specifies that objects in some ontological categories (ANIMAL, PERSON, PLANT) have biological properties. So a simple violation of expectations occurs when we attribute physiological or other biological processes to a category that does not intuitively include a biology. The Aymara people, a community of the Andes, describe a particular mountain as a live body, with a trunk, a head, legs and arms. The mountain is also said to have physiological properties: it 'bleeds' for instance and also 'feeds' on the meat of sacrificed animals that are left in particular places. Sacrifices of llama's hearts or foetuses are made to the mountain and left in special shrines to feed its body in exchange for the fertility of the fields. Diviners 'pump [sacrificial] blood and fat, principles of life and energy, to the rest of the mountain's . . . body'. A whole domain of ritual acts and explanatory assumptions is based on this transfer of biological properties – associated with animals, plants and persons – to what is otherwise identified as an inert natural object.[3]

These people do not have a fantastic ontology where mountains *in general* are live organisms with digestion, in the same way as llamas, people and goats. The supernatural concept specifies that *this* mountain has *some* physiological features. That other mountains are inanimate natural objects, like rocks and rivers, quite literally goes without saying in the Andes as it does everywhere else in the world. Indeed, the notion of *one* mountain having a physiology is attention-grabbing only against this intuitive background.

All animal species, in our intuitive categories, belong to one and only one species. Our intuitions go beyond the surface features of these different species. For instance, everyone (even young children) has the intuition that members of a species have the same 'stuff' inside: the innards of all cows are similar, and so are the insides of all giraffes. Violations of this principle are often found in supernatural concepts, not just in religion but also in myth and folktales. In the Sumerian *Gilgamesh* epic the hero's companion Enkidu is a half-human, half-animal composite. In the Fang epics, some heroes have an iron stomach and liver, which supposedly explains why they are invulnerable. To mention yet another, perhaps more familiar example from religion, the concept of a woman who gave birth without having sex is another instance of this general pattern: same species (she is a human being like other human beings) but counter-intuitive physiological property (she reproduces in a way that is not the same as other members of the species).

Among the Fang some people are said to possess an internal organ called *evur*, which allows them to display particular talent in various undertakings outside the domain of everyday activities. People with great oratory skills or a particular ability in business, people whose plantations are especially successful, are commonly said to have an *evur*. This is usually described as a small additional organ located in the person's stomach. One is born either with or without *evur*, although there is no easy way to find out. Indeed, how *evur* affects the person depends on external circumstances, so that possession of the extra organ is invoked to explain both positive personal features (someone is particularly skilled or attractive) and nasty but mysterious dealings. Most cases of illness or misfortune are connected to *evur*. Some *evur*-bearers are said to launch invisible attacks against other people, drink their blood and bring misfortune, illness, or even death to the victim. In fact, there are few examples of successful people who are not, in one way or another, suspected of having committed such witchcraft murders, in order to steal the others' goods or talents.

The representation of *evur* activates some intuitive biological expectations and violates others. It conforms to expectations in the sense that we routinely produce assumptions about hidden internal features of animal species. Tigers are aggressive but chickens are not, tigresses give birth to live offspring but hens lay eggs. This is not because of where they live or what they eat. We intuitively expect that such salient differences in observable behaviour are caused by internal differences in the ways animals are built. On the other hand, we do not expect such fundamental internal differences between members of the same species. All tigers and all chickens are supposed to have the same organs (with the exception of sexual organs). This is where the *evur* concept is counter-intuitive in assuming that the list of internal organs is different in *some* people.

That species-membership is essential and permanent (once an aardvark, always an aardvark) is an intuitive expectation. So it is not too surprising that *metamorphosis* should be a common supernatural device. People turn into animals, animals into mountains or rocks, etc. Such concepts again illustrate how supernatural imagination is more structured than we would usually assume.

First, note that the transformation is generally not complete. That is, the prince who 'turned into a toad' has not literally become a toad, otherwise the story would stop there. This new toad would carry on doing whatever toads do, which is fine but of no great narrative interest. What holds the reader's or listener's attention in such stories is that we now have *a human mind*, indeed the prince's own mind trapped in *a toad's body*, which is a very different matter.

Second, the choice of species or kinds of objects is itself constrained by intuitive ontology. Psychologists Frank Keil and Michael Kelly went through a mass of mythological and folk-tale material to tabulate what was turned into what and how often. The results show that most accounts of mythical metamorphoses occur between close ontological categories. Persons are turned into animals more often than into plants, in fact into mammals and birds rather than insects and bacteria, animals are turned into other animals or plants more often than into inert natural objects. Both persons and animals are seldom turned into artefacts. Now what does it mean to say that two ontological categories are 'close'? Simply that they have lots of inferences in common. Turning a prince into a frog is all right because frogs are animate beings that go where they want, have goals and intentions, etc. So you can still run all sorts of inferences about the narrative character once it is turned into an animal. You can describe it as *knowing* that it can be saved by a princess, *hoping* to meet one, *trying* to get a kiss, etc. All this would be more difficult to imagine if the prince had been turned into a potted geranium, and far more contrived if he had become a carburettor.[4]

These two features – incomplete metamorphosis and its occurrence between close categories – are connected. They both preserve a source of inferences. Naturally, people are generally not aware of the consequences of such ontological choices. It is just that their intuitive expectations either produce rich inferences or they do not, which makes the difference between good and bad stories.

Now, the notion of metamorphosis is where this account of supernatural concepts, in my experience, sometimes leaves people quite puzzled. 'Surely' (they say) 'there is something wrong in a model that describes metamorphoses as counter-intuitive. Metamorphoses do happen! Caterpillars become butterflies. This is a natural process.' This is where having a precise model (or paying attention to the precise features of the model, if I may say so) is important. Intuitive ontological categories and principles do not always constitute true or accurate descriptions of what happens in our environment. They are just what we intuitively expect, and that's that. The fact that caterpillars become butterflies, if you assume that caterpillars and butterflies are two different species, violates the principle that organisms cannot change species. You can of course accommodate it by considering caterpillars and butterflies as members of the same species seen at different points along a rather exceptional growth process. This, however, violates our intuitive grasp of such processes. We expect growth to produce a bigger and more complex version of the initial body-plan, not two different kinds of animals, each of them perfectly functional but in completely different ways. To cut a long story short, a natural metamorphosis of this kind is, whichever way you want to represent it, counter-intuitive in the precise sense described here. It violates intuitive, early-developed expectations about the ontological category ANIMAL. Many aspects of the real natural world are in fact counter-intuitive relative to our biological expectations.

Counter-intuitive mentation

To turn to a different domain, a very frequent type of counter-intuitive concept is produced by assuming that various objects or plants have some mental properties, that they can perceive what happens around them, understand what people say, remember what happened and have intentions. In chapter 1, I briefly mentioned the Cuna statuettes that serve as the shaman's auxiliaries. A more familiar example would be that of people who pray to statues of gods, saints or heroes. It is not just artefacts but also inanimate living things that can be 'animated' in this sense. The Pygmies of the Ituri forest for instance say that the forest is a live thing, that it has a soul, that it 'looks after' them and is particularly generous to sociable, friendly and honest individuals. These will catch plenty of game because the forest is pleased with their behaviour.

For a more detailed illustration, consider anthropologist Wendy James's account of 'ebony divination', a recent and successful cult of the Uduk-speaking peoples of Sudan. People report that ebony trees have capacities that mark them off from other plants and natural objects. The trees can eavesdrop on conversations people would not care to hold within other people's hearing distance. Because of their position ebony trees are also apprised of other occurrences: '[Ebony] will know of the actions of the *arum* [souls, spirits, including people who were not given a proper burial] and of *dhatu/* [witches] and other sources of psychic activity.'[5]

If ebony trees just archived past conversations, plans and conspiracies in a store which was inaccessible, this would not be of much interest (recall our examples of spirits that forget instantly or of a god who has no idea what is going on around him). But the trees can sometimes 'reveal' what they overheard. To recover the juicy gossip or the witches' schemes, a diviner takes a twig from the ebony tree, burns it and plunges it into a bowl of water. Divination messages are 'read off' in the way the stick burns and in the patterns formed by ashes falling on the surface of the water. The smudges not only indicate the nature of the problem at hand but also a solution, for instance by directing the diviner to the place where a particular soul is held, separated from the person. So ebony trees provide traces of past misdeeds and remedies to current difficulties.

Ebony trees are not the product of an unbridled imagination; they support precise inferences within narrow constraints. For instance the trees cannot record something that did not occur. They cannot record events before they happen. This may seem obvious because I used the word 'record', but here I put the cart before the horse. We (and the Uduk) call this a 'recording' process precisely because these constraints are imposed on the way trees acquire information. Where do the constraints come from? The Uduk are not theologians so very few people there would waste much time over purely speculative questions of this sort. It is clear however that you can have the constraints without having an explicit theory of these constraints. Trees record what happened and not what did not happen because they are so to speak 'impressed' with what happens in the same way that our eyes and ears cannot help but see and hear. Our intuitive concept of a mind suggests that minds form such impressions *as* events occur and *because* they occur, and the same is intuitively assumed of ebony trees.

The mind-concept is such a rich source of inferences that we use it spontaneously even in cases where some of its usual assumptions are challenged. Consider for instance a fairly typical case of possession among Mayotte islanders described by Michael Lambek. During a trance the person 'is absent, no one can say where', so that standard communication with him or her is impossible. This violates a crucial intuition that the mind is the 'executive centre' that plans and controls the person's behaviour. So the idea of someone who is around, is alive and awake yet 'isn't there' in the sense of conscious experience is counter-intuitive. Notice however that people do not stop there. They assume not just that the possessed person's mind has 'gone away' but also that *another* mind has 'come in'. A spirit has invaded the person and is now in control. These spirits take on all the standard assumptions about the mind. People talk with the invading spirit. They generally negotiate its return to its usual base and the return of the dislodged mind to its body. The spirits are assumed to know certain facts, to have beliefs, they are also described as wanting certain events to happen. These complex hypotheses form a necessary background to all the conversations that take place in these counter-intuitive circumstances. Mayotte spirits come in different shapes and behaviours. Some outrageous types always insist on drinking perfume and will not go away until they have taken a swig or two from a bottle of cologne.[6]

This very short tour of a few non-Western notions has taken us through most of my list of unfamiliar religious concepts. Most but not all. It is time to reveal that – to my knowledge at least – one does not find a concept of people who disappear when they are really thirsty or the notion of a wristwatch that keeps an eye on one's enemies. (However, when my friend Michael Houseman did anthropological work in Cameroon he was told of a magical watch that could tell the exact time when your friends would call on you; a nicer, less paranoid conceit that nobody took very seriously.) That incest may trigger all sorts of natural catastrophes is a common theme the world over, but I made up the story of a river that flows upstream. Note that these imaginary concepts are neither more bizarre nor less coherent than the other items listed.

Why put imaginary examples in the list? We want to explain the religious concepts people actually have, the ones that are stable in a culture and seem to be found, in slightly different versions, in many different cultures. The explanation is that successful, culturally spreading concepts are those with specific properties. Now this implies that human minds are receptive, not just to the concepts they actually have, but also to many other possible concepts, provided they correspond to this model. What we want to describe is the envelope of *possible* religious concepts. Indeed, as I will show below, we now have experimental means to test whether new, artificial, supernatural concepts have the potential to spread or not.

Templates in religious concepts: Step 2

The examples illustrate the first step in our recipe for supernatural concepts, the insertion of a violation of expectations. But they also show why this cannot be the whole story. As I said, the counter-intuitive ebony trees have the special feature that they can understand and remember what people say. This is used to produce all sorts of *inferences* about them. These inferences are what makes the concept 'work', as it were. If the trees heard conversations but could not remember them or if they remembered conversations that had never actually happened, the concept would probably not be that successful.

We can now describe more precisely this distinction between 'workable' and 'unworkable' concepts like the following:

[5] There is only one God! He is omniscient but powerless. He cannot do anything or have any effect on what goes on in the world.

[6] The gods are watching us and they notice everything we do! But they forget everything instantaneously.

[7] Some people can see the future but they then forget it immediately.

[8] Some people can predict future events, though only about thirty seconds in advance.

[9] There is only one God! However, he has no way of finding out what goes on in the world.

[10] This statue is special because it vanishes whenever someone thinks about it.

[11] There is only one God! He is omnipotent. But He exists only on Wednesdays.

[12] The spirits will punish you if you do what they want.
[13] This statue is special because you see it here but actually it is everywhere in the world.

These all include violations. [7] is counter-intuitive because our intuitive ontology, as we will see below, has some very strict conditions on what it is to have a mind. In particular, it assumes that minds form perceptions because of actual events that occur in their environments. As a result of these perceptions, minds form beliefs about what happened. In our intuitive concept of a mind there are causal links that go from events to perceptions and from perceptions to beliefs, not the other way around. So a mind that has beliefs or representations of events that have not yet occurred is counter-intuitive all right. The same applies to the other examples. There is a god who perceives everything [5]; this violates our intuitive notion of mind, following which perception is always focused on some objects and has limited access to what happens. [13] is also counter-intuitive because material objects like statues are expected to have one location in the world; they are somewhere or somewhere else but not in two locations at the same time, let alone everywhere at once.

Here is the reason why, though they include a violation, these concepts are not quite satisfactory. Religious concepts comprise (1) an ontological label and (2) a particular tag. In all the 'good' items we have examined so far, the tag contradicted some of the information given by the label. Notice that I was careful to say *some*, not *all* of the information provided by the ontological label. The point is crucial. Consider two of our favourites again:

[24] Some people are dead but they keep walking around. They cannot talk any more, they are not aware of what they are doing.
[36] This mountain over there (*this* one, not that one) eats food and digests it. We give it food sacrifices every now and then, to make sure it stays in good health.

The zombies described in [24] are certainly counter-intuitive in that they are PERSONS but without control of their own actions. (Comatose or paralysed people are a different case because they do not engage in complex series of actions. Zombies go around, carry things, even murder people, etc.) But this counter-intuitive element still leaves many aspects of the PERSON category untouched. This is good, because there is a lot in the PERSON category that tells you what to expect a zombie to be like. Persons are solid physical objects with a mass. Zombies are like that too. Persons have a unique location in space and time. Zombies too are at one place at one time. To turn to more gruesome conjectures, if you chop off a zombie's arm the zombie may carry on living but not the arm! At least you are not given any information to the contrary, so that is a plausible conjecture. The same goes for the mountain. A mountain that eats food still has a unique location, a mass, it is still a solid object. Many inferences that were given for free by the ontological category still apply. This is the gist of a second condition:

> *The religious concept preserves all the relevant default inferences except the ones that are explicitly barred by the counter-intuitive element.*

A good illustration is the familiar concept of a ghost or spirit. This is found more or less the world over, not just in Gothic novels and Victorian seances. The concept is that of a PERSON that has counter-intuitive physical properties. Unlike other persons ghosts can go through solid objects like walls. But notice that, apart from this, these ghosts follow very strictly the ordinary intuitive concept PERSON. Imagine a ghost suddenly materialises in your home as you are having dinner. Startled by this sudden appearance, you drop your spoon in your bowl of soup. In a situation like this your mind creates a whole lot of assumptions that you do not necessarily represent consciously. For instance, you assume that the ghost *saw* you were having dinner so that he now *knows* that you were eating. Also, the ghost probably *heard* the sound of your spoon landing in the soup and can now *remember* that you dropped it. You assume that the ghost *knows* you are here since he can *see* you. It would be unsettling but not too surprising if the ghost asked you whether you were enjoying your dinner. It would be very weird if he asked you why you never had dinner at home or why you never had soup. In other words you assume that this ghost has a mind. All the italicised verbs above describe the sort of thing a mind does: it perceives actual events in the world and forms beliefs on the basis of these perceptions. Furthermore, the ghost's mind seems to work according to definite principles. For instance, we assume that the ghost sees what happens and believes what he sees. We do not assume that the ghost sees what he believes.

All this may seem rather banal – and as the old Groucho Marx joke goes, don't be deceived: it *is* banal. Our notions about the ghost's mind are just similar to our assumptions about the minds we are used to, that is, our own minds and the minds of people around us. Most of our interaction with ghosts is informed by assumptions that we routinely use in dealing with more standard versions of persons. Indeed, the banality of ghost-representations is a rich source of comic effects, as in a Woody Allen story where the hero returns from the dead to visit his widow during a seance only to ask her how long it takes to roast a chicken in the oven. The world over, people assume that such agents as ghosts and spirits have minds.

The general process whereby we combine (1) a limited violation and (2) otherwise preserved inferences from a concept is a very common phenomenon in human thinking, namely *default reasoning*. Consider the figures overpage:

Most people have no difficulty describing these as 'a circle with a dent' and 'a square with a spike on the right-hand side'. But such phrases correspond to no precise geometric features, because a circle with a dent is not properly speaking a circle at all and a square with a spike has lost the standard geometrical properties of a square. This is why computer programs have great difficulty recognising a circle and a square in the above figures. It takes quite a lot of subtle pro-

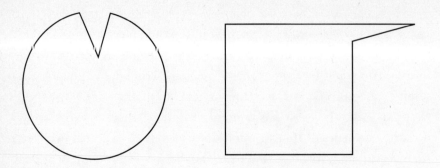

gramming to circumvent this rigidity. Humans, by contrast, spontaneously think of such cases as a combination of (1) an instance of the usual concept and (2) a minor change added to it that only affects some of its properties, which is also the way supernatural concepts are built by using default expectations from ontological categories.

This is important because it explains an aspect of cultural transmission that would otherwise remain mysterious, namely that in the domain of the supernatural, *people have detailed representations even though they are not told much.* Take the example of our familiar ghosts again. You were probably told at some point that ghosts can walk through walls. Similarly, the Fang are told that ghosts often appear in clearings in the forest, out of nowhere, and then disappear in the same counter-intuitive way. But neither you nor the Fang were ever told that 'ghosts can see what happens when it happens' or that 'ghosts remember what happened after it happened'. No one ever says that because no one needs to say it. These inferences that literally go without saying are spontaneously produced because our minds apply a default principle.

In this domain, then, cultural transmission is very easy because the mind provides a lot of information to complete the fragmentary elements provided by other people. It is not too surprising that various people have similar representations about the ghosts' thought-processes, although no one ever talks about it. The representations are similar because the PERSON template in everybody's mind is very similar. Cultural transmission is cheap; it does not require much effort and communication, as long as templates in our mind provide order for free, as it were.

What is intuitive in the paranormal

Many people think that, in some circumstances at least, perception can extend beyond its ordinary limits. One can then guess other people's thoughts, visualise events before they actually occur, receive messages from dead people, travel through time, etc. In some form or other such notions occur all over the world. In the same way, many people also have the symmetrical belief that mere thoughts can cause real effects. Some psychics are said to move objects at a distance or make them disappear by sheer will-power.

A Fang friend of mine once insisted that he had seen a gifted shaman perform an extraordinary feat. The old man had stuck a finger in the ground in his village and had made it re-emerge in another village several miles away, by just telling his finger to get there! When challenged by derisive sceptics in the village ('How can you claim you *saw* it all if it happened in two different places?'), the narrator conceded that he had witnessed only the first part of this dramatic event; but the re-emergence of the finger had been reported by very reliable sources. As this last comment only added fuel to the sceptics' scorn my friend walked off in a sulk.

Such notions crop up in conversations the world over. So, to some extent, does the sceptical reaction. Only in the West have such beliefs become a kind of institution, the very earnest activity of dedicated individuals who compile records of such events, classify them and even perform experiments to try and validate extra-ordinary paranormal claims. Psychologist Nicholas Humphrey has documented this dogged pursuit of the paranormal and the miraculous. Heroically stubborn researchers explore all the possible evidence, exchange masses of information on documented cases, design ever more clever techniques to discover supernatural causation. The sad fact that experiments never demonstrate the intended effects – or do so only when they are not properly controlled – does not in any way dash their hopes. They lose every battle but expect to win the war. The main reason for this unbridled optimism is that there is a strong motivation here, that people really *want* such claims to be true. Why is that so? As Humphrey points out, the cultural impact of science on modern Western societies is certainly a relevant factor. In a cultural context where this hugely successful way of understanding the world has debunked one supernatural claim after another, there is a strong impulse to find at least *one* domain where it would be possible to trump the scientists. Life used to be one such domain, as scientists could not properly explain in a purely physical way the difference between living and non-living things or the evolution of exquisitely designed organisms. Life had to be special, perhaps the effect of some non-physical vital elan or energy. But evolution and microbiology crushed all this and showed that life is indeed a physical phenomenon. What is left, for some people, is the soul, and the idea that mental events, thoughts and memories and emotions, are not just physical events in brains. Hence the hope that they might show that thought can travel in physically impossible ways and have direct effects on matter.[7]

However, Humphrey also shows why this explanation is insufficient. The source of all this fascination cannot be that there are effects of *thought* on *matter* at all, because such effects are not in themselves always supernatural or even surprising. When you are happy and you smile, that's an effect of mind on matter. If you see a photograph of car crash victims or surgical operations, your heart-beat will increase slightly and your skin's electrical resistance will change. These too are effects of mental states on physical events, but no one finds them terribly fascinating. What makes psycho-kinesis so interesting to believers is not that some intention results in some effect, but that it results in *precisely* the effect intended. When the supposed psychic wants the paperweight on the table to move from right to left, it does indeed move from right to left. What is supposed to happen in such cases is a transmission of detailed information coming from the mind, specifying that it is the paperweight, not the glass, that should move and that it should move from right to left, not the other way around. All that information is received by the right target and decoded in the appropriate way; it then results in the right move.

Is that supernatural? In some sense, not at all. To have precise information received by the right targets and result in the relevant effect is something we are all familiar with, since we all control our own bodies in this way. Our intention to move our hand towards the coffee-cup results in the right target (the hand) moving in the right direction. So what is supernatural in the paperweight's motion is not that thoughts direct physical events but that they direct them *outside our bodies*. We do have a powerful intuitive expectation that our thoughts only control our bodies. Indeed, that is the way we learn how to interact with objects in the environment in the first months of life, by reaching, pushing, touching, etc. So the notion that my intentions could control not just my hand but also the door-knob before my hand touches it is a violation of intuitive expectations. This is the counter-intuitive element.

This violation is represented in a way that preserves the intuitive expectation that the effects of thoughts on material objects (our bodies in the standard situation) are *the precise effects described by the intention*. For my friend, it was quite natural that the shaman's finger had resurfaced in the precise village where its owner had decided to send it. This expectation of control-by-description is so natural that believers in psycho-kinesis rarely comment on it or even mention it. But it is indispensable to the supernatural claim, as Nicholas Humphrey shows. Suppose I had a new kind of paranormal belief, for which this was the evidence: first, when I try magically to move my socks to the laundry-bag this invariably propels my tea-cup into the kitchen-sink; second, whenever my friend Jill is in danger I dream of my friend Jack eating cake. This would be counter-intuitive enough (my thoughts move objects, distant events have direct effects on my mind) but the intuitive inferential elements would be absent. I do not think anyone would make much of a career in the paranormal on the basis of such claims.

From catalogues to experiments

The combination of ontological violation and preserved inferential potential explains the family resemblance among supernatural concepts. The common features are not in the concepts themselves but in the templates that produce them, in the recipe that specifies an ontological category, a violation-tag, as well as the use of all non-blocked inferences. This would suggest that there are not that many different templates. To produce a good supernatural concept, you must describe something as belonging to an ontological category. But there are not that many different ontological categories. Indeed, we have some reasons to think that ANIMAL, PERSON, TOOL (including in fact many other man-made objects beyond tools proper), NATURAL OBJECT (e.g. rivers, mountains) and PLANT more or less exhaust the list. Once you have the ontological category, you must add a violation. But we also have evidence that there are not that many violations which can preserve expectations in the way described here. As we saw above, some violations are cognitive dead-ends. You can imagine them but you cannot produce many inferences about the situation described (if this statue disappears when we think about it, what follows?).

This is why there is only a rather short *Catalogue of Supernatural Templates* that more or less exhausts the range of culturally successful concepts in this domain. Persons can be represented as having counter-intuitive physical properties (like ghosts or gods), counter-intuitive biology (like many gods who neither grow nor die) or counter-intuitive psychological properties (such as unblocked perception or prescience). Animals too can have all these properties. Tools and other artefacts can be represented as having biological properties (some statues bleed) or psychological ones (they hear what you say). Browsing through volumes of mythology, fantastic tales, anecdotes, cartoons, religion and science-fiction, you will get an extraordinary variety of different concepts, but you will also find that the number of templates is very limited and in fact contained in the short list given above.

Indexing supernatural themes in this way has all the attractions of butterfly-collecting. We now know where to put various familiar themes and characters in our systematic catalogue of templates, from listening trees to bleeding statues and from the Holy Virgin to Big Brother. There is no reason to stop there. We could go through compilations such as *Bulfinch's Mythology* (1855–62) or various folk-tale indices and check that most concepts actually correspond to one of these templates. However, we have much better things to do. For one thing, we should explain why these combinations of concepts are so good for human minds that the supernatural imagination seems condemned to rehash these Variations on a Theme. Second, we should try and figure out why some of these combinations are much more frequent than others. Third, we should explain why some supernatural concepts are taken very seriously indeed, as representing real beings and objects with consequences in people's lives. Explaining all this is probably more rewarding and certainly more urgent than classifying mythological themes.

A first task was to show that very diverse concepts from different places correspond to a few templates. Now we must explain why this is the case. To achieve this, we do what could be called 'experimental theology'. In controlled experiments, we create new concepts and we see whether concepts that correspond to these templates are really better recalled or better transmitted than other concepts.

Psychologist Justin Barrett and I have been involved in running such experiments for some time now. Our reasoning was that the present explanation of supernatural concepts, on the basis of what we know from anthropology, also implied precise psychological predictions. Cultural concepts are selected concepts. They are the ones that survive cycles of acquisition and communication in roughly similar forms. One simple condition of such relative preservation is that concepts are *recalled*. So Barrett and I designed fairly coherent stories in which we inserted various new violations of ontological expectations as well as episodes that were compatible with onto-logical expectations. The difference in recall between the two kinds of information would give us an idea of the advantage of violations in individual memory. Naturally, we only used stories and concepts that were new to our subjects. If I told you a story about a character with seven-league boots or a talking wolf disguised as a grandmother, or a woman who gave birth to an incarnation of a god after a visit from an angel, you would certainly remember these themes; not just because they were in a story but also because they were familiar to start with. Our studies were supposed to track how memory stores or distorts or discards novel material.

Recall, counter-intuitives and oddities

The results of such experiments are perhaps fascinating, but the detail of the operation is invariably tedious. This is why I only give here a brief report of the relevant findings, as far as violations and other such supernatural material are concerned. Our first result was that violations or transfers indeed fared much better than standard items. Long-term recall (over months) shows that violations were much better preserved than any other material. In these artificial conditions, then, people recall descriptions of artefacts or persons or animals that include violations of intuitive expectations much better than descriptions that do not include them. Violations are certainly distinctive, that is, they are surprising given people's expectations. When a sentence begins 'There was a table . . .', you do not expect to hear '. . . that felt sad when people left the room', and this is certainly part of the reason why such combinations are recalled. But that is not the only reason. Barrett and I also found that violations of ontological expectations – as found in the templates for supernatural concepts – are recalled better than what we called 'mere oddities'. For instance, 'a man who walked through a wall' (ontological violation) was generally better recalled than 'a man with six fingers' (violation of expectations, but not of those expectations that define the ontological category PERSON). Or 'a table that felt sad' was better recalled than 'a table made of chocolate' (equally unexpected, but not an ontological violation).

This last result is not just interesting for slightly obsessive experimental psychologists. It also explains some aspects of supernatural notions in the real world, as it were. We can now explain in a much more precise way why it is misleading to think of religious concepts as 'strange' or 'unusual'. We have kind-concepts ('giraffe') and we have ontological categories ('animal'). You can create strange new concepts by contradicting some information associated with either of these. If you say 'there was a black giraffe with six legs', this violates people's expectations about the kind-concept. If you say 'there was a giraffe that gave birth to an aardvark', this violates expectations about the ontological category (because of the intuitive principle, that animals are born of other animals of the same species). Now consider the following sentences:

[26a] We worship this woman because she was the only one ever to conceive a child without having sex.

[26b] We worship this woman because she gave birth to thirty-seven children.

[27a] We pray to this statue because it listens to our prayers and helps us get what we want.

[27b] We pray to this statue because it is the largest artefact ever made.

[31a] Some people suddenly disappear when they are really thirsty.

[31b] Some people turn black when they are really thirsty.

Items [26a], [27a] and [31a] are all bona fide candidates for inclusion in some religious repertoire. Indeed, two of them are very familiar religious representations. By contrast the corresponding [b] items, though they are about the same categories and include some non-standard conceptual association, are much less convincing. They all include a violation that is *not* an ontological violation. That is, they all contradict some conceptual information, but not that associated with the ontological categories. Your mental entries for people's physiology probably does not include people generally turning black when thirsty, so this is clearly an exceptional state of affairs. However, there is nothing in the mental construal of a person that would rule out the possibility of turning black. The same goes for the woman with thirty-seven children, a really exceptional person but still a PERSON, or the largest artefact ever made. It is intuitively assumed that artefacts have a size, and it follows from this that some artefacts are larger than others and one of them has to be the largest. Again, all these associations are strange and exceptional but the special tag does not contradict the relevant ontological entry. The memory effects – we find better recall for ontological violations than for oddities or for standard associations – seem to explain the anthropological observation – oddities, compared to ontological violations, are not found at the core of supernatural concepts.

I must of course nuance this conclusion a little. Religious concepts do include oddities in this precise sense. Some Mayotte spirits, as we saw, drink cologne instead of water. If you find this a bit lame, consider a more far-fetched example, from Charles Stewart's description of those minor demons one is likely to encounter in isolated places in modern rural Greece, away from the reassuring space of the village. All these *exotiká* are thought to be either incarnations of the Devil or among his minions. Here is a short list (I have omitted some): *daoútis,* a goat-devil that couples with flocks; *drákoi*, huge ogres who abduct young women; *fandásmata,* ethereal creatures that transform themselves into cattle, donkeys, goats; *gelloúdes*, female demons that eat young children; *gorgónes* or mermaids; *kallikántzaroi*, very ugly goblins with tail and horns; *monóvyza*, one-breasted giant women; *stríngla,* an old woman who transforms herself into an owl and drinks the blood of children; *vrykólakas,* a vampire whose flesh is not decayed and generally comes back to haunt his own family; *neráides*, very beautiful dancers seen dancing in outlying places, who drive young men insane; *smerḍáki*, a small demon that attacks flocks; and finally the *lámies*, very beautiful females (writes Stewart) with only a couple of minor blemishes: a cow's foot and a goat's foot.[8]

These odd features, the violations of kind-concept information, are added to ontological violations. They are features associated with the supernatural concept though not indispensable to its representation. For instance, the implications of the existence of spirits would not be changed much if people in Mayotte started believing that spirits drink petrol instead of cologne. But the change would be far more drastic if they became convinced that spirits cannot talk through people because a spirit does not have a mind. In the same way, the crucial feature of the *exotiká* is that they appear and disappear at will, undergo no biological process – they do not get old or die – and are agents of a hugely powerful Devil. That they have cow's feet or goat's horns are details that make them even more salient but do not contribute to inferences about their interaction with people, and this is why such details change a lot from place to place and over time, as Stewart reports. Indeed, anthropologists have long documented short-term changes in surface details of religious concepts, as well as differences within a group. Such changes and differences are generally limited to the surface oddities added to the ontological violation and maintain the crucial violation.

Memory effects do not change (much) with culture

Do such memory effects work in similar ways in different cultures? This was very much taken for granted in my explanation so far. I compared concepts from very different places and suggested that they are produced by recipes that would work in any normal human mind. But we could not just rule out the possibility that our experimental results had been biased by all sorts of cultural factors. The way European and American subjects recalled stories might be influenced by the use of literacy, a formal schooling system, the cultural influence of scientific theories, the existence of mass-media as sources of information and fiction, the presence of institutional religion, etc. This is why cross-cultural replications are indispensable in this kind of investigation.

Doing this does not mean just transporting a protocol to a different location. For one thing, some of the stories would make no sense at all to people used to very different kinds of fiction and fantasy. More important, the very notion of 'testing' someone's memory, indeed of testing anyone on anything, is alien to most people without formal schooling. As many cross-cultural psychologists have noted, there is something deeply unnatural in the idea of academic tests, and of experimental protocols too. In such contexts, the person who is in a position to know the answers (the teacher, the experimenter) pretends not to know them; while the person who is in no such position is supposed to provide them! It takes years of formal schooling to get used to this odd situation.

We first adapted our stories to test recall with Fang people in Gabon, both in the capital city Libreville and in several villages in the forest. Doing this kind of work with Fang people actually turned out to be quite easy. Many Fang people take particular pride in being able to recall very long stories in precise detail. Such people, traditional story-tellers, often challenge others to recall what happened at what point in this or that story. So all we had to do was to present our tests as a not-too-serious version of such a challenge. In one of the villages this actually turned into a competition between the research assistants (Fang university students) and some local youths, to determine which group had the 'better minds'. Obviously, one might fear that this too would introduce a special bias – but remember we do not and in fact cannot eliminate all bias. All we can do is vary the situations so the sources of bias push the data in different directions and therefore cancel each other out. In any case, these experiments were of interest because of the contrast between Fang people and Euro-Americans in terms of exposure to religious and supernatural concepts.

As far as religion is concerned, our Western subjects were used to rather sober versions of Christian concepts. They were also familiar with a whole range of supernatural notions, but these were entirely non-serious, belonging to the genres of fantasy, folk-tales, science-fiction, comic books, etc. Fang people, by contrast, are exposed to a whole range of supernatural objects, beings and occurrences that are taken in a very matter-of-fact way as part of daily existence. Witches may be performing secret rituals to get better crops than you. Ghosts may push you as you walk in the forest so you trip up and get hurt. Some people in the village are presumed to have an extra organ and may prove to be very dangerous. Indeed some people are widely believed to have killed other people by witchcraft, although nothing could be proved. I do not mean to suggest that Fang people live in a paranoid world with ghouls and monsters lurking in every corner. Rather, ghosts and spirits and witchcraft are part of their circumstances in the same way as car-crashes, industrial pollution, cancer and common muggings are part of most Western people's.

To vary contexts even further, I also conducted a small-scale replication in a very different context, among Tibetan monks in Nepal, with some help from Charles Ramble, a specialist of Tibetan Buddhism. The monks, like Fang people, live in groups where religious and supernatural occurrences and concepts are part of their familiar surroundings rather than of distant fiction. However, in the context of Tibetan Buddhism, these concepts are mainly inspired by written sources. Indeed the monks are local specialists in these sources and in the various intellectual disciplines associated with them. So we thought these studies would tell us whether these important cultural differences had much effect on memory for supernatural concepts.

In both places, violations were best recalled, followed by oddities and then by standard items with the lowest recall rate. This suggests that there is indeed a general sensitivity to violations of intuitive expectations for ontological categories. That is, the cognitive effects of such violations do not seem to be much affected by (1) what kinds of religious concepts are routinely used in the group people belong to, (2) how varied they are, (3) how seriously they are taken, (4) whether they are transmitted from literate sources or informal oral communication and (5) whether the people tested are actually involved in producing local 'theories' of the supernatural. This, at least, would be the natural conclusion to draw from the essentially similar recall performance observed in all three cultural environments. French and American students, like Fang peasants and Tibetan monks, are more likely to recall ontological violations than either oddities or standard associations.

Violations remain circumscribed

Barrett and I also tested strange combinations of concepts not usually found in human cultures. This was not just for the sake of running more experiments. If we want to explain why supernatural concepts are found in human cultures we also need to explain why other types are not found. Here is an example of that kind of approach. If what makes a concept salient and potentially well preserved is the violation, then material that combines several violations might be even better recalled. Consider for instance these two violations: Some being has cognitive powers such that it can hear future conversations; some artefact can understand what people say. It would seem that an even better concept could be produced by combining these two, for example, an amulet that can hear what people will say in the future. Other such combinations could be: Someone who sees through opaque walls and only sees what does *not* happen behind them (combining two violations of intuitive psychology); a dishwasher that gives birth to offspring but they are telephones, not little dishwashers (combining a transfer of biology to an artefact with a breach of biological expectations); a statue that hears what you say and disappears every now and then (combining a transfer of psychology to an artefact with a breach of intuitive physics); and so on.

Such combinations are certainly counter-intuitive, but they are not usually recalled very well, and certainly not as well as single violations. Again, individual performance in the lab is analogous to cultural spread in time and space. Anthropologists know that combinations of counter-intuitive properties are rather rare in culturally successful supernatural concepts. When they occur, this is mostly in the rarefied intellectual atmosphere of literate theology. They are all but absent in popular, cultural widespread forms of supernatural imagination. Indeed, most culturally widespread concepts in this domain are in fact rather sober and generally focus on one violation at a time, for one particular category.

To illustrate this, consider a familiar situation. Many people in Europe are Christians. Their concept of God includes the explicit assumption that God has non-standard cognitive properties. He is omniscient and seems to attend to everything at the same time; no event in the world can be presumed to escape God's attention. This means that prayers addressed to God but also to such agents as Christ or the Virgin Mary can be uttered anywhere. The god will hear you, regardless of whether you are in a crowd or on your own, sitting on a train or driving your car. In many places Christians also treat some artefacts as endowed with special powers. People for instance go to a distant place to pray to a particular Madonna, which means standing in front of an artefact and talking to it. (You may find this description rather crude, and retort that no one is really talking to a man-made object; people are considering a 'symbol' of the Virgin, a 'sign' or 'representation' of her presence and power. But that is not the case. First, people are really representing the Madonna as an artefact. If I tell them who made it, using what kind of wood and paint, they will find all that information perfectly sensible, as it would be indeed of an other man-made object. Second, it really is the artefact they are addressing. If I proposed to chop the Madonna to pieces because I needed fire-wood and suggested I replace it with a photograph of the statue, or with a sign reading 'pray to the Virgin here', they would find that shocking.)

Now people who represent these two types of violation do not usually combine them. They have a concept of agents that can hear you wherever you are; they also have a concept of artefacts that can hear you. But they do not have the concept of artefacts that could hear you wherever you are. That is, people who want to pray to the Madonna of such and such a place *actually go there*, and in most cases will take care to stand *within hearing distance* of the statue when they utter their prayers. This is in fact a general observation. All over the world we find concepts of artefacts that hear or think or more generally have a mind; and concepts of minds with counter-intuitive properties are not uncommon. But their combination is extremely rare. This illustrates, again, the fact that a combination of one violation with preserved expectations is probably a cognitive optimum, a concept that is both attention-grabbing and allows rich inferences.

Violations are attention-grabbing only against a background of expectations. But what happens if people routinely produce counter-intuitive representations? If you are brought up in a place where people repeatedly assert that a mountain is digesting food, that a huge invisible jaguar is flying over the village, that some people have an extra internal organ, does that have an effect on your expectations? In the past, anthropologists used to think that the presence of such super-natural representations might have a feed-back effect on people's expectations. But there is no evidence for that. On the contrary, there is experimental evidence to show that ontological intuitions are quite similar. Psychologist Sheila Walker conducted a series of careful experimental studies of both child and adult categories among Yoruba people in Nigeria, and showed how intuitions were not really affected by the presence of familiar counter-intuitive representations. People say for instance that a particular ritual that includes the sacrifice of a dog was successful, although the animal actually given to the gods was a cat. They claim that the animal somehow magically changed species under the priest's incantations. At the same time, however, people are quite clear that such transformations are excluded in normal circumstances, because species membership is a stable feature of animals. Indeed, it is precisely that principle that makes the ritual transformation an index of the priest's powers.[9]

Theological correctness

Finally, let me turn to the way people produce inferences on the basis of ontological violations. As I said above, it seems to be a condition for 'good' supernatural concepts that they allow all the inferences not explicitly barred by the violation. So a spirit can very well go through walls but should have the expected mental functions of a person. Imagine what would happen if you did not preserve this default background. You are told that some trees can eavesdrop on people's conversations. You are not told anything else. If you do not maintain the background, you can now imagine more or less anything about these trees: that they move about, that they fly in the air when they want, that they disappear when someone looks at them, and so on. But that does not seem to be what happens.

This, too, could be tested experimentally. Here is a simple example. People in America have a concept of God. That is, they seem to have organised thoughts about what makes God special, in what way God is different from a giraffe or a courgette or a person like you and me. If we had not learnt our lesson from cognitive psychology, we might be tempted to think that the best way to understand how people think about God is just to ask them: What is God? Indeed, this is what most students of religion have been doing for centuries. Go see the believers and ask them what they believe.

Then Justin Barrett thought that there may be something more to people's thoughts about God than they themselves believed. So he used a very simple, tried and tested method. He got his subjects to read specially prepared stories and to retell them after a while. The point of this is that people cannot store a text verbatim if it is longer than a few sentences. What they do is form a memory of the main episodes and how they connect. So when they recall the text people often distort the details of a story. Between the bits that are actually preserved from the original they insert details of their own invention. For instance, people read in *Little Red Riding Hood* that 'she *went* to her grandmother's house' and a few hours later say that 'she *walked* to her grandmother's house'. Minor changes of this kind or additions reveal what concepts people use to represent the story. In this particular case, they show that people imagined the heroine walking rather than taking a bus or riding a motorbike, although the story did not mention anything about how she travelled about.

So Barrett did two things. First, he asked his subjects to answer the simple question, What is God like? People produced all sorts of descriptions with common features. For instance, many of them said that an important feature of God is that he can attend to all sorts of things at the same time, contrary to humans who by necessity attend to one thing and then to another. After this, Barrett had his subjects read stories in which these features of God were relevant. For instance, the story described God as saving a man's life and *at the same time* helping a woman find her lost purse. After a while the subjects had to retell the story. In a spectacular and rather surprising way, many subjects said that God had helped one person out *and then* turned his attention to the other's plight.

So people both say explicitly that God could do two things at once – indeed, that is what makes him God – and then, when they spontaneously represent what God does, construe a standard agent who attends to one thing *after* another. Barrett observed this effect with both believers and non-believers, and in Delhi, India, in the same way as in Ithaca, NY. These experiments show that people's thoughts about God, the mental representation they use to explain what God does and how he does it, are not quite the same as what they say when you ask them. In fact, in this case, one contradicts the other. In each person there is both an *official* concept – what they can report if you ask them – and an *implicit* concept that they use without being really aware of it.[10]

Barrett coined the phrase 'theological correctness' to describe this effect. In the same way as people sometimes have an explicit, officially approved version of their political beliefs that may or may not correspond to their actual commitments, people here are certain that they believe in a God with non-standard cognitive powers. However, the recall test produces what could be called a certain 'cognitive pressure' which diverts their attention from the desire to express 'correct' beliefs. In such a context, people use intuitive expectations about how a mind works, which are available automatically since they are activated to make sense of people's behaviour at all times. When the task allows for conscious monitoring, we get the theological version; when the task requires fast access, we get the anthropomorphic version. This shows, not only that the theological concept has not displaced the spontaneous one but also that it is not stored in the same way. Very likely the theological concept is stored in the form of explicit sentence-like propositions ('God is omniscient', 'God is everywhere'). By contrast, the spontaneous concept is stored in the format of direct instructions to intuitive psychology, which would explain why it is accessed much faster.

'TC' is a great coinage though perhaps misleading as the effect is much more general than the term 'theological' would suggest. That is, Barrett and Keil tested subjects in literate cultures, where there are theological sources that describe supernatural agents, and there are specialists around who know these sources. But in many human groups, there are neither theologians nor specialised interpreters of texts, nor indeed any texts to describe supernatural agents. Yet the TC effect exists there too. That is, people have an explicit version of what they hold to be the important features of the supernatural concepts: spirits are invisible, ghosts are dead people who wander around, gods are eternal, this woman gave birth without having sex, etc. What make such concepts easy to acquire, store and communicate is not just that explicit part, but the tacit one that is completely transparent to them: for instance, that spirits are like persons in having a mind that works like other minds. So you do not need to have theologians around to think in 'theologically correct' ways.

Silly tales or serious religion?

The supernatural comes in two varieties: more serious and less serious. Serious scholars often ignore the non-serious stuff and they are wrong. So far, we have an explanation of supernatural templates that accounts for a whole variety of concepts: notions of invisible dead people hovering about, of statuettes that listen to people's prayers, of animals that disappear or change shapes at will, of ancient people who lived on a floating island adrift on the ocean, of an omniscient Creator who keeps track of every single person's acts and intentions, of trees that record conversations, heroes with iron organs and plants that feel emotions. That is a pretty mixed bunch, to say the least. Most of this sounds like a catalogue of superstitions, old wives' tales, urban myths and cartoon characters, much more than a list of religious notions.

Religion seems more serious than that, less fanciful than all these strange combinations. Also, religion is far more *important*. Legends about Santa Claus or the Bogeyman are interesting, even arresting, but they do not seem to matter that much, while people's notions of God seem to have direct and important effects on their lives. We generally call supernatural concepts 'religious' when they have such important social effects, when rituals are performed that include them, when people define their group-identity in connection with them, when strong emotional states are associated with the concepts, etc. These features are not always all present together, but in most places one finds both these two registers: a vast domain of supernatural notions and a more restricted set of 'serious' ones. People feel very strongly about God, less so about Santa. In Cameroon where I did fieldwork, people have a popular version of the Bogeyman: a big white man who will kidnap and eat children who misbehave. This is not taken very seriously, while invisible dead people are a real menace and that is taken very seriously indeed.[11]

The crucial mistake is to assume that there is no point in understanding 'non-serious' or 'folkloric' supernatural representations, since they do not create such strong emotional states in individuals, or trigger such important social effects. That would be a mistake, because there is no difference in origin between concepts in the serious and non-serious registers. Indeed, concepts often migrate from one to the other. The Greeks sacrificed to Apollo and Athena and ostracised those who committed sacrilege against these gods. From the Renaissance onwards, the whole Greek and Roman Pantheon was the source of rich but non-serious artistic inspiration. Conversely, Lenin and Stalin were to Russians what De Gaulle was to most Europeans, the stuff of history and ideology. In Gabon the French general became for some time the object of a cult and Russian dictators were among the higher deities visited by some Siberian shamans in their trances.

Serious religion makes use of the same notions found in the non-serious repertoire, *plus* some additional features. To understand how this occurs we need to dig deeper in the way a mind works when it represents concepts. It is all very well for me to suggest that the mind can build complex supernatural buildings out of very simple conceptual bricks – ontological categories, violation tags, inferences – but how do I know all this? Why did I say that ANIMAL or TOOL is an ontological category and is used as a template, but ELEPHANT SEAL or TELEPHONE is not? Why this particular list of ontological categories? Why am I so sure that 'same species, same organs' is an intuitive rule in human minds? So far I have done what no respectable scientist should do: give the conclusions before giving the evidence. When we turn to the evidence, we will see not just why some principles and concepts are intuitive to human minds, but also why some conceptual constructions become so important.

Chapter Three

The kind of mind it takes

About halfway through Jane Austen's *Pride and Prejudice*, the heroine, Elizabeth, and her relatives are given a tour of the house and grounds of Pemberley, the vast estate of her proud acquaintance and spurned suitor Mr Darcy. The place is grand ('the rooms were lofty and handsome, and their furniture suitable to the fortune of their proprietor') and promises pleasures so far unfamiliar to Elizabeth ('to be mistress of Pemberley might be something!'). Being no social historian, Elizabeth is more interested in the many delights of owning these commodious apartments and lush gardens than in the hard work involved in maintaining this kind of household. She lives Upstairs and does not talk much about (or even consider) what happens Downstairs.

But a lot happened downstairs. The efficient running of large households like Pemberley, with stables and fields, gardens and kitchens, guest-rooms and dependants' quarters, required the execution of precisely defined tasks distributed among dozens of specialists – house-steward, housekeeper, groom of the chambers, butler, valet, lady's maid, chef, footman, under-butler, young ladies' maid, housemaid, still-room maid, scullery maid, kitchen-maid, laundry-maid, dairy-maid, coachman, groom, postilion, candle-man, odd-man, steward's room man and servants' hall boy, to name but a few. These specialists all had a precisely defined position in a hierarchy (there were several castes of servants, like the Upper Ten or Lower Five, that dined separately) and specific duties. The chef cooked but had no control over wine. The butler decanted wine, the still-room maid handled the china. With this complex division of labour came a complex chain of command. The house-keeper hired and directed all the women servants but not the lady's maids and nurses; the steward, not the butler, could give orders to the chef; the chef controlled the preparation of food but not its serving which was the butler's domain.[1]

What is truly impressive about this system is how *invisible* it remained to the denizens of upstairs rooms, especially to house-guests. Food and drink would appear magically at the appointed time, freshly shined boots would be brought to bedrooms in the morning. Even the owners of such places had but a vague notion of the complicated hierarchy and distribution of tasks, which was the steward's full-time occupation. As a guest, you would not even perceive any of this but only marvel at how efficiently it all seemed to work. However, another feeling (commonly evinced by visitors to such places) was that getting everything you could possibly need is not quite the same as getting what you want. For the complex hierarchy came with a certain measure of independence and rigidity. Footmen were not supposed to do a valet's work and vice-versa. Kitchen-maids who cleaned floors would not make breakfast for you. Your boots would be shined, but only in the morning – the relevant people were busy at other times. So master and guest could certainly nudge this organisational juggernaut in certain directions but they could neither really direct it nor in fact clearly understand how it worked.

The guest's view of the mind

It is unfortunate, and almost inevitable, that when we talk about religion we quite literally do not know what we are talking about. We may think we know our own thoughts ('I know what I believe; I believe that ghosts can walk through walls') but a good part of religious concepts is hidden from conscious inspection: for instance the expectation that ghosts see what is in front of them, that they remember what happened after it happened, that they believe what they remember and remember what they perceived (not the other way around), etc. I insist on this, because a good part of what makes *all* concepts remains beyond conscious access.

Another misconception is that we can explain that people have particular thoughts if we understand their reasons for holding them. ('They believe in ghosts because they cannot bear the grief of losing people'; 'they believe in God because otherwise human existence does not make sense', etc.) But the mind is a complex set of biological machines that produce all sorts of thoughts. For many of them there is no reasonable reason, as it were, except that they are the inevitable result of the way the machines work. Do we have a good reason for having a precise memory of people's faces and forgetting their names? No, but that is the way human memory works.

Now having a complex brain is like being a guest at Pemberley. We enjoy the many advantages of that efficient organisation, but we have no real knowledge of what happens downstairs, of how many different systems are involved in making mental life possible. The organisation of mental systems is in fact far more complex than anything you would find in the most extravagant household.

At Pemberley, different servants poured wine and tea; in a more modest household, the same person would have carried out both tasks. Because our mental basement usually works very well, we tend to think that it must be simple in organisation. We often have a suburban view of the mind, assuming that a few servants may be enough, but the brain is much more like a grand estate. What makes the system work smoothly is the exquisite co-ordination of many specialised systems, each of which only handles a fragment of the information with which we are constantly bombarded.

To catch a thief (using inference systems)

Systems in the mind are complicated and complicatedly connected. Some of this complexity is crucial in understanding why people have religious concepts. Fortunately, we are already familiar with the most important aspect of mind-organisation that is relevant here. In the previous chapter I mentioned the fact that all objects we encounter are mentally sorted into different *ontological categories* with associated expectations. Having ontological categories is not just a matter of classifying stuff out there in large classes (e.g. most roundish, furry or feathery things → 'animals', flat surfaces and sharp angles → 'machines'). What makes ontological categories useful is that, once something looks or feels like an animal or a person or an artefact, you produce specific *inferences* about them. You do not pick up the same cues or process information in the same way, depending on whether the object is an animal or a person or an artefact or a natural object like a rock. If a branch moves it is probably because something or someone pushed it. If the leg of an animal moves it may well be because the animal is pursuing a particular goal.

This description may give the impression that sorting objects along ontological distinctions and producing category-specific inferences is a matter of explicit, deliberate thinking. Far from it. The distinctions are constantly produced by the mind. We do not have to think about them. To get a sense of how smoothly inference systems work, imagine the following scene:

In a quiet and prosperous suburb, a dapper old gentleman with a hat comes out of the back door of a house and walks across the lawn. He is carrying a big screwdriver and a crowbar which he puts in his trousers' side-pockets. He looks around a few times and then proceeds along the pavement. Not far from there, a child is playing with his huge Labrador that he keeps on the leash. All of a sudden, the dog starts at the sight of a cat in the next garden and gives a sudden pull that makes the leash snap out of the child's hand. The dog dashes after its prey, charges across the pavement and knocks over the old man who trips up and falls flat on his face, his hat rolling in the gutter. The man yells in pain as the screwdriver has sprung out of his pocket and badly cut his arm. The man picks himself up and limps away, massaging his bloodied hand, leaving his hat in the gutter. You were not the only witness of all this; a police officer was patrolling the neighbourhood. She picks up the hat, runs after the gentleman, puts her hand on his shoulder and goes 'Hey, wait!'. As the man turns he recoils in visible shock at the sight of the police officer, looks around as if trying to find an escape route and finally says: 'All right, all right. It's a fair cop.' From his pockets he extracts a handful of rings and necklaces and hands them over to the bemused police officer.

Perhaps not altogether riveting – we are far from Jane Austen – the scene illustrates how multiple inference systems are involved in the perception of apparently simple events. Were you a witness to all this you might be surprised by some events but you would understand all of them. This is not because there is some centre in the brain that is busy understanding 'what is happening to the man, the little boy, the dog and the police officer'. It is because there is a whole confederacy of different systems involved in handling particular aspects of the scene. Consider these:

- *Understanding the physics of solid objects:* The dog yanked the leash out of the child's hand and knocked over a passer-by. The tie between leash and dog-collar is stronger than the child's grip on the leash, and the man is knocked aside because both he and the dog are solid objects that collide when their trajectories cross. This kind of phenomenon is automatically represented in our minds by a set of mechanisms that do what psychologists call 'intuitive physics', in analogy with scientific physics.
- *Understanding physical causation:* In the scene you witnessed, you saw the dog hit the man on its way and you then saw the man

stumble and fall down. But that is not the way you would describe it. What seems to have happened is that the man tripped up *because* he had been hit by the charging dog. Physical events around us are not just one damn thing after another; there often appear to be causes and effects. But you cannot *see* a cause, at least literally. What you see are events and your brain interprets their succession as cause plus effect.

- *Detecting goal-directed motion:* The dog charged across the street in a particular direction that happened to point towards the cat's location. To put things in a more natural way, the dog's *goal* was to get closer to the cat. If all you saw was physical motion, you would think that some invisible force was driving the dog towards the cat. But an inference system in your mind suggests that this invisible force is inside the dog's head, in his desire to get closer to something that looks like a prey.

- *Keeping track of who's who:* The scene makes sense to you as an eyewitness only if you can track the different characters and keep a particular 'file' on each of them with an account of what just happened to them or what they just did. This seems of course trivially easy, if some system in your brain takes a snapshot of every character's face, and then manages to re-identify the different characters, even though faces and bodies change orientation, they are partly occluded, the lighting is different, etc.

- *Linking structure to function:* The screwdriver hurt the man as he fell down. This is not too surprising as this instrument was probably hard, pointed and the blade at the end was probably sharp. We intuitively guess all this, not just because screwdrivers in general are like that, but also because there is a reason for these features: they help in performing particular functions. That we expect tools to have such functional features is manifest in the surprise that would be created if the crowbar or screwdriver happened to be soft as rubber.

- *Understanding mental representation:* This too is indispensable to make sense of what happened to the thief and the police officer.

To us witnesses of what happened, she saw that the man had dropped his hat and wanted to give it back to him. He thought she knew he had broken into a house. But she in fact did not know that, although she immediately deduced what was going on when she saw the jewels. She also realised the thief had not understood that she only wanted to help him. One could go on for some time. The point is that you cannot understand the story if you do not maintain a rather sophisticated account of who thinks what about whom. But thoughts are invisible. You cannot observe them directly, you must infer them.

This is not, by far, a complete list of all the systems engaged, but it should be enough to give an idea of what I want to emphasise here. The most banal scenes of everyday life are replete with facts that seem obvious or simple only because we have a veritable Pemberley in the head, a huge mental basement filled with extremely efficient servants, whose activities are not available for detailed conscious inspection. Each of these specialised systems only handles a limited aspect of the information available about our surroundings, but produces very smart inferences about that aspect. This is why all these systems in the brain are called *inference systems*.

This is where scientific discoveries go against the grain of common-sense. We may think that there is nothing terribly complicated in understanding, for instance, how objects move when they are pushed, what happens when they collide, why an object will fall if there is nothing underneath to support it, in other words what psychologists call an 'intuitive physics'. If I drop an object, you expect it to fall downwards with a vertical trajectory. If I throw a ball against a wall you expect it to bounce at an angle that is roughly symmetrical to that at which it hit the wall. If a billiard ball is on the path of another billiard ball, you expect them to collide, not go through one another. If you throw a tennis-ball as hard as you can, you expect it to fly higher and faster than if you just gave it a gentle nudge. Intuitive physics, like its scientific counterpart, is based on principles. These principles take as input a particular description of what objects are around and what their motion is, and produce expectations about the next step. That we have precise expectations is not something we are aware of. It is made manifest only when some aspect of physical reality around us violates the principles, which is why experimental psychologists often use cheap magical tricks to produce counter-intuitive situations.[2]

Intuitive physics uses observable phenomena (like the motion of objects) to infer what is intrinsically invisible. Consider for instance causal connections between events. If you see a billiard ball hitting another one, you can't but perceive that the second ball moved *because* it was hit by the first one. Indeed, we sometimes think we 'see' such events even when we know that no physical object is involved. If you show people coloured discs moving on a screen, you can make them 'perceive' that one disc 'hit' another one, 'pushed' it along, and so on. This happens even if people know that what are on the screen are just dots of light, so that there is nothing that is hitting or pushing anything. If you adjust the displays a bit, you can make the 'causal illusion' disappear. What people see now are discs moving, other discs moving too, but no 'cause' and no 'effect'. In the 1940s, psychologists Michotte and Heider showed that such 'causal illusions' are very reliable – everybody reports that they 'saw' a cause – and that they depend on precise mathematical relations between the motions of the objects – you can eliminate the illusion or re-create it by adjusting the displays according to precise formulae. More surprising, Heider and Michotte had also shown that dots on a screen can make people believe that what they see are not just solid objects moving and colliding, but animate beings 'chasing' or 'avoiding' each other. Again, by carefully adjusting the timing and spatial characteristics of the dots' relative motion, you can create the illusion of 'social causation'. In the same way as in the simpler experiments, the adult subjects know that what they see are in fact just dots on a screen. But they cannot help perceive them as engaged in a 'chase' or as 'trying to get somewhere'.[3]

In the previous chapter I gave a very simplified account of what it is to have ontological categories. I suggested that we have a mental catalogue of the kinds of things that are around us, with entries like 'animal', 'person' and 'man-made object' and a little theory about each entry. The theory specifies for instance that animals are born of animals of the same species, that the structure of man-made objects is related to their use, etc. But the term 'theory' may be a bit misleading, so here is a more precise description. Seeing or other-wise perceiving an object activates a particular set of inference systems. Not all objects activate them all. The fact that a certain type of objects activates a certain panoply of inference systems is what we mean when we say that it belongs to a particular category.

To return to the thief and the police officer: You formed certain expectations about the *physics* of the dog and the old man. When their trajectories coincided you were not surprised that they collided (rather than go straight through one another). So we can say that looking at the dog and the man had activated your *intuitive physics* system. This is activated also when you look at inert objects like trees or at man-made objects. But the dog and the man and the police officer also activated your *goal-detection* system, which is why you could spontaneously assume that 'the dog was trying to catch the cat', 'the man was trying to avoid the dog', and 'the police officer was trying to catch up with the man'. These persons also activated a more complicated *intuitive psychology* system, which produces subtle inferences like 'she realised that he had not realised that she did not know what he was up to', a description that would never be pro-duced if you were considering a tree, but might be produced in a much simpler form if you were considering a mouse or a worm. That the screwdriver was hard and sharp would be an expectation of your *structure-function* system. This system is also activated by animal or human body-parts: seeing a cat's claws you immediately expect them to be there *so that* the animal can rip open a prey's body. On the other hand, when you see a tool, you immediately activate not just a description of its functional features but also its use by a human hand, for instance the fact that a screwdriver or gimlet is designed to be turned while a crowbar is meant to be leant on.

All this to show that you can replace what I called 'ontological categories with theories' with a list of appropriate inference systems. If something activates physics, goal-detection, as well as some biological expectations I will describe below, then it is what we usually call an 'animal'. If it activates all that plus intuitive psychology, it is what we usually call a 'person'. If it activates physics and structure-function, it may be either a 'man-made object' or an 'animal part'. If it does that plus intentional use, it is what we usually call a 'tool'. Instead of having a complex mental encyclopaedia with theoretical declarations about what animals and artefacts and persons are, all we have are flags that switch on particular systems and turn other systems off.

Our knowledge of inference systems has recently made huge progress because of independent findings in four different fields. Experimental studies of normal adult subjects showed how their intuitions about various aspects of their environment are based on specialised principles – the example of causation is one among many, as we will see presently. Also, the study of cognitive development showed with much more precision than before how some of these principles appear very early in infancy and how they make it possible to acquire vast amounts of knowledge so quickly. At the same time, imagery techniques that track blood-flow, or electrical and magnetic activity in the brain, reached a sufficient level of precision to tell us which parts of the cortex and other brain structures were active in different types of task. Finally, neuro-psychologists discovered a whole set of cognitive pathologies that impair some inference systems while leaving the rest intact, which suggests how the system is organised.

Wheels within wheels: systems in the brain

In this model, then, what makes our minds smart is not really a set of encyclopaedic descriptions of such things as artefacts and animals in general, but the fact that very specialised systems are selectively turned on or off when we consider different kinds of objects. This description is better than the one in terms of encyclopaedic entries, for several reasons. First, it makes sense of the fact that some inference systems are activated by several different kinds of objects. Goal-detection is applied to dogs and to persons. Structure-function is applied both to artefacts and some body-parts. Also, the way I talked of 'ontological categories' as if these were real kinds of things in the world was misleading because many objects migrate from one of these so-called 'categories' to another, depending on the way we consider them. For instance, once you take a fish out of the sea and serve it poached, it has ceased to be only an animal and has become, to some extent, an artefact. If you use it to slap someone's face, it has become a tool. It is of course not the object itself that has changed but the kinds of inferences the mind produces about it. At some point it seemed to be an 'animal', which means that our goal-detection system was activated when we looked at it moving about and spontaneously wondered what it was looking for. When we say that the fish has become an 'artefact', what we mean is that questions like 'who made it?', or 'what for?' are now produced spontaneously. When the fish has become a 'tool', this means only that we produce inferences like 'if it is heavy it will strike hard', 'the tail is narrow and therefore affords a good grip', that is, our structure-function system is active.

A description of our minds as a bundle of inference systems, differently activated by different objects, is better than that of a mental encyclopaedia because it is much closer to the way a brain is actually organised. That is, there is no general 'catalogue of all things' in the brain with their different characteristics; nor is there a division in the brain between the bits that deal with animals, those that deal with persons, those that only consider artefacts, etc. Instead, there are many different functional systems that work to produce particular kinds of inferences about different aspects of our surroundings. This is not just theoretical speculation: that there are different systems, and that they are narrow specialists, is made manifest both by neuro-imaging and by pathology.

Consider for instance the domain of man-made objects. This would seem to be a straightforward ontological category. Many objects in our world were made by people and many were not. If our brain had been designed by philosophers, it would certainly differentiate between man-made and non-man-made stuff in general. But the brain is subtler than that, because it was 'designed' by evolution. When people are presented with novel artefact-like and animal-like pictures, their brains do show different activation. In the case of artefacts, there seems to be enough activity in the pre-motor cortex (involved in planning movements) to suggest that the system is trying to figure out (forgive the anthropomorphic tone: the system is of course not aware of what it is doing) some way of handling this new object. But this only applies if the object is tool-like. In other words, there may not be a category of 'artefacts' in the brain, but there is a system for 'finding out how to handle tool-like objects', which is far more specific.[4]

The specificity is even more obvious in the handling of complex domains like animacy (the quality of things that move of their own accord) and intentionality. In my interpretation of the story above, I simplified matters a great deal when I said that we have a system that computes mental states like *knowing*, *hoping*, *perceiving*, *inferring*, etc., and produces descriptions of these states in other people's minds, as an explanation for (and prediction of) their behaviour. This is simplified because this intuitive psychology system is in fact composed of a variety of sub-systems. The whole scene with the thief – especially the spectacular denouement - only made sense because you grasped some aspects of what was going on in these different people's minds. This is made possible by specialised mechanisms that constantly produce representations of what is going on inside people's heads, in terms of perceptions, intentions, beliefs, etc.

That this requires subtle and specialised machinery is made obvious, indeed spectacular, by the fact that a part of this machinery is impaired in some people. They can compute the trajectories of solid objects and their causal connections, predict where things will fall, identify different persons, etc., but some psychological processes elude them. Indeed, the story of the thief and the police officer is largely inspired from similar anecdotes used by neuro-psychologist Chris Frith and his colleagues to test autistic patients. Children and adults with this condition have great difficulty making sense of such anecdotes. Why the man would give the police officer the jewels and why she would be surprised are events that they register but cannot easily explain. Also, Frith showed that a specific pattern of brain activation occurs when normal subjects listen to such a story. This activation is typical of what happens when these normal subjects have to represent how other people represented a certain scene. But patients have a rather different pattern of activation, which would indicate that their 'theory of mind' mechanism is either not functioning or functioning in a very different way.[5]

This interpretation of autism as a failure to represent other people's representations was originally proposed by three developmental psychologists, Alan Leslie, Uta Frith and Simon Baron-Cohen. Autistic children do not seem to engage in social interaction that is typical in normal children of their age. They develop unusual, repetitive behaviours, can become obsessed with details of particular objects and develop strange skills. Some of their development can be otherwise normal, as some have high IQs and many can talk. Yet they do not understand other people and often treat them like inert physical objects. Their special impairment is made obvious in simple tasks like the 'false-belief test' about puppets on a stage. Puppet 1 puts a marble in box A, then goes offstage. Puppet 2 arrives on the scene, finds the marble in box A, puts it in box B and goes offstage. Now puppet 1 comes back. The question is: Where will he look if he wants his marble? Children over four (and even Down's syndrome children of a comparable mental age) generally answer 'in box A' and sometimes comment 'in box A, because that is where they *think* it is'. Note that this apparently simple task is in fact quite complicated. It requires that you hold two descriptions of the same scene in your mind: there is the actual location of the marble (in B) and the location of the marble as represented by puppet 1 (that's in A). These two descriptions are incompatible. One of them is false and is the one that will direct the puppet's behaviour. Autistic children react like three year olds. They expect puppet A to look for his marble in box B, because that is where it actually is. They do not seem to grasp that the marble could in actual fact be in box B and represented by someone as being in A. Ever since these experiments were conducted in the 1970s many other experiments have shown that the autistic syndrome occurs as the outcome of an intuitive psychology deficit. For instance normal infants at about eleven months start pointing 'declaratively', that is, just to attract other people's attention to some object; they then check that people are indeed looking at the object of interest. Infants who do not do that often turn out a few years later to display the typical symptoms of autism. Normal five year olds, but not autistic children, assume that peering into a box will give them more information about what is inside than just touching its lid.[6]

Simon Baron-Cohen called autism a form of 'mind-blindness', which is both felicitous – autistic people are indeed impervious to something we think we 'see', namely other people's mental states – and perhaps misleading. As Baron-Cohen himself showed, our intuitive psychology is a bundle of different systems with different functions and neural implementations. One of these examines what other people's eyes look like and infers what they are looking at. Another one distinguishes between things that move in an animate fashion from inert objects that only move when they are pushed or pulled. A third one computes the extent to which other agents perceive what we perceive, and in what way their perception is different. But autistic children seem impaired in only one particular sub-capacity, in the representation of other people's representations. They are not blind to all mind-stuff but only to a most crucial part of it.[7]

Representations of other people's actions and mental states may be even more complicated than this description suggests. For instance, studies of neural activation in normal subjects have shown that when we see someone making particular gestures, we generally imagine making the same gestures ourselves. Again, this is something we are generally not aware of. The studies show that the brain areas activated when we see people's gestures overlap with those activated when we actually act in a similar manner. In other words, there is some part of the brain that is imagining performing the action witnessed, although the plan is not made conscious and the motor sequence is inhibited. Infants seem to have the same system minus the final inhibition, which leads them to imitate other people's gestures. This may be the explanation for that famous and rather surprising experimental result, that people who merely *watch* others practise a particular sport actually get better at that sport (not quite as much as those who actually practised, unfortunately). So seeing people move as something *we* might be doing ourselves is the job of another specialised system.

There is now evidence that representing other people's pain is the output of yet another specialised neural structure. Some sets of neurones respond selectively to excessive heat, cold and pressure. Other, neighbouring areas respond selectively to similar events affecting *other* people. The fact that we have specific emotional reactions to seeing pain inflicted on other people may result from the simple simulation produced by this system. That is, the experience of other people's pain, as handled by the brain's dedicated structures, to some extent overlaps with that of one's own pain. Again, there is a system that produces some description of how events affect other persons (in terms of a close simulation of what it would be like for us to experience the events), but is only concerned with a narrow aspect of these events.[8]

To sum up, then, our internal description of other people's mental life is not the product of one general theory of persons but the outcome of many different perceptions, simulations and inferences about different aspects of what they experience. What seemed to be a unified domain of 'intuitive psychology' is in fact a collection of sub-domains with specialised systems. The same would apply to other domains of the mental encyclopaedia. For instance, we seem rather good at detecting that some objects in the world (e.g. animals and people) move in pursuance of various goals, while others (rocks, rivers, trees, etc.) only move because of some external force. Now some simple detection mechanisms seem to distinguish between these objects on the basis of motion itself. That is, the motion of animate beings is typically less uniform in velocity, more erratic in direction, than that of inanimate things. But motion is not the only criterion. Animate beings often provide cues that they are attending to other objects in their surroundings. Animals for instance turn their heads to follow the objects they are interested in. In this domain, again, we find that what seemed to be a simple process – find which objects are goal-driven and which are not – requires the collaboration of several more specialised neural systems.

At several points I mentioned findings about infants and young children. The most striking and fascinating models of the mental encyclopaedia – or rather, of the systems making up what seems to be an encyclopaedia – have come from developmental psychology. This is not an accident. The study of young children asks the most radical of philosophical questions: Where does knowledge come from? How do we ever manage to discover anything about the world around us? But it turns them into scientific questions settled by experimental tests. We know a lot more now about how minds work because we have found out a lot about how young minds grow.[9]

Progress-box 5: Domain-specificity

- Perception and understanding of surroundings require inferences and guesses about different aspects of objects around us.
- The mind is composed of specialised systems that produce inferences about these different aspects.

- Objects in different 'ontological categories' activate different sets of these specialised systems.
- Each inference system is itself composed of even more specialised neural structures.

What every nursery-school child knows

Little children do not seem very bright. Two year olds are clumsy, they have no manners or morals, they (literally) would not find their way out of a paper-bag. They talk with an awful accent and their conversation is, to say the least, rather restricted. Given young children's sadly limited capacities, it would seem that only some miracle could turn them into competent adults. But that is nonsense. Children can learn a lot because they *know* a lot. Scientists can now describe very precisely those mental processes that help children discover (almost) all there is to know, using the very confusing information we make available to them. However difficult to believe, little children may in fact be very bright.

What makes them bright is what makes us all bright: that our minds comprise a variety of specialised inference systems. For psychologists, children are a kind of natural experiment. Although their knowledge of many domains of experience is minimal, they gradually figure out all sorts of pertinent facts about their surroundings. The only way they could do that is by *inferring* some description of their surroundings on the basis of limited exposure. This is possible only if they start with some definite biases about what aspects of the environment they should attend to, and what way they should infer from these cues. For instance:

If you open up a crocodile what will you find inside? Take a (dead) crocodile. Armed with a sharp knife, proceed to dissect the reptile. Inside, you will find bones, muscles and various internal organs. Now here is a truly difficult question: What do you think you would find if you opened up a *second* crocodile? Most people will answer: Very likely a bunch of *similar* bones and muscles and internal organs.

This of course is the right answer. If we want to find out whether crocodiles have lungs, it seems to make little sense to dissect two hundred of them and compare our findings because we are fairly certain that opening one (or a couple at the most, if we can stretch our research funds a bit) is quite enough. But there is not much in our own experience to justify this belief. We just *assume* that all members of a species have similar 'innards' (with the exception of sexual organs, of which we expect two different versions). Now this is a belief that even young children (three or five year olds, depending on how you ask the question) seem to share, even though they have even less experience of animals than we do, and certainly little experience of butchery and dissection. You may find that the question was not so difficult. After all, if we *call* all these things 'crocodiles' it is to indicate that they are all more or less similar. However, children who are so sure that all crocodiles have similar insides are much less certain about the innards of telephones or TV-sets. That these have some common features is not the point. Children can recognise a telephone when they see one, and they know what a TV-set is for. It is simply not that obvious to them that machines are what they are because of what is inside them. The beautiful thing about this principle is that it is entirely abstract. That is, children expect the innards of all crocodiles to be essentially similar, but they generally have no idea of what actually is inside a crocodile, or any other animals for that matter. Psychologist Frank Keil observed that young children have the vaguest notion of what is inside an animal body *yet* are quite sure that whatever is inside one mouse must be inside other mice as well.[10]

There is in fact a deeper and more subtle aspect to these banal inferences. Living species (that in fact are *genera* for biologists: dog, cat, giraffe, etc.) are generally represented in *essentialist* terms, by both children and adults. That is, we assume that cows have some internal property (or set of properties) that is characteristic of the species as a whole and cannot be removed. Psychologists Frank Keil, Henry Wellmann and Susan Gelman have extensively documented this kind of representation in young children, but it occurs in adults too. Suppose you take a cow, surgically remove the excess body mass and remodel it to look like a horse, add a mane and a nice tail, and perform other operations so it eats, moves and generally behaves like a horse. Is it a horse? For most people, including most children, it is not. It is a disguised cow, a horsy cow to be sure, perhaps a cross-cultural cow, but in essence still a cow. There is something about being a cow that is internal and permanent. You can have this assumption without having any representation of what the 'essence' is. That is, most people represent cows as having some essential 'cowness' about them but do not have a description of cowness. All they know is that 'cowness', whatever it is, cannot be removed and creates external features. This is why a cow grows horns and hoofs.[11]

That animals have species-wide essences corresponds to another special characteristic of animal concepts, namely that they are integrated in a taxonomy, a general classification of animals and plants. The terms that designate natural species are mutually exclusive – a given animal does not belong to two classes – and jointly exhaustive – all animals are assumed to belong to one such class. Note that this is not true of kind-concepts outside the natural domain. A piano can be both furniture and a musical instrument (so the kind-concept 'piano' is a member of two higher-level classes). Also, natural kind-terms are grouped into larger classes that correspond to general body-plans, like 'birds', 'mammals', 'insects', etc.[12]

Why do some things move of their own accord? As I said above, dots on a screen can give the impression of chasing each other, rather than just colliding, if we adjust their motion in subtle ways, and even infants seem sensitive to this difference. A while ago, psychologist Alan Leslie showed that infants too fell prey to Michotte's causal illusion, being able to differentiate between 'causal' and 'non-causal' displays in the same way as adults. Another child psychologist, Philippe Rochat, used this kind of experimental set-up with six-month-old babies, and showed that they too are sensitive to the difference between 'physical causation' (push, pull, hit) and 'social causation' (chase, avoid). So it would seem that all these connections between events are somehow represented much earlier than we thought: certainly before the child has acquired the concepts 'chase' or 'avoid' and before she has any experience of either. Older children, say around three, have definite expectations about the difference between self-propelled and non-self-propelled objects in the environment. For instance, psychologist Rochel Gelman tested pre-school children on whether a series of animals and models of animals could move. For her subjects, it was quite clear that real animals can move of their own accord, but that models could not. Children have this intuition but they have no explanation for it. Some of Gelman's subjects explained that the model could not move 'because it had no legs'. When shown that the model did have legs, they argued that 'these were not good legs', and so on. This often happens when testing such deep intuitive principles. Children have the principle, they have the systematic intuitions, yet they have no explanations for them. This is because the intuition is produced by a specialised system that is, even in adults, away from conscious access.[13]

Are there different people out there? Infants start to treat human faces as a special kind of visual stimulus more or less from the word go. It is not just that they note the difference between faces and other objects in their environment. They also pay more attention to differences between faces than to differences between other visual stimuli. The reason for that special behaviour is that the child is quickly building up a database of relevant people. From a few days after birth, the baby starts to build up different 'files' for each of the persons she interacts with, by remembering not just their faces but also how she interacted with them. Psychologist Andrew Meltzoff discovered that infants use imitation to identify people. If the infant has played at imitating a particular gesture with an adult, she will try different ones with other adults. When the previous playmate returns she will return to the previous routines again. In other words, the baby seems to use imitation as a way to check out who she is interacting with, which Person-File she should associate with a given face, smell, etc. What the baby assumes – or rather, what the baby's brain is built to assume – is that the differences between two human-like objects are far more important than those between say two different mice or two different toys. Babies do not start by seeing lots of stuff in the world and noticing that some of them – people's faces – have common features. They start with a pre-disposition to pay special attention to face-like displays and to the differences between them.[14]

Incidentally, the fact that an infant can imitate adults' facial gestures (sticking out their tongue, pursing the lips, frowning, etc.) shows that the new-born brain is equipped with highly specialised capacities. To imitate you need to match *visual* information from the outside with *motor* control from inside. Infants start doing all this before they have ever seen their own faces in mirrors and before parents react to that behaviour. The child does not learn to imitate but uses imitation to learn. Imitation can be used to recognise different people; but it is also crucial to acquire complex gestures, and to some extent to acquire the sounds of your language.[15]

How many objects are out there? In the same spirit of enthusiasm for infants' capacities, why not claim that they do arithmetic? As it happens, they do. Or rather, some mechanisms in their brains, as in ours, keeps track of how many objects are around. These mechanisms react to 'impossible' changes – for example, when two objects turn into one – and produce a reaction of surprise. Show a six-month-old infant an object; put an opaque screen in front of it. Then show them another object and place it behind the screen. You then lift the screen and . . . only one object is left. (Cognitive psychologists often use cheap magicians' tricks in their experiments.) Infants find this extremely surprising, much more so than if the objects have changed colour or shape while they were hidden behind the screen. So some part of the brain is keeping track of how many objects were masked. Note that in an experiment like this they have not yet seen the two objects together. So what surprises them is not that something in the world has changed. It is that something has changed in a way that is not expected.[16]

How do we know all this? Obviously, you do not ask a five-month-old infant whether she finds it strange that $1+1=1$. Experiments with such young subjects rely on ingenious techniques that measure how surprised and how attentive infants are, by tracking their gaze or monitoring the intensity with which they suck a dummy. When infants watch repeated displays that conform to their expectations, they quickly lose concentration and start looking around. If you change what you show them in particular ways you can get them to focus again, which tells you that they noticed the change. Naturally, you do not want to measure their reaction to a mere change, so you change the stimuli in different ways and observe whether these different changes produce the same effect or not. This gives you some indication about which changes are more attention-grabbing than others.

To sum up, then: A young mind is by no means a simple mind. Many of the specialised capacities we find in adults are already present in infants, in the form of particular expectations (e.g. they assume that objects are continuous), preferences (e.g. they pay attention to differences between human faces, ignore those between giraffe faces) and ways of inferring (e.g. if this thing moves of its own accord, try and identify its goal; if it moves because someone pushed it, don't bother). What these early capacities allow is the application of specific inference systems to specific domains of reality. This helps the child acquire a huge amount of information about her sur-roundings, because the mind is biased to ignore all sorts of facts about the world and attend to some of them. Paying attention to all potential connections of all objects would be (if possible) a waste of time and resources. You learn a lot only if you are selective.

Innateness and development

We cannot help assuming that objects around us belong to very different classes, that they have different 'hidden' properties (like an essence if they are animals, goals if they are agents) that explain what they are. Even more striking, we do all that long before we accumulate enough knowledge of the world to realise that these expectations allow us to understand our environment. Infants assume that things that move by themselves have goals, that different faces are crucial to interacting with different people, that the sounds coming out of their mouths must be treated in a different way from noises produced by objects. All this is found in normal minds and all this is found very early. Which of course leads many people to wonder: Whence the principles? Are children born with these ontological categories and inference systems? Are distinctions (e.g. between animates and inanimates) *innate* in the human infant?

This question, unfortunately, does not make much sense. (I have said this already in another chapter, but some dead horses require repeated flogging, as they keep rising from the dead to cause recurrent conceptual confusion.) For instance, we know that pre-school children have different expectations about animals and artefacts. Now could this be an innate distinction? Well, we happen to know that younger children expect most animal-looking things to move by themselves, but not artefact-looking things. Could this be based on some even more precocious distinction? Perhaps, since infants make a difference between animate ('erratic') motion and inanimate ('Newtonian') motion. So it would seem that we can go backwards in time and find the origins of complex conceptual distinctions in earlier and earlier capacities. However, note that the further back we go in time, the more we change the concepts themselves. We started with a concept of 'animal', then moved on to 'animal-looking thing', then to 'self-propelled thing' and 'thing with erratic motion'. So, whatever we will find at birth will not be, strictly speaking, the 'animal' concept but something that (normally) leads to something that leads to something . . . that builds the 'animal' concept.

The same is true of other concepts. You find early precursors of these concepts but the further back you go the less they look like the concepts you are interested in and the more you find generative structures that usually result in the concepts you want to explain. You have to redescribe the concepts as you move backwards in time, and at some point you are certainly studying extremely early-developed structures with huge consequences for the child's future concepts, but these structures do not correspond to the conceptual labels you started with. It is very likely that genetic material has a direct effect on the separation between cortical areas and on the neural pathways that get these neural areas to interact. How brain connections get activated to support inference systems obviously requires a lot of further calibration.

The confusion is created here by our tendency to understand concepts as encyclopaedia entries that describe objects. So we wonder whether infants have some part of the entry that we find in the adult mental encyclopaedia. But, as I said before, the encyclopaedia description is rather misleading. Ontological categories in fact consist in a set of switch settings telling this and that inference systems to get activated, while others are off. As philosopher Ruth Millikan pointed out, concepts are much less descriptions than skills. The 'animal' concept is the skill to recognise actual animals and make appropriate inferences about them. So there is a gradual development here, in concepts as in motor skills; there is no clear cut-off point at which the child has acquired *the* animal concept. Indeed, one can always become better at that particular skill.[17]

Loose talk of 'innateness' seems to imply that we will find in infants the same concepts that we observe in adults. But the actual study of developing minds reveals something more complex: a series of skeletal principles, initial biases and specialised skills that result in adult concepts, if the child is provided with a *normal* environment. This is in fact much clearer if we leave aside concepts for a while and consider bodily development. Children are born the way they are and develop the way they do because the organism's architecture is provided by its genotype. All normal children grow a set of milk-teeth, then lose it and grow the permanent set during middle childhood. But this requires adequate conditions, Vitamin-deprived children may have a different developmental trajectory, to be sure, and we know nothing of children raised in zero-gravity or fed through an intravenous drip instead of on chewable food. We can exclude these circumstances as irrelevant, not just because they are rare (they could become common), but because they were not part of the conditions prevailing when the relevant genes were selected. Whatever genes control modern human tooth-development appeared in an environment where people chewed their food, where that food consisted of plants and animals, where lollipops, candy bars and intravenous drips were absent.

In much the same way, most normal children have a step-wise linguistic development that invariably includes a huge vocabulary expansion between two and five, a one-word-sentence stage followed by two-word utterances followed by the full syntax and morphology of their language. But this again requires a normal environment, which includes people who speak such a language and speak it in interacting with children. Children raised in isolation may not develop full linguistic capacities. To sum up, a normal environment is indispensable to development if you have the right genetic equipment that prepares you to use resources from that environment, to build your teeth out of normal nutrients and to build your syntax out of normal linguistic interaction with competent speakers.

Which leads us to another, much more important question. As I said, particular ontological categories and inference systems are found in all normal human minds, from an early age. I should have emphasised the term *human*. For the particular architecture I just described is indeed characteristic of humans. We intuitively make distinctions like the one between inanimate stuff as opposed to goal-oriented stuff, or between naturally occurring objects (mountains) and created ones (bows and arrows), between human agents and non-human animals. But there is no metaphysical necessity to do it that way. Indeed, many philosophers and scientists would think that some of the distinctions we intuitively make (e.g. between humans and animals) are not that justified. Our intuitive ontology is not the only one possible.

To see this, consider this simple scene. *Mary* with her little *lamb* are resting under a *tree* next to a *lamp-post*. Now imagine how this is processed in the minds of different organisms. For a human being, there are four very different categories here (human, animal, plant, artefact). Each of these objects will activate a particular set of inference systems. The human observer will automatically encode Mary's face as a distinct one but probably not the sheep's, and will consider the lamp-post's function but not the tree's. If a giraffe were to see the same scene, it would probably encode these differently. For a giraffe there is probably no deep difference between the sheep and Mary (assuming that the giraffe does not identify Mary as a predator) because both are non-conspecifics (not members of the same species), and a lamp-post is just like a useless (leafless) tree. Now if a dog were around, it would still have a different take on the scene. Because dogs are domesticated animals, they make a clear distinction between humans and other non-dog animals, so Mary and the sheep would activate different systems in the dog's brain. But the dog would not attend to the difference between a lamp-post and a tree. Indeed, both afford the same possibilities in terms of territorial marking.

So having particular ontological categories is a matter of 'choice' (the world lends itself to many different ways of categorising its contents), and the choice depends on which species you belong to. Consider face-identification again. We automatically register these subtle features that make two faces different, but we ignore these same cues when presented with animal faces. Human babies are born in a state of extreme dependency; they need years of care to be able to survive on their own. Also, they need to co-operate with other human beings to survive, so that recognising who's who in a group is crucial throughout their lives. This is not true only of humans, but it is pushed to an extreme in our species. Our interaction with people depends, obviously, on who we are dealing with. By contrast, our interaction with giraffes, snakes or hyenas does not depend on *which* animal we are chasing or running away from, but on *what species* they belong to, and that may be why our brains are biased not to notice those fascinating differences between giraffe faces. Or again, consider artefacts like tools. Watching a picture of an unfamiliar tool results in very specific brain activity, different from what occurs when people watch pictures of unfamiliar animals. This activity involves some of the motor control areas in the brain. But this is not too surprising in a species of tool-makers, in which organisms have for a very long time created tools far more complex than anything any other species could come up with. Having special inference systems for tool-handling confers a real advantage in this domain, allowing humans fast and flexible acquisition of complicated tool-making techniques.

Progress-box 6: Development and specificity

- Inference systems make us attend to articular cues in environments and produce specific inferences from these cues.
- Skeletal versions of the principles direct knowledge acquisition from infancy.
- All concepts develop as skills, which is why discussions of innateness are often meaningless.
- What principles you have depends on what species you are: which is why evolution is relevant to mental architecture.

The architecture and the designer

Once we realise that different species have a different take on what is around (different categories and inference systems), it makes sense to consider that this must have to do with the history of these different species, in other words with *evolution*. Our inference systems may be there because they provide solutions to problems that were recurrent in normal human environments for hundreds of thousands of years. I insist on these *ancestral* circumstances, that prevailed for much of human history, because these are the conditions under which we evolved as a distinct species: foraging for food in small nomadic groups, where close co-operation is a matter of survival and information is richly transmitted through example and communication. Compared to the many generations of hunting game and gathering food, recent advances, such as agriculture, industry, life in large groups or states or cities, etc., are only a few seconds in evolutionary time. This matters because we bear the traces of this evolutionary past in many features of our behaviour and most importantly in the ways our minds are organised. To take a simple and familiar example, most humans have a marked tendency to have a sweet tooth because sources of sugar and vitamins were few and far between in our ancestral environments. A taste for rich sources of such nutrients – the same goes for animal fat as a source of energy and meat as a source of protein – developed simply because whatever genes caused that propensity were very likely to spread. Bearers of such genes would tend to have more offspring than non-bearers and some of their offspring would carry these genes too.

Problems of adaptive significance come in very different shapes. For instance, you must be able to detect whether there are animate agents around or just mechanical events – whether the movement in the tree was caused by the wind or by an animal lurking up there. But you must also keep track of who interacted with you, when and with what results, otherwise stable co-operation would be impossible – and this requires special memory-stores and adequate face-recognition. These two are not the same problem and it is very dubious that a common system could handle such different tasks. And this is only the beginning of a very long list of specific adaptive problems. Detecting what makes some people reliable for co-operation is not the same as detecting what makes potential sexual partners attractive, which is not the same as evaluating whether a particular food is poisonous or not. It is not just that these problems are different in their subject-matter, but they require different ways of handling information. To be efficient in interaction with people you must recall what each person did and infer their motivation in each case; but if you are dealing with animals you can consider all members of a species as more or less similar.

These considerations led a number of evolutionary biologists to consider that the evolution of a complex organ like the human brain would probably accumulate lots and lots of specialised systems, as well as make the system as a whole bigger and smarter. Indeed, the idea was that being smart consists in having lots of specialised systems that handle only one such problem, rather than just a larger general-purpose intelligence. This would make sense because a large system would be bogged down by irrelevant details. If for instance our face-recognition system kept specific files for each individual animal ever encountered, this would both waste resources and make us rather sluggish when a quick response was needed. The relevant response to the presence of a giraffe or a tiger depends on the species not on the individual. So there was an evolutionary story to suggest ever-increasing specialisation as the origin of complex cognitive capacities like those of higher primates and humans. In this view, smarter species got smarter by having 'more instincts' not fewer than other species. But this remained a conjecture.[18]

The situation changed when, independently from these biological conjectures, developmental psychologists and neuro-psychologists began to demonstrate more and more specialised inference systems (as described above). So one could now combine the psychological findings with their evolutionary background, a combination that is now generally known as *evolutionary psychology*. The main point was that we could better understand how human minds are organised if we took into account what specialised systems in the brain are for, how they are supported by special routines in the brain, and under what conditions they evolved through natural selection. This required one to connect and combine evidence from evolutionary biology, genetics, neuro-physiology, psychology and anthropology.[19]

Tool-kit 3: Evolutionary psychology
Our evolutionary history has shaped our inference systems as evolved responses to recurrent problems in ancestral conditions. So we must (a) reconstitute the particular features of these problems in such conditions; (b) deduce what specific computational principles could solve these problems, and therefore predict some non-obvious design features; (c) examine whether there is independent experimental or neuro-physiological evidence for the corresponding specialised inference system; and (d) evaluate how the special system described by psychologists could have evolved from other systems and whether it would confer reproductive advantage to its bearers.

These stringent requirements explain why evolutionary psychology is still very much in its infancy. We cannot just consider a human capacity (e.g. the capacity to read and write) and invent a story that would make it adaptive (written communication is very convenient). Literacy does not require a specific system in the brain. It just recruits systems that served throughout our history and still serve other purposes (recognition of visual shapes, segmentation of words into syllables, motor control of the hand and wrist, etc.).

In some domains, it is quite clear that the way our inference systems work is an outcome of evolution, because our choices have direct consequences on survival and reproductive success. For example, evolutionary psychologists Don Symons and David Buss have put together a precise account of many aspects of human sexual behaviour: how people choose partners, what they find attractive, as well as how they gauge the reliability of these partners for long-term co-operation and parental care.[20]

Life in ancestral environments was fraught with danger, not just from the obvious predators but also from a variety of microbes, viruses and toxins. Ancestral foods obtained through foraging, scavenging and hunting were quite 'natural' and therefore far from healthy. Many plants are full of dangerous toxins and so are dead animals. Also, many animals carry pathogens that adapt easily to life in a human body. The danger is especially high for a 'generalist' species like humans, that is, one that finds its nutrients in a great variety of sources and adapts to new environments by changing its diet. Being a generalist species requires that you have not just immune defences like most other species but also some specific cognitive adaptations to minimise the danger of contamination and contagion. Rats, too, are generalists; this shows in their extremely cautious approach to novel foods, and in the way they quickly detect the correlation between a new food and various somatic disorders. They detect this better than other non-food related correlations, which shows that the system that produces such inferences is indeed specialised.

Humans too have special cognitive adaptations in this domain. For instance, very young children are open to a whole variety of tastes as long as the food is given by their care-takers, which helps them adapt to the local conditions; they then become rather conservative, which limits their forays into dangerous foods. Pregnant women develop their specific food aversions, mainly to tastes of toxin-rich foods. Morning sickness seems to target precisely those foods that would be dangerous to foetal growth in an ancestral environment. Food is obviously not the only source of danger of this kind. Contact with rotting corpses or with wounded or diseased people, ingestion of faeces or dirt: these are avoided for good evolutionary reasons.[21]

Indeed, the human mind seems to include a specific inference system that deals with such situations and triggers strong emotional reactions to even the mere suggestion of such situations. Psychologist Paul Rozin, who has studied the psychology of disgust, its connections to evolved food-preferences and its relation to the risk of contamination, showed that this *Contagion system* obeys specific inferential principles. First, it assumes that the source of danger is not necessarily visible; what makes a rotting carcass a bad source of food was not detectable before microscopes and microbiology. Second, the Contagion system assumes that even *limited* contact, however brief, with a source of danger transmits the *whole* of the risk. In other words, there is no 'dose-effect' here. Contagious substances do not lose their harmful powers with dilution. Third, the system specifies that *any* contact with sources of pollution will transmit it, although the aversive reactions are especially strong with ingestion.

These principles are specific to the domain considered. The Contagion inference system may in some circumstances seem overly cautious, as when subjects in Paul Rozin's experiments refuse to drink from a glass that once sheltered a cockroach and was then thoroughly disinfected. But the system is tuned to ancestral conditions where there was no such thing as thorough disinfecting.[22]

Life in the cognitive niche

Taking this evolutionary stance leads us to ask very general questions like, What do humans need? What is special about their needs, as opposed to those of giraffes and wombats? Obviously, humans need oxygen to breathe and a complicated cocktail of nutrients to sustain themselves, but that is fairly general among animals. What they specially need, more than any other species, are two types of 'goods' without which human existence is impossible. They need *information* about the world around them; and they need *co-operation* with other members of the species. These two are so much part of our environment that it is difficult to realise to what extent they are, literally, a matter of daily survival; also, it is difficult to realise to what extent our minds have been shaped though millennia of evolution to acquire these commodities and have become ever more dependent upon their supply.[23]

Humans are information-hungry. Human behaviour is based on a rich and flexible database that provides parameters for action. Very little human behaviour can be explained or even described without taking into account the massive acquisition of information about surrounding situations. This is why some anthropologists have described the proper environment of humans as a *cognitive niche*. Just as frogs need ponds and whales need sea water, humans are constantly immersed in a milieu that is indispensable to their operation and survival, and that milieu is information-about-the-environment. The journalistic cliché that this is the 'information age' is misleading if it suggests that in the past, either recent or distant, we did not depend on information. Think of the ordinary life of foragers in small nomadic groups dispersed in a savannah environment, collecting edibles on their way and trying to catch game to supplement their diet. They could not operate without vast amounts of detailed, preferably reliable and constantly updated information about their surroundings. Contrary to what we may imagine, gathering fruit and other vegetal nutrients is not quite as simple as picking foodstuffs off supermarket shelves. One must find out and remember where different species can be found, where past collections were particularly successful, in what season, etc. One must also store vast amounts of knowledge about the different tastes of different nutrients, their shapes, their smells, as well as their similarity with potentially dangerous substances. The same goes for hunting, which requires complex skills but also quite a lot of experience and information. Different species are stalked, approached and attacked in different ways. As far as predators go, humans are not especially well equipped. They compensate their physical weakness not just by low cunning but also by using information acquired in the field and transmitted across generations. Which leads me to the second point.[24]

Humans are co-operators. Humans have for a long time – long enough to make a difference in evolutionary terms – lived in organised groups and in intense social interaction. Humans need co-operation because they depend on rich information, well beyond what individual experience can provide. Other people provide most of this information. Also, most of what humans do requires co-operation. What I said above about foraging and hunting makes sense in the context of *some* people carrying out *part* of an operation and *others* being able to do *their* part because of the first one's actions. This is co-operation not just in the simple sense of 'doing things jointly' but rather as 'doing different things in a co-ordinated manner'. Now co-operation requires specific capacities and dispositions.

These general requirements of human existence have two important consequences:

- Humans, because they only survive through co-operation and because they need information, are generally dependent upon *information provided by other humans*. This is not to deny that humans can acquire vast amounts of information by direct experience. But the fact is, that even this could not be acquired without massive transfers of information from other conspecifics, to a degree that is not equalled in any other species.
- Humans depend upon information and upon co-operation, and because of that they depend on *information about other people's mental states*, that is, what information they have and what their intentions are. No joint hunting expedition, war raid or marriage negotiation can be organised without precise monitoring of what other people want and believe.

Once you are told that whales live in sea water you may not be surprised to find out that their capacities and dispositions were tailored by natural selection to provide a reasonable fit to these conditions. The same is true of human capacities and dispositions, once you understand that the proper milieu of human existence is that of other people's information. This means that we must explore yet another batch of inference systems in the mental basement.

Inference systems in the social mind

That humans live in the cognitive niche, and that most elements of that informational milieu are provided by other humans, results in specific behaviours and capacities. Most of these are very familiar, so familiar indeed that it is sometimes difficult to realise that they require specific cognitive equipment. Here are a few:

A hypertrophied social intelligence. What we call social intelligence in many species are special capacities for social interaction. We have hugely complex social interaction, compared with other species, partly because we have hugely complex systems that represent what others are up to and why. For instance, here are two aspects of social intelligence that are highly developed in humans: (1) figuring out complex embedded states, for instance understanding that 'Mary knew that Peter resented the fact that she had agreed with Paul when he said Jenny was too clever for Mark'; (2) keeping 'files' on various individuals without ever mixing them up. This is so natural that it may be difficult to realise the huge memory stores required. In the above situation, Mary knows something that involves four different individuals. Obviously, the only way to produce such complex thoughts is to have information about these different individuals, keep it in separate files, access several of these files at the same time yet never confuse them. This requires capacities that are developed to this extent in no other species. As I said above, what we call 'intuitive psychology' or 'theory of mind' is a federation of brain structures and functions, each of which is specialized in particular tasks: detecting the presence of animate agents (which may be predators or prey); detecting what others are looking at; figuring out their goals; representing their beliefs. Different species have different sets of these components. Psychologist Daniel Povinelli showed that chimpanzees can certainly follow the gaze of another agent, but they do not seem to have a rich representation of the agent's *intentions* as revealed by gaze direction. More generally, some aspects of intuitive psychology seem to have evolved in primates as a way of catching prey and avoiding predators in a more efficient way. This, in particular, may be the origin of our immediate, emotionally charged detection of animate agents in the environment. But the extraordinary development of intuitive psychology in humans was also triggered by the advantages incurred in individuals who could better predict the behaviour of other human agents, since interaction with other human beings is the real milieu of human evolution.[25]

A taste for gossip. Although we tend to despise it or downplay its importance, gossip is perhaps among the most fundamental of human activities, as important to survival and reproduction as most other cognitive capacities and emotional dispositions. Gossip is practised everywhere, enjoyed everywhere, despised everywhere. Why is that? We can understand these three features better if we recall what gossip is about. Its main focus is information about other people, preferably information that they would rather not divulge, and it centres on topics of adaptive value such as people's status, resources and sex. Gossip loses much of its interest when it strays away from these topics, as is demonstrated by our attitude to people who feverishly acquire and exchange information in other domains. Think of those obsessive fans who exchange information about every track of every record ever issued by their favourite band, when and where the cover photographs were taken, etc. Or consider the more extreme case of British 'trainspotters'. (For non-British readers, these people spend entire weekends watching trains; their goal is to tick as many boxes as possible in a catalogue of all the rolling-stock used by every railway company, including every locomotive and carriage type.) Such characters tattle about matters of no relevance to social interaction. We do not praise them for that; we just think they are not quite normal.[26]

There is no human society without gossip. Yet there is virtually no human group where gossip is praised for its great informative value, for its contribution to social interaction, for its great usefulness. Why is that? This universal contempt for gossip stems from two equally important factors. One is that, for all we want to hear about other people's status and sex and resources, we have equal reluctance to broadcast such information about ourselves. Another reason is that, every bit as much as we like gossip, we also have to represent ourselves as trustworthy. This is necessary if we want to maintain any stable social interaction, particularly co-operation, with other people. We must be seen as people who will not betray secrets and spread information beyond the circle of our real friends. So our ambivalence does not mean that contempt for gossip is hypocritical.

Adaptations for social exchange. Nothing is easier to understand than situations of social exchange. That you will gain a certain benefit (get a share of the meal) if you accept to pay a certain cost (bring a bottle) is so natural that the subtle reasoning behind such situations seems self-evident. The inferences are indeed automatic (if the meal is lavish and your bottle less than respectable, people will not be that grateful) but that is because the inference system is quite efficient. Social exchange is certainly among the oldest of human behaviours, as humans have depended on sharing and exchanging resources for a very long time. Evolutionary psychologists Leda Cosmides and John Tooby pointed out that people become much better at solving complex logical tasks if these are presented as social-exchange problems; it does not matter if the situation is exotic. To check whether members of an imaginary tribe actually abide by the rule 'if people get their faces scarified then they have a right to eat buffalo', subjects spontaneously look for buffalo-eaters with intact faces (rather than scarified individuals who do not eat buffalo). Inferences in such situations follow a specific 'check for cheats' rule rather than a general logic. Indeed, subjects are confused when asked to check an equivalent but non-social-exchange rule, such as 'if people get their faces scarified then they have visited Peking'. Psychologists observed these same experimental results in American college students and Shiwiar hunter-gatherers in the Amazon. That social exchange is a special inference system is confirmed by the fact that it can be disrupted by brain pathology, when other reasoning functions are preserved.[27]

Evaluation of trust. That humans depend on co-operation creates *strategic* problems, where the value (the expected benefit) of a particular move depends on whether someone else makes a particular move (not necessarily the same one). Ideally, one could choose to co-operate only with people who are forced to co-operate. Whenever you pay for something you can of course draw a gun and threaten the shopkeeper to be sure that you get the correct change. This is not really possible in most circumstances, but we have capacities which compensate that. One is that we can decide to co-operate with people on the basis of particular *signals* from which (we think) we can infer that they are co-operators.[28]

Now this part of the computation is crucial but we are not really aware of it. Sociologists Diego Gambetta and Paul Bacharach have studied extensively the signals by which people evaluate other people's trustworthiness in everyday situations. They show that in many contexts (e.g. would you let the person who arrived just behind you into the building, even though she has not dialled the appropriate code or rung the bell?) people are able to evaluate whether certain signals are reliable or not. This requires that they compute both the significance of the signal and the probability that it is faked. All this is done automatically and quickly: not because the inferences are simple, but because we have specialised systems that carry out this computational work.[29]

Coalitional dynamics. This is another common feature of human interaction. People will spontaneously form groups where a certain degree of trust ensures co-operation and mutual benefits. Biologist Matt Ridley coined the term 'groupishness' to describe the human tendency to join groups. Modern ethnic conflicts, but also the harmless social dynamics of fashions or the minor coalitions within any large classroom, office, congregation, etc., illustrate the power of this propensity.[30]

Note that coalitions are a very special form of association. To have a common goal is not sufficient to build a coalition; you and I may wish our streets were cleaner, but that does not bring us into a coalition. It is not even sufficient that people are aware of having the same goal and co-operate to achieve that goal. For instance, factory workers need to co-ordinate their work to produce a manufactured good but they do not construe this as a coalition. The latter pre-supposes an activity in which joining is (presumably) voluntary, defection is possible, benefits can be accrued by co-operation and there is a notable cost in being a co-operator when others defect.

Group action will allow you to reap great benefits as long as everyone is in it together. But then in many situations it may be much more profitable for some individuals to withdraw co-operation at an awkward moment. Your hunting partner might put you in great danger by running for his life precisely when he was supposed to attack. Your comrade in the office conspiracy might spill the beans to please the boss. There is just no iron-clad guarantee that people will not blab or run away or, to put it more generally, *defect* to protect or enhance their immediate interest. This is why so few species actually have coalitions (chimpanzees and dolphins build alliances but not on the same scale and with the same stability as the human version). Coalitions require complicated computation, and therefore the mental capacities to run these computations in an intuitive, automatic way.[31]

To make this clear, it may be of help to list the conditions that must obtain in a coalition: (1) You behave in such a way as to enhance the benefits gained by other members of the group, but not those of non-members. (2) This behaviour towards other members does not require that you receive a particular benefit for helping them. (3) You expect similar dispositions and behaviour towards you from other members (and of course not from non-members). As a result, (4) whether it is a good thing for you to be in the group is computed by taking the benefits and costs incurred in interaction with *all* other members, not with *each* of them. (For instance, in a particular association you may be constantly helping X and receiving help from Y; if this is a coalition you will balance the two and disregard the fact that you are in some sense exploiting Y and being exploited by X.) (5) You represent the behaviour of members of other groups as exhibiting in some sense the whole group's behaviour. (If you are a Tory, and a Labour militant attacks you, you think of that as an attack from Labour, not just from that person.) (6) Your reactions to how a member of another group behaves are directed to the group, not specifically to the individual in question. If the Labour militant has attacked you, it makes sense for you to retaliate by attacking *another* Labour member. (7) You represent the various groups as 'big agents'. For instance, you think what is happening in the political arena is that 'Labour is trying to do this' or 'the Tory Party is doing that', although parties cannot literally be trying to do anything as they are not persons. (8) You are extremely concerned with other members' loyalty. That is, whether the others in your group are reliably loyal to the group or not (regardless of how it affects you directly) is a matter of great emotional effects. This is manifest in several different ways. You feel a desire to punish those people who have defected from the coalition; you may also want to punish those who failed to punish the defectors; you may want to screen people by submitting them to various ordeals, where they have to incur substantial costs to demonstrate their loyalty.[32]

I listed the conditions above in some detail – however painfully obvious they may all seem – because this shows how building coalitions requires complex computation. The fact that coalitions seem such a simple and obvious thing to us shows, not that their functioning is simple, but that we have the kinds of minds that compute all this without much difficulty, which is different. Nobody in any human culture needs much instruction to figure out how co-operation is established between partners or how to detect potential threats to co-operation. Also, note how coalitional behaviour is so easily developed by young children, in the absence of much explicit instruction (and indeed very often against dismayed parents' recommendations).

Incidentally, this discussion in terms of cost and benefit, co-operation and defection, may seem very abstract. We tend to think that we just have 'feelings' about such situations. This is true in a sense: Feelings are the most salient aspect of these reactions we are aware of. But feelings are the outcome of complex calculations that specialised systems in our minds carry out in precise terms. For instance, some of my recently arrived African friends were baffled that people in Europe could get so worked up about parking-space 'theft'. They could understand it, in some abstract way, but they just did not 'feel' the anger. After a few weeks of driving their own cars in the city they displayed the same emotional reactions as the locals. It is not that their abstract 'conceptions' of what matters and what does not had changed. But they had acquired the information that parking-space is a very scarce resource, and their emotional systems had adjusted to that information.

Progress-box 7: Evolution, psychology, social mind

- Specific inference systems were tailored by selection for their contribution to solving particular problems in ancestral environments.
- To describe them it is useful to combine predictions from the evolutionary background and independent experimental evidence.
- Crucial to our species are mental adaptations for social life, as information (notably that provided by others) is our ecological niche.
- The 'social mind' consists of a collection of specialised inference systems for sex, parenting, social exchange, trust, friendship and coalition-building, as each poses specific problems and requires specific forms of reasoning.

Decoupling and constraints

A human mind is not condemned to consider and represent only what is currently going on in its immediate environment. Indeed, human minds are remarkable in the amount of time they spend thinking about what is not here and now. Fiction is the most salient illustration. Reading the above anecdote about *The thief, the dog, the child and the police officer*, you probably entertained precise notions about the thief's and the police officer's mental states, although there was nobody around, only marks on a sheet of paper. But the capacity is of course much more general. One of the easiest things to do for human minds is produce inferences on the basis of false premises, like 'if I had had lunch I would not be so hungry now'. This can focus on future possibilities too. Worried thoughts about what would happen if the roof caved in and came crashing on your head do not require the usual input (e.g. seeing the roof coming down) and do not produce their normal output (an attempt to dash off as fast as possible). This is why psychologists say that these thoughts are *decoupled* from their standard inputs and outputs.

Decoupled cognition is crucial to human cognition because we depend so much on information communicated by others and on co-operation with others. To evaluate information provided by others you must build some mental simulation of what they describe. Also, we could not carry out complex hunting expeditions, tool-making, food-gathering or social exchange without complex planning. This requires an evaluation of several different scenarios, each of which is based on non-actual premises: What if we go down to the valley to gather fruit? What if there is none down there? What if other members of the group decide to go elsewhere? What if my neighbour steals my tools? Thinking about the past also requires decoupling. As psychologist Endel Tulving points out, episodic memory is a form of mental 'time-travel' allowing us to re-experience the effects of a particular scene on us. This is used in particular to assess other people's behaviour, to re-evaluate their character, to provide a new description of our own behaviour and its consequences, etc.[33]

Decoupled cognition appears very early in children's development when they start to 'pretend-play', using a variety of objects as though they were other objects (e.g. a bar of soap as a motor-car, a puppet as a person, etc.). Now doing this requires a subtle mechanism that tells you which aspects of the real environment should be bracketed off, as it were, and which still counts as true in the imagined scenario. Psychologist Alan Leslie demonstrated spectacular aspects of this capacity. Children pretend-pour pretend-tea out of an empty teapot into several cups. (They are careful to align the spout of their teapot with the cup, because in the pretend-scenario liquids fall downwards as they do in the real world. This aspect of the scenario is handled by intuitive physics as if there were real liquid in the pot.) Then an experimenter knocks over one of the cups, laments the fact that the pretend-tea is spilled all over the table, and asks the child to refill the empty cup. Now three year olds faced with this situation, that is, with two (actually) empty cups only one of which is also (pretend-)empty, do not make mistakes; they pretend-fill only the pretend-empty one, not the actually empty one that is still pretend-full. This kind of virtuoso performance is in fact involved in all situations of pretence. The child's cognitive system can handle the non-actual assumptions of the situation and run those inferences of their intuitive ontology that make sense in that imagined context, not in the real one.[34]

Decoupling is also necessary to produce external representations, another universal capacity in humans. Toys, statues, rock-paintings and finger-drawings in the sand are not the same as what they represent. To make sense of them, our inference systems must block certain inferences – the path through the forest is one-inch wide on the drawing but it is not that narrow in actual fact – and maintain others – that the path in the sand turns left means that the actual one turns left too. So the interpretation of external representations can be subtle. Indeed, in many cases we intuitively consider that what external representations stand for depends much more on their creators' intentions than on what they look like. Psychologist Paul Bloom showed that very young children share this subtle assumption. For them two strictly identical drawings are *in actual fact* representations of different objects (e.g. a lollipop and a balloon) if that is what the creators intended.[35]

It is certainly useful to reason away from the here and now; but that works only if such reasoning is tightly constrained. If our inferences ran wild, for example:

> *If we go down to the valley, my dog will lose its teeth*
> *If my brother is sad, this telephone will break into pieces*

they would not provide the basis for efficient behaviour. Note that

these strange inferences are not strange just because their consequences seem outlandish. You could say:

> *If I feed the dog nothing but candy-sticks it will lose its teeth*
> *If you put the telephone in the tumbler-drier it will break into pieces*

So it is the connection between hypothetical and consequence that is
or is not sensible.

The crucial point to remember about decoupled thoughts is that
they run the inference systems in the same way as if the situation
were actual. This is why we can produce coherent and useful
inferences on the basis of imagined premises. For instance, the
sentence 'If kangaroos had shorter legs, they would jump further'
seems implausible, and 'If kangaroos had shorter legs, they would eat
broccoli' seems to make no sense at all. The inference 'If kangaroos
had *longer* legs, they would jump further' seems plausible because it is
supported by our inference systems. Our intuitive physics assumes
that a stronger push will result in a longer trajectory, therefore that
longer legs should produce longer jumps. In the same way, if I tell
you that I saw a tiger in the forest yesterday you will probably infer
that I *was* in the forest yesterday, because your intuitive psychology
requires that condition.

Hypothetical scenarios suspend one aspect of actual situations but
then run all inference systems in the same way as usual. If this sounds
familiar, it is because I already mentioned it in my presentation of
supernatural concepts, which includes one violation of expectations
('if some agents were invisible . . .') and then runs all relevant
inferences in the same way as usual ('. . . we could not see them, but
they would see what was going on'). Supernatural concepts are just
one consequence of the human capacity for decoupling representations. But what makes them more or less important is the kind of
inferences we then produce on the basis of these premises, as we will
see presently.

By-products and salient gadgets

The fact that the brain comes equipped with many specialised inference systems *and* can run them in the decoupled mode, may explain why humans the world over engage in a host of activities that carry no clear adaptive value.

To illustrate this, consider how the auditory cortex of humans must perform several complicated tasks. One of these is to sort out the sounds of language from other noises. Information about noises is sent to associative cortical areas that categorise the sounds and identify the nature of their source. Information about the source's location is handled by other specialised circuitry and sent to specific systems. The auditory system must also isolate the sounds of language. All normal humans have the ability to segment a stream of sound emerging from someone else's mouth in terms of isolated sounds, then send this purified representation to cortical areas specialised in word-identification. To turn a stream into segments, the system must pay attention to the specific frequencies that define each vowel and the complex noises of consonants, as well as their duration and their effects on each other. To do this, the auditory cortex comprises different sub-systems, some of which specialise in pure tones and others in more complex stimuli. All this is clearly part of a complex evolved architecture specialised in fine-grained sound analysis, a task of obvious adaptive value for a species that depends on speech for virtually all communication. But it also has this interesting consequence: that humans are predisposed to detect, produce, remember and enjoy music. This is a human universal. There is no human society without some musical tradition. Although the traditions are very different, some principles can be found everywhere. For instance, musical sounds are always closer to pure sound than to noise. The equivalence between octaves and the privileged role of particular intervals like the perfect fifth and the fourth are consequences of the organisation of the cortex. To exaggerate a little, what you get from musical sounds are 'super-vowels' (the pure frequencies as opposed to the mixed ones that define ordinary vowels) and pure 'consonants' (produced by rhythmic instruments and the attack of most instruments). These properties make music an intensified form of sound-experience, from which the cortex receives purified and therefore intense doses of what usually activates it. So music is not really a direct product of our dispositions but a cultural product that is particularly successful because it activates some of our capacities in a particularly intense way.[36]

This phenomenon is not unique to music. Humans everywhere also fill their environments with artefacts that over-stimulate their visual cortex, for instance by providing pure saturated colour instead of the dull browns and greens of their familiar environments. This has been so for a long time. Our palaeolithic foragers used red ochre, probably for purely aesthetic reasons. In the same way, our visual system is sensitive to symmetries in objects. Bilateral symmetry in particular is quite important; when two sides of an animal or person look the same it means that they are facing you, a relevant feature of interaction with people but also with prey and predators. Again, you cannot find a human group where people do not produce visual gadgets with such symmetrical arrangements, from the simplest make-up or hair-dressing techniques to textile patterns and interior decoration. Finally, our visual cortex includes specialised sub-systems that quickly identify objects in terms of *kinds* rather than individuals, while other systems are more interested in the location and motion of these objects. Artificial stimulation of either or both of these systems – in other words, figurative art – has a long history too, as we know from the spectacular displays of palaeolithic cave-paintings like Chauvet or Lascaux.[37]

These activities recruit our cognitive capacities in ways that make some cultural artefacts very salient and likely to be transmitted. These salient cognitive artefacts can be extraordinarily primitive, like glass beads or pieces of shiny metal whose only merit is to provide an unusual visual stimulus. But ideas too and their abstract relations can constitute such artefacts. Jokes recruit our reasoning capacities and our expectations about situations, often ending with a punch-line that forces us to reconsider the whole situation from a new angle; paradoxes fascinate because there seems to be no way of escaping an unacceptable conclusion.

Once we understand how brain evolution resulted in the design of a brain with these particular inference systems, we can better understand why humans are sensitive to *these* particular artefacts rather than others. That there are pure tones in music and symmetries in visual art is certainly no coincidence, given the way our brains were designed by evolution.

Turning to a domain closer to our supernatural concepts, such evolutionary reasoning may well explain certain forms of magical beliefs. For instance, in many places in India it would be highly polluting to share food with a member of some low castes, say a tanner or blacksmith. Indeed the whole household would need serious ritual cleansing. Most people there have no idea *why* it would be polluting or *in what particular way* this pollution would affect them, but they would certainly avoid such situations. To take a less extreme example, mixing flesh and milk in a dish will make the whole food impure, as far as traditional Jewish regulations are concerned. But again there is no description of why this is so. We anthropologists used to think that such magical thinking was the result of some failure in the mind's usually firm grip on what causes what. People are generally quite good at figuring out the causes of events, otherwise they could not manage their everyday activities. But then in magic they seem to abandon all that. So it would seem that people believe in magic when they somehow relax their criteria of what could count as the cause of what.

This is not too convincing, however, because such magical reasoning is not in fact very different from many ordinary inferences. Many people know that it is better to brown the meat before putting it in the stew but they have no idea why this is the case. They till the soil when they plant seeds but have little knowledge of soil chemistry. Indeed, ideas of purity and pollution seem very absurd if you consider them against *general* standards of what causes what, and much less so if you consider a *special* inference system in the mind, the one that deals with possible contamination and contagion. As I said above, this system seems to have its own principles: that the dangerous substance is not necessarily visible, that the dose does not matter, that any contact with the original source of danger transmits the whole of the pollution. Apparently strange beliefs about touching the hand of a blacksmith are only an application of these principles outside their adaptive domain – that of contaminants and toxins. Once it is suggested that low-caste people contain a specific substance, the Contagion system naturally derives all the consequences: for instance that *any* contact with such a person is polluting, however brief; also, that the danger is there even if it is invisible.

This neatly encapsulates the features of some of these cognitive gadgets that seem to have haunted human minds ever since they were human. First, the whole pollution story is based on a counter-intuitive assumption, namely that although other people are of the same species as us their internal constitution may be different. Second, an adaptive inference system is activated, which naturally produces all sorts of additional consequences, once you represent the initial assumption. Finally, the whole scenario is usually represented in the decoupled mode, as an interesting 'what if' scenario, since people do not in fact share food with polluting castes. This does not in any way hinder the transmission of the belief. Quite the opposite. The notion of polluting people is one of these artefacts that fascinate the mind because it produces relevant inferences from salient suppositions, and that is enough.

All this brings us back to serious religion. We must not assume that cognitive gadgets are confined to unimportant domains, from the real but minor pleasure of jokes to the real but not vital functions of music and visual art. This would be misleading. I used the example of caste pollution to show that once human minds acquire such cognitive artefacts the consequences can be very serious indeed. A great part of social interaction is founded on such notions in many parts of the world outside India. More generally, religious concepts too constitute salient cognitive artefacts, whose successful cultural transmission depends on the fact that they activate our inference systems in particular ways. The reason why religion can become much more serious and important than the artefacts described so far is that it activates inference systems that are of vital importance to us: those that govern our most intense emotions, shape our interaction with other people, give us moral feelings and organise social groups.

Progress-box 8: The mind it takes (to have religion)

- The mind it takes to have religion is the standard architecture that we all have by virtue of being members of the species. (No need for a special kind of mentality or mind.)
- Because of decoupling and specialisation, human minds are sensitive to a particular range of cultural gadgets.
- (To anticipate:) Religious concepts too are probably successful to the extent that they activate inference systems.
- (To anticipate:) They probably activate several different inference systems ('composite relevance').

Chapter Four

Why gods and spirits?

Religious concepts are those supernatural concepts that *matter*. The world over, people entertain concepts of beings with special qualities and special powers. They live forever, in some places they are supposed to be prescient or indeed all-knowing, to govern the elements, to carve mountains, to strike with lightning or to smite the sinner. In all human groups some god or gods or the spirits or the ancestors (or some combination of these different types) stand out from the rest of the supernatural repertoire in that very strong emotional states can be associated with their representation. Thoughts about what the gods want or what the ancestors know can induce strong feelings of fear, guilt, anger but also reassurance or comfort.

What makes these stories so important to so many people? Why is God more important than Santa Claus, or in the Fang context why do ancestors matter so much more than the White Bogeyman? One may think the answer is quite simple: *People believe in God's or the ancestors' existence, not in Santa's or the Bogeyman's.* This, however, is not a cause but a consequence. Some supernatural concepts are represented in such a way that it can seem obvious or at least possible that they refer to real things and agents in the world. The problem is to explain how this happens. This will take several chapters. A first step is to understand what kind of agents gods, spirits and ancestors are.

Religion is practical

Western people, especially educated people, especially students of religion tend to consider religious concepts primarily as the expression of some beliefs about how the world works. Nothing wrong about that in principle, except that it may lead to a *contemplative* view of religion, in which people are said to consider their world or existence in the abstract and realise or imagine that it would make more sense with the addition of some concepts of gods, ghosts or ancestors. In this view, what counts most about the ancestors is that they are the souls of dead people; what matters about God is that he created the world, and so on. But this may not be the most important aspect in people's actual thoughts about these agents. For religion is a rather practical thing.

First, religious concepts are represented by people mostly when there is a *need* for them. That is, some salient event has happened that can be explained in terms of the gods' actions; or someone has just done something that the ancestors probably will not like; or some baby is born or someone just died and these events are thought to involve supernatural agents. In most trains of thought where religious concepts are used, these help understand or formulate or explain some *particular* occurrence.

Also, what are constant objects of intuition and reasoning are actual situations of *interaction* with these agents. People do not just stipulate that there is a supernatural being somewhere who creates thunder, or that there are souls wandering about in the night. People actually interact with them, in the very concrete sense of giving and receiving, paying, promising, threatening, protecting, placating, etc.

The Kwaio concept of spirit-ancestor (*adalo*) illustrates this contrast between contemplative, theological understandings and the more mundane business of representing religious agents in practical contexts and interacting with them. The Kwaio live in the Solomon Islands; most of their religious activities, as described by anthropologist Roger Keesing, involve dealing with ancestors, especially the spirits of deceased members of their own clans, as well as more dangerous wild spirits. Interaction with these *adalo* (the term denotes both wild spirits and ancestors) is a constant feature of Kwaio life. As Keesing points out, young children need no explicit instruction to represent the ancestors as an invisible and powerful presence, since they see people interact with the *adalo* in so many circumstances of everyday life. People frequently pray to the dead or give them sacrifices of pigs or simply talk to them. Also, people 'meet' the ancestors in dreams. Most people are particularly familiar with and fond of one particular *adalo*, generally the spirit of a close relative, and maintain frequent contact with that spirit.

The ancestors are generally responsible for whatever happens in a village: '*Adalo,* a child learns early, are beings that help and punish: the source of success, gratification, and security, and the cause of illness, death, and misfortune; makers and enforcers of rules that must at first seem arbitrary.' Good taro crops and prolific sows indicate that the ancestors are happy with the way the living behave. Illness and misfortune are generally an effect of the ancestors' anger. True, the Kwaio, like most people in the world, accept that some events 'just happen' and have no particular cause. Some illnesses may be interpreted as a straightforward weakening of the body with no special implications; the fact that some ailments are cured by Western medicine shows that they are in that category of mere mishaps. But salient events, particularly remarkable cases of misfortune, are explained as consequences of the *adalo*. As a Kwaio diviner tells Keesing: 'If we see that a child is sick . . . we divine and then we sacrifice a pig [to the *adalo*].' Divination is required to understand which spirit is angry and why. A diviner will take a set of knotted leaves and pull them to see which side breaks first, indicating either a positive answer or no answer to a particular question. The origin of many problems lies in the ancestors' anger at people who broke rules about what is proper and what is *abu* (forbidden or dangerous – from the root *tapu* that gave us our 'taboo'). Ancestors like humans crave pork and demand frequent sacrifices of pigs. Interaction with the ancestors can be quite complex, because it is not always clear which ancestor is causing trouble: 'If it is not really that *adalo* [discovered in divination] that asked for a pig, in order that our pigs or taro grow well, then even though we sacrifice it, nothing will happen.' So people may go through several cycles of divination followed by sacrifice to reach a satisfactory arrangement with the ancestors.

On the whole, there are few situations in Kwaio life that are not construed as involving the ancestors in some way or other. The *adalo* are always around, in most contexts a reassuring but also a threatening presence. Keesing tells how, when taking a walk far away from a village, he was asked by his ten-year-old companion to stop whistling, as this would disturb the wild *adalo* that dwelt there. Keesing jokingly remarked that he did not fear them as he was carrying a big stick, only to be lectured about the futility of such defence.

The Kwaio ancestors are a perfect example of supernatural agents who *matter* to people. Now, this may seem paradoxical, the Kwaio are also remarkably vague as concerns the exact nature of the *adalo*, where ancestors actually live and so on. Keesing notes that people are not even very precise about the process whereby a living person becomes an ancestor. The few who bother to think about such matters only do so as a result of being prompted by an anthropologist, and they have wildly divergent representations of the process. Some people consider that *adalo* are people's 'shadows'. A person stays alive as long as their body, shadow and breath are held together; at death the 'breath that talks' goes to live with other dead people in a remote village. The shadow remains around the village as an *adalo* that interacts with the living. Others maintain that there is probably no village of the dead. The 'breath that talks' just fades away while the shadow remains with the living. Others think that the shadow does depart to the village of the dead; but it soon comes back to its former village. As Keesing notes, most general questions about the *adalo* receive either inconsistent answers or no answer at all: 'How and why do ancestors control events? What are "wild spirits" [the dangerous ones]? Where do they come from? There is no answer to these questions. [However] in those realms where Kwaio need to *deal with* their ancestors, their cultural tradition provides guidelines for action.'[1]

This is in fact a very general characteristic of religious notions, beliefs and norms. This may seem surprising to those of us brought up in modern Western contexts where religion is mostly encountered as a *doctrine* that includes definite statements about the origin of things, what happens to the souls of dead people, and other such theoretical topics. In another chapter I will explain why religion in some historical contexts came to acquire this theoretical emphasis. For the time being, let me just insist that doctrines are not necessarily the most essential or important aspect of religious concepts. Indeed many people seem to feel no need for a general, theoretically consistent expression of the qualities and powers of supernatural agents. What they always have, on the other hand, are precise descriptions of how these agents can influence their own lives, and what to do about that.

Precisely because religion is a practical thing, we may be tempted to think that the solution to our problem is quite simple: Some supernatural concepts are important because people believe that the agents in question have extraordinary powers. The *adalo* matter a lot to the Kwaio because the Kwaio take it as obvious that these ancestors and wild spirits can make them sick or give them good crops. But this is not a solution to the problem, it is just another way of formulating it. We must understand why it is so obvious that the gods and ancestors have those powers. Besides, this explanation would not be generally valid. There are many places in the world where the most powerful supernatural agents are *not* the ones that matter most. The Fang have all these rituals and complex emotions associated with the possible presence of the ghosts-ancestors. They also say that the natural world (meaning earth and sky and all creatures great and small) was created by a god called Mebeghe, vastly more powerful than either the living or the dead. His work was then completed by another god, Nzame, who invented all cultural objects: tools, houses, etc., and taught people to hunt, domesticate animals and raise crops. However mighty, these gods do not seem to matter that much. There are no cults or rituals specifically directed at Mebeghe or Nzame, although they are assumed to be around, and they are in fact very rarely mentioned. The situation is a bit different in Christianised areas where 'Nzame' has become the name of the Christian god and has therefore become more important. But even there people still pay a lot of attention to what the ghosts-ancestors know or want and much less to the supposedly all-powerful gods. This is in fact a common theme in African religions, where a supreme god is both supreme and in actual fact of little importance to people. For a long time, this puzzled travellers, anthropologists and of course missionaries. Many African people seemed to recognise a Creator in the same sense as the biblical one, yet were remarkably indifferent to Him. We will see below the explanation for this apparent paradox. For the time being, let us just keep in mind that what matters is not so much the powers of supernatural beings considered in the abstract, as those powers that are relevant to practical concerns.

Like the Kwaio ancestors, gods and spirits are very generally represented as agents we can interact with, and this shapes the way people intuitively think of their powers. To take a Western example, consider another of Justin Barrett's studies of the God-concept. Barrett asked his Christian subjects to imagine various situations in which they may have to pray to God to save other people from imminent danger. For instance, a ship in high seas has just hit an iceberg and is sinking fast. Praying is in essence asking God to do something about the situation, to tinker with a probable sequence of causes and effects that should result in a wreckage. But there is a variety of ways in which God could help. For instance, God could help the ship stay afloat with a broken hull, or give the passengers the physical strength to withstand a long stay in freezing sea water, or give another ship's captain the idea of changing course so he sees the sinking liner and rescues everyone.

Barrett wanted to find out which of these scenarios would seem most natural to believers, as this may reveal their (not entirely conscious) notion of how God intervenes in the world. Now, although Barrett was careful to make all these possible interventions equally salient, and though they are all trivial for an omnipotent god, most subjects spontaneously choose the third kind of option. That is, in most situations of this kind they would pray to God so he changes someone's mind, rather than nudge physical or biological processes. In some sense, this is not too surprising. People have a 'theologically correct' notion of God as omnipotent but they also use their intuitive expectation, that it is easier for a *person* to change people's mind than to correct or reorient physical and biological processes. But note that this expectation would be irrelevant if God's great powers were the most salient part of the God-concept. The expectation is activated only because people represent God as a person-like agent who interacts with them.

Gods and spirits as persons

In myth and folk-tales, we find supernatural concepts describing all sorts of objects and beings with all sorts of violations: stories about houses that remember their owners, islands that float adrift on the ocean or mountains that breathe. But the serious stuff, what becomes of great social importance, is generally about person-like beings. These invariably have some counter-intuitive properties, like a non-standard biology (they do not eat, grow, die, etc.) and often non-standard physical properties (they fly through solid obstacles, become invisible, change shape, etc.) *but* people's inferences about them require that they behave very much like persons. When people get serious about what is around, beyond what they can actually observe, they tend to furnish that imagined world with persons rather than animals or plants or solid rocks.

That gods and spirits are construed very much like persons is probably one of the best-known traits of religion. Indeed, the Greeks had already noticed that people create gods in their own image. (Admittedly, the Greek gods were extraordinarily anthropomorphic, and Greek mythology really is like modern soap-opera, much more so than other religious systems.) Voltaire echoed this thought with his characteristically wry comment that, were cockroaches to have a notion of God they would probably imagine Him as a very big and powerful cockroach. All this is familiar, indeed so familiar that for a long time anthropologists had forgotten that this propensity requires an explanation. Why then are gods and spirits so much like humans?

Anthropologist Stewart Guthrie reopened this long-abandoned question in a book that anticipated some of the cognitive arguments presented here. Guthrie noted that there is an anthropomorphic tendency not just in visual artefacts, in the art of many different cultures, but also in visual perception itself. That is, we tend to interpret even very faint cues in terms of humans traits; we see faces in the clouds and human bodies in trees and mountains. This, naturally, is also found in concepts of religious agents, many of whose features are strikingly human. A common explanation is that we imagine person-like agents who rule our destinies because this produces a *reassuring* view of our existence and the world around us. We project human features onto non-human aspects of our world because that makes these aspects more familiar and therefore less frightening. But as Guthrie points out, this is not really plausible. Gods and spirits are dangerous and vindictive every bit as often as they are helpful and benevolent. Moreover, imagining barely detectable agents around oneself is in general rather cold comfort if one is scared. Suppose you are on your own in a house on a deserted moor and hear noises around the house. Is it really that reassuring to think that they are caused by someone you cannot see? Is it really better than to imagine that the noise came from branches brushing against the window?

Guthrie argues that the anthropomorphic trend is a consequence of the way our cognitive systems work, and has little to do with our preferences, with a desire to imagine the world in this way rather than that. The solution, for him, is that we imagine person-like agents because persons are more *complex* than other types of objects. In fact, persons are the most complex type of object we know. Now our cognitive processes strive to extract as much relevant information as possible from environments (this is of course an automatic, unconscious process) and produce as many inferences as possible. This is why, when people are faced with ambiguous cues in their environment, they often 'see' faces in the clouds and on the mountains. Our imagination naturally turns to human-like creations because our intuitive understanding of persons is just far more complex than our understanding of mechanical and biological processes. For Guthrie, this also explained the human-like features of gods and spirits, the fact that, however much people want to describe them as different from humans, they are in fact very much created in our own image.[2]

The anthropomorphic tendency described by Guthrie is certainly there. However, before we understand how it contributes to people's notions of supernatural agents, we must make this psychological description a bit more specific. First, note that gods and spirits are not represented as having *human* features in general, but as having *minds*, which is much more specific. People represent supernatural agents who perceive events, have thoughts and memories and intentions. But they do not always project other human characteristics, like having a body, eating food, living with a family or gradually getting older. Indeed, anthropologists know that the *only* feature of humans that is *always* projected onto supernatural beings is the mind. Second, the concept of a mind is not exclusively human. As I said in the last two chapters, it is part of our intuitive expectations that animals as well as humans perceive what is going on around them, react to those events, have goals and form plans, etc. Intuitive-psychology inferences are applied to intentional agents in general, not just persons. So it is quite likely that concepts of gods and spirits are mostly organised by our intuitive notions of *agency in general* (the abstract quality that is present in animals, persons, and anything that appears to move of its own accord in pursuance of its own goals) rather than just human agency.

Supernatural agents and dangerous beasts

The nuance is quite important because in many situations our intuitive systems can detect this generic form of agency without having a description of what kind of agent is around. When we see branches moving in a tree or when we hear an unexpected sound behind us, we immediately infer that some agent is the cause of this salient event. We can do that without any specific description of what the agent actually is. As I said in the previous chapter, some inference systems in the mind are specialised in the detection of apparent animacy and agency in objects around us. These systems are not concerned with whether what was detected was a person or animal or yet another kind of agent (other systems handle this identification task).

According to psychologist Justin Barrett, this feature of our psychological functioning is fundamental to understanding concepts of gods and spirits, for two reasons:

First, what happens in religion is not so much that people see 'faces in the clouds' (in the way described by Guthrie) as 'traces in the grass'. That is, people do not so much visualise what supernatural agents must be like, as detect traces of their presence in many circumstances of their existence. The Kwaio track the *adalo*'s involvement in various people's illnesses or good fortune. Many circumstances of everyday life are seen as consequences of what the ancestors do or think or want.

Second, our agency-detection systems tend to 'jump to

conclusions', that is, give us the intuition that an agent is around, in many contexts where other interpretations (the wind pushed the foliage, a branch just fell off a tree) are equally plausible. It is part of our constant, everyday humdrum cognitive functioning that we interpret all sorts of cues in our environment, not just events but also the way things are, as the result of some agent's actions.

For Justin Barrett, these two facts may explain why agent-like concepts of gods and spirits are so *natural*. This results from the fact that our agency-detection systems are biased towards over-detection. But why is that the case? There are important evolutionary reasons why we (as well as other animals) should have 'Hyper-Active Agent Detection'. Our evolutionary heritage is that of organisms that must deal with both predators and prey. In either situation, it is far more advantageous to over-detect agency than to under-detect it. The expense of false positives (seeing agents where there are none) is minimal, if we can abandon these misguided intuitions quickly. By contrast, the cost of not detecting agents when they are actually around (either predator or prey) could be very high.[3]

Our background as predators and prey is of course rather remote to most of us, although it is certainly crucial to understanding some features of our mental functioning. In fact, another psychologist, Clark Barrett, argued that many aspects of our intuitive psychology stem from predation. We have very sophisticated inference systems geared to describing other agents' mental states and producing plans and expectations from these descriptions. As I said in the previous chapter, most evolutionary psychologists think that we developed intuitive psychology to deal with each other. Ever greater skills at understanding other people were required for ever more complex co-operation. But it is also the case that sophisticated mind-reading is a substantial asset in stalking prey and avoiding predators. For archaeologist Steven Mithen, the evidence available suggests that modern humans had a much better understanding of other animals' mental states than their predecessors, adding to the evolutionary pressure for astute mind-reading. In any case, it is clear that predation constitutes one of the central contexts where our intuitive psychology is activated.[4]

From an altogether different background, many scholars of religion in the past noticed frequent references to hunting as well as the salience of hunting or predation metaphors in many religions. Shamanism is all about hunting for souls, chasing spirits away or avoiding predation by dangerous witches, and these metaphors are found in other types of religion as well. Classicist Walter Burkert described hunting as one of these major domains of our evolutionary past that religion seems to point to. Also, anthropologists have noted the frequent presence of dangerous predators in the mythology and supernatural repertoire of many peoples. The awe-inspiring jaguar of Amazonian cosmologies, in the same way as the were-tigers of Asian myths and beliefs, bear witness to the salience of dangerous predators.[5]

Are gods like predators?

Justin Barrett's notion of agency hyper-detection is based on experimental evidence about our inference systems and provides a context where we can make more sense of some apparently peculiar features of religious agents. For one thing, as Guthrie pointed out, sensing the presence of barely detectable agents is generally not a comforting feeling. Many such agents are dangerous or frightening rather than reassuring, which makes good sense if the systems activated in such contexts were originally geared to the detection of dangerous predators. Also, as I said in chapter 2, the agents described as 'gods' or 'spirits' are mainly represented as persons *plus* some counter-intuitive feature, which always creates some ambiguity as to whether they are otherwise like persons or not. In most human groups and in most contexts this ontological uncertainty is not really resolved (nor does it appear to be of interest to anyone). In what way the ancestors or the gods are precisely similar to or different from humans is largely left unexplored. This is perhaps less surprising if the main inference system activated when representing such agents is agency-detection, triggered by predator-avoidance and prey-detection systems. These systems, as I said above, detect agents but do not specify what type they belong too.

For me, the connection with predation may also illuminate a characteristic of Fang ghosts that I used to find puzzling. The ghosts, as I said, are the fleeting presence of dead souls that have not yet reached the status of ancestors. People who report actual encounters with these spirits often mention that they could watch them but not hear them, or conversely that they heard their voices but could not see their faces. For many people this discrepancy (sound without sight or sight with no sound) is also what made the encounter particularly weird and frightening. This is not special to the Fang. The dissociation between modalities is a frequent feature of encounters with supernatural agents. For a long time I had no idea why this should be especially uncanny and unsettling, but Barrett's ideas about hyperactive agency-detection might suggest an explanation, since predation is one of these contexts where hearing without seeing (or vice-versa) is particularly dangerous. This, however, remains largely speculative so far.

To return to firmer ground, Barrett is certainly right that our agency-detection systems are involved in the construction of religious concepts. But this too needs to be fine-tuned. Consider this: Like everybody else, you must have had many experiences of 'hyperactive agent-detection', that is, of interpreting some noise or movement as the presence of an agent. But in many cases it turned out there was no agent. So the intuition that there was one was quickly abandoned. This is natural. It makes sense to 'over-detect' agents only if you can quickly discard false positives, otherwise you would spend all your time recoiled in fear, which is certainly not adaptive. But thoughts about gods and spirits are not like that. These are *stable* concepts, in the sense that people have them stored in memory, reactivate them periodically and assume that these agents are a permanent fixture in their environment. If Barrett's interpretation makes sense – and I think it does – we now have to explain how such 'over-detection', far from being abandoned when there is little evidence of the agents being around, is in fact maintained and becomes stable.

In particular, we need to see how some intuitions about agents in our surroundings are given a stable form by what people around us say about them. Kwaio people interpret some inexplicable shades in the forest as the presence of *adalo*. Many of my Fang acquaintances reported having seen an animal suddenly disappear in the forest, leaving no trace; and this for them meant that a spirit had taken the animal away. These experiences probably reinforce people's sense that the supernatural agents really are around them. But note that the concepts were there to begin with, as it were, and mainly constructed on the basis of other people's utterances. The Kwaio build most of their representation of *adalo* on the basis of what other people tell them, not of such experiences. The Fang interpret various events in the forest as the result of the ghosts' presence but their ghost-concept is mostly informed by constant warnings of the wandering spirits' menacing presence. Indeed, in both the Kwaio and the Fang cases, and in fact in most human groups, having such experiences is not even necessary. In a similar way, some Christians may have had experiences of God's or the angels' presence but most Christian concepts are not derived from that. It would seem, on the contrary, that it is the prior concept that makes sense of the experience rather than the opposite.

Guthrie and Barrett put us on the right track, because what makes gods and spirits so important really stems from our intuitive understanding of agency. But, as I emphasised in the previous chapter, *many* different mental systems are at work, producing particular inferences, when we think about counter-intuitive agents. Indeed, this is where Guthrie's remark is particularly apposite: supernatural concepts are salient because they generate complex inferences, that is, because they activate many different inference systems. So, accepting for the time being Barrett's claim that agency-detection gives initial salience to concepts of barely detectable agents, how are such concepts made more stable and how is it that they *matter* to people? The connection to a predator-avoidance system may explain some of the emotional overtone of the religious imagination; but people also establish long-term interaction with religious agents. This is where other mental systems contribute their own inferences. To see this in a more precise way, let me take a side-road again and describe imagined agents who are *almost* but not quite like supernatural agents.

Gods and spirits as partners: Imaginary companions and invisible friends

Although we are not aware of it, the inference systems that manage our interaction with other people are full-time workers. We constantly use intuitions delivered by these systems. Indeed, we also use them when we are not actually interacting with people. All inference systems can run in a decoupled mode, that is, disengaged from actual external input from the environment or external output in behaviour. A crucial human capacity is to imagine counterfactuals – what would happen if I had less meat than I actually have? What would happen if I chose this path rather than that one? – and this applies to interaction too. Before we make a particular move in any social interaction we automatically consider several scenarios. It allows us for instance to choose this rather than that course of action because we can imagine other people's reactions to what we would do.

In fact, we can run such *decoupled* inferences not only about persons who are not around but also about purely imaginary characters. More striking, this capacity seems to appear very early in children's development. From an early age (between three and ten) many children engage in durable and complex relationships with 'imaginary companions'. Psychologist Marjorie Taylor, who has studied this phenomenon extensively, estimates that about half of the children she has worked with had some such companions. These imagined persons or person-like animals, sometimes but not always derived from stories or cartoons or other cultural folklore, follow the child around, play with her, converse with her, etc. One girl describes her companions Nutsy and Nutsy as a couple of birds, one male and one female, who accompany her as she goes for a walk, goes to school or gets in the car.

Taylor's studies show that having long-term relationships with non-existent characters is not a sign of confusion between fantasy and reality. Developmental psychologists now use precise tests to determine how children mark off the real from the fantastic. Those with imaginary companions pass these tests from the age of three, and are often better at them than other children. They know perfectly well that their friends, the invisible lizard, the awkward monkey, or the amazing Magician, are not there in the same sense as real friends and other people. Also, children with companions are often better than the others at tasks that require a subtle use of intuitive psychology.

All this led Taylor to the intriguing hypothesis that imaginary companions may well provide a very useful form of training for the social mind. The relationship with such a companion is a stable one, which means that the child computes the companion's reactions, taking into account not just the imagined friend's personality but also past events in their relationship. Taylor's studies show that wishful thinking plays only a minor role in such fantasies. What the companions do or say is constrained by the person they are, and must remain consistent and plausible even in this fantastic domain. A four year old has sophisticated skills at representing, not just an agent where there is none, but also an agent with a specific history and personality, with particular tastes and capacities different from one's own. Companions are often used to provide an alternative viewpoint on a situation. They may find odd information unsurprising or frightening situations manageable. So it is extremely easy, from an early age, to maintain social relations in a *decoupled* mode. Children have the social capacities required to maintain coherent representations of interaction with persons even when these persons are not actually around and do not in fact exist.[6]

It would be tempting at this point to drift into a not-too-rigorous parallel between such imagined companions and those supernatural agents people seem to establish long and important relations with, like guardian angels, spirits and ancestors. Indeed, the very term 'imaginary companion' used by modern-day psychologists seems to echo the 'invisible friend', *aoratos philos*, used to describe the saints in Early Christianity. But the differences are as great as the similarities. First, for many people spirits and ancestors are emphatically not fantasies, there is a sense that they are actually around. Second, believers do not just construct their own decoupled interaction; they share with others information about who the spirits are and what they do. Third and most important, the tenor of people's relations with spirits and gods is special because of one crucial characteristic of these supernatural agents, as we will see presently.

Strategic information

Interacting with other agents (giving or exchanging, promising, co-operating, cheating, etc.) requires a *social mind*, that is, a variety of mental systems specially designed to organise interaction. This is crucial because the social-mind systems are the ones that produce the great similarity between supernatural agents and persons, as well as the crucial difference that makes the latter so important.

We have inference systems that regulate social interaction; as we have seen, they carry out complex computations. Is this person a reliable partner or not? Is this news enjoyable gossip or bland information? Consider, for instance, a couple who interview prospective baby-sitters for their children. Although they ask the candidate many explicit questions, it is quite clear that they are paying attention to (and drawing inferences from) all sorts of cues that have nothing to do, at least at first sight, with the business at hand. If the baby-sitter avoids making eye-contact, if she starts ranting, if she blushes and produces incoherent answers when asked whether she is married, they will probably think that she is not suited for the job. If on the other hand she says she is a Mormon – what I describe here has been observed and studied by sociologists in the United States – they will form a much better impression. For the parents themselves, all this is mixed into a general 'impression' that is either favourable or not, and it seems to be all based on a rather vague 'feeling'. But note that the devices working in the mental basement are anything but vague. Cues like gaze-avoidance are particularly important to a feeling of reliability or trustworthiness between people. This system is found the world over, but it is calibrated in special ways depending on where we live. (In the US eye-contact is required; in other places it is aggressive if sustained; but in either case the system pays attention to this cue and delivers the appropriate inferences, without our necessarily being aware of it.) The reason why a Mormon baby-sitter is a good proposition for many Americans depends on local history, but again it requires some complex computation. The main explanation, the one people are aware of, is that a Mormon upbringing would give people desirable moral dispositions. But there is another important part of the story that is not available to conscious inspection. It is that it would be very *costly* for an immoral or unreliable person to stay a Mormon. That is, to carry on behaving in a convincing way towards other members of that particular community, thought to be rather strict on morals, when you have none of the corresponding dispositions would be very difficult and perhaps impossible. (I am not saying this actually is the case; but this is people's intuitive assumption.)

Social-mind systems handle a variety of cues present in any situation of interaction. But we must note that these systems handle only *part* of the information that is available to our minds. As people are talking, your mind keeps track of where the person is, of your body's position, of various noises around, etc. The same would be true for any other situation of social interaction. If a dinner conversation takes on an overtone of seduction, there is a massive production of complex inferences and conjectures (e.g. 'When she said she liked *Much Ado About Nothing* better than *Romeo and Juliet*, was that a subtle hint? But a hint to what?', etc.) because the inference systems specialised in a particular kind of social relations are activated and produce emotionally charged interpretations of what is going on. But, again, this is only part of the information the mind is handling. The brain is also dealing with other aspects of the scene, which is why, at least in most cases, people in such circumstances manage to stay on their chairs, swallow their food and indeed eat their dinner rather than the cutlery.

To repeat: Information that feeds the social-mind systems is only *part* of the information handled by the mind. It makes sense to distinguish socially neutral information from the specific information that activates the social-mind inference systems. So here is a general definition:

Strategic information is the subset of all the information currently available (to a particular agent, about a particular situation) which activates the mental systems that regulate social interaction.

If the baby-sitter's manic facial expression, absent gaze and chain-smoking are noticed by the parents, then in that particular situation they are pieces of strategic information. If what she was wearing had no consequence for their social-interaction systems – it did not produce any special inference about her reliability – it is not strategic information in that situation. If the literary preferences of your dinner companion had no special effect on the ongoing interaction, then it remains plain information; but it becomes strategic information if it triggers inferences about what to do next.

All this is simple enough but also introduces one salient difference between humans and most other animal species. Many animals exchange information that is relevant to interaction, to co-operation or exchange or mating. But in most cases it is very clear whether a given piece of information is strategic or not. For instance, there are in most species very clear signals to indicate willingness to engage in sexual activities. Hierarchy too can be the object of such unambiguous signals. In chimpanzees, males that want to challenge a leader and establish their own pre-eminence start screaming and shaking branches. When such a behaviour is observed by other members of the band, it is a clear signal that what's at stake is a political challenge. No one would confuse that for a sexual proposition or an invitation to attack another band. For each domain of interaction there is a specific range of signals.

In humans, there is just no way to predict whether a given piece of information is strategic or not. It all depends on the way the different parties represent the signal in question, the situation at hand, the person who emitted the signal and so on. Depending on how I represent the situation, that you have meat in your refrigerator may be non-strategic to me (in most cases) or strategic (if meat was stolen from my pantry, or if I am hungry, or if you always declared you were a vegetarian). In all these latter situations, our interaction may be affected, however slightly, by the discovery. If I am hungry, I may want your meat; if you said you were a vegetarian, I may suspect that what you say about yourself is not always reliable; and so on. In the same way, that you went to another village yesterday may be non-strategic (if all I infer is that you were away) or strategic (if I suspect that you went there to meet a potential sexual partner). That you talked with So-and-so may become strategic if I suspect that the two of you are involved in some plot against me or a potential coalition with me.

Saying that some information is strategic only says that it was treated by a particular person's inference systems for social inter-action. The distinction between strategic and non-strategic depends on a representation of the particular situation. It is in the eye of the beholder. No two beholders behold in quite the same way (and they may well be wrong too) so you cannot easily predict whether a given piece of information has these effects or not. To say that some information is strategic is not to say anything about the information itself, but only about the way it is treated in the mind of the person who considers it. (If you find this a bit abstruse, consider another term that is defined in this way: *reminder*. When we say that a particular object or situation is a reminder of something, we know that it can only be a reminder of a particular fact to a particular person. You cannot enter a room and say in advance which objects will be reminders. But given a particular person, some objects will be in that category, triggering a special memory activity. In the same way, some pieces of information will become strategic or not depending on a particular person's representation of the situation at hand.)

I use the word 'strategic' because it is a standard term that refers to any situation where people make moves (adopt a certain attitude, say something), the consequences of which depend on other people's moves. This technical term does not imply that the information in question is important or vital. For instance, people are generally interested in their co-workers' sexual peccadilloes. This is strategic given our definition, as our social-mind systems track gossip-worthy news and produce minor emotional rewards for acquiring and spreading it. But in most cases this information is of no importance. By contrast, knowing whether it is better to freeze or flee in the face of particular predators is non-strategic (it does not activate any of the special inference systems that regulate social interaction) but it is vitally important.

Humans, being social organisms with complex interaction, not only represent strategic information, they also represent the extent to which other people have strategic information. For instance, given a particular situation where you have something that I want, I auto-matically form a representation, not just of the fact that you have what I want, but also that you may be aware of the fact that I want it, and that this may have some influence on your intentions, etc. Such com-plex inferences are supported by our intuitive psychology which represents other people's mental states and their access to information.

One fundamental principle of our intuitive psychology is that access to information is *imperfect*. Given a situation, and given some information about that situation, we do not automatically presume that this information is equally accessible to everyone. For instance, if I remove your keys from your pocket while you are out of the room, I expect that you will not be aware of what I did. I expect that you will be surprised when you cannot find your keys. As we saw in chapter 3, normal children from the age of four routinely solve experimental tasks that require evaluating such obstacles to information. That your keys are now in my pocket does not automatically imply that you know they are in my pocket. We do not need to run all this reasoning consciously because our intuitive psychology is an efficient system that does its work in the basement. This principle of 'imperfect access to information' is so fundamental that not having it in one's cognitive equipment results in pathologies like autism.

This assumption applies to information in general and therefore to the subset of information which is strategic information. So, given a particular situation and some information about it that is strategic to you (i.e. activates your mental capacities for social interaction), you cannot automatically *presume* that other people, in particular other people involved in the situation, also have access to that information. Here is the general principle:

> *Imperfect access: In social interaction, we presume that other people's access to strategic information is neither perfect nor automatic.*

Suppose you went to the other village last night for a secret rendezvous. The identity of the person you met is, at least potentially, strategic information for other people. (Again, it may be of no real importance.) Knowing that you met So-and-so rather than Such-and-such would activate their inference systems, and could change the way they interact with you. But it is not clear to you to what extent that information is available to other people. That is, you cannot presume that they know. Indeed, you may hope that they do not (for fear of scandal) or wish that they did (so you can brag about the romantic episode).

Humans generally spend a great deal of time and energy wondering whether other people have access to some information which is strategic from their own standpoint, wondering what inferences, intentions, plans, etc. these other people draw from that information, trying to control their access to such information and trying to monitor and influence their inferences on the basis of such information. All these complex calculations are based on the assumption that our own and other agents' access to strategic information is complex and generally imperfect.

Gods and spirits as special persons

The reason for going through these complex definitions and explanations is that if people consider gods and spirits as *agents* with which they engage in interaction, then surely the cognitive systems that shape our regular interactions with other agents will inform interaction with supernatural agents too.

At first sight, interacting with them is very much like interacting with human agents, in that most of our ordinary inference systems are activated and produce their inferences in much the same way as usual. It is worth insisting on this, because that is what makes interaction with these rather discreet agents so *natural*. Gods and spirits have minds, so they perceive what happens, we can predict that they will remember what happened, that they will have particular intentions and do what it takes to get these intentions realised. Also, more subtle aspects of social interaction seem to apply to them. As we saw in the Kwaio example described by Keesing, offering a pig to an ancestor when *another* ancestor was causing trouble is just a waste of one's resources. The offended spirit will carry on making people sick until someone offers him a proper sacrifice. All this is quite natural, indeed the Kwaio diviner cited by Keesing only gives us an elliptic formulation of this reasoning, because all this goes without saying. But it goes without saying only if you apply the relevant inference systems.

More generally, all gods and ancestors and spirits are construed as beings with which we can interact by using our social inference systems. You pray to God because you want to be cured. This requires the assumption that God perceives that you are ill, understands that you wish to be better, desires you to be happy, understands what would make you happier, and so on. (Incidentally, prayers and other utterances addressed to gods and spirits require that such agents understand, not just our language but the way we use it. Saying 'dear God, it would be so much nicer if my relatives could get on with each other' implies that God knows how to translate this indirect form into the direct request 'please make my relatives get on with each other'.) Gods and spirits that *want* something in particular will often try to get it, they will be satisfied once they have it but not before that, they will retaliate if people try to cheat them out of it, etc. The fact that all these statements sound so trite shows how intuitive these assumptions are, if you apply the right inference systems.

So are ancestors and gods just like other people? Not really. There is one major difference, but a subtle one that is generally not explicit in people's statements about these powerful agents. The difference is this:

- In social interaction, as I said above, we always assume that other people are agents with *limited* access to strategic information (and we try and evaluate the extent to which they have access to that information).
- In interaction with supernatural agents, people presume that these agents have *full* access to strategic information.

Supernatural agents are in general credited with good access to information. That they appear at several places at the same time or become invisible gives them the means to hold information that real agents have more difficulty acquiring. This does not mean that such agents are always considered wiser than mere mortals. The point is not that they know *better* but more simply that they often seem to know *more*. Indeed, in the many narratives (anecdotes, memories, myths, etc.) that include such agents as well as human ones, the scenarios in which a religious agent has information that a human agent does not possess greatly outnumber descriptions of the converse situation. God knows more than we know, the ancestors are watching us. More generally: In most local descriptions of spirits and other such agents, we find the assumption that they have access to information that is not available to ordinary folk.

What is made explicit is most often a vague assumption that the spirits or the gods simply know more than we do. But it seems that people in fact assume something much more specific, namely that the gods and spirits have access to *strategic* information (as defined here) rather than information in general. Kwaio people's statements about their ancestors highlight this. At first sight, what they say would seem to confirm that ancestors simply know more: 'The *adalo* see the slightest small things. Nothing is hidden from the *adalo*. It would be hidden from us [living people, but not from them]' or again 'an *adalo* has unlimited vision'. But when people illustrate these statements, notice how they immediately move from 'agents who know more' to the much more specific 'agents who know more about what is strategic': 'An *adalo* has unlimited vision . . . something happens in secret and [the *adalo*] will see it; [if] someone urinates, someone menstruates [NB, in improper places: doing this is an insult to the ancestors] and tries to hide it . . . the *adalo* will see it.'[7]

In other words, although you can say that the *adalo* in general see what humans cannot see, what *first* comes to mind is that they can detect behaviours that would have consequences for social interaction: someone who has polluted a particular place puts others in danger and should perform appropriate purification rites. Whether someone did violate these rules or not is clearly strategic information. When people represent possible violations, this activates their inference systems for social interaction. For them, it also goes without saying that it is *that* particular kind of information that the *adalo* have access to. It may be hidden to people (this is the 'imperfect access principle': people's access to strategic information is not guaranteed) but not to supernatural agents (they have full access).

Here is another example of the salience of strategic information. The shamans are special, say the Batek of Malaysia, because they can turn themselves into tigers with human heads, and then also make themselves invisible! This may sound like a straightforward example of counter-intuitive qualities. But then comes the crucial consequence: because they are now invisible and fly about as they wish, were-tiger shamans can eavesdrop on people's conversations. Nothing that happens can be hidden from them.[8]

This is in fact the way people represent ancestors and gods the world over. People experience particular situations. Some information about these situations is strategic, that is, activates their inference systems for social interaction (cheating, trust-evaluation, gossip, social-exchange, coalition-building, etc.). They also represent that there are supernatural agents around. They spontaneously assume that these agents have access to all the strategic information about that particular situation, even though they themselves may not have access to all of it.

An interesting limiting-case is the concept of gods who know *everything*. The theological, literate version of such concepts stipulates that the god has access to all information about the world from all possible angles. But we know that people's actual concepts often diverge from theological understandings, as Barrett and Keil demonstrated, so we may wonder whether people actually represent gods as literally omniscient. If they did, they would assume that *all* pieces of information about *all* aspects of the world are equally likely to be represented by God. So the following statements would be quite natural:

God knows the contents of every refrigerator in the world.
God perceives the state of every machine in operation.
God knows what every single insect in the world is up to.

In fact, they seem much less natural than these:

God knows who you met yesterday.
God knows that you are lying.
God knows that I misbehaved.

Note that it is all a matter of context. If you are in a context where the first statements actually refer to some strategic information, then they will seem natural. God may in fact be thought to represent the contents of your refrigerator (if that includes items you stole from your neighbours), the state of some machines (if you use them to harm people) and the behaviour of insects (if they are a plague we wished upon the enemy). In such situations that information is strategic. Intuitively, people who represent such situations immediately assume that God represents the information that is strategic to them.

So there is a general difference between our intuitive representation of humans we interact with and our intuitive representation of supernatural agents. The latter are:

Full-access strategic agents: agents whom one construes as having access to any piece of information that is strategic. That is, given a particular situation, and given some information that activates one's inference systems, one assumes that the full-access strategic agent has access to that information.

At this point we might think that we are reading all sorts of complicated thoughts in people's rather simple representation of gods and ancestors as powerful beings. But that is not the case. The complex inferences about what is and what is not strategic, whether another agent represents it or not, etc., are complex only if you try and follow them explicitly, as steps in a conscious reasoning. But this is not the way such inferences are produced in human minds.

Making the distinction between strategic and other information may seem alien: we never do it explicitly. But it does not mean that we do not do it. On the contrary, social psychologists have gathered a great deal of evidence to suggest that people in any given situation are particularly attentive to cues that are relevant to social inter-action, and treat these cues differently from other information. That this is mostly beyond conscious access is not very surprising, because most of our inference systems work like that. Consider, again, our intuitive physics and goal-directed motion systems. When you see a dog chasing a prey both systems are activated and focus on specific cues. The Physics system predicts, for instance, that the dog will hit the fence if he does not change trajectories; the Goal-Directed Motion system notices that the prey has suddenly changed direction and predicts that the dog will do the same. Each system carries out its computations to produce intuitive expectations. But we have no conscious rule that tells us to 'separate what is purely mechanical from what is goal-directed in the situation at hand'. In the same way, we need no rule to tell us to 'pay special attention to some aspects of this situation that may be relevant to our interaction with the other parties'. We do not need this because our inference systems just track that information and handle it in a special way.

The assumption that gods and spirits are full-access agents, that they have access to whatever information is strategic in a particular situation, is not made explicit and need not be transmitted explicitly. As I said in the previous chapter, many important aspects of super-natural concepts are not, strictly speaking, transmitted at all. They are reconstructed by each individual in the course of acquiring the concept. You are not told that spirits can perceive what happens, or that they can make a difference between their wishes and reality. You infer that spontaneously. In the same way you need not be told that the gods (or spirits or ancestors) have access to whatever is strategic in any particular situation. You only hear sentences like 'the spirits are unhappy because we failed to sacrifice a pig for them' or 'if someone urinates in a house, we humans cannot see it, but it makes the *adalo* very angry'. Interpreting such statements requires that the *adalo* (or whatever supernatural agent people in your group talk about) have access to strategic information.

The supernatural agents' extraordinary powers vary a lot from place to place. Sometimes the spirits or gods are said to be invisible, sometimes they just live in the sky, sometimes they go through walls and sometimes they turn themselves into tigers. By contrast, the qualities that allow full-access to strategic information are always there. This may explain what missionaries found so puzzling in African religion: that you can have a concept of an all-powerful Creator-god and pay no attention to him.

In traditional Fang religion the ancestor-ghosts are presumed to have access to strategic information. When people represent a particular situation and the strategic information about that situation, they automatically assume that the ancestors know about it. This is the basis of their inferences and actions towards the ancestors. All this is very similar to the Kwaio situation. On the other hand, Mebeghe the creator of natural things and Nzame the creator of cultural things are just not represented in that way. People have no intuition about whether these gods represent information about situations; there are no anecdotes that require this assumption to make sense. When missionaries managed to persuade some of the Fang that Nzame actually has all this information, that Nzame-God knew about what people do in secret to other people and knows all they know, these Fang found it natural to direct rituals, sacrifices and prayers to Nzame (although the missionaries were often less than happy at the unorthodox way in which people adapted Christian notions – but that is another story). The powerful gods are not necessarily the ones that matter; but the ones that have strategic information always matter.

Relevance in cultural transmission

What is the motivation for having concepts of gods and spirits? It is always tempting to assume that there must be a special *reason* why people conceive of agents with counter-intuitive properties. In general this leads to purely imaginary solutions. There *must* be a desire to include the whole cosmos in some explanation, to make life more meaningful, etc. We have no evidence for these general propensities. As I suggested in chapter 1, it makes more sense to start from what we actually know about religious representations, as well as about human minds and the way they function.

People do not invent gods and spirits, they receive information that leads them to build such concepts. Particular systems in the brain specialise in particular aspects of objects around us and produce specific kinds of inferences about them. Now we may wonder what 'pushes' the systems to pay attention to particular cues in our surroundings and to produce inferences. Part of the answer is that such mental systems are driven by *relevance*. To illustrate this, let me mention a domain where the consequences of relevance are extremely stable and predictable.

Most people born and brought up in modern urban environments have very limited biological knowledge. They can only name a few common species, they only have the vaguest notion how most animals feed, where they sleep, how they reproduce, etc. People who live in a forest environment, on the other hand, generally acquire a huge amount of precise knowledge of plants and animals and this is crucial. Does this mean that the inference systems concerning living things are different in these two situations?

Anthropologist Scott Atran and his colleagues thought that this should be established experimentally, by performing controlled experiments with Michigan students and Itza Maya villagers in Guatemala. They did find the obvious differences in richness and complexity of biological knowledge. The Michigan students, for instance, generally identify pictures of birds as 'birds'. They know a few names for species of birds, but are generally incapable of recognising them from a picture and cannot say anything about their particular behaviour. The Itza always identify birds in terms of particular species and know a lot about what makes them different.

However, in both groups, it is assumed that living things come in different, exclusive groups with special characteristics and that the most important groupings are at the level of folk-species (e.g. blackbird, cardinal) rather than ranks or varieties. In one of Atran's experiments, people were told about a bird of an unfamiliar species and told that it could catch a specific disease. All this had been designed so that both the species and the disease would be new to the subjects. They were then asked whether the disease would also affect other animals, ranging from other members of the same species to close species, to different kinds of birds, to mammals and insects. Similar tests were then conducted with other properties, for example, by telling subjects that a certain animal had a certain internal organ, or a certain kind of bone, etc. In such contexts, Michigan students and Itza Maya react very much in the same way. They assume that behaviour is usually stable within a species, but that diseases can affect closely related species in similar ways, and that internal structure can be similar in large animal families.[9]

For Atran, this confirms that taxonomy is a powerful logical device that is intuitively used by humans in producing expectations about living things. People use the specific inference system of intuitive biological knowledge to add to the information given. They are told that 'this cow aborted after we fed it cabbage' and conclude that other cows could be similarly affected, but perhaps not horses or mice. They are told that this rodent has a spleen and conclude that other mammals may have that organ too, but not worms or birds. (Biological inferences are not always valid. What matters here is how they are created.) This is what we call an *enrichment* of intuitive principles. This form of acquisition, filling out empty slots in templates provided by intuitive principles, is very general. It applies not just to biological knowledge, but also to theories of personality, to local models of politeness, to particular criteria of elegance, and so on.[10]

How does the system 'know' which bits of information to send to which inference systems? In the case of the sick cow and the cabbage, there may be a lot of information about this situation (e.g. the fact that the cow in question was stolen, that it aborted on a Tuesday, that cabbage is green) that is simply not sent to the taxonomy inference system. But when information about the cow circulates through various inference systems, some of them just happen to produce some inferences, because the information meets their input conditions, and some do not. Information is attended to inasmuch as there is *some* inference system that can produce something out of it.

We can in fact go further and say that information in the environment is attended to as a function of the inferences various systems can produce from it. This is a general aspect of inference systems, especially the very abstract ones that are particularly relevant to religious concepts: that they are driven by *relevance*. This notion was first formulated by Dan Sperber and Deirdre Wilson in studies of verbal communication, but it provides a very useful tool in the description of cultural acquisition.

Tool-kit 4: Relevance and transmission
Human verbal communication is not a code-deciphering operation. Every utterance is compatible with many different interpretations and a listener's task (or rather the listener's brain's task) is to infer an optimal interpretation, via a description of what the speaker intended to convey. This can in general be done if the interpretation chosen is one that produces more inferences than others or requires fewer inferential steps, or both. More generally, an optimal interpretation is one that corresponds to a higher inferences/inferential steps ratio than other available interpretations.

The technical aspects of relevance theory are not important here. What is important is that the principle gives us a good approximation of how cultural information can become more or less successful. Some types of cultural input are easily acquired because they correspond to intuitive expectations. In this case the inferential effort required to assimilate this material is minimal. If you are told that poodles are a type of dog, it is very easy to assimilate the consequences of this fact, because the living-beings-as-essential-classes system described by Atran is already in place.

This is quite clear in the domain of supernatural concepts too. As I mentioned in chapter 2, there is a small catalogue of templates. Individual imagination may expand beyond this catalogue but concepts that do not correspond to one of our templates are usually found in marginal beliefs rather than mainstream ideologies, in obscure theological scholarship rather than in popular representations. The concepts built according to these templates were built by relevance-driven inference systems. Someone tells you that there is an invisible presence of the dead in the forest and your intuitive-psychology inference system produces all sorts of inferences about what the dead know and what they want, on the assumption that their minds are like ours. You are told that this statue can listen to you, and that too affords inferences only if your intuitive psychology produces them. So it is quite natural that supernatural ideologies will revolve around invisible gods with a normal mind rather than invisible gods with intermittent existence.

We like to think that we have certain concepts or hold certain beliefs because it is in our interest, because they seem rational, because they provide a sound explanation of what happens around them, because they create a coherent world-view, and so on. But none of these views explains what we actually find in human cultures. It seems more plausible that cultural transmission is relevance-driven. That is, concepts that 'excite' more inference systems, fit more easily into their expectations and trigger richer inferences (or all of these) are more likely to be acquired and transmitted than material that less easily corresponds to expectation formats or does not generate inferences. We do not have the cultural concepts we have because they make sense or are useful, but because the way our brains are put together makes it very difficult not to build them.

Relevance of full-access agents

The fact that most concepts of gods and spirits include this full-access assumption is a result of cultural selection. Over thousands of years, indeed over many thousands of years and in many different social groups, human minds have entertained a huge number of individual representations of gods and spirits. These probably varied and still vary along many dimensions. How does all this affect the way people build concepts on the basis of what others tell them? The presence of such systems has a simple consequence: People build concepts in ways that activate their inference systems most and produce the richest set of inferences with the lowest cognitive effort. Now compare three possible varieties of supernatural agents:

DIVINE BRUTES: They know nothing about what is going on but can make you sick, make your roof collapse, or make you rich, etc. quite inadvertently.

FULL AQUINAS AGENTS: Their minds represent every single fact about the world.

FULL STRATEGIC AGENTS: If some information is strategic to your inference systems they have access to it.

The two first types are not frequent, for obvious reasons. Brutes are easy to understand but their representation generates no inferences. Given a choice between two possible courses of action, the presence of a Brute makes no difference. Aquinas agents do make a difference, but then figuring out what they know would be costly. For every aspect of every situation, you would have to imagine that the Aquinas agent represents it, derives conclusions from it, etc. Very few of these imagined thoughts would be of any consequence. (If a god knows that my toothpaste contains peroxide, what follows?) This is why, even in places where the official theology describes an Aquinas agent, people's actual intuitions do not follow this complicated route, as Barrett and Keil's experiments showed. I am not suggesting that people could not entertain the notion of a Divine Brute or Aquinas

Agent. I am just saying that, over a huge number of cycles of acquisition and transmission of cultural material (stories, anecdotes, explanations of events, comments about situations, etc.) the concepts of full-access strategic agents enjoy a certain selective advantage, *all else being equal*, and that this is sufficient to explain why they are more frequent than others. So what is this cognitive advantage?

It seems, first, that such concepts are relevant because they require less effort to represent than possible alternatives, given the way our cognitive systems work. Remember that we always assume that other people's access to strategic information is imperfect so that we constantly run complicated estimates of what they know, how they came to know it, what they conclude from it, etc., given the obstacles between facts and their knowledge of these facts. I talked to So-and-so yesterday but perhaps you do not know that, because you did not see the people who saw us together, or you met people who would not tell you, and so on. Conceiving of what the full-access agents know means running all these estimates *minus the obstacles*, that is, by going straight from 'I met So-and-so' to 'the ancestors know that I met So-and-so'.

But there is more. Concepts of full-access agents not only require less effort, they also generate richer inferences than other supernatural concepts. To illustrate this, consider the notion, especially widespread in the United States, that aliens from some remote galaxies periodically pay a visit to earth, contact people, deliver stern warnings to humankind or recruit unwilling participants in bizarre medical procedures. Anthropologists Charles Ziegler and Benson Saler have documented the spread of such ideas, showing that these beings are often described in a way that is very similar to religious agents. Stories such as the infamous Roswell incident – an unidentified craft which supposedly crashed in New Mexico, leaving the charred remains of several aliens – bear all the hallmarks of what anthropologists call mythical elaboration, the gradual construction of a 'good' story out of not-so-perfect initial versions by changing some elements, reordering the sequences, eliminating episodes that do not contribute to the general meaning, etc. Also, the popular version of aliens – they have knowledge we do not possess, they have counter-intuitive properties, they have huge powers (give or take the occasional aeronautical mishap) – would make them very similar to most versions of supernatural agents.

Yet, as Saler and Ziegler point out, this is not quite like religion as we commonly know it. Although many people seem to accept the existence of such beings and the surprisingly efficient governmental cover-up, there are no specific rituals directed at the aliens, the belief seems to trigger in most people no deep emotional commitment, no significant change in lifestyle, no intolerant notion that *we* are better because *we* believe in aliens. If I may speculate, I would add that in the most popular version these aliens are simply not described as having what I just defined as strategic knowledge. That is, although the aliens are described as smart fellows with advanced knowledge of physics and engineering, this somehow does not seem to trigger the inference that *they know that my sister lied to me* or *they know that I filed my tax-returns honestly*. The way believers acquire and represent the 'evidence' for alien visits seems to have no bearing on individual behaviour.

In contrast to this, a small number of people actually represent aliens in the same way as gods and spirits. In some cults what the aliens know and want makes a huge difference to people's lives. What you can do and how you do it, the way you live and the way you think are all informed by thoughts about the aliens. This generally happens because an impressive character managed to convince followers that he (less often she) had some direct contact with the visitors, and also managed to trigger the inference that they have strategic access. What matters to the followers' inference systems – how to behave, what choices to make, etc. – is then affected by the aliens' viewpoint on these choices and behaviours. In these cults, beliefs in aliens are much more like religion as we know it. There are rituals, high emotional commitment, a sense that *we* are the privileged believers.[11]

Given this expectation of full-access, it may not be too surprising that in many human groups people are so concerned with *other people's* views of religious agents. To assume that there is a fully informed agent around is likely to change my behaviour. But then if others assume that there are such agents it will change their behaviour too, which is why their representations are of great interest to me. This is one aspect of religion that we cannot under-stand if we stick to the common idea, that gods and spirits are just very powerful persons who can move mountains, send people plagues or good fortune. If that was the main feature of gods and spirits, we could understand why they mattered to a believer; but we could not explain why believers are often so keen to know whether they matter to other people.

In a way, we could translate all this complex cognitive argument into more familiar terms by simply saying that 'people assume that the gods know what is important; if some information is important people assume the gods will know it'. But this trite summary would miss the crucial point. What is *important* to human beings, because of their evolutionary history, are the conditions of social interaction: who knows what, who is not aware of what, who did what with whom, when and what for. Imagining agents with that information is an illustration of mental processes driven by relevance. Such agents are not really necessary to explain anything, but they are so much easier to represent and so much richer in possible inferences that they enjoy a great advantage in cultural transmission.

Chapter Five

Why do gods and spirits matter?

Why do you let some religious doctrine determine what you may or may not do? This is a common question addressed to religious people, generally by sceptics or outsiders. Why indeed should the existence of some supernatural agents – the ancestors or some invisible spirits or a whole pantheon of gods or just a single one – have consequences for what people are allowed to do? When we ask such questions we take for granted a particular scenario about the connections between belief and morality. We assume that religion provides a certain description of supernatural agents and their moral demands ('There are five gods! They hate adultery and will smite the transgressors'). We then imagine that people are convinced, for some reason or other, that the doctrine is actually true. It follows that they take the moral imperatives to heart, given the powers of the gods or ancestors to enforce morality. So there seems to be a simple story here: however fit for treasons, stratagems and spoils, human beings happen to believe in the existence of the gods, but the gods demand a particular behaviour, so people abide by the rules.

Consider another common statement: 'So-and-so became more religious after his accident' (or: 'after his partner had a brush with death', 'after his parents died', etc.). The way this is formulated may be typical of modern Western conditions (in many places everybody just takes it as obvious that there are ancestors or spirits around, so it makes little sense to talk about anyone being more or less 'religious'), but the connection between misfortune and religion is evident the world over. This is one of the principal contexts in which people activate concepts of gods and spirits. Again, we find this natural because we commonly accept a particular scenario about religious doctrines and salient events: that gods and spirits are seen as endowed with great power, including that of bringing about or averting disasters. People struck by misfortune strive for an explanation and for some reassurance, and this is what religious concepts would seem to provide. A simple story again: Accidents happen, people want to know why, if they have gods and spirits they can say why.

But both stories are probably false. The facts themselves are not disputed. People do connect notions of gods with what they may or may not do; they connect misfortune to the existence of supernatural agents. It is the way these connections are established in the mind that anthropology came to see in a very different perspective. Religion does not really support morality, it is people's moral intuitions that makes religion plausible; religion does not explain misfortune, it is the way people explain misfortune that makes religion easier to acquire. To get to that point we need to explore in much more detail the way social inference systems in the mind handle notions of morality and situations of misfortune. That we have evolved capacities for social interaction means that we tend to represent morality and misfortune in a very special way which makes the connection with supernatural agents extremely easy and apparently obvious.

Legislators, exemplars, onlookers

Shiva created all living things, including people, and gave them each a 'headwriting', an invisible inscription on the forehead that specifies the person's character, tendencies and overall behaviour. The particular mix of humours in a person's body is a consequence of this headwriting and explains why different people act differently in similar circumstances. This, at least, is how Tamil people in Kalappur (India) account for personality differences and explain people's behaviour, at least in some circumstances. As anthropologist Sheryl Daniel reports, concepts of morality in fact constitute a 'tool-box' from which people extract whatever element is relevant to a particular situation. The notion of a destiny fixed by the gods is not the only one. Against this stands the idea that people can find in themselves the will to perform good karma deeds, actions that change the balance of their moral account, as it were. Such actions may even affect the balance of humours inside the person (which in Western terms would mean change their personality).

Obviously, the presence of such different accounts of personality create an inconsistent or at least ambiguous theory. But that is not really a matter of much concern to most people. This is not because people do not mind inconsistencies or contradictions. On the contrary, when they are faced with particular situations, they argue vehemently that one of these perspectives, not the other, provides a true explanation for what happened. For example, Kandasany is a thief who was caught making off with the village schoolmaster's chickens. He is arrested and his relatives have to pawn their goods to pay his fine. Unable to bear the shame, he then commits suicide. As Daniel reports, 'a crowd of villagers had gathered [and] openly discussed the case'. Some family members tried to argue that Kandasany was a victim of his fate, that is, of Shiva's *lila* (whim, sport). But to most people this was unacceptable; the thief's behaviour was a matter of personal decision, which made the headwriting irrelevant.

The notion that the gods laid down the moral rules *and* decreed people's destinies makes it difficult to understand serious transgressions. If a god intends people to behave and has the power to instil moral dispositions in the mind, why so much immorality? But again inconsistency is not too problematic. Faced with striking examples of moral violations, one Brahmin tells Daniel: 'We are mere human beings. It is hard for us to understand the *lila* of the gods', which is of course a diplomatic (the word Jesuitical springs to mind) way of dodging the issue. But another informant is more direct: 'What do you expect? . . . Just look at Shiva's family life. One son is a womaniser and the other one refuses to marry. Shiva and Parvati can never stop quarrelling. If even the gods behave like this, what do you expect of men?'[1]

People everywhere have moral intuitions and in most places they have concepts of supernatural agents, but there are several ways to understand this connection. A common one is to think that there are moral principles because the gods or ancestors themselves decided what these norms would be. This is what we could call the *gods as legislators* story. Many theological systems include lists of prohibitions and prescriptions, of varying length, attributed to some direct communication from the supernatural legislature. We must follow moral principles because the gods *decreed* how people should behave. In most literate cultures this is accompanied by some formal and fixed description of the rules in question: there is a text. But people can have the notion of gods and spirits as legislators without having such a description of the particular laws. For instance, the Fang and many other people consider that proper behaviour, towards one's family for instance, is clearly what the ancestors want. However, there is no fixed description of what they want. People intuitively agree that a certain course of action is the right, proper, time-tested way of behaving so it *must* be what the ancestors wanted in the first place.

A second, very common, way of connecting religion and morality is that some supernatural agents provide a model to follow. This is the *paragon* model in which saints or holy people are both different enough from common folk that they approach an ideal, and close enough so their behaviour can serve as a model. This is the way people conceive of individuals with supernatural qualities, such as Buddha, Jesus, Muhammad or the many Christian and Muslim saints as well as the miraculous rabbis of Judaism. The life of the Buddha gives a clear indication of the path to follow: renounce worldly attachment, display compassion, escape from the false appearance of reality.

Another, third, connection is present in many circumstances. This is the idea that supernatural agents are *interested parties* in moral choices. All this says is that the gods or the ancestors are not indifferent to what people do, and this is why we must act in particular ways or refrain from certain courses of action. Interaction with the Kwaio ancestors or Fang spirits is mostly of this kind. We also find the interested-parties model in many world-religions. Most Christians entertain this notion that every single one of their moral choices is relevant to their personal connection to God. That is, God not only gave laws and principles but also pays attention to what people do. For obvious reasons, the notion that supernatural agents are interested onlookers is generally associated with the idea that the gods or spirits are powerful and that it is within their capacities to inflict all sorts of calamities upon people – or help them prosper – depending on their behaviour.

These three ways of connecting gods and spirits to moral choices are not exclusive. In many places people combine them. The Fang think of the ancestors as interested parties but also as law-givers. The Christians may think of Jesus as law-giver and paragon, but also very often as an interested party, in that he is said to hear their prayers, know of their suffering, etc. However, to say that the legislator, paragon and interested-party models are combined is a bit misleading, because in people's actual reasoning about particular situations, in the practical business of judging people's behaviour and choosing a course of action, the interested-party model is largely dominant.

As far as anthropologists know, people in most places conceive of some supernatural agents as having some interest in their decisions. This can take all sorts of forms. The Christians for instance consider that God expects some particular kinds of behaviour and will punish deviation. People who interact with their ancestors, like the Kwaio, have a much less precise description of what the ancestors want, but it is part of their everyday concerns that the *adalo* are watching them. In either case, people do not really represent *why* the ancestors or gods would want to sanction people's behaviour. It is just assumed that they will. When I say that this way of thinking about morality is 'dominant' I simply mean that it is constantly activated and generally implicit. It is the most natural way people think of the connection between powerful agents and their own behaviour. The 'legislator' and 'model' representations are icing on the cake, as it were.

A first reason may well be that both the 'legislation' and 'paragon' accounts of morality are by nature insufficient. For instance, religious codes like the Christian Commandments specify a simple list of prescriptions and prohibitions. But the range of situations about which people have moral intuitions or uncertainties is far greater than this. The same applies however many prescriptions and prohibitions you add to the list, even if you have the 613 *mitzvot* of the Torah. The problem with all religious codes is that they must be general enough to be applicable without change to all possible situations. This is why in most places where you find such religious codes (generally in literate cultures) you also find a whole literature that adds nuance to their application. This happened in Christianity, in Judaism with the development of Talmudic scholarship, and in Islam as well, where the various prescriptions of the Koran are completed with a vast compilation of the Prophet's specific pro- nouncements. Paradoxically, as the divinely sanctioned code is expanded and specified in this way by specialised scholars, we also observe that many believers only have the vaguest knowledge of the original laws. It is a source of some surprise to outsiders that many devout Christians cannot remember the list of Commandments and that many Muslims have a rather hazy grasp of what the Koran actually recommends. But all this should not be too surprising. What matters to people is what is relevant to practical concerns, that is, to particular situations, and that is precisely where the codes lose much of their relevance.

The same problem besets paragon-inspired morality, for symmetrical reasons. The models are always too specific. The stories mention particular deeds of particular people, but there is no way to see how these apply to different situations unless one completes the story with the appropriate inferences. It is all very well to know that a good Samaritan gave away his coat to clothe the naked, but how does that translate given different circumstances? So models are good only if you already have some intuitions about where and when they should be followed, and in what way.

To say that codes are too general and models too specific is only part of the explanation. There must be something else that makes the interested-parties connection quite plausible to human minds. So far, I have described these links from religion to morality as if morality were a simple matter of what is proscribed and what is encouraged. But it is far more complex than that.

Moral reasoning and moral feelings

We all have moral intuitions ('My friend left her purse here, I must give it back to her'), moral judgements ('He should have returned his friend's purse'), moral feelings ('He stole his friend's purse, how revolting!'), moral principles ('Stealing is wrong') and moral concepts ('wrong', 'right'). How is all this organised in the mind? There are two possible ways of describing the mental processes engaged. On the one hand, moral judgements appear to be organised by a system of rules and inferences. People seem to have some notion of very general principles (e.g. 'do not harm other people unless they harmed you', 'do unto others as you would have them do unto you', etc.). These provide very general templates. If you fill the placeholders in the templates with particular values – the names of the people involved, the nature of the action considered – you reach a certain description of the situation with a moral tag. This is called the *moral-reasoning* model. On the other hand, in many cases people just seem to feel particular emotions when faced with particular situations and particular courses of action. Without having a clear notion of why we have a particular reaction, we know that doing this rather than that triggers emotional effects that goad us in one direction rather than the other, or that make us proud to have done the right thing, guilty if we did not, revolted if others did not, etc. This is a *moral-feeling* model.[2]

If we follow people's explicit reasoning about the moral dimensions of a particular situation, we observe a mix of these two processes. The simple argument 'she lied to him, but he's always been perfectly frank with her' is such a mix: it (1) implies that the situation is a violation of the Golden Rule and (2) appeals to the emotional response that should result from this description. Once you construe what she did as 'harming him in a way he never harmed her', a certain emotional overtone is added that should lead to a particular conclusion. When I say that emotion is involved, I do not just mean strong reactions of admiration or disgust. Emotion also includes those very weak reactions, barely recorded by our conscious mind, that lead us to choose one course of action over another. Emotional rewards trigger such behaviours as holding the door open to let your friend in or passing the salt before people ask for it, although the emotional effects are so slight that we often (and wrongly) feel that the behaviours are not driven by emotion. This is why most psychologists say that the opposition between principles and feelings is overstated. The emotions themselves are principled, they occur in a patterned way as the result of mental activity that is precisely organised but not entirely accessible to conscious access.[3]

This explains why it is extremely difficult to elicit general moral principles in many places in the world. For instance, the Fang find the explicit principle 'do unto others as you would have them do unto you' so vague and general that it is virtually meaningless. But these people are certainly not immoral, far from it. They constantly talk about this action being right and that one wrong, as in every human group.

So an abstract moral code, with principles and deductions, may well be a cultural artefact like a writing system or a musical notation. People everywhere have specific musical intuitions, they judge that this or that chord, given the parameters of their musical tradition, is felicitous or not; but it is only in some cultures that people write treatises on harmony to describe these intuitions in a more systematic way. That people have principled moral feelings without explicit moral principles would explain why cross-cultural studies of *explicit* moral reasoning give very confusing results. There are places where such reasoning is familiar and places where people find it baffling.[4]

Consider another difficulty: If moral intuitions came from moral reasoning, then people who are clearly immoral would probably be deficient in that form of reasoning. It might be that they are not aware of the general principles or that they have difficulties applying them to particular cases. The clinical study of sociopaths suggests a rather different situation. These people have no difficulty describing what they did or what they were planning to do as violating moral rules, for instance as hurting people without justification. If anything, some criminal sociopaths seem to have a very keen sense of what is wrong and why, and they often entertain precise descriptions of what effects their actions will have on others. They seem to apply all the rules of moral reasoning but this somehow does not give them the motivation to act differently. To know that some course of action is wrong is not really what we mean by a 'moral' judgement if it does not divert you from doing it.

But then where do the feelings come from? They seem far more complex than other types of emotional reactions, like the fear of an unseen presence or the pleasure of getting more than one expected. Fear alerts us to danger and forces us to focus on a possible source of harm; the pleasure derived from beneficial situations leads the individual to recognise where his or her best interests lie. But there is nothing straightforward about feeling guilty after lying to a friend. There is no obvious danger there. Feeling proud that we did not lie is equally complex. We get no clear reward to behave morally, indeed in many cases we have to forgo some possible gratification. So why should this trigger a pleasurable feeling? One solution is to look at how people acquire moral sentiment, that is, how children gradually identify moral norms in their particular group and form their own system of intuitions.

Early morality

That young children are morally incompetent may seem obvious. They often behave in ways clearly excluded by local moral standards. Adults use a whole panoply of measures (from good examples to threats or coercion) in the hope of correcting this. Children do change and in general gradually acquire intuitions similar to those of adults, so that whatever measures were taken by adults are invariably construed as the cause of these changes. But psychologists know that this is a gross over-simplification. Children may not be totally incompetent in the domain. Indeed, it would be difficult to explain the development of morality if young children did not have some inkling of moral concepts. As philosophers used to say, you cannot derive an ought from an is. There is no simple way to define what 'morally right' means, as distinct from desirable, conventionally agreed, positively sanctioned, approved by the authorities, etc.

Because there were two general accounts of moral judgement, in terms of reasoning from principles and of feelings respectively, psychologists have tried to explain the acquisition of morality, either as the gradual refinement and abstraction of principles, or as the gradual development of specific emotional reactions.

Seen from the first, principle-based perspective, children acquire morality by gradually making their principles more general, less centred on very specific actions. In this view, any child who is attentive enough should find out how to optimise their rewards by behaving the way more powerful others, like parents and older peers, recommend. Then children would gradually acquire a more abstract version of the principles, which would allow them to predict whether a given behaviour would be all right or not. Once the child understands that tormenting a pet is 'bad' but so is maiming a friend or hitting a sibling, they form a more general concept of 'brutal behaviour' as punishable because of its effects. Then children get even more abstract principles about Good and Bad in general.

If on the other hand feelings are the main source of moral understandings, children's development in this domain should be slightly different. Consider a prototypical moral sentiment, like feeling guilty about harming others. Morality gives us a (minor) punishment in the form of an emotion that supposedly mirrors the suffering of others. So children should acquire these feelings as a measure of their capacity to represent the thoughts and feelings of others. This capacity for empathy would gradually extend to others and the norms would become internal to the child's mind.[5]

Both accounts of moral development (children gradually refine abstract principles, or children internalise close people's emotions) explained *some* of the actual evidence, that is, of how children actually use moral concepts. But there were some problems too. First, many such studies were based on interviews designed to elicit explicit moral reasoning. But we know that this method is not quite sufficient. In many domains where we have specialised mental systems, there is a large gap between our precise intuitions and the explicit concepts that would justify them. The gap is even larger in children, who lack the verbal sophistication to explicate their own intuitions, so that subtler experimental techniques are necessary. Here is a simple illustration: Six year olds like adults have the intuition that it is wrong to lie, or rather, that it is wrong to communicate information (either true or false) with the intention of deceiving someone. However, young children also tend to use the word 'lie' in the narrow sense of 'communicating false information', which is why they would sometimes call a genuine mistake a lie, and conversely fail to identify as a lie an elaborate deception that only used true information. Their moral concept of 'lying' is quite similar to the adults' but their use of the word does not correspond with that concept. You will not understand their moral judgements if you just ask them explicit questions like 'Is it wrong to lie?' because of this discrepancy, which may extend to other moral concepts as well.[6]

Indeed, when psychologist Eliot Turiel used indirect tests he found that even young children had sophisticated moral understandings. Turiel wanted to find out whether children make a distinction between violations of *moral principles* (e.g. hitting people) and violations of *conventional rules* (e.g. chattering while the teacher is talking). The violation of a convention disappears if there is no convention; if the teacher did not insist on silence then chattering is no offence. Moral transgressions by contrast are such that they remain violations even in the absence of explicit instruction. The distinction points to what is specific about ethical rules as such. So if children made it this would suggest that they had the first rudiments of a special concept of ethical behaviour.

Turiel found that even three and four year olds had the intuition that hitting people would be wrong both in those contexts where it had been explicitly forbidden and in those where there was no prohibition. On the other hand, shouting in class is perceived to be wrong only if there is an explicit instruction to keep quiet. Slightly older children (but still as young as four or five) also have precise intuitions about the relative seriousness of various violations. They can perceive that stealing a pen is not quite as bad as hitting people; in the same way, shouting in class is only a minor violation of convention, whereas boys wearing skirts would violate a major social convention. But they find it much easier to imagine a revision of *major* social conventions (e.g. a situation where boys would wear skirts) than a revision of even *minor* moral principles (e.g. a situation where it would be all right to steal an eraser). Also, children make a difference between moral principles and prudential rules (do not leave your notebook next to the fire-place!). They justify both in terms of their consequences but assume that social consequences are specific to moral violations.[7]

A possible objection to Turiel's conclusions was that perhaps his subjects were special because they lived in a particular culture. But studies in North Korea and America gave similar results. Or perhaps their attitude to moral transgressions was special to the context of schooling. But psychologist Michael Siegal found that newcomers who had just enrolled in a kindergarten were if anything stricter in their moral attitudes than old-timers (that is, four year olds with two years of day-care). Or perhaps one might think that Turiel's subjects were special because they had a relatively stress-free existence, where serious violations of moral rules were in fact uncommon. But neglected or abused children seem to have similar intuitions.[8]

So experimental studies show that there is an early-developed specific inference system, a specialised moral sense underlying ethical intuitions. Notions of morality are distinct from those used to evaluate other aspects of social interaction (this is why social conventions and moral imperatives are easily distinguished by very young children). To have principled moral intuitions – they only apply to a specific aspect of social interaction, they are directed by particular principles – does not mean that you can articulate them explicitly. Also, obviously, that young children have early moral concepts does not mean that they produce the *same* moral judgements as adults, far from it. Children are different for a variety of reasons. First, they have some initial difficulty in representing what others believe and feel. Intuitive psychology is among their capacities, but it requires a lot of fine-tuning before it can provide reliable descriptions of mental states in other people. So whether you actually hurt someone may not be quite as easy to figure out as adults may think. Second, children need to acquire all sorts of local parameters, for instance the understanding of what counts as 'hurting' in a particular social context. Third, older children and adults have a much larger repertoire of previous situations and judgements about these situations, on the basis of which they can produce case-based analogies.

Despite these differences, it is quite striking that some important aspects of reasoning do *not* really change with development. Our moral intuitions specify that behaviour is either right or wrong or morally neutral; that whether we are able to justify our intuition by invoking abstract principles is irrelevant; that a course of action is in actual fact right or wrong regardless of how the agents themselves explain their behaviour. If you think that stealing a friend's pen is wrong, you think it is wrong not just from your viewpoint but also from anyone else's viewpoint. Whether the perpetrator of this minor offence can invoke self-serving excuses or not is completely irrelevant. Whether the owner of the pen minds the theft or not is equally irrelevant.

This is what philosophers call 'moral realism', the assumption that behaviours in themselves have specific moral values. In general, being a realist consists in assuming that the qualities of things are in the things themselves: if a poppy *looks* red it is because it *is* red. If we place it under blue light it does not appear red any more but we have the intuition that it still *is* that colour, that it has some intrinsic redness that is difficult to detect under these special circumstances. (Obviously, our common intuitions are not always congruent to how a scientist would approach the question, here as in many other domains.) Moral realism is the same, only applied to the ethical aspect of actions, so that wrongness is thought to be as intrinsic to stealing as redness is to a poppy. Moral philosophers are not in general too keen on moral realism because it creates difficult paradoxes. But the children studied by Turiel and others are, precisely, not philosophers. That is, they are not in the business of making ethical principles explicit, testing their application to difficult cases and checking that the overall results are consistent. They just have spontaneous moral intuitions with a realistic bias, and when this bias creates an ambiguity they just live with it.

Now this realist assumption does not change much with development, which is remarkable because in other domains children gradually form more and more sophisticated descriptions of the difference between their own and other people's viewpoints on a situation. This 'perspective-taking' is an indispensable skill in a species that depends so much on social interaction. You have to monitor not just situations as you see them, but also the way others see them and what creates the difference between these viewpoints. So it is all the more interesting that no such change is observed in the domain of moral intuitions. For the three year old as well as for the ten year old and indeed most adults, the fact that a behaviour is right or wrong is *not* a function of one's viewpoint. It is only seen as a function of the actual behaviour and the actual situation.

Dispositions for co-operation

Why do we have this specific domain of understanding, these specific capacities for moral judgements and feelings? When we see that young children quickly grasp some complex distinctions, in the face of fragmented and often incoherent messages from their environment, it makes sense to wonder whether they have special dispositions for paying attention to particular cues in the environment and for deriving particular conclusions from these cues. In other domains we have seen that early principles make learning possible and that this is certainly a consequence of evolution. We have specific dispositions for learning specific kinds of animal concepts and tool concepts. This is not too surprising in a species that depends on interaction with animals for survival and has been in the business of tool-making for hundreds of thousands of years. But what about moral dispositions?

It is tempting to think that social life *imposes* certain norms on individuals. Morality is seen as the opposite of our bestial nature, as it were. We live in groups, which imposes certain limits on people's behaviour; besides, living in groups is possible and advantageous only if individuals are not completely opportunistic, if there is some restraint in the pursuit of individual gain. So it would not seem too surprising that we evolved moral dispositions which are beneficial to social groups. Groups that are composed of people with such dispositions would flourish, while groups of selfish opportunists would not be able to reap the benefits of co-operation.

Unfortunately, stated in these terms the explanation is a non-starter. To say that we have dispositions for a form of behaviour is to say that particular genetic traits lead, given the appropriate environment, to that form of behaviour. But genes always vary and always have varied. This is what makes evolution possible at all. Some variants give their bearers better chances to pass on their genes so these variants spread in the gene-pool. Other variants reduce these chances and therefore tend to disappear. If we had dispositions for socially acceptable behaviour, these should vary too. What would happen then? Some people would have stronger dispositions and become selfless individuals who sacrifice their immediate benefits on the altar of group-prosperity. Others would have much weaker dispositions and would take every opportunity to thrive at the expense of others and of the group. These 'cheats' would have no problem surviving and spreading their genes around, since they would never forgo their individual benefits. This would be particularly easy if most people around them were gentle 'co-operators'. The latter would be less successful at spreading their 'good' genes since they would occasionally sacrifice themselves. This would lead to a gradual extinction of the 'good social behaviour' variant from the gene-pool. So if there are dispositions for 'unselfish' behaviour, these cannot have evolved only because of their advantage to social groups. That is not the way evolution by natural selection generally works, simply because it is organisms not groups that reproduce and transmit genes.[9]

These remarks are just a hugely summarised account of a discussion that has been going on for about thirty years in evolutionary biology and psychology, concerning social dispositions in humans and other animals. This discussion was prompted by the fact that we observe unselfish behaviour in many species. This may be spectacular, as in the case of insect societies where most organisms literally slave away throughout their lives for the benefit of a colony.

In other cases co-operation seems less 'automatic' and more responsive to context. Many birds will put themselves at great risk by attracting a predator's attention just to divert it from their brood. Animals that signal the presence of a predator by special alarm-calls do a great favour to their group but are more easily located. Biologists who studied vampire bats noticed that the tiny animals, after a successful attack on cattle, will often share the harvest with less fortunate companions, by regurgitating some of the blood. Primates too share some of their resources; humans among them are the most dedicated co-operators. The general problem then was to explain how evolution could lead to altruism in animals (including humans). Obviously, the term 'altruism' is misleading if it suggests a course of action that is completely divorced from compulsion, something we do only for the goodness of the act, which of course is not a plausible description of animal behaviour. More difficult, the term suggests that there is *one* phenomenon here and therefore *one* explanation. But animal behaviour is more complicated than that. Indeed, there are no fewer than three different evolutionary routes to selfless behaviours.

The first one is *kin-selection*. When sterile ants and bees work for a colony and defend it, they seem to violate the most crucial biological imperatives, since they forgo all chance of reproduction and even survival. However, if you view the situation in terms of their genes' replication, the picture is quite different. Biologist William Hamilton combined empirical data with mathematical models to show under what circumstances the individual's self-sacrifice would propagate the genes that favour that behaviour. When all workers in a colony are sisters and the queen's offspring share genes with them, when they sacrifice themselves they help propagate genes that they share. Now humans too display *some* dispositions that can be explained in terms of kin-selection. We do not just spend resources and energy for our offspring's benefit but also co-operate with kin much more readily than with non-kin and on terms that are quite different.[10]

Still, kin-selection is obviously not the only factor since humans from times immemorial have engaged in co-operation with unrelated (or very remotely related) individuals. But this, too, is found in other animal species besides humans, and constitutes *reciprocal altruism*, following the principle 'I scratch your back and you scratch mine'. This is the main explanation for such familiar examples as blood-sharing among vampire bats. Biologist Robert Trivers showed how reciprocating strategies could evolve under specific conditions of population, reproduction and use of resources, but also when specific capacities are present in individuals. Co-operation requires that animals can discriminate between loyal partners, who tend to reciprocate a good turn, and free-loaders who do not. Apparently indiscriminate sharing is in fact judiciously measured. This seems to be the case in bats or dolphins or other species with complicated brains, and of course in humans who do preserve memories of past episodes of interaction with other humans. Again, although such strategies are individually unselfish they remain genetically selfish. The genes that carry them stand a good chance of propagating even when other strategies appear in the local gene-pool.[11]

Incidentally, what is called a 'strategy' in these accounts is of course not based on conscious deliberation. The bats that exchange blood do not reflect on the possible consequences of sharing or not. A strategy is just an organised way of behaving. This is the same as 'deciding' how to stay upright. You do not have to think about it, but a special system in the brain takes into account your current posture, the pressure on each foot and corrects your position to avoid a fall. In the same way, these accounts show that specialised cognitive systems register situations of exchange, store them in memory and produce inferences for subsequent behaviour, none of which requires an explicit consideration of the various options available.

Beyond opportunism

Kin-selection and reciprocal altruism are not the only factors involved in human co-operative behaviour. People behave in altruistic ways in many circumstances where no common genes are involved and no reciprocation is expected. They refrain from extracting all the possible benefits from many situations. It would be trivially easy to steal from friends, mug old ladies or leave restaurants without tipping. Also, this restraint does not stem from rational calculation, for instance from the fear of possible sanctions, for it persists when there is clearly no chance of getting caught; people just say that they would *feel* awful if they did such things. Powerful *emotions* and moral *feelings* seem to be driving behaviour in a way that does not maximise their benefits.

These facts are certainly puzzling but their combination may suggest an evolutionary explanation. To date, the best account of these human propensities has come from economists who found such everyday behaviours – tipping in restaurants one will never again patronise, refraining from undetectable cheating, etc. – rather difficult to explain in their standard models. Economist Robert Frank proposed that such behaviour may reveal important aspects of human dispositions for co-operation. Humans depend on co-operation, which creates trust and commitment problems. In many situations you just cannot be sure that others will co-operate rather than defect or cheat. Maybe the baby-sitter is a thief; maybe your business partner is a crook. You have to rely on cues that indicate some degree of reliability. Because we depend so much on co-operation, the problem is equally acute from the other side of a prospective exchange. If you are seeking work as a baby-sitter you need some means to convey your honesty to prospective employers, and the same applies if you want to set up some fair and mutually beneficial business partnership. To have good dispositions is of no great advantage unless you can demonstrate that you have them. These problems have been with us for hundreds of thousands of years. Here I am using examples from modern conditions but collective foraging or hunting expeditions pose the same problems. You sincerely intend to bring back to the camp all the berries you gather and share your pickings with others; but this disposition must be obvious to others for co-operation to begin at all.

Throughout human history, a number of *commitment gadgets* have helped solve such problems. In our modern conditions for instance a travel agent could very well take people's money and sell them bogus tickets, but travel agents set up associations that would immediately expel any member convicted of having done this. Wherever such an association exists any agent who is not a member clearly becomes suspicious and will lose trade. Such legal gadgets are widespread and have been around for a long time. What they do is paradoxical: they restrict our freedom of movement in order to make exchange possible. A good way to show commitment to honest co-operation is to put yourself in a situation where you are actually forced to honour that commitment. You signal your honesty by tying your own hands.[12]

Legal binds and reputation maintenance are not the only commitment gadgets. In many situations, as Robert Frank suggests, passions will do the trick too. Consider another commitment problem. I am a shopkeeper, you are a sales assistant. If you steal from the till I will fire you and sue you. This is the standard way of deterring cheats: threaten them with a punishment that would make cheating very costly whatever the potential benefits. However, punishment too has its costs. I might end up spending vast amounts of money on lawyers and court costs. If I am strictly opportunistic, I will avoid this so even if you are caught I will not sue. So my threat is effectively empty. But now imagine that discovering a thief among my staff is known to put me in such a rage that I will do anything to harm the miscreant at whatever cost. Everyone around me knows that. In this case I am pushed by a passion that I cannot control and does not, apparently, work completely to my advantage. But the very fact that I cannot control myself changes the situation. My threat is now much more credible. I will sue not because it is to my advantage – it is not – but because I just cannot help it. So to be known as someone who is actually in the grip of such passionate feelings is a very good thing as long as they are, precisely, feelings that over-ride rational calculations.

This may explain passionate resentment, but what about other moral feelings and especially a disposition to honesty? Again, con sider the problems faced by a species where co-operation is crucial, where you have to demonstrate reliability to find co-operators. The problem is that being reliable is costly. We are often told that the straight and narrow is not the easy path, and that is true. There is a price to pay: all those tills left unopened, all those friends' wallets left untouched. If people around us were all rational calculators they would sometimes behave well and sometimes cheat. So it would be dangerous to trust them. But what if some people are not rational calculators? What if they are driven to honesty by emotional urges that over-ride their best calculations? These would be precious people to have around because they would be irrationally disposed to honesty even when it is not to their immediate advantage. If there could be clear signals that people have such dispositions, one should choose to co-operate with such individuals rather than the rational calculators. So a disposition to co-operation creates all sorts of opportunities that would not be open to people identified as potential cheats. True, there is a cost too but this is more than offset by the benefits of co-operation.

The disposition must be difficult to fake, otherwise the signal would be of no value. Indeed, there is quite a lot of experimental evidence to suggest that deception is not quite as easy as we generally think. That is, emotional cues such as facial expressions and gestures often give people an intuitive feeling that some deception is going on even before they can clearly articulate what gives them this feeling. Obviously, this is not a matter of complete certainty. The strategy only requires that some signals, on the whole, give a fairly good indication of people's underlying dispositions, and this seems to be the case. Experimental evidence also supports this account. People generally evaluate possible transactions in terms of 'fairness', a set of intuitive criteria that do not seem to match rational economic models. Indeed, business school teachers often try to correct such 'naïve' propensities in their students by demonstrating how they can be dangerous in actual markets.

However, honest dispositions only pay off if certain conditions obtain. First, people should be prepared to punish cheats even if it is costly. So they should have powerful emotions that help them disregard the cost. This is clear in many everyday situations. The anger triggered by queue-jumpers and parking-space thieves is quite disproportionate to the actual damage they inflict. Second, we should be outraged when cheating is not punished even if we did not incur any cost because the existence of 'suckers', by making cheating a viable strategy, is a threat to our own safety. So people should punish cheats, not just because they feel outraged but also because others will feel outraged if they do not. This passion too is a constant in human interaction. The queue-jumper makes you angry even if you are standing in another line. The existence of such dispositions tends to make cheating a low-benefit strategy. That is, even if cheats appear they will not have the smooth ride that would make their behaviour really profitable. This does not guarantee that they will not appear. As we all know, there *are* con-artists and swindlers about. Their strategy works to some extent but not well enough to eliminate all co-operators.[13]

Seeing co-operation as not just a rational problem but also an evolutionary one suggests why these dispositions should take the form of *feelings* rather than rationally motivated cogitation. Many varieties of moral feelings make much more sense once we see them in this light. Guilt is a punishment we incur for cheating or generally not living up to our advertised standards of honest co-operation with others. But then feeling guilt is also useful if it balances the benefits of cheating, making it less tempting. Prospective guilt provides negative rewards that help us brush aside opportunities to cheat, a capacity that is crucial in organisms that constantly plan future behaviour and must assess their prospective benefits. Gratitude is a positive emotional reward associated with encountering co-operation in others in situations where cheating was indeed possible.

Pride, a positive reward for co-operative behaviour, somehow compensates the frustration of missed opportunities to cheat. All these dispositions are all the more beneficial if we have limited control over their emotional effects.

General dispositions, variable judgements

This detour through the evolution and psychology of moral intuitions may help make sense of very general properties of human morality. Our evolved dispositions connect specific emotional states to specific situations of social interaction. This is why specific moral pre-scriptions vary a lot from culture to culture, but their connection to social interaction does not. Many cues tell us whether people are on the whole good co-operators or not, but these cues are often related to particular ways of life. Faced with strangers whose habits and language are different, there is precious little to guide us. Conversely, this means that people with good dispositions can only truly demonstrate them to people who understand them. It is not surprising that the history of tribal mankind is also the history of solidarity within tribes and warfare between them. The likelihood that other-tribe members will co-operate is not that great, given that we cannot read their cues and they cannot read ours. Which is all the more reason for not even trying to co-operate with them.

The connection between morality and social interaction is also obvious in children. Note how the examples of moral violations that four year olds find repugnant, in Turiel's and other psychologists' studies, are often behaviours that disrupt co-operation. Children are angered by disruptive behaviour, for instance throwing all the pieces in the air in the middle of a snakes-and-ladders game. What children need to acquire is a better sense of who should be treated as a likely co-operator and who should not. Such information is not that easy to pick up because it is entirely context-dependent. You cannot adjust your behaviour unless you have lived through enough different situations. We blame children for refusing to share their toys with a visiting cousin. But children also observe that we do not offer all our possessions to perfect strangers. So children must learn to recognise and classify different situations of social interaction in their particular social milieu.

We should not be too surprised that moral principles in all cultures seem both highly commendable in formulation ('peace is most precious', 'a guest is sacred') and less so in their application ('let us raid the next village', 'let us rob this rich traveller'). This is not a symptom of unredeemed hypocrisy but more simply a consequence of the constraints imposed by commitment and co-operation. In such situations one has to consider the trade-off between offering co-operation (at the risk of being swindled) and denying it (at the risk of missing out on mutual advantage). So peace is genuinely valued in general but this has to be weighed against the perceived threat of inaction against dangerous neighbours. In the same way guests are honoured but less so if there is no conceivable expectation of further interaction with them. Westerners can afford to find tribal warfare and systematic nepotism unpalatable because they are to some extent protected from these evils by the judicial system and other state institutions. Between warring tribes and Western suburbs the moral understandings are similar but not the perceived safety of offering co-operation to unknown partners. So, against the wisdom of many moralists, the milk of human kindness is not in short supply; but it is apportioned in a principled manner.

Full-access agents and moral intuitions

Moral intuitions are part of our mental dispositions for social interaction. But why are they connected to gods, spirits and ancestors? To understand how the latter fit in moral understandings, consider two facts I mentioned very briefly in the course of this psychological journey. First, our moral intuitions suggest to us, from the youngest age, that behaviours are right or wrong *by themselves*, not depending on who considers them, from what point of view. Second, gods and spirits and ancestors are generally considered *interested parties* in moral choices and moral judgements, rather than providers of codes and rules. These two facts are just two aspects of the same mental processes.

Imagine this situation: You know (a) that there is a banknote in your pocket and remember that you stole it from your friend's wallet. This situation may produce a specific emotion (guilt). Let me change the context. You took the banknote from your friend's wallet but also remember (b) that *he* stole money from you in the first place. This new context will probably result in a rather different emotional reaction, perhaps a mixture of reduced guilt, outrage at his behaviour and partly quenched resentment. So your emotions are very much a function of the information you represent about the situation at hand. But, that is the crucial point, in either case you assume that the emotion you feel is the only possible one given the situation. A disinterested third party who knew the facts about (a) would agree that stealing the money was shameful; whoever knew about (a) *and* (b) would share your outrage and your sense of justice done. This at least is what we assume and why we invariably think that the best way to explain our behaviour is to explain the actual facts. That is why, were your friend in situation (b) to complain about your behaviour, you would certainly explain to him that it was only a just retribution for his own misdemeanour. Most family rows are extensive and generally futile attempts to get the other party to 'see the facts as they really are', i.e. how you see them, and *by virtue of that* to share your moral judgements. This rarely works in practice but we do have this expectation.

So we intuitively assume that if an agent has full access to all the relevant information about the situation, that agent will immediately have access to the rightness or wrongness of the behaviour. When I talk about 'information' I naturally mean 'strategic information' since all this is relevant to our social-mind inference systems. Whether the banknote was crumpled or not, whether it is not in your left or right pocket are non-strategic pieces of information that do not enter into these thought processes.

Now remember that supernatural agents are tacitly represented as having full access to strategic information. That is, people who have thoughts about these agents and represent a particular situation tend to assume that the agents represent all the strategic information, all the aspects of the situation that are relevant to the social mind. To illustrate this, consider the example above. In such a case, people who have a concept of god or spirit will probably not wonder whether the god/spirit knew that the banknote was crumpled. But they will probably assume that the god/spirit knows who has the banknote, knows that they took it and knows why they did what they did.

This is why supernatural agents are quite naturally connected to moral judgements. If you have a concept of agent that has all the strategic information, then it is quite natural to think of your own moral intuition as identical to that particular agent's view of the situation. This is the way religious moral judgements work in practice. To Christians for instance it is obvious that in the situation (b) above God knows all the relevant facts and *therefore* knows that it is a (partly) justified theft. People with other kinds of supernatural concept would run similar inferences. As we saw in chapter 4, the Kwaio consider it a major moral violation to defile other people's shrines, in particular to utter words that are *abu* (forbidden) in these shrines. Whenever this happens ancestors know about it and *therefore* know that it is a bad action. Our moral intuitions suggest that if one could see the whole of a situation without any distortion one would immediately grasp whether it was wrong or right. Religious concepts are just concepts of persons with such an immediate perspective on the whole of a situation.

So concepts of gods and spirits are made more relevant by the organisation of our moral understandings, which by themselves do not especially require any gods or spirits. What I mean by relevant is that the concepts, once put in this moral context, are both easy to represent and generate many new inferences. For instance, most people feel some guilt when acting in a way which they suspect is immoral. That is, whatever their self-serving justifications, they may have the intuition that an agent with a full description of the situation would still classify it as wrong. Thinking of this intuition as 'what the ancestors think of what I did' or 'how God feels about what I did' provides an easy way of understanding our own mental states. That is, most of our moral intuitions are clear but their origin escapes us, because it lies in mental processing that we cannot consciously access. Seeing these intuitions as someone's viewpoint is a simpler way of understanding why we have these intuitions. But this requires the concept of an agent with full access to strategic information.

All this may explain why the interested-party notion is vastly more widespread, and more active in people's actual thinking, than the 'legislator' or 'exemplar' connections. The interested-party model is just the assumption that gods and spirits have access to all relevant information about what we do and *therefore* have the moral opinions that we experience as intuitions. As I said at the beginning, we know that religious codes and exemplars cannot literally be the origin of people's moral thoughts. These thoughts are remarkably similar in people with different religious concepts or without any such concepts. Also, these thoughts naturally come to children who would never link them to supernatural agency. Finally, even religious people's thoughts about moral matters are constrained by intuitions they share with other human beings, more than official codes and models.

To sum up, then: Our evolution as a species of co-operators is sufficient to explain the actual psychology of moral reasoning, the way children and adults represent moral dimensions of action. This requires no special concept of religious agent, no special code, no models to follow. However, once you have concepts of supernatural agents with strategic information, these are made more salient and relevant by the fact that you can easily insert them in moral reasoning that would be there in any case. To some extent religious concepts are *parasitic* upon moral intuitions.

Witches and misfortune
When I was working in Cameroon I heard of hundreds of cases of

accidents and suspicious deaths that could only be explained, in people's view, by the action of witches. So-and-so had fallen off a tree, although he was a good climber. Such-and-such still had no children though she did all that was required. Someone had almost drowned in the river when a dug-out canoe capsized. Someone else had been even less lucky and was run over by a truck. I was told that 'there was more than meets the eye' in each of these cases; and the 'more' in question only meant that some people, probably equipped with *evur* (the mysterious organ that gives them witchcraft powers), would profit from the accident or death. Who the witches were, and how they operated, was of course clouded in mystery.

Witchcraft seems to provide an 'explanation' for all sorts of events: many cases of illness or other misfortune are spontaneously interpreted as evidence for the witches' actions. Fang people say that witchcraft has become so general and so diffuse, modern transportation and communication have made their work so much easier, that you could be attacked from anywhere. A whole variety of rituals, amulets, secret societies and spells can provide a measure of protection against witches. But this is only cold comfort when you see evidence of the witches' powers at every turn. In the Cameroon, there may be little witchcraft activity but discourse about it is constant and frames the way people think about misfortune.

Anthropologist Jeanne Favret-Saada documented the converse case, where witchcraft activities are all too real but no one will talk about them. As she started working in the Bocage in western France, Favret-Saada observed that most people denied the very existence of witchcraft. Whenever she broached the topic people would often concede that there 'used to be' witchcraft, or that it still happened in other regions, but all would plead ignorance. One major reason is that *others* talk far too much about it. Journalists, psychiatrists, social scientists, schoolteachers and government officials are all too eager to supply the anthropologist and other visitors from the city with lurid accounts of the peasants' supposedly backward beliefs. As Favret-Saada points out, these officials do not in fact have much knowledge of what goes on in their district and are in fact quite keen on ignoring as much as possible, substituting folkloristic stereotypes of bats, black cats and muttered incantations for genuine information. There is witchcraft; but it is not a matter of old legends and narrative frisson, for the fights between witches and their victims may be, quite literally, deadly.

The first sign of a witchcraft attack is that a household is struck by repeated misfortune. Single events – a cow aborts, a member of the family gets ill, someone has a car-crash – are things people can take in their stride but repetition is what alarms them. At some point, someone has to open their eyes to the fact that they are being attacked, that the enemy will not give up until they are thoroughly ruined or dead. This 'announcer' also discloses the identity of the putative witch, very generally a neighbour or close relation. This disclosure and explicit description of the situation immediately make him or her an ally of the victims. So in this case the nature of bad news seems to disinfect the teller, so to speak, but also puts them in great danger. The fight between witch and 'unwitcher' is a deadly one. What is at stake is to deprive the witch of his vital force, to force him to desist; in other words anti-witchcraft fights are witchcraft operations. This is another important reason why no one ever talks about it. Talking about witchcraft, for the people concerned, means talking about a particular case, and this in turn implies taking sides. Saying that So-and-so is not actually bewitched means siding with their aggressors; accepting that they are is tantamount to declaring war on their enemies. Disinterested discourse is not an option, which is why Favret-Saada only found out about such fights when she was enlisted by friends as a knowledgeable and therefore potentially powerful ally against witches.

The actual rituals, helping prayers, magical formulae and protective amulets used by people vary a lot. Their detail may be less important than the fact that people can now reconsider all sorts of past and present occurrences in terms of the fight against an overly powerful agent. Witches are described as having an excess of 'strength' or 'force'. While normal people's strength is invested in their farm and household, that of the witch flows over and invades the domains of others, supposedly to the point where it will kill them. The struggle comes to an end only when the witch realises that he has found his match. This is why it is crucial to counter the witch's threat by sending clear signals of defiance. Every time the witch looks at you, people say, you should sustain his gaze; looking down is a defeat.[14]

What anthropologists call witchcraft is the suspicion that some people (generally within the community) perform magical tricks to plunder other people's health, good fortune or material goods. Concepts of witches are found in more or less all human groups, although in different forms. In some places there are explicit accusations and the alleged witches must either prove their innocence or perform some special rituals to pay for their transgression. In general, however, suspicion is conveyed through gossip, seldom coming out in the open. (Note that in anthropology the term 'witchcraft' is used exclusively for those situations where being a witch is being a criminal, so that very few people would admit to having used witchcraft. Those who confess do it in highly dramatic rituals. This is totally different from a form of modern 'pagan' religion that calls itself 'witchcraft', takes inspiration from popular European ideas about witches and gives them a more positive twist. What I am talking about here is only the negative, fantastic witchcraft that is found the world over.)

Evil eyes and angry gods

Witchcraft beliefs are only one manifestation of a phenomenon that is found in many human groups, the interpretation of misfortune as a consequence of envy. For another example of this, consider the widespread, although to a varying degree, belief in an 'evil eye', a spell cast by envious people against whoever enjoys some good fortune or natural advantage. In some human groups it seems that *any* difference is likely to attract the evil eye, so that people need to be forever on their guard against possible attacks. In his description of a Gujarat caste in North India, David Pocock gives a detailed description of such a situation. The *najar* or curse from the envious is a constant threat. People can cite hundreds of cases. A friend of Pocock's is distressed because her infant has got a bad rash. After a few days of enquiries, this is finally connected to an uncle's visit just after the baby's birth. This uncle had commented on how lively the child was, how he seemed to understand what was happening around him. So the jealous uncle must have cast the evil eye on the precocious child.

In some cases the effects of *najar* are even more direct: 'A man bought a new hookah of the portable kind and was walking back from the town with it. A passer-by asked him where he had bought it, and it broke at once. A woman had a child and another asked to see it. It died.' The fear of the evil eye ruins the simplest pleasures. A man complains to the anthropologist that he cannot buy apples for his children in Bombay because other children do not receive such delicacies and this difference would certainly attract a curse. Indeed, this is perceived as almost automatic and that is why people generally accept that one can cast a spell of this kind without realising it. The perception of difference automatically triggers envy which triggers the evil eye even though the originator of the curse may not be aware of what happened.[15]

In many places, people also explain illness, bad crops, accidents and other catastrophes as the direct action of the gods or spirits. This is very clear in the Kwaio case. As Roger Keesing reports, 'when an illness or misfortune occurs, a father or neighbour will break knotted strips of cordyline leaf, talking to the spirits to find out which one is causing trouble and why'. People want to know which ancestor is involved and why. It goes without saying that some ancestor *is* involved. This is in fact a most common situation, from ancestors causing bad crops to God punishing people's lack of faith or other misdemeanours by afflicting them with plagues and lean years.[16]

According to some 'origin of religion' scenarios, people have religious concepts because some salient events require urgent attention, yet cannot be explained. The spirits and gods fill the explanatory gap. But why is that the case? What makes it convincing or plausible that supernatural agents are the source of misfortune? The first reason that springs to mind is that gods and spirits are described as powerful agents that can cause bad crops or other problems. People are told that God can make people sick or that the ancestors can make you fall off a tree. That is precisely what makes them different from ordinary mortals.

This obviously is not a very good explanation, for it takes us straight back to square one: Why are the gods and spirits described as having such powers in the first place? To anthropologists, it is clear that people's reasoning actually goes the other way around, that people attribute great powers to gods and spirits *because* the latter are frequently mentioned as the origin of misfortune. That is, you *first* hear about particular cases of illness and accidents which people interpret as the consequence of the gods' or spirits' actions and you *then* infer that they must have whatever powers it takes to do such things. Naturally, these two kinds of representations feed each other. A description of the gods as powerful makes them plausible origins of misfortune. Their description as causes of misfortune makes it plausible that they are powerful. So, again, why are these representations combined so easily? Why do people interpret misfortune in 'magical' or supernatural ways? Why are they so keen to see the vagaries of misfortune as the whim of malfeasance?

Misfortune as a social thing

In the past, anthropologists sometimes suggested that most people were not very good at understanding natural correlations or the work of random variables. In some groups *most* cases of disease or death are ascribed to witchcraft. Surely, the argument goes, statistically minded people would notice that more or less everybody catches some disease at some point, that not all operations are always successful, and that in the long term we are all dead. Failing to appreciate these contingencies, people resort to magical explanations for events that are in fact perfectly ordinary. This is what we generally mean by 'superstition'. People see patterns and causes where there is just chance.

However, anthropologists know that people the world over are in fact rather good at detecting statistical regularities in their environment. Indeed, even the simplest techniques depend on such detection and this has been the case for as long as humans were around. Early Humans could not successfully maintain a rich food supply as foragers unless they could detect which fruit and tubers could be found where, with what frequency, in what season. People cannot hunt animals without detecting which habits and behaviour are true of a species as a whole and which apply only to particular exemplars. So it seems difficult to maintain that contingencies and random events are not really understood.

Also, people who attribute magical and supernatural causes to events are in general aware of the immediate mechanical or biological causes of these events as well. I mentioned in chapter 1 the incident of the collapsed roof and the debate between Evans-Pritchard and his Zande interlocutors. For the anthropologist, the house caved in because of the termites. For the Zande, it was quite clear that witchcraft was involved. However, the Zande were also aware that the termites were the proximate cause of the incident. But what they wanted to know was why it happened at that particular time when particular people were gathered in the house.

In much the same way, many Fang people are perfectly prepared to entertain both a biological explanation and a witchcraft interpretation of illnesses. Sure, So-and-so died of tuberculosis because the disease made his lungs non-functional. But then, why him? Why then? When people find supernatural causes it is not because they have ignored the work of mechanical and biological causes but because they are asking questions that go *beyond* these causes.

Causes and reasons of misfortune

This leads us to a second explanation for the fact that people explain so many events in terms of supernatural causes. The idea is this: Some events are such that they naturally suggest questions (Why me? Why now?) that are simply not answered in terms of ordinary causal processes. That is, people who do all this know perfectly well that disease strikes *most* people at some point or that mud-huts will eventually collapse in a termite-infested village. No one could be unaware of these general principles. But general principles are, precisely, *general*. That is their weakness. They have nothing to say about particular cases. People are understandably concerned with the particulars of each case, not its general aspects. Hence the value of supernatural explanations, which are relevant to the particulars of the situation.

In the paragraph above I called some questions 'natural' and this raises another question: What makes them natural? We might think that there is no great mystery here. The reason why our minds consider such questions as 'Why did the roof cave in when *I* was underneath?' or 'Why did the ancestors send *me* this illness?' is that these questions are the ones our minds *must* consider if they are well-designed. Focusing on the specific chain of events that brought about a particular misfortune may be the best way to avoid a repeat. Once bitten, twice shy: but only if you know what bit you and how in the first instance.

But is this a sound explanation? People's ways of talking about misfortune do not seem to correspond to this model. When people say that gods smite miscreants or cause a particular illness, they represent not the precise powers of these supernatural agents but their *reasons* for acting the way they do. In such contexts people are often extremely vague about the powers but much more precise about the reasons. God decided to punish the heathen and send them plague. Notice how no one describes *how* he did that. In fact, no one seems even to think about that aspect of the question! In the same way, the ancestors make people ill. In most places where people entertain this kind of notion, they only have the vaguest notion of how the ancestors do it. They do not even consider this a relevant or interesting question. In general, people do not think about the *ways* in which the powerful agents act, but they are very precise about their *reasons* for acting in a particular way. Indeed, these reasons always have to do with people's interaction with the powerful agents. People refused to follow God's orders; they polluted a house against the ancestors' prescriptions; they had more wealth or good fortune than their milieu could tolerate; and so on.

This is odd. If our thoughts about misfortunes were designed to avoid further occurrences, it would make much more sense to focus on the proximate causes, on the actual ways in which we are made to fall ill or risk our lives. So even if the question itself, Why did I fall ill? is natural, the particular way in which people formulate it requires some explanation. We ask questions in a particular way because our inference systems suggest the *format* of a possible answer. Questions do not spring by themselves out of events; they only appear in a mind that is already considering the events from a particular angle. For instance, the question 'Why did they make this fork out of rubber?' is natural because we have a special system in the mind that connects artefacts to possible functions, and therefore perceives a discrepancy between the usual function of forks and the features of this particular utensil. The same may well apply to our spontaneous way of thinking about misfortune.

Misfortune as social interaction

This is commonplace among anthropologists: misfortune is generally interpreted in *social* terms. We have social relations, we have been in complex social interaction for hundreds of thousands of years, because we have the specialised mental capacities that social life requires. We have special equipment to recognise our kin in a group, we know how to deal with group-members as opposed to outsiders, we have intuitions about whether people are trustworthy or not, we have inference systems that pay special attention to cheating and defection and produce specific emotions when principles of social exchange are violated.

Consider our examples in this light. The Kwaio say that ancestors sent people a disease in order to receive a sacrifice. In some cases people admit that they should have performed the sacrifice to start with, that they neglected a particular ancestor or failed to maintain proper relations with him. Note that these are clearly construed as *exchange* relations. Ancestors provide some form of protection and people provide roasted pigs in sacrifice. In some cases people tend to think that the ancestors are 'pushing it' a bit and they feel justifiably resentful. This is the kind of emotion we find in situations where one party seems to be receiving increased benefits without paying increased costs. The relationships with ancestors are represented in a mental system that is usually activated by situations of social exchange.

Notions about the evil eye activate this mental system too. At first sight, it would seem that all that is involved in evil eye beliefs is straightforward jealousy and the fear of jealousy. As Pocock says of the *najar* in Gujarat, the danger is in other people's gaze: 'Whenever you feel that someone is looking at you, immediately pretend to take great interest in some worthless object, and so direct his attention towards that.' People construe other people's envy as a force whose effects are unpredictable.

But the situation is not in fact quite that simple. If the fear of jealousy was the only factor here, all social differences would create it. After all, people are likely to feel envious of whatever difference they can detect between their lot and that of others. Now, as Pocock insists, some social differences are in fact *not* a source of apprehension. A rich landlord can strut along in his finest clothes without really fearing much from the evil eye: '*najar* seems to be apprehended more from those with whom one is, in most other respects, equal, or has reason to expect to be'. What attracts the evil eye are unexpected differences of good fortune among people of similar status.[17]

So what you fear is not that people may be envious, but that they may mistake you for a *cheat*, for someone who managed to get some benefit without paying a cost. This is relevant when the differences occur between people who exchange directly with each other, so that any difference between them *might* be a consequence of some cheating. But vast differences of social status and wealth are interpreted in this particular context as the consequence of one's essence (made manifest by caste-membership) and moral destiny. These are not construed as the result of exchange at all, which may be why they do not activate the social-exchange inference systems; the cheat-detection that creates the evil eye is therefore irrelevant.

Finally, social-exchange considerations are obviously central to the representation of witches. People invariably describe witches as individuals striving to reap benefits without paying the costs. This is precisely what people like the Fang and many others say about witches: They are the ones who take but never give, who steal other people's health or happiness, who thrive only if others are deprived. Fang people also compare witches to a particular species of tree, that starts out as a modest shrub and gradually takes out all the nutrients from its surroundings at the expense of all other trees around.

This social-exchange model explains why people's models of witchcraft in Africa have changed so much to adapt to changing economic conditions. In traditional beliefs the witches were relatives or in-laws; one had to identify them to solve the problem. In more modern developments the witches are anonymous, and rituals offer a general protection against their attacks. The traditional version was clearly inspired by village-based forms of exchange, where people co-operated mainly with kin or kith and knew them personally. The modern version follows a general transition to market economies and a constant influx of people into the cities, changing the format of social exchange. In both contexts the way you exchange directs the way you construe the arch-cheats.

In a similar way, in the French case described by Favret-Saada, the witch's tricks are *always* construed as attacks against the economic potential of the family. Favret-Saada notes that the husband-father, as the head of the household and the person who needs 'strength' to keep it working, is the prime target. This interpretation is general and unproblematic, as is the notion that the 'strength' is something that is usually invested in economic exchange. Non-witches invest their strength in growing crops, raising cattle, selling their produce. Witches are pushed by their excessive strength to cheat and reap benefits for which they have paid no costs.

Supernatural agents as exchange partners

To sum up, then, it is quite easy to understand the emotional intensity associated with misfortune – people are considering the possible loss of possessions or health or even life. But the particular *ways* in which they represent these situations is framed by their social-interaction inference systems; evil spirits are enforcers of unfair deals, the angered ancestors are enforcers of fair ones, evil-eye people are over-reacting cheat-detectors and witches are genuine cheats.

So why put gods and spirits in your explanations of misfortune? It is clearly not *just* because gods and spirits are powerful. First, people sometimes explain misfortune without any reference to any special agents: this is the case in evil-eye beliefs. Second, even when people consider agents with special powers they do not bother to imagine how these powers work. They are simply not interested in the process. But then consider the question in a slightly different way. People have inference systems for social interaction, which for instance guide their intuitions about exchange and fairness. We know that these systems are constantly active. In a social species like humans, many occurrences of good and bad fortune are the result of what others are up to. Your social environment is the source of protection, benefits and danger.

As a consequence, whenever a striking occurrence is represented in the mind, this produces an interpretation in terms of 'someone' acting. A scenario like this is generally entertained in the decoupled mode, as a conjecture that would make sense of what happened. Once it is entertained, such a scenario would make whatever representations you may have already about powerful agents out there much more relevant. If these representations describe supernatural agents (witches, gods, spirits) with special defined powers, this may be all the better as it provides a convenient identity for the 'someone' in the conjectural scenario.

So it is true to say that notions of gods and spirits help people understand misfortune. True but insufficient, because gods and spirits would be irrelevant if people had not *already* construed misfortune in such a way that it makes sense to include gods and spirits in its explanation. If your representation of misfortune generally treats it as an effect of violations of social exchange, it will potentially include any agent with whom you interact. But spirits and gods are precisely represented as engaging in social interaction with people, especially in social exchange. More important, they are represented as having all the strategic information relevant to interaction between people. So they are among the potential candidates for sources of misfortune, just like neighbours, relatives and envious partners, except more so. Gods and spirits in such a context are relevant but far from indispensable.

That misfortune is seen in terms of social interaction explains not just that supernatural agents are a source of danger but also that they can be perceived as protectors. This is a major theme in many religious doctrines. Indeed in some of them it is the major theme in people's representations of powerful gods. In the Psalmist's words, 'I will fear no evil, for thou art with me, thy rod and thy staff will comfort me' (Psalm 23:4). This is not exclusively a Christian notion, far from it. The Kwaio ancestors too are often considered as protectors. Comparing familiar doctrines with less familiar notions of ancestors helps understand that the emotional interpretation (there is a god who loves the believer) is only one possible variation on a theme that is much more common: that gods and spirits have a stake in what happens to people.

Gods and spirits are parasitic

Religious concepts are particularly successful because representing them requires mental capacities that we would activate, religion or not. At the beginning of this book I mentioned the way religious concepts are *parasitic* upon intuitive ontology. If you have all the inference systems that are found in a normal human brain, then some concepts become particularly easy to represent and generate all sorts of salient inferences. This is what makes a floating island or a bleeding statue or a talking tree likely to have some cultural success. But then we also have social-mind inference systems. We have a system of moral inferences that produces very special representations. It suggests that some qualities of behaviour in the context of social interaction are completely clear to any agent that has all the relevant information. Once you have such assumptions, as all normal children and adults do, the concept of an agent with full access to information becomes both very easy to represent – the necessary system is already in place – and rich in consequences. And this is why, far from religion supporting morality, as we might think, what happens is that our intuitive moral thinking makes some religious concepts easier to acquire, store and communicate to others. In the case of misfortune, our propensity to think of salient events in terms of social interaction creates a context where supposedly powerful agents become more convincingly powerful. In both cases religious concepts are parasitic, which is just a colourful way of describing what technically would be called a relevance effect. The concepts are parasitic in the sense that their successful transmission is greatly enhanced by mental capacities that would be there, gods or no gods.

Chapter Six

Why is religion about death?

Dead people, like vegetables, can be pickled or preserved. You can also abandon them to the beasts of the field, burn them like rubbish or bury them like treasure. From embalming to cremation, all sorts of techniques are used to do something with the corpse. But the point is, *something must be done*. This is constant and has been so for a long time. Early modern Humans, our direct ancestors, buried their dead from the Palaeolithic onwards. Even our Neanderthal cousins may have buried theirs, although the facts are still disputed. For obvious reasons, it is not easy at all to distinguish purposefully buried bodies among the sets of bones found under layers of sediment. For modern Humans, however, the evidence is much clearer, since people were buried or laid down with flowers, tools or other artefacts. Some archaeologists have pointed out that burying the dead may have been a measure of protection against scavengers attracted by decaying bodies. However, one must remember that early Humans were nomadic foragers, which would make it easy for them to avoid such invasion. Be it as it may, the fact that early Humans did decorate corpses, laid down the bodies in particular postures or buried them with flowers, aligned horns or tools would support the notion that some ritualisation of death is a very ancient human activity.[1]

Ancient findings are often reported as evidence for the claim that early modern Humans or even Neanderthals 'had religion'. Whether valid or not – I will return to that in another chapter – the inference shows how confused our common ideas about religion can be. We assume that burying the dead in a ritual way is evidence for supernatural concepts – ancestors, spirits, gods – because we find a connection between these two phenomena in most human societies. But what is that connection?

All religions, or so it seems, have something to say about death. People die but their shadows stay around. Or they die and wait for the Last Judgement. Or they come back in another shape. The connection between notions of supernatural agents and representations about death may take different forms in different human groups, but there is always *some* connection. Why is that so? One straightforward answer is that our concepts and emotions about death are quite simply the origin of religious concepts. Mortality, it would seem, naturally produces questions that religion answers and emotions that it helps alleviate.

We know that human minds are narrative or literary minds. That is, minds strive to represent events in their environment, however trivial, in terms of causal *stories*, sequences where each event is the result of some other event and paves the way for what is to follow. People everywhere make up stories, avidly listen to them, are good judges of whether they make sense. But the narrative drive goes deeper. It is embedded in our mental representation of whatever happens around us. Also, humans are born *planners,* their mental life is replete with considerations of what may happen, what will result if we do this rather than that. Having such decoupled thoughts may well be an adaptive trait, allowing a much better calculation of long-term risks than is available to other species, but it also implies that we represent vastly more life-threatening situations than we actually experience, and that the prospect of death is a very frequent item in our mental life.[2]

The notion of religion emerging from a primordial and universal fear of mortality is one of the most popular scenarios for the origin of religion. But it makes sense to ask some difficult questions that the common scenario glosses over. Do humans really fear mortality in general? Are religious representations really about what happens after death? How does a human mind represent a dead person? How does the mind recognise the difference between the dead and the living? What do concepts of supernatural agents add to our notions of death and dying?

Displaced terror and cold comfort

The most natural and the most common explanation of religion is this: Religious concepts are *comforting*, they provide some way of coping or coming to terms with the awful prospect of mortality by suggesting something more palatable than the bleak 'ashes to ashes'. Human beings do not just fear life-threatening circumstances and strive to avoid them as much as possible – this much is true of all animals, as a measure of how sophisticated they are at perceiving real and potential danger. Humans are also aware of the generality of death and of its inevitability.

Indeed, social psychologists observe that the very thought of general and inevitable mortality induces dramatic cognitive effects, often very remote from the topic of death itself. In experimental studies, subjects are asked to read a story or magazine article that highlights the inevitability of death. They are then presented with an apparently unrelated task, for instance to measure what would be the appropriate sentence for a particular theft, whether a minor offence should be punished, whether a description of some people's behaviour is consistent with their ethnic background. Their reactions are compared to those of subjects who read an innocuous piece of prose with no mention of mortality. The difference between these groups of subjects is always striking. Those who have read 'mortality-salient' stories tend to be much harsher in their reactions to socially deviant behaviour. They are less tolerant of even minor misdemeanours and would demand longer sentences and post higher bail. They react more strongly to offensive use of common cultural symbols like the American flag or a crucifix. They also become more defensive towards members of other groups and more prone to stereotype them, to find an illusory correlation between being a member of another social group and being a criminal. They develop stronger antipathy towards members of their own group who do not share their views. Awareness of mortality seems to trigger a socially protective attitude, where anyone who is even slightly different from us and any behaviour that does not conform to our cultural norms induces strong emotions. Why is that so?[3]

Some social psychologists speculate that our attachment to social identity, to the feeling that we are members of a group with shared norms, may in fact be a consequence of the terror induced by mortality. In this 'terror-management' account the principal source of motivation for human beings as for other animals is the evolutionary imperative to survive. Many cultural institutions – shared symbols, shared values, a sense of group-membership – may provide 'buffers' against this natural anxiety. According to terror-management theorists, cultural institutions are used as a (somewhat illusory) remedy to such feelings because they provide safety and protection. Criminals, outsiders and dissenters are all perceived as enemies of these institutions and therefore threats to our safety, which would explain the experimental results. Also, proponents of this explanation suggest that many cultural institutions, above all religious institutions, promise some kind of escape from death conditional on good behaviour, that is, on adherence to the local norms. Terror-management seems to provide a sophisticated and experimentally tested version of our common intuition that religion does provide a shield against mortality anxiety. After all, what religions seem to say about death is invariably that it is but a passage.[4]

However, the explanation is not really plausible. The connection between emotions, cultural institutions and our evolution is real. But to understand it we must consider more seriously the way evolution by natural selection fashions individuals and their dispositions, including their representations of death and mortality. The 'survival imperative' is not quite as self-evident as it seems. True, humans and most species avoid life-threatening circumstances, but is that really because there is an evolved drive to survive at all cost? Evolutionary biology suggests that the explanation for many behaviours and capacities lies not in the organism's drive to survive but in a drive to pass on its genes. Some environments frequently present an organism with a choice between either surviving but failing to pass on its genes or preserving the genes without surviving. In such situations self-sacrifice genes spread, as explained in the previous chapter.

So if human emotions are explained by the history of the species, we should expect a more complex set of fears and anxieties, as there are many different kinds of threat to genetic transmission. The potential loss of offspring would be one major component of this panoply, but so would a failure to attract one's parents' attention and investment, the absence of a sufficiently high level of trust in one's social network, the fact that one is not considered attractive or the fact that one is clearly at the bottom of the social ladder. All these present a definite threat to genetic transmission and are clearly connected to anxiety, *but* these situations are all specific and require specific strategies. Complex organisms do not survive by having a general 'death-avoidance behaviour' programmed into their minds, because different life-threatening situations require different responses.

Although terror-management is too primitive an explanation, it helps us frame the question in a way that will prove fruitful. There *are* emotional programmes and mental representations associated with death. The representations are complicated and not entirely consistent, because different mental systems are activated by death-related thoughts. It is only against this background that we can

understand how religious representations of death become significant.

Considering this mental background should help us solve several
mysteries in the religious treatment of the topic. Anthropologists are
generally unimpressed by the idea that religion provides comfort,
and this is for good reason. First, they know that in many human
cultures the religious take on death is anything but reassuring. We do
not need to use exotic examples to prove the point. A serious
Christian with a serious belief in predestination does not really
illustrate the idea that religion provides a buffer against anxiety. In
fact many religious rituals and religious myths provide little comfort
against an anxiety that they seem to emphasise and enhance rather
than dampen. Second, most religions simply do not promise a
premium in the form of salvation or eternal bliss to well-behaved
citizens. In many human groups, dead people become ancestors or
spirits. This is represented as the normal outcome of human life, not
as a special prize awarded for high morality. Finally and most
importantly, what religions say about death is very often not centred
on mortality in general, but on very specific facts about dying and
dead people. Which is why we should embark on a short
anthropological tour of the evidence.

Death-rituals: something must be done

In every single group where they have worked, anthropologists have
been able to elicit some description of what happens after death
(often from baffled people wondering why anyone would ask such a
question) and what is to be done when people die, a much more
sensible question. As I have said several times, few people in the
world indulge in speculative theology. Their representations of death
are activated when particular people die and *because* of that event, not
as a form of contemplative reflection on existence. Also, people's
explicit notions only give us part of those mental processes. What
goes without saying generally goes unsaid. This is why anthropologists do not just ask people about their conceptions of life and

death but also observe how the death of a group-member triggers particular behaviours. In any human group, there are prescribed rules and common implicit norms about what is to be done upon such an occasion. There is a wide spectrum here, from places where such prescriptions are minimal and the representations associated extremely bare, to places where far-fetched death-rituals are associated with precise and complicated descriptions of what death is.[5]

Hunter-gatherers, whose economy depends entirely on wild plants and game, generally have fairly simple death-rituals for the simple reason that they have few resources to invest in complex ceremonies. Their peasant neighbours, who generally despise and fear them, say that they just abandon corpses to wild beasts. (This is what my Fang interlocutors often said about Pygmies.) This, however, is a gross distortion. Consider for instance the funerary ceremonies of the Batek, a loose federation of hunting-gathering groups of Malaysia. The corpse is wrapped in the finest sarong available, bedecked with flowers and leaves, and placed on a comfortable sleeping mat. The mourners then carry the body on a stretcher to a distant place in the forest, far away from familiar paths. The men build a platform and lay down the corpse there, after it has been covered with sweet-smelling herbs. The family generally put a number of artefacts on the platform, such as a smoking-pipe, some tobacco, a blowpipe and darts, etc. They blow tobacco smoke on the head of the deceased. After the stretcher has been lifted on top of the platform, people plant sticks around the base and recite spells over them to deter tigers from shaking the platform. The family then come back periodically to check the corpse and monitor the process of decomposition, as long as there are any remnants of the body. On such visits they generally burn incense next to the platform. This lasts until even the bones have disappeared, probably taken away by scavengers. Note how seemingly simple practices of this kind are in fact ritualised. You do not just take a corpse to the forest. You must do it as a group, people sing and recite particular spells, they must place particular objects next to the body.[6]

One frequent characteristic of more complex death-rituals is the practice of *double-funerals*. The first set of rituals is organised immediately after death, it is concerned with the fact that the dead body is dangerous, and in practice it generally concludes with a first burial. The second part, which may occur months or years later, is supposed to turn the deceased body into a more stable, proper, less dangerous entity. In many places this is the point at which people disinter the dead, wipe the bones clear of any remaining flesh and put them in their final resting place. The Berawan in the Philippines have such double rituals described by anthropologist Peter Metcalf. After death, the corpse is exposed on a specially constructed seat in front of the house, so all close and distant kin can come over and inspect it or touch it. During this period the rest of the community are supposed to gather every night, sing and dance and generally make as much noise as possible. People frequently talk to the corpse, asking why he or she 'chose' to leave, offering the corpse a cigarette or some food. This is concluded by the burial proper. In some cases the corpse is placed in a coffin and laid down in a graveyard. In other cases relatives put the body in a jar to accelerate the decomposition. A pipe is inserted in the bottom of the jar to collect fluids. As Metcalf notes, this procedure is also used for making rice-wine, except that here the object of interest is the solid sediment, not the fluids. After a period of weeks or months, decomposition has gone far enough for the remains to be taken out of the jar or coffin, and the bones separated from whatever flesh is left. This marks the beginning of a new ten-day ritual and much chanting. The songs call for the deceased to wash, put on nice clothes and journey up a river towards the land of the dead. The bones are finally either buried or conserved in a wooden mausoleum.[7]

Why such complicated rites? Anthropologist Robert Hertz noted that double-funerals make death-rituals very similar to *rites of passage*, like marriage or initiation. In initiation for instance, a first ceremony usually marks the opening of the transformation process that turns, for instance, boys into men. There is then a period of seclusion, during which all sorts of prohibitions are imposed on the young candidates, as well as various ordeals. Lastly, a formal re-entry ceremony marks their accession to a new status. They have become fully-fledged adults. Double-funerals seem to work according to the same logic. A living person is, obviously, a member of a social group. So is a dead ancestor, since the dead provide the connection between various living people, as well as authority (We must behave the way the ancestors want) and power (Misfortune is often a result of offending the ancestors). Now the *passage* between these two stages is what the rituals emphasise and organise. The transition is made conceptually clearer by emphasising the departure and arrival points.[8]

After this stage, representations about the dead are markedly different. In some groups the dead are not construed as part of social relations any more. Their social role lasts no longer than people's memories of the dead. Describing representations of the souls of the dead in the Amazon, anthropologist Edoardo Viveiros de Castro writes: 'The participation of the dead in the discourse of the group lasts only as long as the experiential memory of the living. A deceased soul only remembers those who remember him and only reveals himself to those who saw him alive.' In other places the dead remain as ancestors, but most features of their personal histories are lost. The dead as ancestors often become generic. As anthropologist Meyer Fortes put it, 'Ancestors behave in exactly the same ways, in the ways expected of them and permitted to them in the ancestral cult, quite irrespective of what their lifetime characters might have been. The ancestor who was a devoted father . . . is divined to be the source of illness, misfortune and disturbance in his descendants' lives in exactly the same way as is an ancestor who was a scoundrel and spendthrift.' What remains is their genealogical identity, serving as a reference point to the social group: knowledge of who the dead were supports our inferences about relations with close or distant kin. This is why, as anthropologist Jack Goody noted, ancestor-cults are particularly important where people inherit material property from the ancestors, especially so in groups where they must manage that inheritance as a collective.[9]

The body as the issue

Whatever their variety, behaviours that accompany death highlight several general traits of human thinking in this domain:

People have vague notions about death and the dead in general. Although people in many different societies are in constant interaction with the dead, their conceptions of what the dead are like, where they are and what they do is often extremely vague. To return to the Kwaio ancestors, Roger Keesing noted how very few people bothered to think about the exact process whereby those who die get to become ancestors. The ones who did consider this had personal intuitions, often less than coherent, but most did not see the point of such questions. Note that these are people who talk to the ancestors every day and interpret most events of their lives in terms of what the ancestors want and what they do. As David Pocock puts it, 'the villagers of Sundarana [in Gujarat, North India], like the majority of peoples known to social anthropologists, were very vague about the after-life'.[10]

. . . but people have more detailed representations of the recently dead, of what they can do to the living. The presence of the recently dead is more likely to be dangerous than reassuring. For one thing, people have many accounts of how the dead are not quite dead; in some form or other their presence is still felt, but this is not, as the comfort theory implies, a welcome presence, far from it. As for the really dead, as it were, the people who have gone beyond that stage, the theories are often very vague. This is true even in places with literate specialists and theologians. For instance, the famous Tibetan *Book of the Dead* is called *Bar-Do*, which means 'between-two' and is, precisely, about the transition between this world and another one, not so much about the details of that other one. Most representations about death and the dead are concerned with the transitional period between the event of death and some further state. The dead are 'sent off on a

journey', they are 'prepared for the voyage' and so on. The metaphors change but their essential point is similar. The rituals are about a transitional period.

Rituals are about the consequences for the living. This is important because it does not quite fit the notion that our conceptions of death are all about the anxiety of mortality. People have feelings about their own eventual death, and they have rituals about death, but the rituals are about other people's deaths. In case you find that self-evident, compare with fertility rituals. People are worried about their crops and they have rituals supposed to help crops grow. But in the case of death we find a very different situation. If mortality anxiety really was the point of all this, we would expect the rituals to be about how to avert death or delay the inevitable. But that is not the case at all. The rituals are about what may happen to the living if they do not handle the corpses as prescribed.

The rituals are all about corpses. What we call funerary rituals are overwhelmingly about what to do with the body. In these rituals, it seems that what creates anguish or other such emotional states is very much the presence of dead bodies. Again, this may seem self-evident but it is not clear how all this would fit the 'anxiety' account. Why does it matter so much that the dead should be thoroughly broiled or carefully pickled? There are of course local explanations for each particular prescription. But since we find *some* prescription in all human groups there must be some more general reason.

What makes anthropology worthwhile is that it forces us to question what would seem self-evident. We know that people the world over follow special ritualised recipes to handle dead bodies. We do not usually look for the causes of that behaviour, because we think the rituals in question express some definite, explicit beliefs about death and mortality. But then it seems that in many places beliefs about death are in fact quite vague; only beliefs about dead bodies seem to be definite. So instead of adding our own vague hypotheses to people's vague concepts, we should perhaps consider the facts that are right under our nose. The reason why people feel the need to handle corpses, the reason why they have done so for hundreds of thousands of years may well be *something to do with the corpses themselves*. Or rather, something to do with the way a human mind functions when faced with that very particular kind of object.

Obviously, the body of a close relative is the object of intense and complex feelings; the body of an unknown person may trigger different kinds of emotion, but is unlikely to leave us indifferent. Because these reactions are intense and emotional, we may think that they have nothing much to do with computations and with the way the brain represents information. But that would be wrong. Emotions are complex programmes in the mind. They are activated when other systems in the mind produce particular results. So it might be of help to consider the different systems involved in representing a dead person. I say 'different systems' because, as we saw in previous chapters, any situation (however trivial) is treated by different inference systems that handle different aspects of it. What shapes the emotional reaction is a *combination* of different mental processes. A dead body is a biological thing. We have special systems in the mind that handle some biological properties of living things and they are probably active and describing that object too. Also, it is a biological thing in a very special state, and some mental systems may be activated by what corpses look like. Finally, a corpse is a person. The mental systems that describe persons will be active too. All these special representations produced in the basement may better explain what is so special about dealing with a corpse.

Pollution and its causes

As John Ruskin once put it, perhaps under the influence of a strong stimulant: 'I don't believe any one of you would like to live in a room with a murdered man in the cupboard, however well preserved chemically – even with a sunflower growing out of the top of his head.' Quite. But the question is to explain, perhaps with less flamboyance but more scientific precision, this general aversion, not just to murdered men but to corpses in general.[11]

Although modern ways of life somehow shield us from the ghastly facts, dead bodies are biological objects in a process of decomposition. This is not lost on human minds, hence the widespread notion that corpses are intrinsically impure or polluting. As an ancient Zoroastrian text stipulates, anyone who touches a corpse is polluted 'to the end of his nails, and unclean for ever and ever'. This notion of being 'polluted' by contact with corpses is of course variable in its intensity, but it is fairly general.[12]

Corpses are even said to contaminate the air around them. Among Cantonese Chinese, 'white affairs' specialists (a euphemism for undertakers) are said to be so polluted by their work that most other people will not even talk to them for fear of receiving some of that pollution back. A dead body contaminates the environment by releasing 'killing air'. When there is a death in the village people promptly take home their young children, and even their domestic animals, thought to be particularly sensitive to such pollution. This is of course not confined to China. Describing the death-rituals of the Merina in Madagascar, Maurice Bloch notes that 'as long as the corpse is still wet and decomposition is therefore still taking place it is supremely polluting and any contact however indirect requires ritual cleaning'.[13]

In some places the disgust and danger of dead bodies is seen in a way that requires the intervention of specialists, supposed to wallow in the pollution and absorb it. In the old kingdom of Nepal, upon the death of the king a priest would be called, whose duty was to sleep in the king's bed, smoke his cigarettes and use his possessions. He could also order his way around the royal household. However, the royal cooks would contaminate all his food with a paste made from bones of the deceased king's head. The point of all this was that the priest would (quite literally in this case) incorporate the corpse and its impurity. Only a high-caste Brahmin could be pure enough to absorb that much pollution. After this period of bizarre intimacy with the king's Body Natural, the Brahmin was promptly expelled from the kingdom, indeed frog-marched to its borders and often beaten up, probably to make sure he would not stop on his way or consider coming back.[14]

The pollution of the dead is also the reason why, in so many places in the world, grave-digging and the handling of corpses are carried out by a specialised, ritually avoided and generally despised caste. This is the case in West Africa, where these specialists are generally considered unclean, must marry within the caste and avoid direct contact with regular folk. The same people also forge iron and make pots (both are considered undignified occupations), but the contact with corpses really is what makes them impure and dangerous. In central Africa where blacksmiths are not in charge of burials, they are high-status craftsmen with no pollution. There is evidence for similar norms in the Mediterranean. For instance Artemidorus of Daldis wrote that dreaming you are a tanner is a bad omen because tanners are also undertakers. In many places undertakers are confined to special neighbourhoods outside the walls of the city lest they pollute the rest of the community.[15]

People find all these concepts, however vague, intuitively adequate because they already have the intuition that there is something to avoid in a decomposing corpse. Notions of pollution seem a direct expression of intuitions delivered by the Contagion system described in chapter 3. This system is mainly concerned with the fear of contact with unseen contaminants. It obeys special principles that are not found in other mental systems. It specifies that the source of danger is present even if it cannot be detected; that all types of contact with the source may transmit the contaminant; that the 'dose' of contaminant is irrelevant. Now these are very much the implicit inferences people use when dealing with corpses. What makes undertakers impure or revolting is that they handle corpses. It does not matter that no one has a precise idea *why* corpses would be polluting. In the same way, it does not really matter whether these specialists touch the corpses or breathe fumes from the decaying bodies, or have any other kind of contact with the corpses. It does not really matter either how much actual contact takes place or how often. All these assumptions are completely self-evident to most human minds, and I think this may be explained simply by the fact that contact with the body is immediately perceived as similar to contact with any obvious source of pathogens.

This is why it may be misguided to see too much symbolism or magical thinking in the quasi-universal avoidance of corpses. People's contagion system is activated, not because the dead are polluting for some metaphysical reason, but more directly because they *actually* are a dangerous source of pathogens. What makes the avoidance sound symbolic or mystical are the explicit notions ('bad air', 'impurity') people invoke to explain intuitions they had to start with. The concepts are notoriously vague and this is not too surprising, because we often have very vague explicit concepts in situations where our mental basement systems produce very precise intuitions. For evolutionary reasons humans may be rather good at detecting definite sources of contamination, yet remain very vague in their explicit reasons for avoiding them.

Activation of the contagion system may well be one major reason why we find these special attitudes to dead bodies the world over, why special handling of corpses is present from the earliest stages of modern human cultures, and why it takes on this overtone of urgency and great though undefined danger. But this is not the whole explanation. People do not perform elaborate rituals to dispose of all sources of biological pollution. Another, obviously important component of people's emotional reaction is that a corpse is not just a mass of polluting agents, but also a living thing that is not live any longer, a conspecific, and very often a previously known person.

Death, predation and intuition

The connection between representations of death and representations of supernatural agents is often considered as a question of metaphysics, of how people consider their existence in general. But notions of death are also based on a mental representation of biological processes. A good way to evaluate our intuitive understanding of such processes is to study how this develops in young children. Psychologists used to think that death was virtually incomprehensible to young children. It is true that such questions as 'What happens at death?' or 'Where do dead people go?' will leave most young children baffled. On the basis of this kind of reaction Jean Piaget and other developmental psychologists concluded that the whole domain was beyond the grasp of children.

However, this is unfair to the children, for several reasons. One is that you cannot really test a cognitive system by asking explicit questions. Children may have intuitions about death without being able to explicate them. Second, many of the questions Piaget and his colleagues asked children were of a kind that no adult could really answer in a precise and satisfactory manner. Even if you have a very definite theological answer, the question Where do dead people go? really is a difficult one. There was another complicating factor in these tests. Psychologists were wondering whether children had the concept of death as a biological phenomenon. But they asked questions about *people*. Now children's concepts about live things often require a sharp distinction between people and other animals. In some cases the psychologists tried to make the questions more natural or easier by asking the child to think about dead people they had known, which should in fact confuse matters even further for reasons I will explain below. In other words, the results seemed plausible but the methodology may have been flawed.

Indeed, children produce much more precise intuitions when they are tested indirectly, for instance if they are asked to predict the outcome of a particular chain of events, or determine which of the characters in a story (some of whom have been killed) are still able to move, or will continue growing up, or will be able to talk, etc. For 'dying' is a complex concept that combines the end of biological processes like growing up, the impossibility of animate motion, the absence of goal-directed behaviour, the absence of mental representations. These different aspects are handled by different mental systems, so understanding what is special about a corpse may also require different types of inferences.

A direct effect of this combination of various systems is that children tend to produce different intuitions on scenarios of human death (where all the systems mentioned above are activated at the same time) and animal death (where animacy is the main focus). Developmental psychologist Clark Barrett pursued this difference and tried to evaluate the extent to which children's intuitions are particularly focused on contexts of *predation*. Reasoning from an evolutionary standpoint, Barrett thought that it would be very strange indeed if a young mind was really unable to produce inferences on such a crucial problem. Humans and their hominid ancestors have been both predators and prey for a very long time. They probably have mental dispositions for understanding what happens in such contexts. Indeed, Barrett found that children's intuitions about predation stories reveal a much more sophisticated understanding of death than had previously been thought. Even four year olds seemed to understand that what happens as a result of successful predation is that (1) the prey cannot move any more, (2) it will not grow any more, (3) it will not be active and (4) this is irreversible. In other words, in this limited context, children seemed to activate the precise expectations that constitute the adult understanding of death.[16]

If children have such intuitions from the age of three or four, why is it that they are so confused when they are asked about the death of *people*? In particular, about their relatives? And why is it that even adults find theoretical questions about death so confusing? Barrett's results confirm that death is handled by different cognitive systems, so that you can elicit clear intuitions from children only by getting them to focus on one particular aspect. This is true for adults too. To get a better picture of all this, we must move on to another crucial aspect of the dying process, the connections with our implicit conception of what a person is.

What is a person?

For a long time, anthropologists have been intrigued by cultural differences in how people define what a person is, what makes her or him different from inanimate objects, from animals, from other persons. As happens frequently in anthropology, what seems a simple enough question reveals very complex thoughts, not all of which are easily expressed. I could say that I have life, which a rock does not have, that I have sentience, which a worm does not seem to have, that I am a particular person, which sets me apart from other human beings, that I have a body which is also different from other bodies. To be a person, then, one needs to have these different *components*: life, sentience, personal identity. Losing life would make me a corpse, losing sentience would make me a zombie, and losing my body would turn me into a ghost.

The way these components are described differs a lot from one place to another. For instance, Keesing reports that the Kwaio see a person as composed of a body, a 'breath-that-talks' and a 'shadow'. It is the 'breath-that-talks' which goes away with death and then resides with the ancestors. Among the Batek of Malaysia there are slightly different concepts. A person is made up of *lih* (the body), *ñawa* (life) and *bayang* (shadow). Only humans and other breathing animals have *ñawa*. The *bayang* is not just the shadow, for plants do not have it. It is 'a soft, transparent entity which inhabits the entire body', as Endicott reports, that leaves the body upon death and defines personal identity.[17]

People generally use conventional metaphors to describe the various components, which is not a surprise as it is quite difficult to express what defines identity. Different individuals may have a slightly different take on how the metaphors should be understood. For instance, some people assume that the 'breath' that defines life is what makes living things live, while others think that breathing is just an effect of being alive. Also, when people make statements about such matters there is a lot which for them just goes without saying, and therefore is not said at all. For instance, the Batek do not *say* that each person has an individual shadow, although this can be inferred from what they say.

There is one major reason, in my view, why such concepts are often vague and their interpretation idiosyncratic. They are about domains of reality for which we have very specific intuitions that are not delivered by conscious, deliberate processes. So our explicit notions of person-components may be a feeble attempt to describe explicitly some processes that happen intuitively (in the same way as our common notion of 'momentum' is a feeble attempt to explain our very precise physical intuitions).

The first inference system involved in our intuitions about persons is the *Intuitive-Psychology system*. When we interact with people, it is on the basis of what this system tells us of their representations. That is, the system creates automatically a particular description of what a situation is like as seen by the people we interact with. It also leads us to imagine what inferences they are likely to draw from what happens and from what we say, and so forth.

Another important system is the *Animacy system*. This is quite different from the Intuitive-Psychology system because it does not require the same input and does not produce inferences about the same aspects of the person. The Animacy system is activated by the sight of any object that moves in a purposeful manner. It produces expectations and inferences about animals and persons. For instance, as Clark Barrett's experiments suggest, the Animacy system would produce very different expectations for an animal that has been the object of successful predation and one that escaped. The former is not expected to move, to react to what's around it, to act in pursuance of any goal, to grow, to move of its own accord, etc. The one that escaped is intuitively expected to move about, have goals, etc.

Another crucial dimension of any interaction with people is, obviously, who the person is, who we are dealing with. This is so completely obvious to all human minds that it is difficult to realise that this is to a large extent a consequence of the kind of animals we are. The main system that helps us understand who we are dealing with constitutes what we could call a *Person-File system*, a kind of mental address-book or *Who's Who?* of the person's social environment. This system keeps 'files' on every single person we interact with, with memories of past interaction episodes. The system also files people's general dispositions, facts about their histories, etc. It keeps records of different people as different entries in a vast biographical encyclopaedia. Keeping a file is no use unless you can retrieve it at short notice, and retrieve the right one.

Several other systems provide information that help the Person-File system identify the person we are dealing with: there is a *Face-Recognition system* that can store thousands of different faces and associate the relevant file with the relevant face-appearance. (Note what a great effort it requires to remember the names of all the people we meet socially, yet what an easy task it is to associate the faces with what they said, what they do, how we like them and so on.) Other information can be used: we also identify people's voices quite distinctively, as well as their gait and other such cues.

When different systems are not in harmony

Different systems produce inferences from different cues and produce expectations about different aspects of a person or animal, but they all exchange information. This requires that this information is coherent. For instance, if the Face-Recognition system delivers information that a person is familiar, the Person-File system should try to retrieve a file for the person. If the Animacy system states that the person is moving in a goal-directed manner, the Intuitive-Psychology system should produce inferences about what the goals are, based on what information is accessible to the person. In general, information from one system also helps correcting or fine-tuning information from another one. If your Person File says that So-and-so is an avid eater, the fact that they charge right across the room to the kitchen when they come to see you is immediately translated in terms of goals (getting to the refrigerator) and mental representations (a hope that some delicacies will be found in there).

This picture of the mind as orchestrating different sources of evidence and different inference systems would predict that incoherent output from any system, or a lack of collaboration between these systems, will wreak havoc with ordinarily smooth operation. This is indeed what happens in a variety of pathological forms of brain impairment caused by infection or strokes or closed-brain injury.

Prosopagnosia is one of these pathologies. Patients cannot recall who people are by looking at their faces. It is not that their visual abilities are generally impaired. Indeed, in all sorts of other visual tasks, they can discriminate between different shapes and images, and they can recall associations between images. It is only faces that pose a special problem. Note that this deficit is generally limited to *human* faces. One patient who became a sheep-farmer after becoming impaired, could correctly identify the individual 'faces' of his own sheep. The impairment is not extended to all aspects of persons, as voices and other contextual information are still identified correctly. A spectacular demonstration of this limited impairment is that patients are sometimes better than non-patients at particular tasks. For instance, faces seen upside-down are particularly difficult to identify for most people. (To test that, open a newspaper upside-down and look at the photographs of various politicians or film-stars. The chances are you will not be able to recognise them till you turn the paper the right way up.) Patients are presented with several faces the right way up and asked to match them to various upside-down images. They are sometimes better than normal subjects at this task. Why is that? In normal subjects, face-information is not handled by the same systems as other complex visual shapes. It is sent to special brain areas. These require a particular configuration of features (eyes above nose, etc.) and are just confused by stimuli that do not conform to these requirements. By contrast, in patients the face-information is sent to brain areas that deal with complex visual shapes in general. These brain areas are quite good at handling rotation, inversion, etc., which would explain the patients' good performance with inverted stimuli. In prosopagnosia, the Face-Recognition system either does not deliver any output any more because it is off or delivers output that the Person-File system for some reason cannot handle. We do not know exactly how the brain injury translates into this strange impairment, but it clearly affects a separate system for human face-recognition.[18]

In a rarer form of impairment, patients recognise the faces (they identify the person), the Person-File system retrieves the relevant information, yet something goes wrong. The patients have a strong intuition that the person they are dealing with cannot be the *real* one. In this Capgras syndrome, the patient ends up suspecting that the 'real' person has been abducted by aliens, is possessed by spirits, has sent a clone or look-alike or twin to take her part, etc. In this case, there are indices from face-recognition (as well as other consistent cues, such as voice) that the person should be identified as XYZ, but the Person-File system still does not deliver a clear answer to the question of who the person is. This kind of problem may be caused by the fact that two distinct systems are activated in Person-File: one system simply keeps track of the facts about the person we are dealing with, the other system associates emotional responses to activating one file rather than another. The pathology, in this model, would stem from the fact that if the emotions are absent, then the Person-File system does not accept the identification delivered by the Face-Recognition system. (Incidentally, Capgras syndrome patients sometimes have these delusions about a pet, showing that the Person-File and its connections to emotional response are not exclusively geared to actual persons, but to living things treated by the brain as persons.) In a dramatic form of such delusions, some patients find their whole environment strangely unreal which leads them to think they may be actually dead.[19]

In chapter 3, I described a third kind of person-interaction pathology: the inability of the Intuitive-Psychology system to provide adequate descriptions of other people's mental states. This is found typically in autistic subjects. This too is a very specific impairment.

Autistic children seem able to recognise some goal-directed action. But they have great difficulty in representing other agents' beliefs or objects of attention. This may be because one of the systems (Intuitive-Psychology) is not operating, or does not deliver inferences in a format that other systems could handle, or does not have access to the representations created by the other systems. Again, it is difficult to judge, in the present state of neuro-psychological knowledge, which of these is the case. However, what we do know is that the impairment is limited and that it affects only particular types of inferences in social interaction. People who are mentally retarded are not autistic: they may have difficulties com-puting complex social situations, but they are attuned to the social nature of such situations, they know that other people see the world from their own perspectives, and so on.

To sum up, interaction with other people requires delicate inter-connection and calibration between different systems that focus on different aspects of a person. I have described conditions in which this breaks down, which are all pathological. But there are objects in the world that can put us in such dissociative states, that is, objects that can trigger incompatible intuitions and inferences in the different systems.

Corpses induce dissociation

Like metamorphosis, dead bodies are to some extent counter-intuitive yet real. The difference is that biological metamorphosis is a familiar and amusing but not too consequential part of our natural environment. Dead bodies on the other hand are a vastly more important part of our social environment. They are represented in ways that both warrant some common inferences about social interaction, but at the same time contradict these inferences. So they create the kind of dissociation that in other contexts we see in people with brain damage or other forms of cognitive impairment.

Being faced with dead persons triggers a complex set of inferences from various systems, and these do not seem to match. The sight of a dead person certainly activates particular inferences from the Animacy system. When we see dead animals, we have similar intuitions. We intuitively assume that there is a time at which the animal will cease to move for good, and that it does not have goals or objects of attention after that. For persons, the situation is a bit different because the Animacy system and the Intuitive-Psychology system typically exchange lots of information with the Person-File system.

Now something happens with the death of known people that is both familiar as an experience and rather strange once it is described in terms of these systems. On the one hand, the Animacy system is quite clear in its output concerning such persons. They are ex-persons, they have no goals, etc. On the other hand, it seems that the Person-File system just cannot 'shut off'. It keeps producing inferences about the particular person, on the basis of information about past interaction with that person, as if the person were still around. A symptom of this incoherence is the hackneyed phrase we have all heard or used at funerals: 'He would have liked it this way'. That is, he would have approved of the way we have conducted his funeral. As many people have felt as they uttered this, there is something compelling and yet absurd about such an idea. Judging whether ritual arrangements are appropriate is a typical action of live beings, the only way you can have your own funeral is by becoming a dead body, and dead bodies do not pass judgement on things, indeed do not do anything. Still, the thought occurs and seems somehow natural because our Person-File system is still active and its inferences are produced without using the information provided by the Animacy system. It is when we confront the two sources of information that the sentence becomes absurd.

Another symptom of this dissociation between inference systems may be the feeling of guilt that so often surrounds funerals. Why feel guilty when we bury relatives? No good explanation springs to mind. Perhaps this familiar experience makes more sense in terms of cognitive dissociation. Disposing of the corpse is mandated by some mental systems for which this makes sense because the body is represented as an inanimate object (Animacy system) and as a signal of danger (Contagion system, Predation system). But disposing of the corpse is also handling a person who is *not* yet absent, as far as our Person-File systems are concerned.

We all run Person-File based inferences on dead people. We are angry at dead people, we approved of what they did, scold them for having done this or that and very often resent them for dying in the first place. Now note how all these feelings are about beings for whom the Animacy system would undercut such inferences immediately. In other words, being faced with a dead person whom we knew is very much like being affected by one of the dissociative pathologies I described above. That is, one of the inference systems is busy producing inferences while another delivers output that excludes such inferences.

Philosophers and anthropologists often assume that death poses a special conceptual problem to humans mainly because humans are incorrigible *dualists*. That is, we all intuitively feel that body and mind are things of a different nature. This would make it difficult to understand how a mind can disappear as a result of the body's destruction. But the cognitive puzzle created by corpses is in fact much more specific than that. It does not result from abstract conceptions of the body and the mind but from our intuitions, and from the particular way in which some of our inference systems work. You could very well be a dualist and accept that minds go extinct as bodies cease breathing. What creates a special problem is not the notion that the 'person' goes on, but the conflicting intuitions delivered by two systems, both focused on persons, one dealing with animacy and the other with person identification.

We can now better understand why there are so many death-rituals and why, although they take so many different forms, they generally centre on prescriptions for what is to be done with the dead body. This is indeed the central question. People's representations are focused on the dead body's passage to another state of being, rather than about detailed descriptions of the afterlife. Also, this account makes better sense of the two stages of death-passage often noted in such rites. These two stages may correspond to two different periods in terms of psychological activity: a first period during which the living are still in the discrepant state described here, followed by a second stage where they simply have memories of the dead person, but these are gradually fading and do not create Person-File inferences any longer.

Focused grief and fear vs. general terror

Grief is the aspect we usually mention first when thinking about representations of death, yet it makes sense to consider it last. Grief is a very special emotion because it is about the kind of dissociative object I described here, about a person about whom several mental systems give inconsistent intuitions. This naturally does not explain grief, only its special tenor where dead people are concerned.

Why we feel grief at all is not really very well understood. However, taking our evolutionary history into account makes sense of some aspects of the feeling. Losing a child, but also losing caring parents or losing grandparents who care for your offspring, are obvious genetic catastrophes. In these seemingly cold-hearted genetic calculations, losing a young child is a real disaster; but losing an infant is less damaging (because a lesser investment is wasted); losing a teenager is the worst possible situation (all investment is lost *and* a source of genetic transmission is gone); and losing an aged parent should be less traumatic. There is some evidence that the relative intensity of grief (always a difficult thing to measure, but large-scale comparisons allow some statistical inferences) does correspond to these predictions. But these are not the only people we lose. Because we are an intensely social species, and because we have lived in small groups for so long, the loss of any member of a group is a huge loss in terms of valuable information and potential co-operation.[20]

All these evolutionary considerations may illuminate why we

grieve for some people rather than others, but they still do not explain why we should experience such intensely negative feelings in the first place. Biologists speculate that many negative emotions probably help fine-tune behaviour. That we mull over what might have been may help in making subsequent choices. For instance, that we bitterly regret having mistreated someone may provide the emotional urge to accommodate other people better in the future. All this should be irrelevant since the dead will not be partners in any actual social interaction any more. However, this last point may be precisely what is not entirely obvious to human minds. As I suggested, in the presence of a dead body some mental systems still function as if the person was still around. So we have no general explanation for grief, but we may better understand it if we realise that death is simply represented as a termination only by *some* parts of our mental systems.

Grief is not the only process whereby dead bodies create strong emotional effects. As Clark Barrett's experiments showed, our understanding of death is mostly based on intuitions of animacy developed in the context of predation. Although modern-day children have little if any familiarity with the actual situation, this is the context where their intuitions are most readily elicited and most definite. This provides us with a different context in which to under-stand the emotions involved. Proponents of 'terror-management' theory claimed that mortality in general is a source of terror. The actual study of inference systems would suggest that being a prey is a much more salient source of intuitions and emotions. In actual fact, dead prey are only a subset of dead bodies. But for our intuitive systems it may be the other way around; a prey is a well-understood object, so that other dead bodies are represented in terms of an analogy with prey. So inasmuch as the sight of a corpse triggers associations with anguishing realities, this may be because a dead person is, to some extent, represented as the victim of a successful predation.

Dead bodies and supernatural agents

In the first chapter I suggested that many religious phenomena are around because of a conspiracy of relevance. That is, once a particular theme or object triggers rich inferences in a variety of different mental systems, it is certainly more likely to be the object of great cultural attention and elaboration. This certainly seems to be the case for dead bodies. Their presence activates different systems for different reasons. They are thought to be polluting because this is a relevant conceptual interpretation of the intuitions delivered by our Contagion system; they are fascinating because different mental systems deliver inconsistent intuitions about them; they are emotionally salient because of our personal relations to them; they are scary because they activate mental schemas for predator-avoidance.

Consider again the catalogue of supernatural templates. One of the categories was that of an inanimate object, generally an artefact but also a part of the environment, that is said to have intentional properties. For instance, people will pray to a particular statue. In Severi's examples, a Cuna shaman talks to a row of statuettes supposed to understand what he says in their special language. In many places, people will consider that a particular rock or a tree has the capacity to understand various situations and how people behave. All these supernatural notions require special effort because their counter-intuitive qualities are, to a large extent, largely unpersuasive. To think that a madonna can cure the sick or that statuettes will fight against spirits requires that people combine many counter-intuitive stories in such a way that the object indeed becomes attention-grabbing. This is hard work, as it were.

But dead bodies are special because they are not created by people, it requires no special effort to encounter them, and they inevitably create obvious cognitive effects. Dead bodies are salient whatever we want to think about them. They create special cognitive effects by the very fact that different systems involved in the representation of persons create incompatible representations, with the added intensity of grief, combined with the fear of predation.

We do not need to imagine any special 'metaphysical' reasons in people's minds that would lead them to fear the recently dead and to find any contact with them awe-inspiring or polluting. These intuitions and emotions are delivered by evolved systems that would be there, whether or not we had any special religious conception of the dead. In the same way, we do not need religious ideologies to have a confused notion that the recently dead are both indubitably present and remote. This confused impression stems from two systems in our minds that deliver incompatible intuitions about dead persons. None of this really depends on religious concepts. Dead persons are special objects because of a combination of different intuitions. While one system in the mind represents them as dangerous sources of unseen and barely describable danger, another system is producing inferences about interaction with them, yet another assumes they cannot have any goals or interaction, and finally the circumstances of their death may themselves inspire fear.

We should not be surprised that the souls of the dead or their 'shadows' or 'presence' are the most widespread kind of supernatural agent the world over. This equation

the dead as seen by our inference systems = the supernatural agents

is the simplest and therefore most successful way in which concepts of supernatural agency are transmitted. In many places, obviously, this simple equation is combined with more complex representations of other agents like gods or spirits that are not ex-persons. But it seldom happens that such complications actually *replace* the direct equation.

In some cases, representations of the dead are associated with supernatural concepts in a special way, as in the doctrine of 'salvation' that seems so natural to Christians, Jews and Muslims, and to some extent are translatable into Hindu or Buddhist notions. This is by no means a general feature of religious representations about death, but rather a specific ideology that combines a particular notion of a *soul* with personal characteristics, a special *destiny* attached to that soul, a system whereby moral worth affects that destiny, and a complicated description of what may happen to the soul as a result of past actions. All this is found in *some* places in the world, mainly as an effect of particular literate theologies, a point I will discuss in chapter 8. But it is just that: one ideology among the many types that get high cognitive salience by recruiting emotions and representations we naturally have in the presence of dead people.

The properties of corpses provide material that makes some supernatural concepts *relevant* for reasons that are quite different from our need for comfort. So religion may well be much less about death than about dead bodies. The dead are by no means the only available source of intuitions about powerful agents with strategic information and counter-intuitive physical presence. But they are a rich source of such intuitions, given the organisation of our minds and the tragically lavish supply of these real and counter-intuitive objects.

Chapter Seven

Why rituals?

On the appointed day, the villagers gather near a shrine dedicated to Buyut Celi, a long-departed hero who is now a powerful spirit and a were-tiger. People who pray to Buyut sometimes see him appear as a gigantic and threatening tiger-head. Others have seen him in the form of a dog. He is said to stand up and walk on his hind legs when nobody is watching. The shrine contains several relics: a spearhead, small bracelets, a few copper plates with barely legible inscriptions, a bronze beaker. The caretaker of the shrine takes these, still wrapped in white cloth, from a shelf near the shrine and hands them over to his assistants who carefully unwrap the relics and place them on a pillow. The other participants are now assembled around the pillow. The caretaker starts cleaning each of the relics, first rubbing a split lime on it, then sprinkling a few rice husks and rubbing the spearhead with bamboo shavings. This is repeated three times, then the relic is passed on to the other participants, each of whom cleans the spearhead in the same way before passing it on to the next

person, anti-clockwise, for anyone who handed it over in the other
direction would probably die. Then each of the other relics is
inspected, every participant holding it against his forehead while
praying. The relics are then given to the women so they get a share
of their blessing and protection. Then the caretaker stores all the
objects in the reliquary until next year's ceremonial cleaning.[1]

In honour of the goddess Chandli, devotees take a goat to her
temple to have it purified by a priest who pours consecrated water
on the animal's body while addressing prayers to the goddess. The
priest then presents flowers, incense, rice and water to the goat,
worships it and whispers prayers into its ears, promising the animal
that its soul will be soon liberated. He also worships a special sword
supposed to contain divine power. Another participant raises the
sword and chops off the goat's head in one stroke. The head is taken
to the altar to be offered to the goddess. The man who offered the
animal takes it away to share with friends and relatives.[2]

Everyone gathers to witness the formal induction of the new
shaman. During a long series of dances led by senior shamans, the
new specialist is led repeatedly back and forth between a small pole
erected in one of the houses and a tall one in the middle of the village.
He is then instructed to 'play', in fact struggle with a ram, trying to
open its mouth and bite its tongue. The villagers follow all this until
another ritual officer enters the mêlée, cuts the head clean off the
ram and rips open the chest to give the new shaman the palpitating
heart. The new shaman, now blindfolded, puts the heart in his mouth
and climbs to the top of the pole where dangerous witches, it is said,
will try and make him fall off. An assistant climbs behind him and
unties the blindfold. The shaman is now formally recognised as
strong enough to fight witches and evil spirits.[3]

In a secluded space outside the village, the candidates for initiation
– young boys who will become full men as the result of a year-long
series of rites – are told about their imminent death during the
impending ritual. They are advised not to struggle when the time
comes, for if they do so they might get killed for real. They are taken

by the grown men to a large pool and held under the water, gasping for air. The women gather at a distance and try to peer between the rows of men hiding the candidates. Then the 'killer' appears holding a small blade with which he touches the bellies of the boys. He goes off and returns with a large spear, and this time plunges it right through the stomach of each boy (or so it would seem from a distance). The boys, supposedly dead, are then taken away on their elders' shoulders and brought to their initiation camp where they will stay for a year.[4]

Actions of great moment (and less meaning)

These examples were taken from Java, India, Nepal and Central Africa, but I could have chosen virtually any other continent or religion to illustrate the point. Rituals of various kinds are found in most human groups, and notions of supernatural agents are associated with them. Indeed, it is rare that people have concepts of gods or ancestors without prescriptions for particular sequences of actions to be performed at specific times and with the expectation of particular results.

Why do people spend their time and resources doing all this? Rituals are often described as the occasion for people to commune with gods and spirits, to partake in a transcendent world through highly emotional experience. Rituals are said to communicate profound meanings about gods and spirits, so that the real significance of supernatural concepts is conveyed through some special experience. In a less exalted way, rituals also seem to be the occasion for people to interact with gods and spirits, both to ask for help and to demonstrate worship and loyalty. Indeed, in many places people have some confidence in the actual efficacy of ritual, in its power to bring about good rainfall or crops. All these give us precious indications of how people see their own rituals, but that is not enough. There are rituals in all human groups and as we shall see presently they have some important features in common. What we should try to explain is why ritual is such a *general* human activity.

The most obvious feature that distinguishes a ritual from an ordinary action is that specific rules organise the performance. First, the participants are each given a specific part to act, as it were. The priests of the Hindu sacrifice described above are Brahmans, which explains both that they can consecrate the various elements and that they cannot kill the animal themselves. In the same way, the cleaning of Buyut's relics is primarily the business of a caretaker, in charge of the shrine and the relics, and of the men of the group. The women are not part of the circle and only handle the relics after they have been cleaned by the primary participants. This division between men and women is even more clear-cut in the case of Gbaya initiation of Central Africa, as each sex is assigned a specific role to play in the ceremony. Second, the place is also special: a specially erected platform near Buyut's shrine, a Hindu temple dedicated to the local goddess, a pole in the middle of the village, a pond in the forest. Third, each of the actions has to be performed in a special manner. Blessing the goat and worshipping it require specific formulae. The order in which various ingredients are rubbed onto the relics is supposed to be particularly important. Fourth, the instruments of ritual, a consecrated sword or select relics, are special objects that cannot in principle be replaced by more convenient substitutes. Finally, the script, the particular ordering of actions, is of course crucial. One is not allowed to behead the goat and then bless it, handle the relics before the caretaker has cleaned them, or get the shaman to fight a ram after he has climbed up the pole.

People perform rituals to achieve particular effects (receive the gods' protection, turn boys into men), but the connection between the actions prescribed and the results expected is often rather opaque. The Javanese assume that cleaning the relics and handling them will have some beneficial effects, but that does not explain the connection. Also, why handle the relics in a particular order? Why circulate them anti-clockwise? Many rituals come with no explanation for the specific actions. The Kham Magar apparently do not explain why the new shaman should try and bite a ram's tongue as opposed to a chicken's foot. When there are local explanations, they are often like religious explanations described in the first chapter — they explain one element by producing another one that would itself require explanation. For instance, people in Java circulate the relics anti-clockwise because of the widespread Indonesian belief that this motion concentrates some element (in this case the blessing of the relics) while clockwise motion would disperse it. But there is no account of why this is the case.[5]

We often say that ceremonies are *meaningful* to the people who perform them. Through ritual, people perhaps grasp or express important messages about themselves, their relationships to each other and their connection with gods and spirits. This indeed may well be what some ritual participants themselves offer as a justification for performance. But do rituals really convey much meaning? To be blunt, what on earth does it mean to bite a ram's tongue or to get some mean-looking character to pretend he is killing your children? What is the information transmitted? Not much, apparently. If you asked people what they had learned or expressed through participation in such rituals, they would find the question rather strange. In most human groups people have all sorts of rituals but no good explanation of why they should be performed, especially of why they should be performed in the specific way prescribed. (Even in places where theologians produce such interpretations – Hindu ritual would be a good example – most people pay very little attention to that exegesis, being far more interested in exact performance.)

Indeed, we can predict what will happen in a ritual much better if we consider that the whole enterprise is geared to reducing the amount of information transmitted. Anthropologist Maurice Bloch pointed out that most ritual language is either archaic, so no one has a clear idea of what it means, or formulaic, so that you are mandated to repeat the same words as in previous performances. Together with the rigid prescriptions for action and the lack of a clear connection between what is done and what should result, this turns rituals into occasions where there is much less meaning conveyed than in other situations of social interaction. True, you can certainly associate various ideas with what is being done, as you can when faced with more or less any human action. But this is mostly a matter of free interpretation, and the associations are certainly not the explanation of action. You can associate a vast number of notions to each ritual action and still have no clear justification for performing *this* action rather than that. Which is why people's exegesis of their own rituals is often vague, circular, question-begging, mystery-ridden and highly idiosyncratic.[6]

Salient gadgets

As anthropologist Roy Rappaport pointed out, even if some meaning was conveyed through rituals, this still would not explain why it has to be conveyed that way. That is, we would be left with the same question as before: Why these rigid requirements on place, script, actors and instruments? Suppose we say that a Christian wedding means that the father transmits his authority over his daughter to the groom, with God as a witness. Even if this was a valid interpretation, it would only tell us what people could have communicated *without* a ritual, which is unfortunate if we want to explain why they felt the need for a ritual. Since Chandli is presumably au fait with what is going on in the village, why not just kill a goat and tell the goddess to drop in and take her share whenever convenient? If the relics of Buyut Celi protect people, why not lease them to whoever feels in need of protection? When a shaman has completed his training, why not just have the elders test him and proclaim the results, instead of going through all this complicated, dangerous and clearly irrelevant rigmarole? Since boys do grow up eventually, why not just assemble the whole village and have everyone agree that they are now full men and should be treated as such? These crude questions spring to mind when we consider exotic ceremonies, but they are equally pressing with more familiar ones. Why have the groom wait at the altar while the bride and her father are walking up the aisle? Why invite friends and relatives to witness this event? Why baby-showers, baptism, ordination or funerals? Why bother with all this?[7]

The problem, then, is to explain why people feel the need to resort to what seems to be a particular *mode of action*, as anthropologists Caroline Humphrey and James Laidlaw put it. Since the phenomenon is so general, it would seem that we need a psychological explanation for this human propensity. However, ritual is not an activity for which we can easily demonstrate some specific disposition or a special adaptive advantage. It is difficult to explain, even as a speculative exercise, how people would develop a capacity or an urge to organise collective ceremonies, how the genes that create this drive would spread better than a non-ritualistic genotype. True, some anthropologists have proposed extremely speculative origin scenarios for the appearance of rituals in early human societies. Performing a ritual together implies that you act in a co-ordinated manner, as each person does his or her bit as directed by the ritual script. This *might* have made groups more cohesive, and it *might* have allowed some coalitions to wield more influence in a group. If that was advantageous to each individual, the capacity or inclination to do all this *might* have become entrenched in human dispositions.[8]

However, such scenarios are rather shaky. This is not just because it is difficult to reconstruct what happened in early human groups, but also because of a crucial gap in the explanation. Evolution does not create specific behaviours; it creates mental organisation that makes people behave in particular ways. For all these scenarios to work, we would have to establish that people do have a 'ritualistic disposition' and describe what this amounts to. But we have no evidence for a special 'ritual system' in the mind, at least not so far. Even if we found it, we would still have to explain why people use rituals in some circumstances rather than others. Rituals are used to a bewildering variety of purposes, or so it would seem: to give good crops and keep disease away, to celebrate birth and marriage, to cure the sick and help the dead reach another world, to ordain priests and initiate young folk, to appease the gods' anger or secure their protection. So this would imply that ritual is an *atavism*. In this view, humans first performed rituals for one particular reason (to ensure social cohesion, to wage war, to negotiate relations between men and women) and *then* extended this to other circumstances. Even if there was good evidence for this historical sequence, it would not tell us why rituals are compelling *now* on occasions other than the original ones. As I said in chapter 1, origin scenarios of this kind do not really explain present behaviour.

Perhaps the mistake is to assume that a *unique* capacity or propensity in human minds accounts for the existence of prescribed ceremonies in all human groups. As I have emphasised several times already, many cultural creations, from visual art to music to the low status of tanners to the fascination of corpses, are successful because they activate a variety of mental capacities, most of which have other, very precise functions. In other words a lot of human culture consists of salient *cognitive gadgets* that have a great attention-grabbing power and high relevance for human minds as a side-effect of these minds being organised the way they are.

This may be the case for rituals as well. Indeed, I think we can explain in this way at least three important properties of this kind of action:

First, acting in rituals is not quite the same as acting in other contexts, as any participant or observer feels quite clearly. However, this feeling is particularly difficult to describe. Although what you do is supposed to have some direct effect, ritual is not quite like ordinary work because the connection between what you are doing (e.g. biting a ram's tongue) and its supposed effect (turning you into a real shaman) is not terribly obvious. Although there is a lot of acting (e.g. pretending to kill the young boys), it is not quite like theatre as the consequences of the performance are all too real. What makes many rituals special is that they combine these elements of work and play with a sense of urgency, that is, an intuition that you should perform them in the correct way otherwise something terrible may happen, but there is often no explanation of how correct per-formance averts that danger (or indeed of what the danger actually is). This is the *sense of urgency* problem, which I think is easily solved if we take into account other situations where human minds feel that particular emotion.

Second, many rituals have consequences for social interaction: the wedding makes an honest family of two former lovers, initiation makes a man out of a boy, sacrificing a sheep to the ancestors seals your alliance with another village. This is the *social effects* problem, which is not so much of a mystery once we understand how human minds understand (and often misunderstand) the web of social relations around them.

Third, perhaps most important for our purposes, notions of supernatural agents are included in many rituals; the wedding ritual takes God or the ancestors as witnesses, the sacrifice is directed at the spirits. This *supernatural participation* problem is better understood if we realise that the participation in question is really optional, as witness the number of rituals without any gods or spirits. In other words you can understand what gods are doing in ritual, so to speak, once you realise that they are an add-on to a human activity that does not really require them. As we will see, belief in gods and spirits does not really entail that you have rituals, but since people have them for other reasons, gods and spirits are much more convincing once they are somehow included in these salient activities.

On all three counts, I think it is possible to highlight the reasons why ceremonies are significant to human minds. Not all rituals have these three properties, but the ones that do are optimally relevant and successfully transmitted. This may help us understand why religious concepts are usually accompanied by at least some ritual.

The intuitive sense of urgency
People acquire ritual prescriptions by observing what others are doing and by being told that certain ritual recipes are appropriate in certain contexts. The requirements of ritual come in the form of

specific rules, for instance, 'if you want to give a goat to Chandli, the Brahman must first bless the sword', 'if you want the spirit's protection, circulate the relics anti-clockwise (otherwise you will die)'. So we might think that ritual rules are just another example of social conventions. We know that humans are extremely good at acquiring a vast amount of seemingly arbitrary social rules. But if ritual prescriptions are mere conventions, like wearing a suit at a job interview, it is difficult to understand the feeling of urgency that accompanies them. A Brahman who killed the goat himself would be polluted, offering a goat without first consecrating the sword would be insulting the goddess, mishandling the relics could kill. So ritual prescriptions are examples of what psychologists call *precautionary rules*, they are presented as what you must do in order to avert a danger.[9]

What would create this impression? A first explanation would be that the rituals are addressed to or involve powerful gods and spirits. The latter are seen as powerful agents who can affect your health and good fortune, without whose blessing or co-operation you cannot get good crops, many children, a peaceful society or protection from natural disasters. However, this is a little misleading. People are not born with the notion of powerful gods and spirits. They get that from other people, from hearing what others say and observing how they behave. The performance of rituals is one of these external elements that you can observe long before you acquire complex notions of gods and spirits. So it may well be the case that rituals are not so much a *result* of people's representation of the gods' powers as one of its many *causes*. That is, rituals are organised in such a way that they give a particular shape and tenor to people's notions of supernatural agents and make more plausible the gods' involvement in their existence.

The special flavour of ritual that we can find in so many different cultural contexts is not just a matter of special rigidity but also of the particular elements introduced in ritual sequences, summarised here by anthropologist Alan Fiske: 'a focus on special numbers of colours;

concerns about pollution and purity and consequent washing or other purification; contact avoidance; special ways of touching; fears about immanent, serious sanctions for rule violations; a focus on boundaries and thresholds; symmetrical arrays and other precise spatial patterns'.[10]

Among the common features of ritual in vastly different cultural environments, we find this obsession with marking boundaries, for instance by marking off some part of the ceremonial space as special. Indeed, as historian of religion Veikko Anttonen points out, this obsession with limits is probably the only common thread in otherwise very different concepts of 'sacred' space and objects. Another extremely common theme is that of purity, purification, of making sure that participants and various objects are clean, etc. The Javanese handling of relics, itself presented as a cleaning operation although the objects are not actually cleaned in the usual sense of the word, is preceded by a ceremonial meal. The chickens reserved for this meal should all be perfectly white and they are washed three times by the shrine caretaker before preparation and again after plucking. The cooking should be done by a mature woman, past menopause since menstruation is seen as polluting. The flowers brought to the ceremonial meal should also be flawless and no one should sniff them as this would probably pollute them.[11]

Obsessive rules

What psychological capacities are involved in all this? Rituals are not like ordinary behaviour. They seem much closer to the automatic and compelling actions endlessly and pointlessly performed by patients with Obsessive-Compulsive Disorder (OCD). These people feel for instance a compulsion to wash their hands hundreds of times a day, or to check several dozen times that they locked the door, or to perform complicated sequences of meaningless actions before they start the day. Many OCD patients realise how irrational their compulsion is. But they also feel that they cannot help it. It is quite beyond them to stop doing their repetitive actions. Indeed, the very thought of not carrying out the exact sequence can fill them with anguish.[12]

Many authors have noticed the similarities between this condition and ritual performance, although it was very difficult to draw any conclusions from the parallel. Some described ritual as a form of collective obsession and others saw obsession as a private religious ritual. Neither view made much sense since very little was known about the mental processes involved in these two kinds of repeated and compulsory sequences. What motivated the comparison was the presence in both situations of actions that make little practical sense but must be performed, as well as the repetition of similar actions over time. Most anthropologists concluded that such similar features may well be a coincidence.

Then anthropologist Alan Fiske reopened the question, showing that the similarities between ritual and OCD are deeper than mere repetition of non-practical actions. Beyond this, we can also find a striking similarity in the concepts and emotional states activated. Comparing hundreds of ritual sequences with clinical descriptions of OCD cases, Fiske showed that the same themes recur over and over again in both domains. Indeed, Fiske's list of common themes in rituals could be used as a clinical description of the common obsessions in these patients. In both situations, people are concerned with purity and pollution; pollution can be averted by performing particular actions; there is no clear representation of why these particular actions should have that result; the actions consist in repetitive gestures; there is a sense that great dangers lie in not performing these routines, or deviating from the usual script; finally, there is often no obvious connection between the actions performed and their usual significance: in rituals people can rub bamboo shavings on a blade and say that it 'cleans' it, in the same way that obsessive-compulsive patients will avoid treading on the lines of the pavement and assume that this protects them in some way.[13]

This argument appeared at the same time as the neuro-psychology of OCD, its causes in brain function, became much clearer. The condition is not due to an arbitrary combination of fear and strange concepts. It comes from a specific dysfunction of some planning functions of the brain and responds rather well to medication. The condition is associated with abnormal activation of particular brain areas that mediate the combination of plans and emotions. Some of these areas are generally involved in producing emotional responses to possible as well as actual situations. They are indispensable to normal everyday function, because we are constantly choosing between various courses of actions, to which these functional systems give higher or lower values. Also, we are constantly considering possible outcomes of what we are doing, so that we must monitor all sorts of consequences of each course of action. In particular, we cannot operate normally without a keen sense of the possible dangers involved in performing each action, as a result of possible intervening circumstances. The sense that danger lurks in each of our everyday actions is something that is taken for granted by such systems, except that in most circumstances this is not made conscious. Suppose you are standing by the train door as the train is about to stop. The mental system involved in planning and controlling motor behaviour may well consider a plan to jump off onto the platform before the train has pulled up. This system rejects such a plan because of the possible consequences. It then gives the intention of jumping off a slightly negative emotional valence, which is barely perceptible but diverts us from such a course of action. Various plans for actions are considered and most of them are rejected by higher planning functions without our being aware of this selection. It is not yet entirely clear how the abnormal activation of such systems takes place in patients but the discoveries of neuro-imagery and physiology suggest that OCD may amount to a small tweaking of normal function. In patients such systems seem to talk loud enough, as it were, to drive actual motor behaviour — people cannot help performing the routines — and to drive emotions as well, so that non-performance creates a strong feeling of fear or anguish.[14]

Urgency and ritual precautions

The similarities highlighted by Fiske do not mean that rituals are obsessive behaviours. But they suggest that some elements of rituals trigger activation of those particular mental systems that work on overdrive, as it were, in obsessive disorders. In particular, many elements of ritual scripts include cues that activate the Contagion system, the specialised system that deals with undetectable contaminants, already mentioned at several points. That it is dangerous to handle dirt, excrement or putrefying carcasses is an intuition delivered by this system. This is all very easily acquired during early childhood and then quite impossible to discard. The system triggers a powerful emotion of fear and disgust and a strong desire to avoid the substances in question, without providing a description of what the danger is. It also leads people to imitate other people's precautions against potential danger, even if they have no available explanation of how the precautions work. This is why people in many human groups are easily convinced that the preparation of certain foods requires extensive precautions, and they rarely venture to try out different methods.

Many elements in ritual scripts activate the Contagion system. The insistence on cleansing, making a particular space safer, avoiding any contact between what is in that space and the outside: all these are cues that suggest possible contamination. This may be why we find parallel emotions and behaviours in many rituals. That there is a potential danger is intuitively perceived although no danger need be explicitly described. That specific and very precise rules must be followed seems compelling although there is no clear connection between them and the danger that is to be avoided. The overall sense of urgency may then be a consequence of the fact that one of the mental systems activated is one that happens to specialise, outside ritual contexts, in the management of precautions against undetectable hazards. Any cultural artefact, like a ritual prescription, that alludes to such situations and presents what are usual cues for this Contagion system, is likely to be highly attention-grabbing. So it is perhaps not surprising that people feel emotionally bound to perform rituals *in the right way* and that they fear dangers that are not directly detectable. This is what the Contagion system is all about. These obvious features of ritual are not so much features of ritual as features of the system that makes rituals highly salient cognitive gadgets.

This is only one aspect of the phenomenon. Behavioural gadgets may be attention-demanding but they are used for particular purposes. As I said at the beginning, people have all sorts of reasons for performing a particular ritual at a particular time. The reasons generally focus on the effects of the ceremonies, on what is alleged to result from correct performance. So what could rituals do, that other forms of action cannot achieve?

Exchange with sleeping partners

The world over, animals or other offerings are presented to gods, spirits or ancestors to ward off illness, to ensure good crops, to make rains fall or, more generally, for propitiation. The example mentioned at the beginning of this chapter is of this kind. Hindu goddesses are involved in daily events, they can prevent misfortune or bring it about. So it makes sense to sacrifice a goat and to consecrate it so it becomes worthy of sacrifice. The relative emphasis on sacrifice as opposed to other ceremonies varies a lot, from Hinduism where an extremely complex system of sacrificial rites is central to religious observance, to Islam where it is a major ritual but confined to annual celebrations, to Christianity where it is marginal.

The Kwaio frequently sacrifice pigs to their ancestors during elaborate ceremonies that 'dedicate' the animal to a particular *adalo*. As Keesing reports, there are all sorts of reasons why the ancestors would require such a sacrifice. First, the ritual is meant to appease them in cases of ritual violations, such as people walking through an area of the village that is *abu* (forbidden to them). Also, various cases of illness or misfortune are brought about by ancestors who feel neglected and crave the pork meat that the living can still enjoy.

Finally, the Kwaio also raise special pigs for one particular ancestor on whose protection they depend.

The general ideology of sacrifice, the justification for its performance, is almost invariably the notion that misfortune can be kept away, as well as prosperity or health or social order maintained, if the participants and the gods enter into some mutually beneficial exchange relation. The ancestors, to follow the Kwaio case, will forgive a ritual violation if given a pig and they will agree to protect those who give one preventively. The logic whereby a slight can be compensated or future co-operation established is clearly available to people the world over, without further explanation, since such inferences are provided by our social-mind systems. So far, nothing mysterious.

However, as an exchange procedure sacrifice is of course para-doxical. Although it is all presented as giving away some resources in exchange for protection, the brutal fact remains that the sacrificed animals are generally consumed by the participants. This irony is not lost on the Kwaio, some of whom pointed out to Keesing that it is a kind of 'cheating' to promise the ancestors a pig, since they cannot actually share in the feast. In many places people find some clever way of finessing this conceptual difficulty. They say that the gods crave the smell of meat, that they ingest the smoke, that they eat the soul of the animal, etc. Outsiders often consider these explanations as so many ways of avoiding the embarrassing fact that the beneficiaries of the ceremony cannot actually receive anything. But I think there may be more to these explanations.

Sacrifice is often offered in exchange for better crops or plentiful game. However, people also have the intuition that the outcome of their agricultural or hunting operations mainly results from their own action. Indeed, whatever the ritual guarantee, farmers and hunters never dispense with all the empirical measures that increase their likelihood of success. You may give a goat to the gods but you still plough your fields to the best of your abilities. The ways in which the gods actually confer benefits are not really described or even thought about. Inasmuch as people get good crops or game, this may well be, in their view, because of the sacrifice, but this is only a conjecture with very little obvious support. In such situations, then, people give resources to the ancestors, but the part that the ancestors receive is not obvious, or not visible, or not material. In exchange people receive protection, but this is not obvious, or not visible. So there may be an intuitive correspondence between what people think they give away (it is after all possible, though counter-intuitive, that some agents feed on smoke or eat souls) and what they think they receive (it is after all possible, though difficult to establish, that the gods really help).

Another reason why the ceremonies make intuitive sense is that, in many cases, people's attention is focused, not so much on the potential exchange with invisible partners, as on the actual exchange or distribution of resources among the actual participants. In many cases sacrifices are occasions of communal sharing. Kwaio people do not just 'dedicate' a pig to the ancestors and eat it. They share it with the whole group. Sacrificial rituals are very often performed in this spirit of unconditional sharing, in contrast with ordinary social exchange. For instance the Muslim annual sacrifice of a ram should be a collective affair and the meat should be shared between families. Those who cannot afford to perform the ritual can count on gifts from neighbours or even perfect strangers. (Conversely, in many places it would be strange to have any communal sharing of costly resources without 'dedicating' at least some part of the feast to the ancestors, gods or spirits. Where I worked in Cameroon, people who open a bottle to share with their friends must spill a few drops on the ground for the ancestors. The banal fact of sharing resources unconditionally with actual people is turned into exchange with imagined partners.) In other sacrifice rituals, people pay great attention to the way the animal is divided up. The Fang pay great attention to who receives which part of a sacrificed goat, each part being assigned to a person who stands in a particular genealogical relationship to the head of family, who offers the animal to the ancestors.

Creating people

There may be all sorts of official justifications for performing the ceremonies, and there may be some notion of what effects they bring about, but it is difficult to understand why people take all this as intuitively plausible, unless you consider the *social relations* involved. This means not just the pre-existing relations between the people who get together to perform a particular ceremony, but also the particular ways in which these relations are created or modified by ritual.

Many rituals produce important changes in social interaction, but not always those changes presented as the reason for performing the ritual in the first place. Here is an example. Consider the initiation rites illustrated at the beginning of this chapter by some details from the Gbaya rituals of Central Africa. In many places adolescents have to go through long and often painful initiation ordeals to be considered full members of the group. Such rites are generally far more complex and are more widespread in the male-only version. Boys can be 'trained' for years before they return to society as full men.

Anthropologists have always found these complex rites fascinating because of their length and complexity, but also because of apparent discrepancies between their performance and their official justification. A familiar explanation for initiation rites is that young boys must acquire the secret knowledge and skills that define real manhood. However, going through initiation is very far from either attending college or going to summer camp. The secret knowledge is more often than not either vacuous or paradoxical. In many rites the candidates are taught that the secret of the rite is precisely that there is no secret at all, or that they will not be told what it is until they reach a further stage of initiation. The rites seem to promote what anthropologist Fredrik Barth called an 'epistemology of secrecy', a notion that knowledge is intrinsically dangerous and ambiguous. The Baktaman rituals of New Guinea studied by Barth comprise several different stages, performed at a few years' interval, which should gradually convey to young men important secrets and the hidden key to various rituals. But at each step the solution provided contains yet more mysteries that a further ritual should illuminate. The few who reach the end of the cycle have not learnt much, except that secret knowledge consists in a series of recursive secrets, probably with no clear end-point. Although initiation is sometimes said to turn immature boys into competent hunters or warriors, no real skills are acquired during these long periods of seclusion. Military drills or strategy are clearly not the most important aspect of the ceremonies. Indeed, many initiation rites comprise long series of painful ordeals and episodes of torture that do not at first sight seem to enhance much the fighting capacities of young boys. Making the penis bleed or dislocating toes may have a great effect on the boys, but it could hardly count as preparation for serious engagement.[15]

Indeed, anthropologist Michael Houseman has shown that paradoxical events, which create a kind of cognitive blur, are central to male initiation. In the Beti male initiation in Cameroon, studied by Houseman, the boys are for instance told to wash in mud puddles. If they oblige they are beaten up for getting dirty; if they refuse they are of course beaten up for staying unwashed. The boys are told that if they go through all the ordeals they will be rewarded with a sumptuous meal of antelope's meat and fat. But all they get is a mixture of rotting meat, semen and excrement. They are instructed to go hunt in the forest but they are the ones stalked and attacked by the elders. More generally, there is also a paradox in the overall organisation of the ritual. The men declare that they will take the children away and secretly kill them to turn them into adults. Once the children are in the camp, they are told that this is all a deception organised for the benefit of naïve women and outsiders; the truth is that there is no real killing. Before the candidates can relax, however, they are thrown into a series of unannounced, violent ordeals, that have nothing to do with the official 'secret'.

This way of instituting a real and painful shock within a declared but empty deception is very common in such rites, according to Houseman. It seems to create a strange 'relational catch' in the sense that the candidates are given two incompatible versions of what happened. The older men are both their tormentors and their partners in an elaborate deception directed against women. The Gbaya boys, before they join the initiation camp, sing 'Father, are you tricking me?'. Even after they have completed the ritual this remains an open question. As most participants in such rituals comment, there is no way to understand what happened but it is clear that something *did* happen and that it did change them in some way.[16]

So why go through all this? The discrepancy between the official goals (initiation is supposed to produce adult men) and the means employed is quite striking. The official goal itself is more complex than it may seem. As many participants will say, one is not really a man, or a 'real' man, or a 'full' man unless one has gone through the rite. But this would not make much sense if taken literally. Everyone around the candidates knows perfectly well that boys will become men, come what may, ritual or no ritual. So the statements express a norm, not a fact. They point to the kind of interaction that *should* occur between adult men but is not guaranteed by mere biological growth. In the tribal environments where such rites are found, this interaction consists in participation in collective hunting, as well as in coalitions and warfare, in the defence of the group, and in some cartel-like arrangements in marital strategies. These are all situations where success depends on co-operative interaction, where it is difficult in advance to assess people's dispositions to co-operate, where defection might be tempting and would endanger all non-defectors, and where it would be difficult to punish a defector after the fact.

The ordeals make more sense if we take into account that warfare and tribal solidarity activate mental systems for *coalitional* behaviour. One difference between coalitions and ordinary groups, as I explained in chapter 3, is that coalitions can launch extremely risky operations if certain conditions of interaction are met. Each member of a coalition must signal that he will co-operate, regardless of the cost. Initiation rituals seem to play on these intuitions. The best way to assess whether young men are prepared to pay a heavy cost as members of the coalition is to make them pay some of it up front, as it were, in the form of accepted pain. But that is not the only effect. A necessary requirement for all successful co-operation in the form of coalitions, is not just that people accept to pay a price for membership but also that they trust others to co-operate too. Initiation does not seem to confer much benefit on the young participants, and in fact it costs them a great deal. But it also confirms (or makes more plausible) to each of them that the others are indeed loyal members. So what is going on during these rites and produces real effects has little to do with changing the participants themselves and a lot to do with making possible the building of risky coalitions with other men.

There is more than meets the eye in such rituals, indeed more than meets the eye even of the participants, who are both baffled and fascinated by the special 'relational catch' of these rituals: You thought you were conniving with older men to deceive the women, children and other outsiders, but what happens in secret is nothing to do with that. What I call a relational catch is a way of acting towards other people that is difficult to understand or describe to oneself, often quite fascinating, but intuitively related to the effects of the ceremony. Without clearly knowing why, the participants feel that the special 'game' they are playing produces important changes in their relations. Which it does, although people could not readily explain how it works.

Marking and creating occasions

Social relations are changed through ritual in a way that is not entirely clear to the participants. This is true even in very familiar rituals, far away from the complexities of initiation. Consider for instance the many rituals whereby people 'mark an occasion', ceremonies organised around events that would happen anyway. A new child is born, two people are now a family unit. People say that the child is not 'really' born until some birth ritual has been performed, or that the couple are not a family at all before the wedding. These same people also know very well that children get born and are alive before any ritual is performed. In many places a ceremony marks the official 'birth'; before that it would be unseemly to declare that a child is born. But the emotional reactions of parents and other interested parties are of course not bound by these official regulations. In the same way, wedding rituals are practically universal, but people know perfectly well that any two adults could enter into some long-term sexual and economic partnership without the rites. Again, this is all a matter of norm rather than fact. But why then mark these occasions with ritual gadgets?

The standard anthropological answer – which I think is roughly on the right track – is that, however 'private', such events have direct implications for the communities where people live. Indeed the very notion of childbirth as a private event or of marriage as involving only two partners would be a very odd one in most human groups. By having children people are putting themselves in a new situation as regards resources and social exchange. Children are the focus of greater investment from their biological parents than from anyone else. The urge to feed and protect one's children rather than others is a general human tendency, for obvious evolutionary reasons. Naturally, the nature of the resources and protection vary a lot from one group to another, from foraging groups to industrial environments, and so does the way they are acquired, from communal operations to private enterprise. But the fact remains that co-operation with people will vary a lot depending on whether they have children, how many, how old, etc.

This is why a birth is a social event and why many birth rituals (baptism, early circumcision, formal christening, etc.) happen some time *after* birth. In many societies there is an official doctrine that the child is not 'really' born before such ceremonies. This would seem paradoxical if the biological birth of the child really was the event celebrated. But note that in most human environments up to modern times, having a child delivered only provided a chance that there would be a child to invest in, because of high infant mortality. So the delay between birth and ritual seems to confirm that such rituals are relevant once it becomes clear that the child is here to stay and that people's interaction will indeed be recalibrated to accommodate parental investment.

A similar anthropological argument explains why marriages are intensely public and publicised events. Again, the details of wedding celebrations vary a lot with differences in family organisation, in the relative status of men and women, in the degree of autonomy of women and in the particular rules of marital exchange. However, *some* ritual is felt to be necessary in most human groups and virtually everywhere it is made as evident as possible. The cheapest way of celebrating a marriage is to make a lot of noise. Where resources allow, using visual pageantry is another common way of making sure the new union is noticed by all and sundry. To consider marriage a 'private' arrangement between two individual parties is the exception rather than the rule.

A simple reason is that any marriage produces a situation that changes the whole sexual and reproductive landscape for the rest of the group, by removing two persons from the pool of possible mates and by creating a unit where sexual access and parental investment as well as economic co-operation are bundled up together in a stable pact. This means that people's co-operation with each of the individuals concerned, in terms of sexual access, economic co-operation, social exchange or coalitional loyalty, must be 'realigned' to take account of this situation. This creates problems of co-ordination. First, at what point should other members of the group change the way they interact with the individuals concerned? Stable couples may be the outcome of a long and gradual process, so there is no clear cut-off point at which others should start to reorient their behaviour. Also, if other members of a group modify their behaviour to take into account the new solidarity that exists between two people, they should all do it at the same time in the same way. If you start treating the new family precisely as a family when others are still treating one of the members as if there was no marriage, you may for instance miss out on sexual opportunities. Or if you mistakenly think a person's resources will now be principally geared to their stable monogamous union you may miss out on occasions to borrow or use some of these resources. So it is convenient that there should be a clear-cut distinction between before and after, as well as a convention that the group's behaviour should change at that precise moment. Even in the West, people immersed in an intensely individualistic ideology still have the intuition that social interaction is what makes the ritual relevant.

The interaction that occurs during a ritual is quite strange and creates social effects for which people have no ready description. But this raises a very difficult question: Why do people resort to *ritual* performance in such circumstances? Why all this ceremonial noise around social relations, if social relations are our most familiar environment? What makes the ritual gadgets relevant? To understand all this we have to take into account a most surprising fact about human beings. Although they have constant experience of social life they just do not understand it, or not very well.

Game-theory is for aliens

In previous chapters I described various psychological aspects of social interaction: for instance a model of moral feelings as an adaptive strategy or of cheat-detection as a way of maintaining co-operation. In each case I made use of concepts that are constantly used in biology and psychology, like *strategy*, *signalling*, *defection*, *utility*, etc. Now this way of describing social interaction strikes most people as rather alien. That is, we understand the arguments, in a fairly abstract and intellectual way, but what they describe is just not the way we *feel* when we are engaged in social interaction.

For instance, a mixture of positive moral feelings towards co-operation together with a very strong angry reaction to cheating, as well as anger towards people who do not punish cheats, constitutes an optimal strategy for co-operators. However, when we engage in co-operative endeavours with people we just feel that they are intrinsically *good, reliable, nice people* or alternatively that they are *devious, unreliable, creepy,* etc. We do not see our dispositions as a strategy.

To take another example, people tend to cluster in solidarity-based groups. In some societies this kind of group is given for free, as it were, in that you are born in a particular lineage or village. You co-operate with your kin and kith and mistrust outsiders. But we are not limited to such groups. In most large settlements or institutions, where thousands or millions are thrown together, people tend to re-create small-scale solidarity networks. After a few months or years in a company or in a town, people identify a number of others with whom they talk, whom they can trust in case of need, as well as a number of neutral outsiders and some potential enemies who should not be trusted. Sociologists now find that these networks are of the same size and involve similar emotions, regardless of the country, language, size of the institution or town, and other differences. Again, however, people often do not think of such networks as coalitions at all. They just find that in their institution, company, neighbourhood, some people are intrinsically likeable and others less so, some people seem trustworthy and others do not. How all this is evaluated in terms of co-operation and trust is not quite accessible to conscious inspection.

Why are we not all sophisticated game-theorists? Why do we have vague concepts (this person is *likeable,* this group is *friendly*) rather than be aware of the precise calculations that we perform without realising it? There are several good reasons for this lack of conscious access to inference systems. First, our mental systems are designed to produce strong motivation and they do this by providing us with rewards in the form of emotions. We would not invest great effort and resources in picking Mr or Mrs Right if this were not an intensely emotional experience. Emotions goad us in the right direction much more easily than abstract descriptions of what would happen if we made the wrong choice. Second, our inference systems are very complex. Choosing Mr Right or selecting reliable co-operators in a large company is hugely complicated because there is no such thing as 'the right person' in the abstract. It all depends on the context, on what we need and what we have to offer, on what others need and may offer, and it all changes as these parameters change. Attending to vast numbers of relevant cues and constantly reassessing their significance may well be too complicated for our sluggish deliberate thought. Finally, our systems for social interaction never evolved in the context of vast groups and abstract institutions like states, corporations, unions and social classes. We evolved as small bands of foragers and that kind of existence is the context in which we developed the special features of our social mind.

The magic of society

Humans live in very different social conditions: in small foraging groups in a savannah, or in villages of sedentary peasants, or in towns where many people do not actually grow the food they eat, or in modern urban environments where people depend upon a vast number of other people for every aspect of their lives. In all these different contexts, people have some explicit description of what society is like, what groups compose it, why this is so, and so on. For instance, people the world over categorise their social environment. That is, they do not just think they interact with individuals, but tend to see them as members of more general classes like families, social class, ethnic group, caste, race, lineage or gender. Also, in all human groups people have consciously accessible concepts of social relations, folk-theories about how they are built and maintained, culturally specific ways of construing them. They have explicit understandings of what friendship is, what exchange ought to be, how power is attained and maintained in complex groups, in so many words: How society works.

All these understandings, obviously, differ with the kind of social world people live in. But they have one feature in common. They are very often based on concepts that seem extremely poor and vague, compared to the actual interaction that takes place, and even compared to people's intuitive grasp of what they should do in any social context. To give a few examples: First, the way people categorise social groups is very generally by assuming that there are *natural* differences between them. In a caste system, people of different castes are said to carry very different 'essences', which supposedly explains why they should not intermarry or even come into close contact. In racist ideologies too, the basic assumption is that some differences are founded in nature although they are not always visible. Second, people faced with any complex interaction tend to use *anthropomorphic* concepts. Villages or social classes or nations are described as *wanting* this, *fearing* that, *taking decisions*, *failing to perceive* what is happening, etc. Even the workings of a committee are often described in such psychological terms: the committee realised this, regretted that, etc. To think that a village, a company or a committee is a big agent spares us the difficult work of describing the extraordinarily complicated interaction that occurs when you get more than two people together.

Anthropologist Larry Hirschfeld coined the term 'naïve sociology' to describe such understandings of social groups and social relations. 'Naïve' does not mean that these understandings are primitive or necessarily misguided but that we develop them spontaneously without the systematic training that we need to acquire scientific concepts. Naïve sociology is what you get when you combine (1) the intuitions that we have by virtue of having social-mind systems and (2) the concepts that we use to create social categories, folk-theories of social interaction, and so on. Such concepts, obviously, are adapted to the social realities we have to explain: people who live in nomadic bands of foragers have little need for a *social class* or *caste* concept. However, they are also constrained by expectations about the nature of society that we develop very early. Hirschfeld's developmental studies show how even young children have some expectations about social groups. For instance, children assume that kinship terms (aunt, father, sister, etc.) refer to something more than the mere fact of living together. They (and adults) tend to guess that some undetectable, internal 'essence' is shared by people with a common genealogy, a bit like they (and adults too) assume that all tigers share some internal tiger-hood. Young children also have some understanding that a *family* (or whatever this kind of unit is called in their society) is therefore logically different from a collection (e.g. the pupils in a class, the flowers in a bunch).[17]

Children also seem prepared to think of social groups as founded on such undetectable common properties. This makes them and adults extremely receptive to ideologies that describe a whole group of people as internally, naturally different from others. Both children and adults acquire this ideology effortlessly, suggesting that it is at least congruent with some general expectations about social groups. This does not mean that children are born racist. Indeed, Hirschfeld's studies demonstrate the opposite. Not only are young children often remarkably impervious to the emotions and attitudes that accompany ethnic classification in their social environment; they do not even seem to pay much attention to the external traits (skin tone for instance) that are the supposed 'foundation' of racial distinctions. In other words they and we all seem prepared to think of social groups in terms of natural differences, but the racist notion that a particular occupation or skin-colour are the index of such differences requires some special cultural learning.[18]

Our naïve sociology, then, is an attempt to make sense of our own intuitions about the social world around us. But it is often flawed. The accessible, explicit concepts lag far behind the intuitions they are supposed to explain. Villages do not *perceive* situations, committees cannot *remember* what happened, companies have no particular *desires*, simply because all these groups are not persons.

This gives many aspects of social interaction a magical character. Because people live in a social context, they are constantly surrounded by social events and processes that their concepts do not fully explain. These events and processes are real and their consequences are real too. But how they came about is something that cannot really be explained using the concepts of naïve sociology. They all seem to require hidden forces and processes that cause all the effects we can see.

For instance, people are members of particular clans or villages. It is quite clear to everyone that these groups were not created by their current members, neither will they disappear with them. It seems that the lineage or the group have a life of their own. Indeed, people are constantly faced with situations where being a member of this clan or that village matters because of how *previous* members of these units acted. If your village has always fought (note the anthropomorphic term) against the next village, then in a sense the interaction transcends the existence of its participants. So it makes perfect sense to think of villages and other such units as abstract persons or living organisms, because that helps explain stable interaction. People often say that all members of a village or a clan have the 'same bones', that they share some essence that is the eternal life of the social group. As Bloch points out, belonging to such groups is 'not at all like joining a social club'. Bloch shows that the biological understandings that are so often used in naïve sociology – 'we share the same bones' or 'the essence of the clan is inside us', etc. – are not loose metaphors. They express the intuition that stable political units do transcend individual people's transient roles, even in small-scale social arrangements.[19]

The 'magic' of society is just the fact that our naïve sociology cannot explain such stable or complex aspects of social interaction. We are left with explanations such as 'we in the village act in this way because we share the bones of our ancestors' or 'we have inflation because the middle classes have decided to ruin us'. These explanations are magical in the sense that there is no explicit connection between the hidden causes that are described and their effects. No matter how detailed your notions about the ancestors' bones, such concepts just fail to explain why, for instance, a feud between two villages can be extraordinarily stable or why you intuitively trust members of your clan more than outsiders.

Relevance of ritual gadgets

I started with a puzzle: Why does it seem obvious that performing particular actions in a prescribed, rigid manner will have particular effects, for example, creating a new family or turning boys into men? We might think that there is a simple solution, which is that everyone around *believes* that rituals have such effects, so that in the end they do have the effects. If everybody sees the boys returning from initiation camp as fully-grown men, then it seems that the ritual did give them a new identity. If everybody treats the newly-weds as a family, then they have become one. But there is a problem here, which is to explain why this belief is convincing at all, and why it always focuses on rituals.

I think this becomes less puzzling if we take into account the weakness of our intuitive sociology. People enter stable relationships in which sexual access, reproduction and economic co-operation are bound together; children are born so that resources are allocated in a different way; people grow up so that their contribution to social-interaction changes. All these processes have been part of our social life for a long time. They are all bound to happen in the kinds of group humans live in. But these processes are seen by people through the concepts of naïve sociology, which just cannot explain what happens and the connections between different social processes. People for instance have the intuition that a stable sexual-economic arrangement between two members of their group has consequences for everyone else, but they may not have the concepts to describe why this is the case.

Let us consider what happens if people have the same interaction, that is, they are faced with these social phenomena without a conceptual explanation, *but* they accompany these situations with a specific ritual gadget. When two people become a stable pair, there now is a special set of actions to perform, with a prescribed list of words, a prescribed cast of actors, etc. This has to be done in public. When boys slowly change from nurtured, immature individuals to potential allies in coalitions, this is marked by ordeals that emphasise the cost of defection. The way the required actions are presented suggests that not doing these things or not doing them the right way might be detrimental or dangerous.

Rituals are not necessary to social processes but they are certainly *relevant* to people's thoughts about these processes. That is, once you see your cultural elders associating a given set of prescribed actions to social effects that would otherwise appear magical, this association has some staying power because it is both easily acquired and constitutes a rich source of inferences. It is easily acquired because the intuitions are already there: that an otherwise unmotivated set of prescribed actions should be followed very precisely to avoid an undefined danger is a very easy intuition to create in human beings, because of our Contagion system. The ritual gadgets also produce rich inferences. For instance, attending a wedding may well give you the intuition that your relations to the newly-weds will now be different, and that this may be the case for other participants too; but having a ritual may give you a simple representation of why these changes are so clearly co-ordinated in all participants, since the event is itself a salient and mutually manifest reference point.

Rituals do not *create* social effects but only the illusion that they do. When people perform rituals, they combine some ritual gadget – easily acquired because it activates our Precaution-Contagion system – and a particular social effect – for which they have intuitions but no good concepts – in one single package. Thoughts about the social effect and thoughts about the ritual sequence are combined since they are about the same event. So rituals are naturally thought to produce the social effects.

This illusion is strengthened by the fact that not performing a particular ceremony, when others do, very often amounts to defecting from social co-operation. For instance, once you attach a particular ritual (initiation) to full co-operation between men, or another one (wedding) to mate-choice, not performing the ritual amounts to a refusal to enter into the same social arrangements as other people. In a place where everybody signals their openness and reliability by keeping their windows open, drawing your curtains is a clear signal of non-cooperation. So the illusion that the ritual is actually indispensable to its effects, although untrue if you consider human societies in general, becomes quite real for the people concerned, as their choice is between performing the actions prescribed – which seems to confirm that the rituals are *sine qua non* – or defecting from co-operation with other members of the group, which is not really an option in most human groups.

Banal transcendence: an opening for gods and spirits

Students of religion used to think that rituals in general were the expression of some emotional religious attitude, that they expressed people's awe of the spirits and gods, a mixture of fear, respect, submission and trust that is consistent with the perception of gods and spirits as immensely powerful. This is still very much the way B-films and comic strips represent religious ceremonies, with an exotic priest muttering opaque incantations to the gods amid a crowd of crazed believers, inebriated by loud drum-beat and mind-altering substances. There are rituals like that, but many, indeed most are quite sober affairs. The performance is not always that fascinating, and its effects not always dramatic. Emotional involvement varies a lot. The induction of a new shaman in Nepal or the staged killing of young boys in Central Africa, described at the beginning of the chapter, are certainly spectacular; but the handling of relics in Indonesia or the sacrifice of a goat in India do not exactly set the pulse racing.

Most importantly, the supposed presence of gods and spirits is an optional feature of rituals. The sacrifice of a goat is construed as a gift to the goddess; the presence of this invisible exchange partner is part of how people represent the ritual. But young boys among the Gbaya are initiated by older men, through a complex series of rituals and mysterious performances that do not involve the ancestors.

One might want to say that there are two kinds of ritual, religious and non-religious. Ordaining a priest would be religious because God is assumed to be around, while a wedding at the registrar's office would be non-religious. Armed with such a distinction, we could then try and observe the differences between the two types. This, anthropologists know from bitter experience, leads to difficult problems. First, there are many intermediate cases where supernatural agents are mentioned but peripheral. Second, there are no very clear general differences between the two types of ritual (except, of course, the alleged presence of supernatural agents in one type). Many civil weddings follow a script that makes them very similar to the religious version.

So let us see the situation in more concrete terms. People are brought up in a particular human group, where gods are mentioned, rituals are performed, and some rituals are performed with a mention of the gods. If this latter association is stable, it must be because it is easily acquired at each generation. In other words, there is something in the representation of rituals that makes it relevant, though not mandatory, to include supernatural agents in their description.

As I said at the beginning, the way a ritual produces particular effects is mysterious, not least to the people concerned. They have no idea why saying this or doing that as the ritual prescribes should make people married rather than get them cured of a disease or some other effect. People who have gone through a painful initiation of the kind described by Michael Houseman have a strong intuition that they have become different and that boys that did not follow the initiation path are indeed 'incomplete' or 'unfinished'. But they have no idea why this is so. The causal link is obvious but its mechanism is difficult to describe. Some undeniably real but inscrutable cause is thought to have produced a visible effect. There is something in initiation that turns boys into men, although no one can say what it is. There seems to be something in the wedding ceremony that really turns people into a couple, in a way that remains mysterious.

All this is quite familiar to anthropologists. It is the reason why we often say that rituals have a definitely *transcendent* flavour. They seem to activate some source of causation, some mysterious forces that people can sense but not describe, let alone explain. There is 'something else' to the ritual than the mere sequence of actions, for how could a few gestures and words really produce such important and undeniable effects? You cannot perform the rituals seriously without assuming that a prescribed series of actions will have a certain result *and* guess at the same time that the series of actions as such cannot explain the result.

To say that rituals suggest some transcendence seems to imply deep mystical attitudes and a propensity to magic. But things are much simpler. That people think in terms of hidden and inscrutable causes is not in itself particularly mystical. On the contrary, transcendence of this kind is found in a great number of perfectly ordinary situations. As I said several times in previous chapters, most of the intuitions that we get from our inference systems imply some mysterious causation of this kind. For instance, we know that objects that are thrown hard will get further, and we explain this by saying that they have more 'momentum'. But this term is largely vacuous unless you have learned physics. In a similar way, we assume that there is something inside the developing organism that pushes it to be similar to other members of the same species. This species-specific 'essence' is what makes courgettes and sprouts develop their particular shape and taste.

Unless we do science, the way we explain our ordinary intuitions very often refers to inscrutable causal processes. In this sense there is much transcendence in our concept of aubergine. This limited sense of 'something unobservable that causes the observable effects' is also what we find in people's thoughts about ritual effects. People have the thought that the ritual created some social effect and have some intuition that the actions themselves are not the whole explanation, so something else must be involved.

This empty slot in our representation of ritual in many cases remains empty. This is very much what happens for many male initiations. People say that it changed the boys into men. When asked how this happened, they just say that it happened and that's that. The married couple are now different from what they were before the wedding. But we do not know why. It just happened.

Now an empty slot like that can also be filled by whatever representation you have that could be connected in some relevant way to the unexplained effect. This is why concepts of gods and spirits and ancestors are often activated in such contexts. People then think that the people were changed by the wedding because the gods were witnesses to their pledge. The apprentice turned into a shaman because the ancestors operated some mysterious change in his body.

Obviously, such explanations do not literally explain much but they certainly are relevant comments on the situation. Since the rituals produce effects without clear causes and the supernatural agents are not clearly detectable, there is no great effort in putting the two together. Also, this produces inferences about the results of rituals. For instance, the intuition you have that there is some social danger in people's extra-marital affairs takes on a new flavour if you assume that this is because the spirits are watching everyone's behaviour. So we can better understand what gods and spirits are doing in rituals, so to speak, once we realise that their participation is a salient but unnecessary *addition* to the mental representation of the ceremonies. This way of seeing the situation is of course less inspiring than the notion of a human urge to worship the divine, but it is more faithful to what actually occurs in minds acquiring cultural knowledge.

What gods do (and what is done to them)

This way of understanding religious ritual helps us understand, not just why gods are associated with rituals at all, but also what precise roles they are supposed to play in these occasions. As Thomas Lawson and Robert McCauley point out, performing a ritual is not or not just a matter of being in some vague relation to gods and spirits, but also of doing things to them (giving them objects, addressing statements to them) or of getting them to do things (like possessing people, providing rainfall or curing the sick). The supernatural agents' specific role is very precisely described in people's mental representations of their ritual sequences. If we have a ceremony to ask the gods for good crops, this specifies for instance that we will say things to them, we will sacrifice a pig, they will listen, we hope they will decide to protect our crops. When we ask the ancestors to turn this young man into a shaman, they are said to descend upon him and change him for good. Nothing vague or mystical here. People know (or rather have some representation of) what the ancestors and gods are doing.

Lawson and McCauley developed a very precise account of these possible roles of supernatural agents. In the mental representation of religious rituals there is both a representation of the series of acts prescribed (what they call an 'action-description'), and a particular point where concepts of gods and spirits are inserted. Performing a ritual is like cooking a stew. The recipe is an action-description (brown the meat, put it aside, sauté the onions, put the vegetables in, put the meat back in, reduce heat, etc.) which specifies the various elements involved (the cook should be a person, the meat a dead animal, etc.) as well as some syntax: some actions come before other ones and some actions *require* other actions. In religious rituals too you have such action-descriptions: for instance, the priest dons special robes, takes crucifix in hand, blesses the crowd. Here too you can say that there are specific labels (the priest must be a person) and syntactic rules (the ordaining of the priest should come before he starts blessing things or people). What makes religious rituals different is only that some of the elements in an action-description are described as 'special', as Lawson and McCauley put it, that is, connected to supernatural agents. In this case, *priest* implies *special*

298 ⌒ Religion Explained

person, ordained, and crucifix is special object, representing crucifixion, etc.[20]

Now rituals differ in terms of *where* you put the *special* elements. When a priest blesses a crowd, it is the main agent, the priest himself, who is labelled as connected to divinity, while the crowd is not special at all; anyone (indeed anything) can receive a blessing. On the other hand, if you are offering a pig to the gods, the agents are not special but the 'patient' (the one affected by the ritual) is special, in the sense that she or he is supernatural. Some rituals are *agent-special* (the gods or their representatives or someone specially affected by them is performing the action); some rituals are *patient-special* (the gods or their representatives are the ones on whom the ritual is said to have an effect).

Lawson and McCauley realised that this difference had important effects on people's intuitions, and also on the general style of ritual performance. Rituals with special agents, in particular the ones where the gods and spirits are themselves said to be doing things, are performed rather rarely, in fact generally only once for a given person. Think of wedding, initiation, birth rituals, etc. Rituals with special patients by contrast are often repeated. People offer a sacrifice to the ancestors, but they have to do it repeatedly to guarantee that the ancestors oblige (with good crops or protection).

There is another difference. According to Lawson and McCauley, rituals with special agents usually trigger high emotional arousal, often by using time-tested techniques like loud music, mind-altering substances, feasting or fasting, etc. Rituals with special patients (we act upon the gods) are generally much more sober. Naturally, this is only a *relative* difference, given the particular ambience of each religious tradition. You certainly find more colourful rituals in Voodoo than in Methodism and more visible excitement in Brazil than in Finland. But within each particular tradition, agent-special ceremonies generally turn up the emotional volume, relative to what you find in patient-special rituals. Why is this? Why should we have higher or lower levels of sensory stimulation in ritual, depending on which role the superhuman agent is playing in the script?

A tempting answer would be that some rituals are 'louder' because that makes them more convincing. After all, gods and spirits are generally discreet. The claim that they really were involved in turning the boys into men or these two people into a family is, at first blush, difficult to believe. So perhaps having lots of sensory stimulation is a way to make such effects more plausible. The patient-special rituals, on the other hand, where people do things to gods and spirits, would not face this difficulty. It does not require much effort to believe that our own actions have effects on distant, generally invisible agents, since after all many of our actions have effects on persons not present.

This is not a very sound answer, for it presupposes that which we want to understand. True, people in many places use cheap gadgets (loud musical instruments, drugs, masks, etc.) to accompany the supposed presence of the ancestors or other such agents. Gewgaws and music may well strengthen your impression that the gods are around (I doubt that, but let us accept it for the sake of argument), but that will work only if you already assume that they are around. Otherwise they just remain gadgets.

The connection between rituals and social effects may offer a better explanation. One-off rituals, performed in principle only once for a given person, are centred on the social changes introduced by people becoming a couple, by children being born, by people growing up to adulthood and dying. These changes by nature happen only once. Because of our naïve sociology's weaknesses, they are rather difficult to understand and they require, as I said before, that everyone co-ordinate their actions to accommodate the change in the same way, at the same time. These are enough reasons to make loud and striking rituals more intuitively apposite than sober ones. The point about weddings is not just that people should take the new relationship into account but that everyone should do it, preferably at the same time. By contrast, other rituals trigger social effects that require repetition. Sacrifice seems to establish an exchange between gods and people, but all humans intuitively construe exchange as an iterated game, that people will play repeatedly with the same partners. People also have the intuition that the terms of exchange with a partner are independent from those that obtain with another. That is, that my exchange with the gods is vastly in my favour so far is not changed by the fact that the gods have swindled someone else. In such circumstances the loud gadgets that ensure co-ordination between people and similar effects on them all would be superfluous. So the correlation observed by Lawson and McCauley (one-off, loud rituals have the gods themselves acting; repeated, sober rituals have the gods acted upon) may well stem from a difference between the social effects of the ceremonies. (As a belated caveat, let me repeat that this is speculation; it is a sad but true fact that we simply do not have enough experimental evidence so far, as concerns people's representation of the gods' and spirits' roles in ritual.)

Whether rituals are thought to have long-lasting social effects (changing people and their relations) or transient ones (curing the sick, guaranteeing good crops), in both cases the participation of supernatural agents adds relevant elements to the mental representation of the ceremonies, but it is not indispensable. Indeed, in many places the hidden 'something' that explains the ritual effect is *Society* or *The Lineage* or *The Community*. This, incidentally, is the way non-religious people often explain their own participation in religious performances like weddings, bar-mitzvahs and funerals. They do not 'believe', they say, but they accept that such ceremonies are important, that they have effects, that people's sense of being a community requires continued performance of the rites even if the metaphysics loses its persuasive power. I would suggest that these people are perhaps much closer than they realise to the mind-set of religious believers. What matters to rituals and makes them relevant is that one construes the social effects as the *result* of the actions prescribed. This inevitably creates a causal gap. Because of the massive salience of agency in our mental systems, most humans fill this gap with concepts of agents; but an abstraction like 'our tradition' or 'society' can play much the same role.

What we know is not the explanation of rituals

We are very far from having explored all the connections between our evolved psychology and the use of ritual conceptual gadgets. So a reasonable strategy is to identify the common mechanisms of some rituals and explain how these are particularly catching for the kinds of mind that we have. The Contagion cues, the relational gadgets and the openings for gods are such devices. They are not found in all rituals but they are present in a number of them and may explain why these apparently pointless behaviours are so common in human groups.

Why do people get together and pretend they are offering the goddess a goat which they then cut up and eat? Why do they gather in a circle and hand around a were-tiger's trinkets? Why should a new shaman try to bite a ram's tongue, a difficult enterprise in any circumstance, then climb up a pole blindfolded and with the animal's heart in his mouth? Why for that matter do people gather in a special building, listen to accounts of a long-past torture-session and pretend to eat the flesh of a god? I chose to open this discussion with unfamiliar examples because this gives us a general sense of the difficulty of such questions. The Catholic Mass (which I just described in very succinct terms) is no more mysterious than the other cases. But as far as familiar religious performances are concerned, we often think that the answer is the official one given by the believers themselves or the authorities: We have these Sunday sessions in order to commemorate a crucial event, partake of supernatural blessings, celebrate a particular supernatural agent and renew a special contract with that agent.

This cannot be the explanation. These thoughts are all perfectly relevant to the situation in question, but they are not a description of the mental processes that make a Mass, or any other ritual, a salient event that people somehow assume they should perform again and again in the same specific way. The explanation for the cultural success of rituals is to be found in processes that are not really transparent to practitioners, and become clearer only with the help of psychological experiments, anthropological comparisons and evolutionary considerations.

People sacrifice the goat in the way prescribed, they circulate relics anti-clockwise and force a young shaman to climb a pole for the same reasons that make a whole variety of other rituals compulsive: because these are *snares for thought* that produce highly salient effects by activating special systems in the mental basement. Human minds are so constituted, with their special inference systems for unseen danger, their weak social concepts and social intuitions, and their notions of counter-intuitive agents, that these very special performances become quite natural.

Chapter Eight

Why doctrines, exclusion and violence?

Here is a simple scenario. People in a group tend to have a similar description of supernatural agents, a local doctrine of what gods or spirits are up to. The very fact that people in a group share this religious identity and perform important rituals together sharpens their perception that they are indeed a group with clearly marked boundaries. Worshipping the same gods creates a community and by implication gives that extra edge to the feeling that people with different gods or spirits really are potential enemies. Indeed, people who become deeply involved in religion, for whom it is a matter of vital importance that their doctrine is the only source of truth, will not hesitate to massacre the ones who seem not to acknowledge this obvious fact or whose commitment is too lukewarm. The most heinous of crimes will be a celebration of the True Faith. This is how gods and spirits lead to group-cohesion, which leads to xenophobia, which leads to fanatical hatred.

Practically everything in this scenario is misguided. Each of the steps describes phenomena we are all familiar with: that religion is the concern of social groups, that there are different doctrines, that there are exclusive and incompatible claims to truth, that fundamentalist violence is a real threat in many parts of the world. But the devil is in the details, not so much in the facts described as in what leads from one fact to another. It is by no means an academic question, whether there really is a historical slippery slope down which religion is bound to slide. Precisely because the scenario is of more than theoretical interest, it makes sense to examine it in some detail.

One doctrine too few

No question, it seems, could be more straightforward than this: What is your religion? Many people will readily answer that they have *a* particular religion, indeed they *belong* to a religion with a particular *doctrine*. People identify themselves as Jains or Protestants or Buddhists and can usually describe the differences as a matter of doctrinal assumptions, of holding for instance that dead people can come back and show us the true path of salvation, that a unique god is watching our every action, that it is abhorrent to destroy any living thing however humble, that the gods can protect you against illness or misfortune, etc. So far, so simple.

But the question is not that 'natural', as many people in the world would not even understand what it means. Here is an illustration: For the Buid people of Mondoro in the Philippines most religious activity consists in communicating and interacting with friendly spirits, and enlisting their help to combat other, dangerous spirits. This is achieved by mediumship. Several times a week, people gather together and start singing to attract their *lai* or personal spirit. At some point they sense that the *lai* are coming over, leaping across mountain tops to come over and visit them. Each singer climbs on the back of her or his supernatural friend. Together, they hover above the mountains and watch the evil spirits swarming around the village. The *lai* are specially helpful in driving away these unwanted visitors. For the Buid most people can master these songs, and there is nothing exceedingly difficult about riding a spirit – it is all a matter of practice. However, in this as in other domains, some individuals are better at it than others. This becomes important in cases of illness or death, when people feel that a great number of evil spirits must be lurking around and a larger seance is required. In such cases reputed singers are called from neighbouring settlements and asked to help in driving away the intruders.

Contrary to what we would find in Christianity, Islam or Buddhism, the Buid have no systematic doctrine of supernatural agents. Everyone assumes that the *lai* have supernatural qualities – they fly over mountains and remain invisible – but there is no received theory of what these agents are like, what they do, where they reside, etc. The Buid have a notion of mediumship but not a concept of 'religion' encompassing all the notions, norms and activities connected to supernatural agency. There is no official school or group of religious specialists. Anyone can sing and attract friendly spirits. Finally, the Buid would not assume that practising mediumship makes them members of a wider community. Whether other people in the world have personal spirits or not, and how these other people construe them, is not a matter of great interest.[1]

Having religion does not necessarily imply that one has 'a' religion with a particular doctrine. Those features that we find straightforward and natural are in fact the outcome of a very specific history. In some historical conditions, religious specialists group themselves in institutionalised associations (churches, castes, etc.) and diffuse a particular description of what their function is. It then becomes clear to everyone, first, that there is such a thing as 'religion' as a special domain of concepts and activities; second, that there are different 'religions', that is, different possible ways of practising religion, one of which is more valid; third, that adopting a particular religion means joining a social group, establishing a community of believers, emphasising the demarcation between us and them.

Several doctrines too many

The fact that people sacrifice to their local spirits or ancestors, that they participate in common ritual, would seem to strengthen common identity, which in turn supports cohesion and co-operation. But is this really the case? Again, we must not mistake official norms for actual fact. This connection between having the same gods or the same practices and being a community may be more a statement of what should happen than a description of what does happen.

Religious concepts and practices in Java illustrate this difference between norms and facts. Several religious traditions combine here. First, many people, especially in the countryside, are mainly concerned with various ancestor and local cults that outsiders call *abangan*, in contrast to literate religion. Second, there has been for centuries a strong Muslim influence, such that a majority of the population define themselves as such. Muslim schools and institutions are more present in cities, they have more direct influence on traders and city-dwellers than on peasants, but Islam remains the majority 'religion'. Many people on the other hand define themselves as Hindu, attend the appropriate ceremonies and perform worship in Hindu temples. Finally, some mystical 'Javanist' cults seem to represent a modern version of traditional village concepts, although they have probably been influenced by Sufi cults. The real mix of influences is in fact even more complex than that. For some Indonesians, the mystical Javanist cults are a genuine but eccentric form of Islam; for others, the real gap lies between local, Javanese elements and foreign (Muslim or Hindu) influences.

People, at least officially, all belong to *one* of the groups defined by these doctrines. I use 'officially' because, as anthropologist Andrew Beatty points out, the division between Muslim, Javanist or Hindu is to some extent 'internal' to most individuals. That is, the various viewpoints and normative ideals that can be identified with these different traditions are tools that people combine much more freely than a description in terms of 'affiliation' would suggest. Muslims attend Hindu rituals and consider Hindu temples as sacred places. Self-declared Hindus include Muslim saints and ancestor-cult references in their rituals. In the village where Beatty did his field-work, about a fifth of the adult villagers (both Muslim and Hindu) were also members of the mystical Javanist sect Sangkan Paran, which they did not identify as religion because it was less concerned with an abstract theology of the afterlife than with well-being and good fortune here and now.

A good illustration of these combinations is the ritual *slamentan*, a formal meal that is at the centre of most religious practices in Java. This is organised in conjunction with a variety of ritual occasions, such as circumcision, if the hosts are Muslims, but also harvest feasts or any other salient event. *Slamentan* is organised to reunite village factions, in cases of serious misfortune, and often to redeem a vow. People who feel grateful for some good fortune organise it to celebrate the gods, God, spirits or ancestors to whom they are indebted. As Beatty describes it, 'the host makes a speech in High Javanese explaining the purpose of the meal to his guests, incense is burned, an Arabic prayer is recited by the guests . . . the speech invokes the host's ancestors, place spirits, Muslim saints, Hindu-Javanese heroes, and Adam and Eve in a polytheistic jumble'.[2]

This is what students of religion generally call 'syncretism', a situation where there is a 'mixture' (the original sense of the word) of heterogeneous elements. The term is literally exact, for the elements that people insert in the *slamentan* are indeed borrowings from various sources: the teachings of the various Muslim schools, the court rituals of old Javanese kingdoms, local ancestor cults as well as Hindu concepts. But the term 'syncretism' is also misleading if it suggests that people are *confused*, that is, build these creative new combinations simply because they are not taught properly the differences between religions. The people who perform a *slamentan* or attend various Muslim rites or visit Hindu temples are anything but confused. The history of Javanese and other Indonesian kingdoms is one of rivalry between political factions, often clearly identified with one of these religious strands. They all created institutions such as temples, schools and a local literate élite. The Javanese are aware of the origins of all these institutions.

It seems that 'belonging to one religion', something that would seem quite straightforward to most Westerners, is problematic for the Javanese. As Beatty puts it, 'it is at birth or death that the individual is stamped, unprotesting, with a religious identity, and at marriage that he or she is the focus of maximum social pressures (often conflicting ones) to proclaim a religious identity'. In such a situation, it is clear that one must 'choose' a religious affiliation in the sense of joining a particular coalition. By joining the Muslims you identify with a particular faction in a particular political context (where 'political' includes family relations and village politics as well as the general Indonesian situation). By joining the Hindu 'camp' you are joining another coalition. In fact people are rather reluctant, for reasons that their history explains all too well, to be formally identified as members of this or that coalition. This is precisely because they perceive the risks associated with this kind of coalitional game. Once you have joined a particular faction, you probably miss opportunities that would have been available at some further juncture.[3]

To compare these two cases: The Buid seem to have one religious doctrine too few. Their notions of spirits and mediumship are coherent but not expressed as one consistent and generally applicable theory. The Javanese by contrast would seem to have several schools too many, as they strive for a potage of doctrines that religious institutions naturally try to curb.

I use these contrasted examples because they illustrate several fairly simple facts that challenge the simple 'scenario' with which I started this chapter: First, concepts do not necessarily form a doctrine; it takes people, in particular religious specialists, to build an explicit set of religious understandings. Second, it is only in very special circumstances that specialists can do that, as we will see presently. Third, what is at stake in the diffusion of religious concepts is very much a matter of social interaction, of coalitions and politics, filtered through people's social mind-concepts.

All these facts are fairly complex and interconnected, so I will start with an apparently naive question: Why are there religious specialists at all? Nothing in the representation of supernatural agents makes specialists a necessary feature of religion. The agents' powers are such that they affect everybody, and it would not in principle be difficult to assume that everyone has the required capacities to handle interaction with them, as the Buid seem to do. As it turns out, the fact that there are specialists, and the special way in which they organise themselves as a group, have important consequences for the creation of religion as something one can *believe in* and *be a member of*.

Local specialists

To anyone brought up in the context of world religions, the presence of specialists such as priests, ministers, *'ulema*, rabbis and monks goes without saying. But priests or scholars recruited, trained and sanctioned by a special institution, are not a universal feature of religion. In many contexts a specialist is just someone who, more than others, is thought capable of handling the delicate relations people entertain with spirits and gods.

Consider the Fang situation. One major concern is to avoid witchcraft attacks. Some people are said to have the internal organ *evur* that flies away at night and performs various magical tricks to damage its victim's goods and health. Many cases of misfortune are interpreted as the result of such attacks, and in such cases one should resort to a specialist called a *ngengang*. This person also carries an *evur*, but he or she is supposed to use it for the common good in fighting against the witches. Often, people become *ngengang* as the result of an illness or a tragic accident in their youth. They are then treated by a specialist who identifies the source of their problems: their *evur* is much too powerful and possibly out of control. They go through special rituals in order to channel the *evur*'s power to the benefit of the group. After a specific apprenticeship they can then cure or protect others; such specialists must be competent in both ritual and medical knowledge.

This kind of notion is quite general, apart from the Fang case: the very problems that led to a specialist's intervention are the ones that made a person capable of helping others – the same capacity that is involved in witchcraft and in anti-witchcraft. This naturally leads to a great uncertainty in people's attitudes towards such specialists. It is not absolutely clear that they do have the special quality in question. More worrying, it is not really clear either that they will use it *only* for defensive purposes, or indeed that the distinction really means much. For what you see as a vicious witchcraft attack against you may also be described as a pre-emptive strike against your own witchcraft. So it is not always clear which side the specialist is on. Most of my Fang friends were quite definite that they did not want to have too much to do with such characters, except in a case of real and urgent need.

What makes a *ngengang* different is not something that you could observe or deduce from unambiguous cues. Indeed, it sometimes happens that people lose confidence in one of these specialists and conclude that he probably never had *evur* to start with. But it is clear to everybody that there is a fact of the matter, that each person either has or else does not have an *evur*. Being a specialist is not just being able to perform certain rituals, for the rituals would be pointless if performed by persons without *evur*. It is not even a question of actually achieving particular results. University trained physicians are known to cure (some) illnesses but no one thinks this is because they have a special organ. In this sense the difference between *ngengang* and other people is represented very much in the same way as the difference between natural species. We assume that there is something inside tigers and giraffes that makes them develop and behave in different ways, but we do not usually have a description of that inherited 'essence'. In the same way, people assume that some individuals have a special quality that makes them shamans or healers or mediums.[4]

The presence of specialists clearly recognised as different from other people stems from a much more general tendency to create co-operation between individuals with different perceived abilities. As soon as certain people are perceived, for some reason or other, to be able to provide a particular service better than others, there is the potential for creating a minimal division of labour. To illustrate this, let me return to the example of the Buid. They seem to have the most democratic religion imaginable, in the sense that everyone is thought to be capable of mediumship. However, even in this situation, people do recognise differences between individuals, a first step towards the creation of local specialists. This in indeed what happened among the Taubuid, a neighbouring group, where efficient singers have become specialists who derive prestige and material benefits from their reputation, as well as some political influence. These Taubuid mediums generally control exchanges between their settlements and the outside world. With their specialisation comes an ambiguous reputation, as many people suspect them of gaining power and influence through witchcraft. Even this seems to work to their advantage, as people in a Taubuid settlement would not want to get on the wrong side of a dispute against them. There is little difference between Buid and Taubuid, as far as religious concepts are concerned. The Taubuid are simply more representative of a very common process. Once a difference in ability is detected or imagined, it leads to a minimal division of labour, where people are called upon in particular contexts. It is only a matter of opportunity for these people to accrue additional benefits on the basis of that reputation, and thereby create a rudimentary religious specialisation.

In such contexts, the people supposed to take a special position in dealings with supernatural agents are represented as having a particular, though invisible, quality that sets them apart from others. In some cases this is said to be inherited, in other cases acquired through disease or accident or some other equally dramatic experience, or to be conferred by the gods or spirits. But in all these cases the special quality of specialists is internal, difficult to detect, and the performance of rituals and other such religious actions is only an index that the quality really is there. That is, one does not become a shaman or healer by being told to perform the rituals and being reasonably efficient at it. In people's conceptions, one probably has that specific quality which would make such rituals efficacious.

Another general characteristic of such specialists is that their authority or authenticity is *locally* guaranteed. In the case of lineage priests this is a matter of course, since the religious activities they supervise or conduct are relevant only to their own group. In the case of shamans, healers, diviners, one either knows them personally or knows some of their past customers. So the specialists' claim to a specific role in dealing with superhuman agents only depends on their position or reputation in a given group. This is why it is quite natural for most people to think that such specialists generally interact with supernatural agents who are local too: the group's ancestors, local demons or spirits who own a particular territory, control a particular animal species or reside in a particular place.

The Fang know that there are many *ngengang* and they also know that each of them has his particular technique and co-operates with particular spirits. It makes perfect sense to resort to one *ngengang*'s services if another fails to solve the problem at hand. The way these specialists describe what they do and why it supposedly works can vary a lot. Since their role depends so much on their particular, individual qualities, on their reputation in a particular group, there is no clear sense that they are representatives of a general way of dealing with supernatural agents.

All this is quite different from what we find in established religions like Christianity or Islam. Those Fang people who became familiar with either of these religions found, first, that specialists in these religions are not defined in terms of some internal essence; the Christian priests or Muslim scholars are simply people who under-went special training; second, that the competence of specialists is guaranteed by a large organisation, not established at the level of a village community; third, that the services offered are uniform: what you get from one Catholic priest is very much what you would get from any other.

Why this difference? The standard answer — put forward by

religious institutions themselves – is that there are institutions because there is a distinctive 'faith' expressed as a doctrine. To diffuse that unique doctrine and organise activities connected with it, a special organisation was then founded, with the result that ritual is standardised. But there is every reason to think that the evolution of religious institutions is more or less the opposite of this standard picture. Doctrines are the way they are because of the organisation of religious institutions, not the other way around.

Origins of the guilds

Millions of pilgrims, devotees, priests and holy men throng the city of Benares. Funerals conducted there are said to confer the deceased a better destiny. The main point of the long rituals performed by specialised Brahmans is to turn the soul of the dead person from a *pret*, a malevolent ghost, into a *pitr* or ancestor. During a ritual cycle that extends over eleven days, the Brahman gradually incorporates the substance of the deceased person, in particular the impurity of the dying process, into his own body. The Brahman receives many 'gifts' on behalf of the deceased. This in fact is a euphemism, for the priests are notoriously rapacious, as anthropologist Jonathan Parry points out. They will haggle for hours over their fees for each segment of the ritual. Their advice to each other is to try to 'wring the neck' of their clients, that is, extort as much money as possible from them. The received wisdom among priests is that the customer who agrees to a price probably was not squeezed hard enough. Conversely, the clients know the value of their money but cannot be sure whether the ritual is really effective, which leads to tenacious haggling on both sides. On the whole, however, the priests know how to extract the greatest benefit from their position, largely dominant if not monopolistic, on this market for highly valued ritual services.[5]

It may seem strange to talk about markets, services and commercial negotiations in the context of ritual services. Not that we believe such phenomena to be absent from religion – we all know that religious institutions provide particular services and receive specific benefits in exchange – but we generally tend to think of these economic aspects as *consequences* of religious organisation rather than as its source. That is, we assume that doctrine comes first, and its implementation leads to particular economic and political behaviour. This may be misguided. Indeed, some crucial aspects of religious institutions make sense only if we understand what the market for religious services is like, what kind of commodity religious knowledge and ritual constitute. To describe this in more detail, we must consider the vast historical process that led to the emergence of religious organisations, and started with the appearance of large state societies with literacy.

Literacy was invented three times in human history, in the Middle East, in China and in the Maya empire, and all present scripts are descendants of one of these. Literacy evolved out of various symbolic systems designed to represent particular facts (a number of notches along a stick to stand for a particular debt, a series of traces on a bone to represent various animals, etc.). But the real revolution, that allowed the storage and retrieval of unlimited amounts of information, was an inventory of signs that could represent *speech* rather than facts or ideas. The new system thereby inherited all the richness and flexibility of a natural language, and could express whatever language could express. The changes that resulted were stupendous for religion but also for the economy and for the administration of large states. Indeed, early scripts were mostly used for administrative purposes, for book-keeping, legal and commercial documents, before they were extended to other types of texts, private correspondence, religious texts, literature, etc. The use of written documents gradually spread the world over, but until recently the standard situation was restricted literacy, where only a small group of specialists handled such documents. In many places, beginning with the Sumerian Middle East and Egypt, as well as China, and then extending to most Eurasiatic states, such literate specialists were also involved in the production of religious texts.

In all these places literacy appeared in *complex states*, in polities where people's decisions were made in the context of large networks and institutions. So literacy and a complex social organisation spawned another important development, that of stable associations of religious specialists. This happened in the Middle East, in Egypt, in India and China, and finally in all Eurasiatic societies. There were written religious texts, ritual prescriptions, lists and tables of moral prescriptions and prohibitions, because religious specialists were transformed into an organised social group, akin to a *corporation* or *guild*. This social transformation had profound effects on the nature and organisation of the concepts that such specialists produced and diffused.[6]

A religious guild is a group that derives its livelihood, influence and power from the fact that it provides particular services, in particular the performance of rituals. In this way it can be compared to other specialised groups, like craftsmen. In a city-state or even an empire, craftsmen can afford to spend most of their time away from subsistence activities such as tending herds and growing food, because they provide goods and services and receive some payment for these.

Such groups often try to control the market for their services. Throughout history, guilds and other groups of craftsmen and specialists have tried to establish common prices, common standards and to stop non-guild members from delivering comparable services. By establishing a quasi-monopoly, they make sure that all custom comes their way. By having common prices and common standards, they make it difficult for a particularly skilled or efficient member to undersell the others. So most people pay a small price for being members of a group that guarantees a minimal share of the market to each of its members.

One might think that the services provided by religious scholars, like ritual performance and scriptural knowledge, are essentially different from making shoes or tanning leather. But this precisely makes the general tensions associated with imperfect markets even more relevant. For religious goods and services are indeed different but in a way that makes their position much more fragile than that of other groups. Specialised craftsmen often have no difficulty maintaining exclusive supply, either because other people are reluctant to perform their dangerous and polluting tasks (gathering garbage, burying the dead, butchering animals, etc.), or because these tasks require technical knowledge and a long apprenticeship (most crafts). By contrast, religious specialists supply something – rituals, a guarantee that they are efficient in dealing with supernatural agents – that could be provided easily by competitors. Indeed, in most places with such castes of religious specialists there *are* other providers: local witch-doctors, healers, shamans, holy men and knowledgeable elders (in other words all the 'local' specialists described above), who can always claim that they too offer some interaction with supernatural agents or protection against misfortune.

This is one of the reasons why religious castes or guilds very often try to gain maximal political influence. Not all religious guilds achieved control over the whole political process as the Christian Church did for a large part of European history. For instance, the Indian groups of scholarly Brahmans did to some extent impose a specific form of religious practice but they did not displace the political supremacy of kings. The Chinese 'schools' (Taoism, Confucianism, Buddhism) never imposed themselves as paramount political forces. However, all these groups in these different circumstances did wield considerable political influence.

The fact that religious groups are so involved in political intrigue and manage to find a political niche in most places with centralised authority is very familiar to all of us, so familiar indeed that we may forget that it is a *special* characteristic of such groups. For instance, castes of craftsmen also try to garner some political support and lend their weight to various political factions, but they are not usually as important as groups of religious scholars. This is not because the goods and services provided by craftsmen are less indispensable or important. In fact the reason may be exactly the opposite. Since the services of literate religious groups *are* dispensable, the religious schools that do not yield some measure of political leverage are very likely to end up as marginal sects, a process that has happened repeatedly in history. So priests and other religious specialists are not necessarily central to large-scale political organisation. But the ones that do not manage to gain some political leverage fall by the wayside. (Incidentally, this is why it is both largely true and somewhat misleading to construe religion as the ally of the oppressors, as an institution that invariably supports centralised political power and offers supernatural justifications for the established order. This is true in the sense that many successful religious guilds were successful precisely because they adopted this strategy. But it is misleading in the sense that organised religious guilds of this kind are not the whole of religion. Indeed, they choose this strategy precisely because the competition is constant and in fact highly successful too.)

Given the elusive nature of the services they provide, literate groups of religious specialists always remain in a precarious position. The difficult training and special knowledge make sense and can subsist only if there is some guarantee that people will actually need the special services. At the same time the services in question are very easily replaced, or so it would seem. Perceiving all this and reacting to it appropriately does not mean that you have expert knowledge of political economy. In all such groups, people have a precise though intuitive grasp of their group's position in the market. It does not require much sophistication to realise that your position as a priest or religious scholar is potentially threatened by the alternatives offered by shamans and local healers.

One solution is to turn the guild's ministration into a *brand*, that is, a service that is (1) distinct from what others could provide, (2) similar regardless of which member of the guild provides it, (3) easily recognisable by some particular features and (4) exclusively provided by one particular organisation. A Catholic priest offers rituals that are quite different from the ancestor-based rituals his Fang congregation were used to; but Catholic rituals are also quite stable from one priest to another; some observable features make it easy for most Fang observers to distinguish between say a Catholic Mass and what is offered by rival guilds. There is nothing intrinsically demeaning in saying that some services are offered in the form of a particular brand. This is likely to occur whenever an organised group of producers is in competition with both local, independent producers and rival organisations. The creation of recognisable brands of religious services has important consequences for the kinds of concept put forward by religious institutions.

The concepts offered by literate guilds

Concepts of supernatural agency, as well as the norms of behaviour that come with them, are presented by the guilds as an explicit doctrine. In order to offer a unique kind of religious services *and* a stable one from one religious specialist to the next, a guild requires a description of what it offers. Clearly, putting forth a doctrine implies that there could at least in principle be several doctrines and that one of them is valid. Even though a guild is keen to present its concepts and norms as the only set that really makes sense, or the only true set, by the very fact of claiming this it makes it possible to think that there could be others. (In fact some guilds include in their presentation a detailed denunciation of other guilds and their claims, so that the existence of alternatives becomes even more obvious.) This aspect of religion is very familiar to most of us, but is not necessarily present in all human groups. Those Kwaio who resisted missionaries, and the Fang before massive colonisation, did not think of their ancestor-cults as a special option. They just saw them as a (supposedly) time-tested and obviously efficient way of interacting with the ancestors.

Literate guilds promote texts as the source of guaranteed truths. They tend to downplay intuition, divination, personal inspiration, orally transmitted lore and 'essential' persons because all these naturally fall outside the guild's control. The use of texts as authority strengthens the notion that true descriptions of supernatural agents come in the form of a stable and general doctrine, rather than on-the-hoof, contextual solutions to specific problems. A typical question in local religious activities is 'Will the ancestors be satisfied with this pig and help this child recover?'. A typical one in a literate religion would be 'What animals must be sacrificed for what types of illnesses?', and the answer to that is a *general* answer.

Also, the use of texts tends to make religious doctrines more coherent, in the sense that all the elements that constitute the description of supernatural agents can be brought together for consideration much more efficiently than when they are stored in individual people's memories, in the form of particular episodes. Guilds offer an account of gods and spirits that is generally integrated (most elements hang together and cross-reference each other), apparently deductive (you can infer the guild's position on a whole variety of situations by considering the general principles) and stable (you get the same message from all members of the guild). This last feature is particularly important for diffusion. Even complex concepts can gradually become more and more familiar to the illiterate masses through consistent sermons and recitations.

Obviously, the work of religious scholars not only creates coherent doctrines but often spawns abstruse and paradoxical theology as well, that is, literate versions of the supernatural concepts that do not connect with any of the supernatural templates listed in previous chapters and do not activate inference systems either. Also, literate guilds sometimes foster forms of mysticism supposed to resolve the paradoxes created by literate religions. Theories created by theologians are to some extent comparable to philosophical systems, although the latter do not offer mystical contemplation as an escape from the puzzles they create. The divorce from common supernatural templates and inference systems is one major reason why such systems are often either ignored or blithely distorted by most congregations, as we will see presently.[7]

All human groups have some rituals to deal with corpses and some notion of how the 'soul' or presence of dead people must set off on a journey, to be separated from the living. In many places this is associated with concepts of particular ancestors, local heroes who settled the group, founders of the dead person's clan, gods of particular places and spirits connected to particular families, which means that these gods and ancestors are specific to each group, or even to a village. This local god demands incense and flowers, that one requires sacrificed chickens, and the divinities of each particular mountain or river are likely to be the object of different ritual procedures.

As a guild claims to offer similar services throughout a large polity, it cannot claim to have a particular connection to *local* supernatural agents, such as ancestors and local spirits. The agents that the institution claims to interact with must be such that any member of the guild, wherever they are, could be said to be in contact with them. This is one of the main reasons why such 'small' gods and spirits are usually demoted in the doctrines of religious institutions and replaced with more general, cosmos-wide agents. The Fang have ancestors who, they say, interact with them and usually protect them; they are also plagued by evil spirits. Both the benevolent and malicious spirits are members of the same social groups as the living people they interact with. Christianity attempts to replace all this with a unique supernatural agent that *anyone* can interact with, provided they resort to the Church's offices.

This is why organised literate guilds tend to promote a very specific understanding of death and the destiny of various com-ponents of the person. What happens to the soul is presented as a consequence of *general* processes that apply to all humans. Religious guilds replace the intrinsically local notions of 'establishing' the ancestors, turning them into mountains or pillars of a house, with a general and abstract notion of salvation conditioned by moral behaviour. Such a notion is found in most written religious doctrines, with important differences in how salvation is defined and what kind of morality is attached to such definitions. The Jewish and Christian versions imply proximity to God as well as a very vaguely defined (especially in the Jewish case) afterlife, while the Indian (Hindu or Buddhist) versions imply an exit from the cycle of reincarnations and the elimination of the soul as a self. These are among the variations on a theme found in many literate traditions. Death should not be construed only as a passage to the status of ancestor but also as a radical leave-taking from society. This makes sense, as the doctrine is offered by specialists who have no particular service to offer in terms of local cults to local characters, or in any case nothing that could be seemingly better than the services of local shamans and other religious specialists.

All these features are very general to religious guilds, although I must insist that the history of such groups presents many variations on these themes. Anthropologists who have noticed these features have often debated whether they were straightforward consequences of the technology of literacy, or a result of the special political role of religious guilds within large polities.

For anthropologist Jack Goody literacy does result in a different cognitive style. The use of literacy changes cognitive operations, in the sense that the written text is used as an external memory. For instance, literacy allows complex mathematical operations during which some intermediate results must be stored. It allows elaborate arguments because it allows people to make long lists of elements that prove a particular point. It allows people to think of various conceptual structures as visual templates. In this way the 'sketchpad' aspect of writing is every bit as important as its long-term 'storage' function.

Some features of literate religion do support this interpretation. For instance, enumerating the 613 *mitzvot* of Jewish law or the thousands of omens recorded in Sumerian and Egyptian texts would obviously require some forms of written aid. Complex theologies, ritual prescriptions for thousands of different occasions, collected texts of various wise men, compilations of oracles and moral rules, all this was of course one of the side-effects of using scripts to store and retrieve data.

But some changes in religious style are also a consequence of the fact that religious specialists are grouped in state-wide groups rather than recruited locally on the basis of personal qualities. The insistence on abstract gods rather than local ancestors, or the notion of individual salvation substituted for contracts with ancestors, are not a direct consequence of literacy as such but rather a consequence of having literacy applied to religion by organised groups of religious service-providers. The two factors, literacy and complex polities, are naturally intertwined, since literacy as the specific technology of a whole group could not develop without complex societies.

Perhaps more important (and in any case more tractable) than the question of ultimate causes is that of the *effects* of literate religion. The above survey might be misleading in suggesting that there was a clear cutting-off point in human history, when religion was taken away from local specialists and became the business of an organised group of scholars, when concepts of local gods and spirits were replaced by more abstract and coherent versions, and when death was reconstrued in terms of salvation. Indeed, this is the way religious institutions themselves often try to present the situation, with a clear-cut distinction between 'before' and 'after' their emergence. The real situation is far more complex than that.

The mirage of theological correctness
However great the control religious guilds impose through political means and widespread diffusion of their doctrines, there *always* seem to be some non-standard beliefs and practices left 'sticking out'. For instance, many Hindu scholars contrast what they call *shastrik* elements of the religion – the belief and practices supposed to be the definition of Hinduism – with the *laukik* or local, popular and con-textual versions. The *shastrik* elements should apply everywhere, regardless of the particular time or place: this is a typical claim for a literate religious group.[8]

However, people always add to or distort the doctrine. The same phenomenon is found in Buddhism, where scholars are scandalised by the many pagan practices they must witness, tolerate and in which they are sometimes forced to participate. The history of early Christianity also includes many difficult conflicts between the competing claims of a still fragile Church with considerable political backing and a host of local cults that somehow deviate from the doctrine. In the case of Christianity, the great difficulty at first was to decide exactly what the doctrine was. The essentials of the doctrine did not originate in a scholarly group but were those of a messianic, revolutionary movement, a loose federation of groups with not entirely compatible interpretations of not entirely similar accounts of the Revelation. When the movement did become an organised religious guild with great political leverage, this created a series of complex struggles between political factions that identified themselves in terms of these different interpretations of revelation and morality. Hence the long succession of Councils supposed to establish, once and for all, coherent foundations for the doctrine, and therefore determine who was in and who was out.

In some ways, Hinduism achieved a more balanced equilibrium between the general, literate version and the inevitable local variants and additions. This was realised mostly through the convenient division between great gods of cosmic significance and local deities, more generally goddesses, that are mainly relevant at the local level. More or less every settlement has its own goddess who is specially concerned with the inhabitants of that special place. Such deities are no less 'Hindu' than the great gods but this arrangement gives people some leeway in the creation of concepts and ritual practices that are not entirely defined by the religious guild. However, tensions remain even within this apparently stable division of labour between deities. As anthropologist Chris Fuller notes, 'there is clear evidence that deities particularly favoured by Brahmans, who are offered only vegetarian food and are worshipped in Sanskrit by Brahman priests, are disparaged by some low-caste Hindus, who see them as much weaker than other deities such as village goddesses, who are offered animal sacrifice and praised in the vernacular by Non-Brahmans'.[9]

This process of addition, re-creation and modification of concepts is *constant* and in all likelihood destined to go on as long as there are organised groups of literate religious scholars. People may well resort to the services of various literate guilds, and even identify themselves as followers of that guild; this does not mean that their supernatural concepts are really organised by the messages delivered by these specialists. Actual religious concepts always seem to stick out, as it were, distort the official message or add all sorts of officially incorrect interpretations. This is in fact inevitable, because the official messages themselves must be understood by people; which means that they must produce inferences to make them coherent or relevant; which in turn implies that their mental constructions must complete, often in divergent ways, messages that are by nature fragmentary, in this as in other domains of cultural constructions.

As I said in chapter 4, people tend to construe gods and spirits as agents with strategic knowledge, and therefore explain their moral intuitions as the fact that supernatural agents are monitoring their actions. Some literate guilds accept that notion, but they generally try and promote a more abstract and internally coherent account of morality, in terms of precisely listed rules and prohibitions. But this somehow never replaces the notion that the gods or spirits are around and concerned with people's behaviour. Indeed, when the literate account is too abstract, people just *add* to it the notion that their ancestors and some spirits are around and concerned with people's actions anyway. It is very difficult for literate groups to counter people's tendency to make their religious concepts more local *and* more practical. People are never quite as 'theologically correct' as the guild would want them to be.[10]

The tragedy of the theologian

Why this tendency? Given the coherence, large diffusion and stability of a guild's message, it seems surprising (not least to the religious guilds themselves) that this influence is constantly threatened by less organised, less coherent and less general versions of religious concepts. But, as anthropologists have suggested, these latter features may well be the very reason why non-standard versions arise and become successful.

Sociologist Max Weber emphasised this phenomenon, contrasting a routinised version of religious authority, where everything is defined and described by the appropriate religious officials, with periodic outbursts of charismatic or revolutionary activity. The latter are generally centred on inspiring individuals who rekindle people's religious passion – blunted by the repetitive and bureaucratic teachings of the religious guild – around spectacular rituals and renewed enthusiasm. Indeed, many religious traditions seem to oscillate between such poles. This oscillation has been documented for Islam and various Hindu and Buddhist movements, as well as Christian movements.

According to anthropologist Harvey Whitehouse, these different modes of transmission in fact activate different cognitive processes, and that may be why periodic outbursts of dissidence are inevitable. For Whitehouse there are in general two ways in which religious concepts are acquired. One is the *imagistic* mode, where people perform 'loud' rituals with high sensory stimulation and vivid imagery. The initiation rites I mentioned in chapter 7 would be a good example of this mode. People go through dramatic performances that leave evident traces in memory, but whose meaning is often unclear to most participants. Whitehouse contrasts this with the *doctrinal* mode of transmission that is found in the activities of most religious guilds. This provides no high drama but a coherent, systematic and frequently repeated set of verbal messages. It is usually characteristic of literate guilds whose activities are based on a set of texts, although this may not be the only circumstance where this mode of transmission is given pride of place. Indeed, Whitehouse himself has described Melanesian cults based on such endless recitations of commandments and exposition of their logical consequences, although without the help of literacy.

Religious guilds generally provide many contexts for acquiring consistent propositional messages through repetition and systematic teaching, but very few contexts where salient episodes, what Lawson and McCauley called 'sensory pageantry' can be recruited as an aid to memory. A consequence emphasised by Whitehouse is that the guilds gradually lose their influence, because of what could be called a tedium-based decay-function. That is, people become gradually more and more familiar with the doctrine, but this familiarity removes much of the motivation for talking part in the guild's rituals and other activities. As a consequence the more religious institutions favour the doctrinal mode of transmission, the more vulnerable they are to periodic outbursts of imagistic dissent.[11]

Religious institutions are invariably keen to support the doctrinal activities and contain the imagistic ones. Christian Churches have always been happy to accept past miracle-makers in their fold but rather reticent with new ones. Churches embrace some displays of religious fervour but also try and contain them as much as possible. Why should this be so?

Memory processes are not the only force driving religious institutions. The market for religious services also imposes particular constraints. The most important imperative for a religious guild is to make its own services stable and distinctive. Imagistic practices challenge the stability of these services. Revelation, trance and other forms of enthusiastic ritual are all difficult to codify and control, which is why they are viewed by religious institutions with considerable suspicion. Also, such rituals offer great scope for enterprising individuals to set up their own particular cult in competition with the guild. Finally, the services of the guild are made stable and distinctive by the systematic use of written manuals and codified messages. But what makes the guild's brand recognisable – an intrinsically positive effect – also makes its rituals entirely predictable.

This, then, is the real tragedy of the theologian: not just that people, because they have real minds rather than literal memories, will always be theologically incorrect and will always add to the message and distort it, but also that the only way to make the message immune to such adulteration renders it tedious, thereby fuelling imagistic dissent and threatening the position of the theologian's guild.

Common gods create a community (or do they?)

Why is it that some people can find it perfectly all right, indeed morally compelling, to exclude or kill people because they are not members of the 'right' religion? Religion, or so it appears, creates a community. It seems to go without saying that holding the same concepts and norms as other Christians, for instance, does make people members of a group, with some degree of solidarity that can be expected from other members and a general distrust towards non-members. People describe themselves as 'members' of this or that religious group, with important and often tragic consequences for their interaction with other groups. This, it would seem, is found not only in places where religious guilds provide an explicit description of what 'the' religion is about, and also explicit criteria for membership. Even in groups without literate guilds, it would seem that communal sacrifice to the ancestors or joint participation in various other rituals enhance the cohesiveness of the group.

Again, however, appearances may be deceptive. The idea that common gods result in a common identity seems fairly plausible because it is based on a correlation. Many groups that have a fairly strong sense of being, precisely, groups apart from the others, *also* use religious norms and practices as signals of that common identity. Because several factors are present at the same time, it is difficult to figure out their exact relations. Note that some of the examples described here seem to go against the simplistic link between common gods and a community. The Buid's main religious activity is a form of mediumship that is found in many neighbouring groups as well. But the Buid are a distinctive group, they see no particular connection to or kinship with other practitioners of this form of religion.

Saying that having the same gods creates solidarity just begs the question of why and how religious concepts can have such an effect. Why should you feel closer to someone who happens to have similar supernatural concepts? In other words, if common gods and spirits are not really necessary for group cohesion, how can they be used for that purpose?

Signals of group membership, especially of *ethnic* group-membership, are very diverse although not indefinitely variable. They consist in features that are both easy to distinguish and difficult to fake, such as residence in a particular territory, mode of sub-sistence, language, accent, dietary preferences or willingness to undergo gruesome rituals. Although there may be great emotional import in these signals, they are none the less construed as nothing more than *symptoms* or *indices* of an underlying set of qualities. People say that they all share the bones of their ancestors, that they have common blood, etc. All these metaphors express what psychologists would call an *essentialist* assumption. That is, one assumes that there must be something in common between all the individuals con-cerned, though one may only have vague or metaphorical understandings of what that thing actually consists of. Members of an ethnic group defined along such lines can readily imagine the improbable yet possible case of an outsider who would manage to speak the language with the right accent, prefer the correct food and in general display all the signs of membership, yet would of course remain an outsider. Membership is defined in terms similar to what I described in chapter 3 as a basis for our understanding of animal species. For a group of people, participating in the same rituals is a simple consequence of sharing some undefined but real quality present in all of them but not in outsiders.[12]

Inference systems have particular input conditions, that is, they get activated whenever information with a certain format is presented. For the essential system, input conditions include the following: (1) some living things are presented as having common external features – a prototype; (2) they are all born of other members of the same category; and (3) there is no reproduction outside the category. This is obviously the case for living things. But social categories are often presented in this way too. In many places in Africa and Asia craftsmen are members of endogamous (marrying only within clan or tribe) castes, thought to be inferior, polluting and dangerous. These groups are explicitly construed as based on *natural* qualities: the people in question are thought to be essentially different from the rest by virtue of some inherited, internal quality. Blacksmiths in West Africa are recognisable, they are all descended from blacksmiths – you cannot *become* a member of that category – and they only marry blacksmiths. Once a social category is construed in this way it should probably activate, in a decoupled manner, the essential inference system.

But this, too, raises difficult questions. So far, we have described the mechanics of *essentialism*, the way it activates inference systems we all have by virtue of the way our brains are constructed. But this is not enough to explain why essential construals of social groups appear so convincing and why they trigger such enormous emotional effects. That social groups are often defined as essentially different is simple enough to understand, given the way our brains work. But why is it so easy to trust members of one's own group and distrust outsiders, even without any actual experience of how they behave? We may think that people are just told that outsiders are not reliable co-operators. The problem is to explain why this idea is so easy to acquire that it hardly needs any teaching.

Essence concepts and coalitional intuitions
One of the most solid and famous results of social psychology is that it is remarkably easy to create strong feelings of group-membership and solidarity between arbitrarily chosen groups. All it takes is to divide a set of participants and assign them to say the Blue group and the Red group. Once membership is clearly established, you get them to perform some trivial task (any task will do) with members of their team. In a very short time, people are better disposed towards members of their group than towards the others. They also

begin to perceive a difference, naturally in their group's favour, in terms of attractiveness, honesty or intelligence. They are far more willing to cheat or indeed inflict violence on members of the other group. Even when all participants are fully aware that the division is arbitrary, even when that is demonstrated to them, it seems difficult for them not to develop such feelings, together with the notion that there is some essential feature underneath group-membership.[13]

These well-known results demonstrate the extraordinary strength of the human propensity towards group solidarity, what Matt Ridley called 'groupishness'. Humans just seem desperate to join some group and to demonstrate loyalty. But the results also show how easy it is to trigger essential understandings of groups, and even to get those understandings to translate into actual behaviour, *in the context of a coalition*. That is, the groups in question are invited to collaborate more with members of their group than with outsiders. They quickly develop intuitions and emotions about trust and reliability, connected to group-membership, described in chapter 5 as necessary to coalition-building.[14]

I think artificial laboratory conditions and actual social behaviour converge here to suggest why essence-based understandings become salient and emotionally important: They are *the concepts we spontaneously use to describe intuitions that are in fact not about social categories but about coalitions.*

This may be abstruse in formulation but the point is really simple. Our naïve view of social interaction around us is that we are often dealing with people with whom we share some essential features. They are our lineage, our tribe, our fellow-believers, and so on. But I think we can get a better sense of how such interaction is actually built if we realise that many of these groups are in fact coalitional arrangements, where a calculation of cost and benefit makes membership more desirable than defection and therefore more stable. In previous chapters, I mentioned the flexible, *ad hoc* coalitions found in many social contexts, from the informal alliances and friendship networks between co-workers to the hunting parties organised by nomadic hunter-gatherers. Coalitions require very sophisticated computations of other people's reliability, based on signals that are often ambiguous and sometimes could be faked, as well as estimates of the costs and benefits that result from joining a coalition. Yet people generally do not need to make these computations explicit. Rather, they justify their behaviour by thinking and saying that some people are intrinsically reliable and others are not. We can usually work on the basis of such gut-feelings because they are the result of subtle calculations in our specialised systems, away from conscious inspection.

Now, in some contexts, the social relations people build on the basis of these coalitional intuitions are made much easier by the fact that the groups are defined as *essential*. In laboratory studies, people were given an arbitrary coalition to co-operate with, and as a result started imagining essential differences between groups. But in real social life the opposite is very often the case. People are presented with social categories that seem essential – castes of blacksmiths or lineages – and use them for coalitional purposes.

Because they are extremely stable coalitions, these essence-based groups do not *seem* to be coalitions at all. That is, for all the members as well as outsiders, the alleged essence is what drives people's behaviour. But I would suspect that actual behaviour is more directly driven by people's coalitional intuitions. Take for instance the case of lineages in an African group like the Fang. Lineages are certainly defined in essential terms, not just in the sense that people are putative descendants of a single ancestor but also because they are said to share some essential features. When I worked in Cameroon, people frequently told me that the So-and-so were easy-going, the Such-and-such were trouble-makers, etc. Fang lineages are also a centre of intense, unconditional co-operation, so that you can rely on fellow-members to help you out but should not expect similar solidarity from non-members, even though they may live in your village. Fang lineage-based groups are spread over huge territories, so that everybody has lineage 'cousins' they seldom interact with. In these rare cases, essential understandings of lineages would suggest that you can trust them (these people are the same substance as you are, you know their personality-type and therefore their reactions), while coalitional intuitions would recommend caution (since this is a first-time interaction and will probably remain a one-off occasion, why should they do you any favours?). People in such cases generally follow their coalitional intuitions, but then reconcile this with their essential concepts by saying that they are not in fact certain that these people *really* belong to their lineage.

So the point is that some social categories appear to be based on essences — *essential concepts* are the ones that come to mind when thinking about these categories — but actual behaviour is piloted by more complex cues: *coalitional intuitions* are not made conscious but give us precise intuitions about what to do. This may seem something of a metaphysical distinction, as far as most social groups are concerned. But the difference becomes crucial when social hierarchies and dominance are involved.

This is clear in the hierarchies created on the basis of what sociologists Jim Sidanius and Felicia Pratto call 'arbitrary set distinctions' like race or ethnicity. Here too there seems to be a discrepancy between explicit concepts of social groups and intuitions that guide behaviour.

Consider the explicit concepts first: That most members of minority groups are dangerous or unreliable is construed as an essential feature of these groups by racists and deplored as lamentably unfair stereotyping by non-racists. Both constituencies agree on one assumption: that attitudes towards various social groups are based on people's understanding of the essential features of these groups. In this view, all it would take to establish better relations would be to convince most dominant-group members that minority people are essentially similar to them. For instance, if children were trained to realise that people do not really behave like their stereotypes, they would perceive the moral ugliness of discrimination.

But then Sidanius and Pratto marshal an impressive amount of evidence to the effect that there is more to dominance than stereotyping, suggesting that the latter is often a consequence rather than a cause. In fact, they demonstrate that many behaviours stem not just from the desire to stay with one's group or to favour one's clan, but also in a more insidious way to favour one's group in a way that maintains the other group's lower-status position. That is, what drives people's behaviour is a coalitional structure where it is actually advantageous to try and keep members of other groups in a lower-status position, with distinctly worse benefits. Racial stereotypes are among the representations that people create to interpret their own intuition that members of other groups constitute a real danger: that is, these outsiders threaten the insiders' own coalitional advantages. Obviously, one possible reason for this blindness to coalitional structures is that they often conflict with our moral standards. This may well explain why many people prefer to consider racism as a consequence of sadly misguided concepts rather than as a consequence of highly efficient economic strategies.[15]

We should not be surprised if many social categories are both maintained by coalitional solidarity and explicitly construed in essential terms. This is another illustration of the *social magic* described in chapter 7. People may well have finely tuned coalitional capacities, but they do not necessarily have access to how these work. The cues that make some people appear reliable and others less so are computed in ways that often escape conscious attention. In the same way, the fact that defection is a threat to me even if it only directly hurts someone else is something that most people grasp intuitively, but they have very poor concepts to explain it. So the notion that blacksmiths or undertakers are naturally different is particularly relevant when it explains why non-blacksmiths and non-undertakers maintain a high solidarity that excludes these craftsmen, but such a notion is not the *cause* of such divisions; the interests of the groups, seen through human coalitional thinking, are the main cause. In this domain of social interaction as in others, people create powerful notions of what groups are, to some extent because these provide a plausible and relevant interpretation of their own intuitions.

To return to religion: I have tried to show that there is nothing *special* about gods and spirits, when it comes to creating communities or establishing efficient levels of trust. But we cannot stop there, for then we would have no explanation for the extreme enthusiasm with which members of some religious groups offer selfless co-operation to other affiliates and see members of other faiths as dangerous, disgusting or distinctly sub-human. The solution lies in the human capacity for coalition-building in and the flexibility of these capacities. The mental systems involved are not specially geared to religious concepts, but the latter can in some circumstances become fairly good indicators of where coalitional solidarity is to be expected.

This may be why many religious guilds try to emphasise affiliation as a radical choice, not open to further negotiation. All sorts of mechanisms in religious corporations reinforce this sense that one is a member for good. Naturally, in most places the notion that there is a 'choice' is theoretical. That is, you do not really 'choose' to be a Muslim and identify with the Muslim *'umma* if you are born in Saudi Arabia, no more than you have much of a choice when you identify yourself as a Christian in America. But the point is that, in each case, you can vary the extent to which you want to declare this identity and make it a source of coalitional commitment and coalitional benefits. Some people have a low-commitment strategy, whereby they accept to be members, pay the various taxes and perform the various services demanded of members, but that is more or less it. Others choose a more involved strategy, where they go further in declaring their allegiance, often volunteer for extraordinary actions on behalf of the faith, and get in return some goods, power, prestige and a guarantee of solidarity from other members of the corporation. Others, still, take a much more risky path and are prepared to kill or risk their lives for the group.

Fundamentalism and the price of defection

In the most diverse traditions (American Christianity, Islam, Hinduism, and even more surprisingly Buddhism) one can find movements entirely focused on a *return* to the religious values promoted by the religious guild and supposedly perverted by further developments. Although such movements are as diverse as the contexts in which they arose, there are some common trends and the legitimisation of violence in the service of a religious restoration is one of them.

We often hesitate between two different explanations for the existence of organised groups that seem prepared to use extreme violence (or 'heroism' as seen from the insiders' perspective) to coerce a wider community into proper religious attitudes. On the one hand, it is tempting to think that this is *all to do with religion*, that is, fundamentalist extremism is simply an excessive form of religious adherence, a caricature of ordinary behaviour in the relevant religious communities. This is a common theme in Western liberal reactions to fundamentalist Islam: religious leaders and their henchmen are seen as just 'more Muslim' than ordinary Muslims, a view that fits the old and persistent antipathy to Islam in the West. This also fits our common notions about religious identity. If you assume that supernatural concepts naturally create identity and solidarity, as well as powerful emotional bonds between people, then it would seem that having a stronger commitment to such concepts would result in extremist behaviour. A second interpretation, equally common though at odds with the first one, is that religious extremism has *nothing to do with religion*. For instance, fundamentalism is seen as a brazen attempt to gain social control on the part of small groups to reach the influence, power, prestige that society is reluctant to give them. This view is often put forward by people from the countries where such movements are active. Muslim intellectuals argue that fundamentalist movements are a caricature of a more authentic, nobler and more generous Islam (and they use considerable scriptural authority to back this argument). In

the same way, many Christians, Jews and Hindus react with horror
to the assimilation of their religion with such movements as Bible-
belt fanatics, ultra-orthodox rabbis, or mosque-burners in India.
Both interpretations, in my view, fail to explain what is special about
such movements. For one thing, even if fundamentalism were just an
extreme form of religious persuasion, this would not tell us anything
about the reasons why some people in some circumstances are led to
this particular version of their religious tradition. Also, the notion
that fundamentalists are simply lusting after power fails to tell us why
they seek it in that particularly dangerous, costly and often
ineffective way. I think the movements really are about religion – but
describing them as 'fanaticism' just begs the question of what leads
people to such behaviour – and they really are about power – but this
does not tell us what power these people are after and why this seems
the only way to get it.

As I said, fundamentalism is a modern phenomenon and mostly a
reaction to new conditions. But this does not mean that the movements are *just* a reaction to modernity. Indeed, as many specialists
have pointed out, groups of this kind are not enemies of things
modern in general. They use modern mass-media – schools, news-
papers, radio and TV stations. Some of these movements create
schools and social networks for mutual help that make good use of all
the available machinery and resources of modern technology. There
must be other features of modernity that create this violent reaction.

A tempting explanation is that the modern world is one of strident
cultural diversity, where you are constantly made aware that other
people live in different circumstances, have different values, worship
other gods, have different rituals. This would suggest that the
reaction is mostly against religious and cultural competition,
specially acute in the case of Third-World societies confronted with
powerful, ex-colonial Western influence. In this view, fundamentalists want to return to a (largely mythical) past when local
values and identity were taken for granted, when no one was aware
that there were other ways of living.

I think this view captures an essential feature of such movements – competition really is the main point here – but we need to go further in explaining the psychology of such reactions. For it is not totally self-evident that people will naturally want to preserve the common 'cultural values' of their group. Why would that be the case? What is the motivation? We commonly assume that people have a strong desire to preserve their own cultural ways because these give them a sense of identity and therefore of solidarity. But that is question-begging; as I said above, some cultural concepts and norms are used in this way in some conditions. You just cannot take for granted that they all are, always. It is even less self-evident that this desire would lead to violence, which is precisely what we want to explain.

We can get a better sense of fundamentalist reaction if we describe more precisely what is so scandalous about modern influence in a religious milieu and if we take into account that the reaction is a matter of coalitional processes. The message from the modern world is not just that other ways of living are possible, that some people may not believe, or believe differently, or feel unconstrained by religious morality, or (in the case of women) make their own decisions without male supervision. The message is also that people can do that *without paying a heavy price*. Non-believers or believers in another faith are not ostracised, those who break free of religious morality, as long as they abide by the laws, still have a normal social position, and women who dispense with male chaperones do not visibly suffer as a consequence. This 'message' may seem so obvious to us that we fail to realise how seriously it threatens social interaction that is based on coalitional thinking. Seen from the point of view of a religious coalition, the fact that many choices can be made in modern conditions without paying a heavy price means that *defection is not costly* and is therefore *very likely*.

To give a more dramatic illustration of what this means in a coalition, think of a platoon in times of war. This kind of group can only function – that is, undertake extremely dangerous operations with some probability of success – if mutual trust is very high, so that each individual can take great risks to protect the others, knowing that they will do the same. Everyone must be confident that implicit trust over-rides considerations of immediate interest; otherwise members of the group would be tempted to defect when the going gets rough. There is usually a heavy price to pay for defection, stipulated by official codes and enforced by threats of court-martial, prison or execution. But people in such groups frequently persecute, brutalise or ostracise *in advance* those individuals who show signs of being less than altogether committed. Armies are rife with spontaneously organised ordeals that pre-emptively discourage and in fact exclude those less-reliable individuals long before they are actually put to the test of real engagement. Soldiers are often eager to ridicule, beat up and publicise the plight of those who fail to show their daring. From the point of view of strict rationality, this would seem a waste of time. Once you have established that someone is a chicken, you should simply not trust him in dangerous situations and that's that. Since you think he is not good soldier material, this will not change him in the least. All the energy and time spent browbeating and punishing the potential defector is wasted. But the effort makes sense if we realise that it is probably directed, not at the victim, but at all the others. That is, it sends a powerful and memorable signal that defection is very costly. This is intuitively perceived as one way to reduce the likelihood that others may defect. All this is a straightforward consequence of the coalitional principles described above. It is dangerous to join a coalition that others can defect from without paying much cost. The more you put at risk by joining the coalition, the higher you want to raise the price of defection.[16]

Fundamentalist violence too seems to be an attempt to raise the stakes, that is, to discourage potential defectors by demonstrating that defection is actually going to be very costly, that people who adopt different norms may be persecuted or even killed. I offer this as a slight modification to the 'reaction to modernity' interpretation, because the coalitional background seems to me to make the psychology of such reactions more realistic, and also because it explains several features of extremism that would otherwise remain puzzling.

First, note that many fundamentalist groups are predominantly concerned with control of *public* behaviour: how people dress, whether they go to religious meetings, etc., even though their religious doctrine often is primarily concerned with personal faith or commitment, and in some cases explicitly condemns the temptation to establish oneself as judge of others' behaviour (this is particularly salient in fundamentalist Christianity and Islam).

Second, some fundamentalist groups have shown a great propensity to make the punishment of what they see as immoral behaviour much more public and spectacular than it would have been in their respective traditions. At first sight, there is no clear rational explanation for the public denunciation of named individuals, for violent demonstrations in front of planned-parenthood clinics or for the public stoning of adulterers. This emphasis on public and spectacular punishment makes sense if it is in fact directed at potential defectors, to make it all the more obvious how costly defection can be.

Third, a good part of fundamentalist violence is directed, not at the external world but at other members of the same cultural, religious communities. The most imperious domination is exerted inside the community: by leaders over mere members, by dedicated followers over non-committed people, and above all by men over women. If the movement was all ethnic-religious, it would concentrate its attacks on outsiders. Again, however, coalitional dynamics would predict that whatever outsiders do is of little concern to fundamentalists. What matters is what other members of the group are likely to do.

Fourth, the main target of many fundamentalist movements is often a *local* form of *modernised* religion. This is quite obvious in American fundamentalism – both Christian and to some degree

Jewish – which obviously cannot be a reaction to colonial or foreign influence, but is directed against liberal versions of these creeds. But we can observe the same phenomenon in other places. The mass-media description of fundamentalist Islam or Hindu violence in India would suggest that we are dealing here with a simple conflict between external modernity on the one hand and internal tradition on the other. But that is not the case. In Islam and in Hinduism too, for over a century there have been many popular movements that adapted religious norms to modern conditions. These movements were particularly popular with the educated, urban middle classes and therefore represented a real political danger for those whose authority is purely grounded in religious hierarchies.

To sum up, then, fundamentalism is neither religion in excess nor politics in disguise. It is an attempt to preserve a particular kind of hierarchy based on coalition, when this is threatened by the perception of cheap and therefore likely defection. If court-martials were to become more lenient towards deserters, and if this was known to soldiers in action, I predict that the spontaneous and illicit search for and punishment of potential deserters would become much more vicious and demonstrative. The same psychology may explain why some people are led to extreme violence in the service of their religious coalition. The mental systems engaged are present in all normal minds, but the historical conditions are special, which is why there is nothing inevitable about this process. Not all religious concepts are used to create ethnic markers, not all ethnic markers are used as coalitional signals, not all coalitions are faced with cheap defection and not all members of such a threatened coalition react by hiking the price of defection. Indeed, the fact that the price is pushed so high clearly shows that these groups are well aware that popular sentiment does not lean in their direction. Which, unfortunately, is no obstacle to political domination if the coalitions are cohesive enough.

Chapter Nine
Why belief?

Some Fang people say that witches have an extra internal animal-like organ that flies away at night and ruins other people's crops or poisons their blood. It is also said that these witches sometimes assemble for huge banquets, where they devour their victims and plan future attacks. Many will tell you that a friend of a friend actually saw witches flying over the village at night, sitting on a banana leaf and throwing magical darts at various unsuspecting victims.

I was mentioning these and other such exotica over dinner in a Cambridge college when one of our guests, a prominent Catholic theologian, turned to me and said: 'This is what makes anthropology so fascinating and so difficult too. You have to explain *how people can believe in such nonsense.*' Which left me dumbfounded. The conversation had moved on before I could find a pertinent repartee — to do with kettles and pots. For the question, How can people possibly believe all this? is indeed pertinent but applies to beliefs of all hues and shades. The Fang too were quite amazed when first told that three persons *really* were one person while being three persons, or that all misfortune in this vale of tears stemmed from two ancestors eating exotic fruit in a garden. For each of these propositions there are lots of doctrinal explanations, but I suspect the Fang find the explanations every bit as mystifying as the original statements. So the question remains: Why do people adhere to such propositions? What makes them plausible? and most importantly, Why do some people believe and not others? What persuades *some* of us to accept a variety of claims about gods and spirits, the evidence for which is, shall we say, tenuous at best?

As I said in the first chapter, it makes little sense to try and explain how people believe in supernatural concepts when we have no clear description of what these concepts are, how they are acquired and organised in human minds. So are we better equipped to answer them now? I think we are, but the explanation is *not* going to be one of those quick, shoot-from-the-hip solutions that many people, religious or not, seem to favour. There cannot be a magic bullet to explain the existence and common features of religion, as the phenomenon is the result of *aggregate relevance*, that is, of successful activation of a whole variety of mental systems. This is also the case for belief.

Indeed, the activation of a panoply of systems in the mind explains the very existence of religious concepts *and* their cultural success *and* the fact that people find them plausible *and* the fact that not everyone finds them so *and* the way religion appeared in human history *and* its persistence in the context of modern science. I realise it is a bit foolhardy to promise to kill so many birds at once, especially when the stone seems so awkward to handle. What do I mean by 'activating various systems'? What I do *not* mean is that 'there are many aspects to religion', 'it is a complicated domain', and 'many factors are involved'. In fact my ambition in writing this book was precisely to escape from such bromides and extract clear explanations from cognitive science.

What I mean is far more precise. There is some experimental

evidence for different inference systems with their specific domain of input. Religious concepts trigger activation of a particular list of these systems, which increases the likelihood that concepts of this kind get built in human minds, that they appear intuitively plausible, that someone agrees with their explicit formulation, that they are left untouched by such corrosive influences as that of science. But note how all this is not so much *caused* as *made more likely* by the cognitive processes I described.

What we know from evolutionary biology, psychology, archaeology and anthropology is a set of factors that constitute the collective and invisible hand of cultural evolution. We humans are generally not very keen on *invisible hand* explanations. As philosopher Robert Nozick once pointed out, we tend to prefer *hidden hand* scenarios, where there is a real conspirator: the masters of the universe who pull all the strings, or in this case a particular feature of the human mind that creates the whole of religion, a central metaphysical urge that is the origin of all religion, an irredeemable human propensity to superstition, myth and faith, a special emotion that only religion provides, and so on. I can safely predict that there will *always* be a market for such explanations, but I also think we have evidence that they cannot be true. So let us see why what I called aggregate relevance is such an important feature.[1]

Accommodating airy nothing: a matter of undue laxity?

People who ask questions such as *How can one believe that?* are of course not among the believers. It is a hallmark of a genuine belief that we generally care little for its origin, for the ways in which it became a denizen of our mental household. For instance, most of us believe that salt is white and steel is tough, but we do not generally know how we acquired these beliefs; nor do we care. Asking where beliefs come from, in the context of religion, has generally been the preoccupation of sceptics. This does not invalidate the question, far from it, but may explain why it is generally answered in a particular way that I find insufficient and actually misleading.

It does not require much effort to have religious beliefs. The Fang people who insist that there are witches flying about on banana leaves, like the Christians who assume that a hugely powerful agent is watching them, do not in general need to work hard to persuade themselves of such claims. Which is why sceptics tend to see belief as a form of *mental negligence*. People are said to believe in supernatural agents because they are superstitious, they are led astray by their emotions, they are not mentally balanced, they are primitive, they do not understand probability, they are not scientifically trained, they are brainwashed by their culture, they are too insecure to challenge received wisdom. In this view, people believe because they fail to (or forget to, have no time to, are unwilling to, or just cannot) censure ill-formed or poorly justified thoughts. The beliefs would vanish if people were more consistent in applying common-sense principles of mental management like the following:

- *Only allow clear and precise thoughts to enter your mind.*
- *Only allow consistent thoughts.*
- *Consider the evidence for a claim before accepting it.*
- *Only consider refutable claims.*

What the Fang say about their ghosts seems unclear at the very junctures where precision would be essential. People say that the ghosts are not material, they are somehow 'like the wind', and also that they have left their body. The ghosts are described as generally invisible but people have very different views about what this means and are seldom confident that their own interpretation is correct. A ghost is construed as what is left of a person once the body is no more. But then the ghosts are also said to *see* what people do. How can they see without eyes? Christians are told that man was created in God's image but as most religious statements this is ambiguous enough to receive many different, contextually appropriate interpretations.

Also, most religious traditions routinely flout the requirement of consistency. Indeed, some religious claims are precisely *designed* to violate it. Sceptics are baffled by the Christian notions that three persons are one person, that God is omnipotent but we are free agents, and by many other apparently inconsistent claims. When they ask for clarification they are generally given extremely confusing answers that seem to avert inconsistency at the price of, again, violating the requirement of clarity.

As for evidence . . . whatever believers consider to be 'evidence' for the existence of gods, spirits and ancestors, as well as their powers, has always struck outsiders as evidence for no such thing. In fact, it is evidence only at the price of violating the requirement that we should only have refutable beliefs. If you are told that a high dose of vitamins can help the body fight an infection, the only evidence that really counts is a test that could refute the claim: if for instance clinical tests showed that patients treated with vitamins had no better recovery than those without vitamins, this would cast doubt on the alleged benefit of such a treatment. Religious claims are not refutable at all in this sense.

The situation may in fact be even worse than this. For centuries philosophers have described the failures of mental management that supposedly led people to unwarranted beliefs. But philosophers only had the tools of introspection and reasoning to figure out how minds worked. When psychologists replaced all these with experimental studies, they found a whole menagerie of mental processes that apparently conspire to lead us away from clear and supported beliefs. Consider for instance the following:

Consensus effect: People tend to adjust their impression of a scene to how others describe it; they may see for instance a face as angry, but if various people around them see is as 'disgusted' they too say they perceive it as expressing that emotion.

False consensus effect: This is the converse effect, whereby people tend wrongly to judge that their own impressions are shared by others, for instance that other people's emotional reaction to a scene is substantially similar to theirs.

Generation effect: Memory for self-generated information is often superior to memory for perceived items. In a particular scene you imagined, the details you volunteered will be recalled better than the ones suggested by others.

Memory illusion: It is easy for experimental psychologists to create false memories, whereby people are intuitively certain they did hear or see some item that was in fact imagined. Also, imagining that you perform a particular action, if that is repeated often enough, may create the illusion that you actually performed it.

Source monitoring defects: People in some circumstances tend to get confused about the source of particular information (was it their own inference or someone else's judgement? Did they hear it or see it or read about it?). This makes it difficult to assess the reliability of that information.

Confirmation bias: Once people entertain a particular hypothesis, they tend to detect and recall positive instances that seem to confirm it, but they are often less good at detecting possible refutation. Positive instances remind one of the hypothesis and are counted as evidence; negative instances do not remind one of the hypothesis and therefore do not count at all.

Cognitive dissonance reduction: People tend to readjust memories of previous beliefs and impressions in the light of new experience. If new information leads them to form a particular impression of someone, they will tend to think that they had that impression all along, even if their previous judgement was in fact the opposite.[2]

The list is by no means exhaustive. The experimental literature describes many more varieties of departures from normative reasoning, from the way we should think in order to think coherently and efficiently. Minor irrationality of this kind is very common in all sorts of circumstances, including the acquisition of information about supernatural agents. A person brought up in a Kwaio environment is surrounded by people who seem to assume that there are ancestors around (consensus effect); she would tend to think that her own impressions are shared, for instance that most people feel the way she does about a particular shameful action and the ancestors' disapproval (potential false consensus affect); some of her representations about ancestors are self-generated, leading to good recall; this is also the case for religious specialists who must tell other people how to perform rituals and how to interact with ancestors, in effect improvising all sorts of new details about these agents (generation effect); whether a certain event was directly perceived or reported might become uncertain after a while (memory illusion, source monitoring defects); once she assumes that ancestors do intervene in people's affairs, occurrences that confirm this may become more salient than others, thereby lending some support to the original assumption (confirmation bias); and even if some definite prediction about the ancestors was refuted by experience, she might well revise her memories of her own past beliefs (cognitive dissonance reduction). Indeed, this latter notion was developed to explain how members of apocalyptic cults managed to cope with the fact that the appointed date for Judgement Day had passed and nothing had happened. What social psychologists found so striking was how a refuted prophecy seemed to deepen commitment rather than shake it. Naturally, gods or a unique God would be the same as the Kwaio ancestors from the point of view of such psychological processes. The contexts in which people acquire religious representations and communicate about such matters seem particularly likely to result in such deviations from sound reasoning.

Belief and the judicial model

All this is probably true, but is it sufficient? As I suggested in chapter 1, such arguments are useless when we want to understand why people believe in particular kinds of supernatural agency rather than others. People have stories about vanishing islands and talking cats but they usually do not insert them in their religious beliefs. By contrast, people produce concepts of ghosts and person-like gods and make use of these concepts when they think about a whole variety of social questions (What is moral behaviour?, What to do with dead people, How does misfortune occur?, Why perform rituals?, etc.). This is much more *precise* than just relaxing the usual principles of sound reasoning.

But there is another, even more serious, problem with the negligence explanation. So far, we have assumed that there are some bits of information represented in the mind, which people then believe or reject. In this view, what happens in the mind seems to require two different functions or organs. One of them is the Representations' Attorney and the other one is the Belief-Judge. The Attorney produces various representations in all their detail, with their connections, their claims and their justification. This is for the benefit of the Mental-Judge, who considers them and hands over his verdict. Some representations win their case. They are then allowed to carry on doing their work in the mind. Some are dismissed as unbelievable and therefore consigned to a mental rubbish-heap.

To some extent, we all have experience of this kind of process. Suppose someone tells me that flamingos are different from other birds because they can only reproduce after breathing exhaust fumes from a diesel engine. I consider this interesting hypothesis for a while. Inside my mind, the Belief-Judge weighs the (probably rather slim) evidence, asks pertinent questions ('then would Counsel explain to us how flamingos reproduced *before* such engines were invented?') and throws out the case. Or, I am told that the earth's magnetic field changed orientation several times in the past, so that the Antarctic was near magnetic North for some time. My Mental-Judge weighs the evidence and concludes that this may be a plausible explanation for various geological facts. The representation is therefore allowed to stay in the mind.

However familiar all this may seem, does it really describe what happens in a mind when information is acquired and used as a basis for action? The judicial model seems to break down if we take a look at the various systems that collect and report information in a brain. Among the hundreds of special systems that compose a normal brain, many seem to be their own Attorney and Judge at the same time.

That is, mental systems do not present their evidence in front of a mental-judge or jury. They *decide* the case even before it is presented to any other system. Indeed, many mental systems do not even bother to present a coherent and unified brief. They just send bits of evidence to other systems, presenting them as fact rather than in the form of an argued brief.

Consider how the visual system works. It seems to do a very good job at presenting its version of events. When we see things we just believe we see them and we believe they really are out there. (I am not talking about exceptional circumstances, but banal scenes. You are at the zoo and there is a tree out there and an elephant next to the tree.) However, the visual system does not present the rest of the brain with a scene. It takes apart chunks of information coming from the optic nerves and handles them separately. One system transforms the two-dimensional information on the retina into a possible three-dimensional representation of volumes, another one evaluates their respective distances, a third handles their colour, a fourth sends information to a database of common shapes for identification, etc. (I am simplifying a great deal: for instance, metric properties are not handled by the same system as the relative positions of objects, and small details of objects are probably treated separately from global shapes.)

One might expect that there will be a place in the brain where all this information is then collated to produce a little 'mental picture' of what you see. But there is no such place. The visual system persuades all the other systems in the brain that there is a tree and an elephant out there without even making its case in a complete brief. It just sends the appropriate information to the appropriate systems, and in each case these systems accept what the visual cortex is telling them without considering the evidence.

So we have two quite different pictures of how a mind reaches a verdict. On the one hand, we sometimes weigh evidence and decide on its merit. On the other hand, there seems to be a great deal of underground belief-making work going on that is simply not reported. When we discuss religious concepts and beliefs we tend to assume that these are processed in the mind along the lines of the first model, a kind of Judge and Attorney system in the mind. We assume that notions of supernatural agents, what they do, what they are like, etc., are presented to the mind and that some decision-making process accepts these notions as valid or rejects them. But this may be a rather distorted view of how such concepts are acquired and represented.

Simple beliefs in a complex mind

What happens in a mind to produce beliefs? To get a better idea of this, it may be of help to leave aside the emotionally charged domain of religion and consider humble beliefs that we all share. For instance, most of us usually assume that children are less capable than adults, that their mental equipment is not yet fully developed. Why do we find this idea so natural? There are many situations where the child's immaturity seems obvious to us. When we utter simple sentences, infants do not seem to understand them. Even once they speak the language fluently, young children do not seem to get jokes. We have moral intuitions which most young children seem incapable of grasping. And so on and so forth. In many situations our intuitive systems produce precise inferences (about the meaning of a sentence, the point of a joke, the morally repulsive nature of an action) that escape children. So it is almost impossible not to represent young children as adults *minus* some important mental abilities (instead of seeing them, for instance, as aliens with a very different world-view).

These common beliefs illustrate several important facts about mental functioning:

First, to avoid confusion we should always be careful to distinguish between the *implicit* processes of our inference systems on the one hand and our *explicit* or reflective representations on the other. What happens in the mental basement is not accessible, it does not consist in sentences, so we cannot be aware of the processes involved. For instance, most adults, especially care-givers, adjust their speech when talking to young children, using a restricted vocabulary and simpler syntax. Even ten year olds are known to use simplified utterances when addressing their younger siblings. (In fact most people greatly underestimate toddlers' linguistic capacities, but that is another question.) Also, most parents walking in a street with their children automatically scan their visual environment and identify various sources of hazard for their offspring. The sight of a large dog coming up towards them, or of a truck approaching, will trigger a specific emotional response and probably make them grasp the child's hand more firmly. But all this has happened quickly and automatically, because of intuitive expectations. In many situations our minds deliver inferences about children implying that they are immature. But then it is only in some circumstances that we actually make all this explicit in the form of a mental statement such as 'children are undeveloped versions of adults'.

Second, what is contained in the explicit thought – what we usually call a 'belief' – is very often an attempt to justify or explain the intuitions we have as a result of implicit processes in the mental basement. It is an *interpretation* of (or a report on) these intuitions. We all behave towards children in a way that is different from our interaction with adults. The reason for this is that we have intuitions about children's mental states. Seeing a two year old, we cannot help assuming that he has certain limitations. This prompts us to say 'yes' when people ask us 'Are children less competent than adults?'. It would be strange and unrealistic to think that the mental processes work the other way around, that we start with some explicit beliefs about children's immaturity and then adapt our behaviour as a consequence. In fact there is a lot of evidence that people spontaneously adjust their behaviour without having the explicit beliefs that would justify the change. Although they adapt their syntax to (their intuitive view of) the toddler's capacities, adults do not generally have a precise, explicit notion of the child's linguistic capacities. Ten year olds often do not even realise that they use a simplified syntax with their younger interlocutors. If we ask adults why they do all this, they will certainly produce some version of the statement above ('children are adults minus some capacities'). This belief is, to them and their interlocutors, a plausible interpretation of their own intuitions, a way of making sense of their own behaviour.

Third, the implicit representations are often handled by *several* inference systems, each of which has its own logic. The moral-emotional system finds the child's behaviour difficult to understand and yields the representation that he is not moved by moral intuitions. The verbal communication system yields the representation that he did not understand what we said. The intuitive-psychology system tells me that he did not foresee what may happen if he pets a large dog. Each of these systems seems to deliver inferences that support the general, explicit interpretation ('children are immature'), but each of them does that for different reasons and in different situations. These multiple inferences about the two year old are on the whole *consistent* with the explicit interpretation.

So what does it mean to say that someone 'has' a belief? Superficially, it means that they can assent to a particular interpretation of how their mind works. If I ask my friends whether they expect their three-year-old daughter to grasp the finer points of moral reasoning or the subtlety of poetic meaning, they admit for all their parental pride that such intellectual feats are still beyond her. But if we want to go beneath the surface and explain why my friends react in this way, we realise that each of these simple beliefs is the outcome of several processes in the mental basement that they are not really aware of.

It would be slightly odd to ask my friends *why* they believe that their daughter is not mentally fully developed yet, what their *evidence* is, what *reasons* they have to believe that. They could of course mention various occasions that illustrate the phenomenon. But they and I would know that they had the belief before they could think of these illustrations, because it is an intuitive belief that their minds just produced.

The crucial point is this: All inferences delivered by specific systems are *compatible* with an explicit interpretation like 'this child is like an adult but with underdeveloped capacities'; but none of these systems actually handled the general, explicit question, 'Are children like adults but with underdeveloped capacities?' So this is a statement that people would agree with although it has not been treated in that general format anywhere in their minds.

Special beliefs, special people, special neurones?

Our explicit beliefs about children are quite clearly a justification for consistent intuitions delivered by specialised systems, away from conscious inspection. But when people tell us that invisible spirits are lurking around or that some people have an extra organ that flies off at night, we assume that the explicit belief must be produced exclusively by such explicit processes as considering evidence, weighing it, examining alternative explanations and coming to a conclusion. Why this difference?

We do this because we tend to think that religious beliefs are *special*, that the processes underpinning everyday judgements and the ones involved in supernatural matters must be different. When William James, one of the pioneers of modern psychology, turned his attention to religious concepts, he naturally adopted this stance too. He assumed there had to be something really special about mental functioning as far as gods and spirits and ancestors were concerned. But what was this something special? James realised that it was not so much in the concepts themselves, for they were quite similar to those of fiction, dream and fantasy. So what made religious concepts special might be a particular kind of *experience* that prompted people to acquire these concepts and find them self-evidently true. This is indeed why James's book was called *Varieties of Religious Experience* and dealt with faith, mysticism, visions and other kinds of exceptional mental events.

Accepting this also led James to focus on exceptional people, that is, on mystics and visionaries. After all, these people seemed to have more of these religious mental states than others. In most human groups there are people who claim some special connection to supernatural agents – they fall into trance, proffer inspired divination, renounce all worldly matters or devote their lives to deepening their contact with gods – while the majority are content to perform the rituals as prescribed and hope they will work as expected. For James, the common version of religion, where most concepts are accepted out of usage rather than conviction, where people trust there must be supernatural agents but do not experience direct contact with them, was only a degraded form of these special people's experience. Only the latter would tell us why there was religion around.[3]

This reasoning – (a) religion is certainly special, (b) what makes it special is experience, (c) exceptional people have a purer version of that experience than the common folk, (d) common religion is just a bland, diluted form of the original experience – is not limited to James's psychology. It is in fact a very common way of thinking about religion, and leads many to think that all discussion of religious *ideas* is misguided and that an exaggerated interest in concepts is a Western bias. Among the many (non-Eastern) people who find special fascination in Buddhism or other Eastern teachings, it is generally assumed that these are precious because of their focus on experience rather than argument. (Incidentally, there may be an ironic misunderstanding here. After all, most Eastern teachings are primarily about correct performance of various rituals and technical disciplines, rather than personal experience as such. Some variants of these teachings do emphasise subjective experience, but they may have been strongly influenced by Western philosophy, by phenomenology in particular, so that what disenchanted Westerners find most fascinating about them might be a distant echo of their own philosophy.) The assumption is quite widespread, which is why it seems that we will learn a lot about religion by asking mystics or devotees about their specific experience, about its special features, about the way it connects with other thoughts.[4]

The notion that religious experience is special is so powerful that it seems to persuade even some cognitive scientists. For some time now, the tools of neuro-psychology – measuring brain activation, studying brain pathology, examining the effects of particular substances – have been applied to religious experience. Cognitive scientists usually measure brain activity as subjects perform exceedingly boring tasks, like deciding whether a word is printed the right way up, whether a picture is of a tool or an animal, whether an image is new or was already presented before. Compared to all this, it would of course be more exciting to visualise or otherwise measure what is happening in a brain processing religious thoughts. But again (and this is where the Jamesian assumption creeps in, so obvious that it goes unnoticed) it would be even better if the religious thoughts in question were quite intense. So people who have visions or those who are intensely religious should be the favoured subjects in such experiments. Is there some religious centre in the brain, some special cortical area, some special neural network that handles God-related thoughts?

Not really. It is certainly possible to measure some specific brain activity during visions and other such extreme episodes which people usually interpret in religious terms, but then this is found also in subjects who have similar visions but no religious interpretations for them. In a more promising way, other neuro-scientists have found that particular micro-seizures, where some part of normal communication between cortical and other brain areas is impaired, do give people a subjective sensation very close to those described by mystics. That people can experience a sudden feeling of peace, of communion with the entire world, or even the presence of some hugely powerful agent, all these can be to some extent correlated with particular brain activity, in the same way as out-of-body or near-death experiences. These are very fragmentary and ambiguous results – but then so are most results in neuro-psychology. We will certainly gain a better knowledge of the neural processes underlying 'religious states'. Consider, for instance, the fact that intense religious experience is very often about the presence of some *agent*, rather than some undefined force. One might predict the neuro-imaging studies will show how religious experience of this kind relies on brain structures involved in thinking about other people's thoughts (those structures I called 'intuitive psychology').[5]

Is exceptional experience a source of belief?

But is this a promising research programme? That is, should we expect such studies to give us a better understanding of why there is religion and why it is the way it is? I think we will continue to learn more by studying the brain and getting to understand its function better, but this requires that we know what it is that we want to understand, which is less than clear in this case. Consider an analogy. We want to understand how processes in the brain give us good ballistic capacities. Compared to most other species, humans are extremely good at throwing projectiles at targets, and they are also better at getting better at it; training can make them very good. Indeed, there are archery and darts champions whose capacities are quite impressive. Now if you want to explain the difference between humans and chimpanzees in this domain, will you study only the champions? It is of course interesting to see how they manage their feats, but that is not the issue. Since all children are endowed from an early age with some talent for throwing objects, as most parents know all too well, it is clear that the champions' capacities are *derived* from this common potential. It is obviously not the champions' feats that create the toddlers' eye-hand co-ordination.

William James and many others after him thought that religion worked the other way around, that some exceptional people created the concepts and the multitude degraded them. In this view, the notion of an invisible supernatural agent, or of a soul being around after the body is dead, or of unconscious zombies remote-controlled by witches, or of extra organs flying about on banana leaves, all this was *first* created by some gifted individuals with intense experience, and *then* proved to be convincing or arresting enough to be adopted (though in a blander, less experiential form) by other people.

But this is rather misguided. First, note that we have no real evidence of this happening for most religious concepts. For all we know, the notion of *evur* in people's stomachs may have been gradually refined over thousands of episodes when people told others fantastic tales, the way urban legends and popular rumours gradually take on a stable form, rather than put forth by an inspired Fang prophet. But even on these occasions when exceptional individuals come up with some new versions of the religious repertoire, it is still the case that these specific versions would make no sense, they would have no effects at all, unless people already had all the cognitive equipment that helps them build such concepts. Even if prophets were the main source of new religious information, that information would still require ordinary non-prophets' minds to turn it into a precise religion. You can always proclaim that traditional ancestors and Christian angels are the same persons, as some inspired new prophets teach in syncretic African religions. It takes people with a prior disposition for concepts of invisible supernatural agents to make sense of such pronouncements. This is why we will probably not understand the diffusion of religion by studying exceptional people, but we may well have a better grasp of religion in general, including that of prophets and other virtuosos, by considering how it is derived from ordinary cognitive capacities.

As I have pointed out repeatedly, building religious concepts requires mental systems and capacities that are there anyway, religious concepts or not. Religious morality uses moral intuitions, religious notions of supernatural agents recruit our intuitions about agency in general, and so on. This is why I said that religious concepts are parasitic upon other mental capacities. Our capacities to play music, paint pictures or even make sense of printed ink-patterns on a page are also parasitic in this sense. This means that we can explain how people play music, paint pictures and learn to read by examining how mental capacities are recruited by these activities. The same goes for religion. Because the concepts require all sorts of specific human capacities (an intuitive psychology, a tendency to attend to some counter-intuitive concepts, as well as various social-mind adaptations), we can explain religion by describing how these various capacities get recruited, how they contribute to these features of religion that we find in so many different cultures. We do not need to assume that there is a *special* way of functioning that occurs only when processing religious thoughts.

Indeed, to be the egregious anthropologist, I should point out that this notion of religion as a special domain is not just unfounded but in fact rather ethnocentric. It is the view of religion put forward, for obvious reasons, by what I described in a previous chapter as religious guilds, that is, the organised groups of religious specialists typically found in complex states and literate cultures. Throughout history people have been told that the services provided by religious specialists concerned a different domain from that of ordinary, practical matters. The official description of supernatural agents as being of 'another world' implied that mental states directed at these agents were of a special kind too, as would be any experience of their presence. That many religious believers, following these guilds, come to share this assumption is of course quite natural, but it is more surprising to notice that it has often spread to people who study religion. Even more striking, some of the ardent enemies of religion seem to share this view, assuming for instance that the kind of unreason or irrationality which in their view explains religious adherence is entirely specific. But we can understand religion much better if we take into account that the processes underpinning 'belief' are the same in religion and in everyday matters.

Agents are relevant to many systems

Throughout the previous chapters I have emphasised that notions of gods and ancestors are a matter of *practical* concerns, because this is crucial and often ignored. That religion is practical means that most representations of supernatural agents are not primarily about their general properties or powers but about specific instances of interaction with them. Among the many representations of such agents that get activated in people's minds, only a very small part are general interpretations, such as 'the ancestors live underground', 'God knows what people are up to', etc. The religious furniture of the mind is cluttered with far more specific representations: 'God punished So-and-so and that's why he is ill', 'this particular ancestor was not pleased with our sacrificed pig', and so on.

It may be of help to see how this works in the case of Kwaio notions of *adalo*. The ancestors are constantly present. As Roger Keesing's vivid descriptions make clear, this sense of a constant presence does not mean that people live in fear or awe or that they are perpetually lost in metaphysical reflections. As the ancestors are always around in some way or other, people's attitude to them are almost as varied as their attitudes to each other. People respect and sometimes fear the *adalo,* but they also think about them as recently deceased people and grieve for them; sometimes people resent their intrusion, or question their protection, or wonder which ancestor will help them or could harm them.

This does not mean that the Kwaio have no coherent concept of ancestors, but that the concept is distributed among a whole variety of systems in the mind. When people think about what the ancestors know and perceive, they have intuitions produced by their intuitive psychology. When they think that the ancestors will resent the sacrifice of a smallish, unimpressive pig, this intuitive judgement is delivered by a social-exchange system. When they feel guilty about a transgression of proper behaviour towards the ancestors, for instance when someone urinates in a place that is *abu*, this intuition comes straight from a moral feeling system. Sometimes a sacrifice fails to have the desired effect, for instance fails to cure a sick person. People think that this is because they sacrificed to the wrong ancestor, to an *adalo* that was not actually responsible for the problem in the first place. Such an explanation comes naturally if you have a social-exchange system (you intuitively assume that people do not deliver the goods, as it were, unless *they* get the payment) and a Person-File system (you assume that the ancestors are not a corporation, they are distinct persons with their particular utilities).

I chose to illustrate this with the Kwaio example because inferences about *adalo* should by now be familiar. But, *mutatis mutandis*, the same description would hold for religious concepts in most human groups. Most Christians for instance live in social contexts saturated with explicit religious doctrine. They constantly hear clear, coherent and systematic presentations of the doctrine by professional specialists. It would seem that their religious representations must be some distillation of this information. But, as Justin Barrett's 'theological correctness effect' shows (see chapter 4), the situation is in fact more complex. People's intuitive understanding of God, often at odds with the official version, drives their inferences about particular occurrences. These inferences are what makes the real difference between believers and non-believers. The former have thoughts about God's possible reactions to this or that action, have the intuition that a particular behaviour is shameful in the eyes of God, trust that God will protect them in this or that dangerous circumstance, wonder why God tried them with misery, and so on.

These thoughts, here as in the Kwaio case, are non-theological; by this I mean that they are not concerned with the general question of God's existence or powers, but more understandably with practical questions: what to expect now and what to do next. And in the same way as among the Kwaio and indeed all people with religious notions, these practical thoughts require activation of diverse mental systems. When people pray this activates the mental system that handles intuitions about verbal communication. When they promise God that they will behave in the future, their social-exchange system gives the intuition that you do not get a benefit (protection) without paying a particular cost (submission in this case). When they assume that God perceived what people did, this is because their intuitive psychology is activated. When they see immoral behaviour as an offence to God, this requires intuitions from their moral-emotional system.

To sum up, then: A whole variety of systems seems to make use of the assumption that there are ancestors around, or that there is a God. Does this get us anywhere nearer answering the question, Why do people believe all this? Yes. I think it is in fact more or less the answer.

What makes supernatural agents more plausible

What makes us assent to a general statement like 'children are underdeveloped versions of adults' is not that we carry out a sweeping assessment of the evidence, but rather that various mental systems, out of sight as it were, produce intuitions compatible with that general statement. None of the systems is busy considering whether it really is the case that children are underdeveloped adults, but most of them produce inferences that contribute to make the general statement relevant.

This is quite similar to what happens when people entertain particular thoughts about ancestors, gods or spirits. Since people's thoughts about ancestors are focused on a variety of different situations, it is not too surprising that many different systems are involved. The intuitive-psychology system treats ancestors (or God) as intentional agents, the exchange system treats them as exchange partners, the moral system treats them as potential witnesses to moral action, the Person-File system treats them as distinct individuals. This means that quite a lot of mental work is going on, producing specific inferences about the ancestors, without ever requiring explicit general statements to the effect that, for example, 'there really are invisible ancestors around', 'they are dead people', 'they have powers', etc. Naturally, most of the inferences I have mentioned are *compatible* with these general assumptions. But none of the systems involved was busy deciding whether the general statements are true or not. Indeed, none of these systems is designed to handle such abstract questions. For instance, when people offer a pig and expect protection in return, the intuition that this behaviour is appropriate is supported by their social-exchange system, which only says this: if there is an exchange partner and if that partner does receive a benefit, then you can expect the partner to send some benefits back to you. But that system is not in charge of deciding whether the partners are really around or not. When you see that other people are sacrificing pigs to get protection, this activates your social-exchange system because that is the most relevant way to make sense of what they are doing.

In other words, what we know of cognitive functioning suggests that our common view of religious belief has things diametrically wrong. We would assume that some explicit decision ('there are ancestors around', 'there is an omniscient God') comes first, which helps people make sense of particular situations. But in the religious as in the everyday case, several mental systems have already delivered intuitions which make sense in the light of those general assumptions. So you do not really *need* to consider the question of the ancestors' or gods' existence to produce interpretations of specific situations, or plans for future courses of action, that include them in the picture.

In the example of beliefs about children, I insisted on the fact that *several* distinct systems are delivering intuitions about situations, all of which are compatible with a general interpretation. This, I think, is crucial to understanding the dynamics of belief.

Our inference systems produce intuitions driven by relevance, that is, by the richness of inferences that can be derived from a particular premise. But in many cases the premises are only con-jectures. Again, it helps to consider simple, everyday beliefs and inferences. If you ask a three year old 'Who did you say the teacher failed to blame for telling her friend not to bring her lunch-box?', the only response may well be a baffled expression on the child's face. In such a situation you may, without having to think about it, rephrase the question in a way that is simpler to parse. This would be because your intuitive-psychology system has noticed the failure to respond and has produced the intuition that the child probably did not understand the question. This is only a hypothesis. It is a sound one, as it would make sense of the child's reaction. It will become a stronger conjecture if the child understands the subsequent, simpli-fied version of the question. But, again, all this is conjectural. It may be that the child was inattentive, tired, deliberately obtuse, had suddenly become deaf or aphasic. Even without considering out-landish possibilities, there are many possible premises that could equally well explain the facts. But a specialised system like our intuitive psychology only produces a limited set of intuitions, based on premises that are both least costly (they are for instance plausible) and richest in inferences (like making sense of what happened). Such systems automatically produce interpretation on the basis of some premise, however tentative. Also, they often produce *several* competing interpretations based on different premises.

So consider again the general statement that children are under-developed versions of adults. There are many situations in which one or several of your inference systems produced interpretations of children's reactions that also supported this general statement. Your agreement to the statement will get stronger and more consistent, as you experience *more* of these situations and they involve *more diverse* systems. The intuitive plausibility of the idea – children are like us minus some crucial properties – becomes greater as more and more different systems produce intuitions compatible with that general interpretation.

This, it seems, works in the same way for religious assumptions. The moral system makes sense of people's statements about moral actions by imagining the ancestors or God as witnesses to actions, but this is only a conjecture that makes other people's behaviour more relevant. In the same way, the inference that an ancestor or God is around is produced as a relevant interpretation of the fact that people sometimes seem to be talking to nobody in particular. But this is only a conjecture that would make their behaviour relevant to the intuitive-psychology system. The premise that the ancestors or God have rescued the dead person's soul explains some of the inconsistent intuitions we have about this person, but that again is only a premise which is used by a special system to make sense of our own reactions and of other people's behaviour. The fact that *similar* premises (e.g. the ancestors are here, God is watching) are used by *different* systems to produce inferences may well strengthen their salience in each of these systems.

This in a way is counter-intuitive, because it suggests that a concept of gods or spirits is all the more likely to do inferential work in the mind if it is *not* entertained as a unified concept, kept apart in a religious domain separate from other mental structures. On the contrary, it is likely to have direct effects on people's thoughts, emotions and behaviours if it is distributed among different systems in the mind. This seems surprising because we are used to a special kind of cultural environment, where religious beliefs are the object of *debate*, that is, are considered explicitly, defended in terms of evidence, plausibility, desirability, beneficial effects, or conversely in terms of their lack of evidence or intrinsic absurdity. But this is a very special kind of culture, as I emphasised in the last chapter. Even in this special environment, it is quite likely that people who do have religious beliefs have them because a lot of inferential work in the basement makes them apparently plausible.

So my advice to religious proselytes would be to avoid bombarding people with cogent and coherent arguments for particular metaphysical claims, and to provide them instead with many occasions where the claims in question can be used to produce relevant interpretations of particular situations. But religions do not need expert consultants for they all do this anyway. This distribution among systems is in fact a familiar feature to anthropologists, who know that religions the world over tend to be multi-media, multi-system affairs. That is, we know that religious concepts are transmitted in a variety of ways and contexts in any single human group. People sing, tell anecdotes, use moral intuitions, use evocation of dangerous situations, dance, take drugs, fall into trance, etc. Naturally, the particular panoply of techniques used varies a lot from one group to another, but there is generally no religion that is confined to one and only one kind of experience.

Why individual belief is mysterious

As Richard Dawkins once remarked, there seems to be one simple process whereby people 'get' their religion and that is *heredity*. After all, the best way to predict people's religion is to find out their parents' religion. Now this does not mean, obviously, that being a Buddhist or a Mormon comes with a particular chromosomal configuration. Dawkins's tongue-in-cheek remark was meant to emphasise something religious people often take for granted but is a source of constant amazement to outsiders: that people generally adhere to the specific religious commitments of their community and ignore other variants as largely irrelevant.

This is one of the recurrent themes in the interminable debates between religious and non-religious people in modern conditions. The insiders produce all sorts of ingenious reasons why a materialistic or non-religious world-view is incomplete or dispiriting, and why religion offers a better or richer outlook on human existence. The outsiders want to know why these general metaphysical worries so often lead people, as if by some extraordinary coincidence, to espouse precisely the same variety of religion as their forebears, parents or other influential elders.

The fact that people tend to adopt their parents' concepts (meaning, more broadly, the concepts used by many people around them) is also a consequence of this activation of many systems in many different circumstances. Most Christians spend little time pondering the mystery of the Trinity, the resurrection of the flesh and other such theological wonders. Most religious thoughts are about particular situations, particular people, particular feelings. This means that such concepts are indeed activated in a variety of different circumstances for different inferential purposes. But this also implies that it would require extra effort to acquire religious concepts in a way that is fundamentally different from what is familiar to one's social milieu. To produce moral inferences using a particular God-concept, as well as Contagion-based inferences, as well as intuitive-psychology inferences, etc., one must have experienced a variety of contexts where the concept was used. This requires a milieu of people who use that concept too. It is not just that people want to have the same concepts as their group. It is that some concepts are so tightly connected to social interaction that it would be bizarre and in fact unlikely to be the only person in a group not to hold them.

This leads us back to a central question: Why do some people believe and not others? I have described religion in terms of cognitive processes that are common to all human brains, part and parcel of how a normal mind functions. Does this mean that non-believers are abnormal? Or, to put a more positive slant on this, that they managed to free themselves from the shackles of ordinary cognition?

We would very much like to have a precise and meaningful answer to the question, Why does So-and-so have religious beliefs that leave others perfectly indifferent? We would like that because we (human beings, not just psychologists or anthropologists) are fascinated by personal differences. More, we are *designed* to pay attention to individual differences, as interaction with other people is our prime resource and interaction depends to some extent on what others are like. (This is why first-year psychology students are often vastly more interested in theories and findings in personality studies, about what makes the difference between you and me, than in the rest of scientific psychology, about what makes humans different from refrigerators, oysters, cockroaches, giraffes and chimps.) This powerful urge to understand what makes individuals unique is the source of much reflection, speculation and informal hypothesis-testing in people's conversations the world over.

But the fact that we *want* some explanation does not guarantee that one is available. Indeed, I think this question is very likely to remain unsolved, at least in the crude formulation I gave above. So-and-so seems to use the premise of the ancestors' presence constantly, in many different contexts, while another does not. So-and-so also has an explicit interpretation of his own mental processes, that says 'yes, I am confident that there are ancestors around', while his friend would say, 'I am not sure there are such agents at all.' Now how shall we explain the difference between our two interlocutors?

We will not and in fact we cannot. This is not because religion is a difficult or complicated domain. It is for a much simpler reason, to do with the explanation of individual events and processes. To make this clearer, take another kind of individual difference, for instance that Mary is much taller than Jane. Mary has tall parents so she probably inherited genes for a tall body, which is not the case for Jane. But genes are only one of the factors. Mary's mother, not Jane's, never smoked or drank during pregnancy. Mary, not Jane, was a well fed child and took lots of vitamins. Does all this explain the difference between Mary and Jane? Only in a certain sense, and the nuance is capital. What these different factors explain is that people like Mary on average tend to be taller than people like Jane. But that is only a probability. If the question of relative heights was really fascinating, we would perhaps want to explore more and more of these factors in Mary's actual history that made her taller than Jane. Indeed we could find more factors, but in each case all they would tell us is something about 'people like Mary', not about Mary as a unique individual.

The same goes for the difference in religious attitudes. Psychologists and social scientists have now gathered vast amounts of data on those factors that increase the likelihood of religious 'belief'. All this is of great interest if you are like me a social scientist, that is, if you want to explain vast trends in human groups. But it will not answer the original question about So-and-so compared with others.[6]

The probability of a single event does not satisfy our appetite for explanations, which hankers after a definite causal chain that would have led this person to have this particular religious attitude. But if the intuitive plausibility of religious concepts is a matter of aggregate relevance, of activating different systems in different ways, then it is *in principle* futile to try and identify that causal chain. All we can describe are trends in groups, and that is certainly frustrating.

Immovable natural failure meets irresistible unnatural success

To people in the West, the most familiar version of the question How can people believe? is this one: How can people believe in supernatural agents, when there is science around? After going through lengthy descriptions of the mental processes involved in the acquisition and representation of religious concepts, we know that it is rather misleading to talk about 'religion' as a real object in the world. It is not a very good starting point to oppose, say religion vs. science, or indeed religion vs. anything, because it is by no means clear that there is such a thing as 'religion' in the abstract. There are many mental representations entertained by people, many acts of communication that make them more or less plausible, many inferences produced in many contexts.

For the same reason, it is very misleading to talk about 'science' as if that was a real object in the world. Science too is a cultural thing, that is, a domain of mental representation which happens to be entertained by a number of human minds. There is no science as such but rather a large set of people with particular activities, a particular database that is stored in the scientific literature, as well as a particular way of adding to or modifying that database. Which of these are we talking about when we consider science vs. religion?

Consider the database. The religion and science debate took a special turn in the West because of the existence, not just of doctrinal religion, but of a monopolistic doctrinal religion that made the crucial mistake of meddling in empirical statements of fact, providing us with a long list of particularly precise, official and officially compelling statements about the cosmos and biology, supposedly guaranteed by Revelation, that we now know to be false. In every instance where the Church has tried to offer its own description of what happens in the world *and* there was some scientific alternative on the very same topic, the latter has proved better. Every battle has been lost and conclusively so. This is of course inconvenient. Obviously, a few people manage blithely to ignore what happened and to live in a fantasy world where biblical sources are a good instrument of geological knowledge and palaeobiology. But this requires a lot of effort. Most religious people in the West prefer the escape clause, that religion is indeed a special domain, and addresses questions that no science could ever answer. This is often the foundation of some decidedly woolly pop-theology, to the effect that religion makes the world 'more beautiful' or 'more meaningful', that it addresses 'ultimate' questions.

Another way of escaping from the conflict is the attempt, especially popular among some scientists, to create a purified religion, a metaphysical doctrine that saves some aspects of religious concepts (there is a creative force, it is difficult for us to know it, it explains why the world is the way it is, etc.) but remove all traces of inconvenient 'superstition' (e.g. God is hearing me, people got a disease as a punishment for their sins, accomplishing the ritual in the right way is essential, etc.). Is such a religion compatible with science? It certainly is, since it was designed for that very purpose. Is it likely to become what we usually call a religion? Hardly. In the actual history of human groups, people have had religious thoughts for cognitive reasons in practical contexts. These thoughts do some work. They produce relevant comments on situations like death or birth or marriage, etc. Metaphysical 'religions' that will not dirty their hands with such human purposes and concerns are about as marketable as a car without an engine.

But the conflict is not just about the database. Science shows, not just that some stories about the formation of planets are decidedly below par, but also that there is something dramatically flawed *in principle* about religion as a way of knowing things, that there is a better way of gathering reliable information about the world.

Religious concepts, as I said, invariably recruit the resources of mental systems that would be there, religion or not. This is why religion is a *likely* thing. That is, given our minds' evolved dispositions, the way we live in groups, the way we communicate with other people and the way we produce inferences, it is very likely that we will find in any human group some religious representations of the form described through these chapters, whose surface details are specific to a particular group.

By contrast, as biologist Lewis Wolpert suggests, scientific activity is quite 'unnatural' given our cognitive dispositions. Indeed, many of the intuitive inference systems I describe here are based on assumptions that scientific research has shown to be less than compelling. This is why acquiring some part of the scientific database is usually more difficult than acquiring religious representations.

What makes scientific knowledge-gathering special is not just its departure from our spontaneous intuitions, but also the special kind of communication it requires, not just the way one mind works but also how other minds react to the information communicated. Scientific progress is brought about by a very odd form of social interaction, where some of our motivational systems (a desire to reduce uncertainty, to impress other people, to gain status, as well as the aesthetic appeal of ingenuity) are recruited for purposes quite different from those relevant to their evolutionary history. In other words, scientific activity is both cognitively and socially very *unlikely*, which is why it has only been developed by a very small number of people, in a small number of places, for what is only a minuscule part of our evolutionary history. As philosopher Robert McCauley concludes, on the basis of similar arguments, science is every bit as 'unnatural' to the human mind as religion is 'natural'.[7]

How we became modern (and religious): a footnote to the epic scenario

Who invented these gods and spirits, when and for what purpose? Obviously, we all know that it is slightly absurd to wonder who invented religion, or when this happened, since what we call 'religion' is a composite reality. We know that people in most human groups have notions of counter-intuitive objects. We also know that such objects include physically counter-intuitive agents, and that such agents matter a lot to people by virtue of the strategic information these agents have. But, as far as we know, these various elements may have had different histories. So the question When did humans get religion? only makes sense if *you* decide which parts of this composite reality are crucial to religion.

But there is a more interesting way to proceed. Religion as we know it probably appeared with the modern mind. It is convenient to date the appearance of modern-type cultures to the symbolic 'explosion' that occurred some time between 100,000 and 50,000 years ago. After 50,000 BP, we find many more artefacts, more efficient and more varied, some of which are of no practical utility. People start using red ochre, painting cave walls and burying their dead with elaborate ceremonies. An important difference with earlier cultural manifestations lies in the diversity of objects and representations, which may indicate the emergence of those group-level similarities and between-group differences that we call human cultures.

What prompted this outburst of creativity and diversity was certainly a change in mental activity. This is why it is tempting to think of modern hominisation as some kind of *liberating* process, through which the mind broke free of evolutionary shackles and became more flexible, more capable of novelty, in a word, more open. Many scenarios of cultural evolution give pride of place to this kind of cognitive breakthrough, understood as a new capacity for symbolic reference and a newly acquired flexibility in decoupled representations. The psychologist Michael Tomasello argues that perspective-taking, which produces intuitive inferences on the reasons why others behave the way they do, was crucial in this change. It was for instance indispensable in the domain of technology. Modern human tools and tool-usage show incremental, cumulative change; the artefacts created required that cultural learners could figure out other people's intentions. In many domains of acquired culture it is simply not possible for developing subjects to consider cues provided by cultural elders and to produce relevant inferences about them without representing those elders' communicative intentions.

Archaeologist Steven Mithen proposes an even more precise

description of those changes that led to modern culture. He starts from the description of the modern mind, by evolutionary and developmental psychologists, as consisting of a variety of specialised inference systems. These systems have clear input conditions, that is, they only attend to and handle information in a particular domain, such as intuitive physics or intuitive psychology, but also more limited domains such as cues for parental investment, mate-choice, coalition-building, living-kind categorisation, etc. For Mithen, the cultural explosion is the effect of significant changes in cognitive architecture, in particular the appearance of cognitive fluidity, in other words, of multiple information exchanges between modular capacities. The difference between early and modern Humans is not so much in the operation of each specialised capacity (intuitive biology, theory of mind, tool-making, intuitive physics, etc.) but in the possibility of using information from one domain in the course of activities monitored by another domain. So artefacts are used as body-ornaments, serving social purposes; biological knowledge is used in visual symbols; tool-making develops local traditions and makes efficient use of local resources, tapping information from intuitive biology.[8]

And this is relevant to our question, because such transfers of information between domains are exactly what supernatural concepts require, as we saw in chapter 2, and as Mithen himself points out. The time when human brains established more connections between different inference systems, as we know from their hunting and tool-making techniques, was also the period when they created visual representations of supernatural concepts. Cave-paintings and artefacts began to include evidence of totemic and anthropomorphic representations as well as chimeras. The archaeological evidence, then, supports two important elements in our psychological description of supernatural concepts: that they require decoupling (to draw a chimera one must learn to represent something that never could be perceived) and that they violate intuitive expectations at the level of ontological domains.

So it would seem that we now know when people 'invented' religion: when such representations could occur in people's minds and exert enough fascination to be painstakingly translated into material symbols. Things are a little more complicated, however, because religion as we know it is not just a mater of counter-intuitive concepts. Religion is not just about flying mountains, talking trees and biological monsters, but also about agents whose mental states matter a lot, about connections with predation and death, about links with morality and misfortune.

We do not really know when these other essential features of religion appeared, because we know very little of the prehistory of the inference systems concerned. All we can say with some confidence is that they probably have a long evolutionary history, given their common features in all human minds. Most archaeologists and anthropologists assume that early modern Humans did what humans now do the world over: use massive stores of information to extract resources from their environment, form exceedingly complex social systems, join coalitions, speak a complex language, seduce other people, protect and nurture their offspring, fall for fashion and snobbery, manufacture tools, deal with politics and find other people's customs ridiculous. The list of such uniquely human activities should of course be much longer; the point is simply that many apparently modern behaviours, like fashion or petty politics, probably have a long evolutionary history. Since all this is evidence for capacities that *also* happen to shape religious thoughts and beliefs as we see them today, it is probable that the latter too have a long history.

The psychological evidence mentioned in the previous chapters also adds a cautionary note to the notion of hominisation as a liberation. It is tempting to think that people acquired religious thoughts because they somehow made their minds more flexible and open. But the evidence gathered by anthropologists, archaeologists and psychologists suggests a slightly different vision. Human minds did not become vulnerable to just any odd kind of supernatural beliefs. On the contrary, because they had many sophisticated inference systems, they became vulnerable to a very *restricted* set of supernatural concepts: the ones that can jointly activate inference systems for agency, predation, death, morality, social exchange, etc. Only a small range of concepts are such that they reach this aggregate relevance, which is why religion has common features the world over.

Cosmic gossip

One thing that modern Humans did and still do vastly more than any other species is exchange information of all kinds and qualities, not just about what is the case but also about what should be or could be; not just about their emotions and knowledge but also about their plans, memories and conjectures. The proper milieu in which humans live is that of information, especially information provided by other humans. It is their ecological niche.

This truly special behaviour creates a huge domain of information that has been passed on over centuries and millennia, with millions of messages lost, forgotten, misheard or ignored, while others were passed on, slightly distorted or sometimes well-preserved, and others still were invented from scratch. If we consider this whole domain of information over time we have a gigantic 'soup' of representations and messages. The messages are constantly changing because the contexts change.

However, we also find that there are lumps in this soup of messages, that is, bits of information that seem to appear in rather similar form at different times and in different places. They are not strictly identical but we find a small number of templates that seem to organise them. Religious concepts and behaviours are like that. To understand why we find these recurrent themes, we do not have to imagine that they are particularly good or useful or that the human mind needs them in any particular way. There is a simpler explanation. They are such that acquiring them activates some mental systems, produces some inferences in the mind, *a little* more than other possible concepts. This is enough to create a huge difference over time, because people are more likely to acquire and transmit these concepts than others. If they do not transmit them, such concepts are more likely to be rediscovered somewhere else, some other time, than other possible concepts. This is why, although we have little tangible evidence for popular concepts of past human groups, one can with some confidence construct the following scenario:

Final progress-box: The full history of all religion (ever)

Over the vast time-scales I am talking about, people have naturally talked about millions of exceedingly parochial and contextual matters, but also about some objects and concepts that are not directly observable. It is after all a hallmark of the 'modern mind' which we have had for millennia that we entertain plans, con-jectures, speculate on the possible as well as the actual. Among the millions of messages exchanged, some are attention-grabbing because they violate intuitions about objects and beings in our environment. These counter-intuitive descriptions have a certain staying-power, as memory experiments suggest. They certainly provide the stuff good stories are made of. They may mention islands that float adrift or mountains that digest food or animals that talk. These are generally taken as fiction, though the boundary between a story and an account of personal experience is often difficult to trace. Some of these themes are particularly salient, because they are about agents. This opens up a rich domain of possible inferences. When you talk about agents you can wonder to what extent they are similar to the unseen and dangerous presence of predators. You can also try to imagine what they perceive, what they know, what they plan and so on, because there are inference systems in your mind that constantly produce such speculations about other people. Among these accounts, some suggest that counter-intuitive agents have information about relevant aspects of interaction between the people

376 ～ Religion Explained

exchanging these messages. This gives speakers and listeners a strong motivation to hear, tell, perhaps challenge such stories. This also allows a further development, whereby people can combine their moral intuitions with the notion that such agents are indeed informed of the morally relevant aspects of what they do and what others do to them. When counter-intuitive agents are construed in this way, it becomes easy to connect them to striking cases of misfortune, because we are predisposed to see misfortune as a social event, as someone's responsibility rather than the outcome of mechanical processes. So the agents are now described as having powers such that they can visit disasters upon people, which adds to the list of their counter-intuitive properties and probably to their salience. People who have such concepts will end up connecting them with the bizarre representations and emotions triggered by the presence of dead people, because this presence creates a strange cognitive state in which predation-related intuitions, as well as the diverse mental processes concerned with the identification of persons, produce incompatible intuitions. We sense both that the dead *are* around and that they *cannot* be around. If you have concepts like this, at some point it will make sense to connect them with the various repeated and largely meaningless actions that you often perform with some fear that non-performance will result in grave danger. So there are now rituals directed at these agents. Since many rituals are performed in contexts where social interaction has non-obvious properties, it will become easy to conceive of these agents as the very life of the group you are in, as the bedrock of social interaction. If you live in a large enough group, there will be some people who seem better skilled at producing convincing messages from the counter-intuitive agents. These people will probably be considered as having some special internal quality that makes them different from the rest of the group. They will also end up taking on a special role in ritual performances. If you live in a large group with literate specialists, these will probably at some point start changing all these concepts to provide a slightly different, more abstract, less contextual, less local version. It is also very likely that they will form a manner of corporation or guild with attendant political goals. But this version of concepts is not really optimal, so that it will always be combined in most people's minds with spontaneous inferences that are not compatible with the literate doctrine.

This brief history of world religion is not really history at all. There is no single line of descent whereby people would have started with a variety of counter-intuitive concepts and then gradually refined them, ending up with what we now call religion. The selection process was constant, because the human production of messages is constant and therefore each single version of each god-concept or spirit-concept is slightly different from all others. But the variants, after many cycles of communication, seem to come back to the various themes I mentioned here. This is because all these human minds carry the systems that produce the small selective advantage I have described. Among these systems are a set of intuitive ontological expectations, a propensity to direct attention to what is counter-intuitive, a tendency to recall it if it is inferentially rich, a system for detecting and over-detecting agency, a set of social-mind systems that makes the notion of well-informed agents particularly relevant, a set of moral intuitions that seems to have no clear justification in our own concepts, a set of social categories that poses the same problem. We are no longer surprised that religious concepts and behaviours have persisted for millennia – probably much longer – and display similar themes the world over. These concepts just happen to be optimal in the sense that they activate a variety of systems in a way that makes their transmission possible.

A frustration of invisible hands

When the story of religion is told this way, it seems to amount to an extraordinary conspiracy. Religious concepts and norms and the emotions attached to them seem *designed* to excite the human mind, linger in memory, trigger multiple inferences in the *precise* way that will get people to hold them true and communicate them. Whoever designed religion, or designs each religion, seems to have uncanny prescience of what will be successful with human minds.

But there is of course no designer, and no conspiracy either. Religious concepts work that way, they realise the miracle of being exactly what people will transmit, simply because other variants were created and forgotten or abandoned along the way. The magic that seems to produce such perfect concepts for human minds is merely the effect of repeated selective events. A complex organ like a mind produces a multitude of mini-scenarios, evanescent links between thoughts and new concepts that quickly degrade. This maelstrom of elusive thought is certainly not what we are aware of, because in a sense the only thoughts that we entertain consciously have already passed a number of cognitive hurdles. But even the explicit thoughts we entertain are not all equally likely to produce similar thoughts in other people, far from it. One of my Fang friends thought that spirits were two-dimensional and always stood sideways when facing human beings lest they would be detected. But this ingenious notion was perhaps too complex. Most people quickly forgot it or distorted it. Other inferences have more staying-power. You must remember that in the domain of inference-production, *many will be called and few will be chosen.*

I have explained religion in terms of systems that are in all human minds and do all sorts of precious and interesting work, but were not really designed to produce religious concepts of behaviours. There is no religious instinct, no *specific* inclination in the mind, no particular disposition for these concepts, no special religion centre in the brain, and religious people are not different from non-religious ones in essential cognitive functions. Even faith and belief seem to be simple by-products of the way concepts and inferences are doing their work for religion in much the same way as for other domains.

Instead of a religious mind, what we have found is a whole frustration of invisible hands. One of these guides human attention towards some possible conceptual combinations, another one enhances recall for some of these, yet another process makes concepts of agents far easier to acquire if they imply strategic agency, connections to morality, etc. The invisible hand of multiple inferential systems in the mind produces all sorts of connections between these concepts and salient occurrences in people's lives. The invisible hand of cultural selection makes it the case that the religious concepts people acquire and transmit are in general the ones most likely to seem convincing to them, given their circumstances.

I call this a frustration because religion is portrayed here as a mere consequence or side-effect of having the brains we have, which does not strike one as particularly dramatic. But religion *is* dramatic, it is central to many people's existence, it is involved in highly emotional experience, it may lead people to murder or self-sacrifice. We would like the explanation of dramatic things to be equally dramatic. For similar reasons, people who are shocked or repulsed by religion would like to find the *single* source of what is for them such egregious error, the crossing at which so many human minds take the wrong turn, as it were. But the truth is that there is no such single point, because many different cognitive processes conspire to make religious concepts convincing.

I am of course slightly disingenuous in describing this as a frustration, when I think it is such a Good Thing. That we fail to identify hidden hands and simple designs and instead discover a variety of underlying processes *that we know how to study* sometimes happens in scientific endeavours and is always for the better. The progress is not just that we understand religion better because we have better knowledge of cognitive processes. It is also, conversely, that we can highlight and better understand many fascinating features of our mental architecture by studying the human propensity to religious thoughts. One does learn a lot about these complex biological machines by figuring out how they manage to give airy nothing a local habitation and a name.

Further Reading

1. What is the origin?
To get a better view of the diversity of religion as actually practised by people around the world, the best place to start is John Bowen's *Religions in Practice* (1997). An excellent summary of how and why anthropologists, psychologists and religious scholars approach religion is found in the first two chapters of Lawson and McCauley's *Rethinking Religion* (1990). That many concepts of religion have to do with ancient survival problems, including hunting and the fear of predators, is the theme of Walter Burkert's *Creation of the Sacred* (1996), based on extensive description of Greek and Near-Eastern ritual and belief. Susan Blackmore's *The Meme Machine* (1999) presents the view of culture as a large set of replicated 'memes'. Dan Sperber's *Explaining Culture* (1996) presents the alternative notion of culture as epidemic similarity in mental representations.

2. What supernatural concepts are like

There are many books on the subject of magical and religious concepts, but few good catalogues of their variations and common themes. Lehmann and Myers's *Magic, Witchcraft and Religion* (1993) is the most readable and reasonable survey. Mark Turner's *Literary Mind* (1996), although it is not exclusively about supernatural notions, provides a very good account of the structures of imagination, literary and mythical. As concerns the paranormal, Susan Blackmore's *In Search of the Light* (1996) is a very readable and funny account of a scientist trying to make sense of the evidence. Nicholas Humphrey's *Leaps of Faith* (1996) presents a general explanation for the fascination of paranormal phenomena.

3. The kind of mind it takes

Among the many excellent books on the mind and the discoveries of cognitive science, the most exciting one is certainly Steven Pinker's *How the Mind Works* (1997), with its highly detailed account of various inference systems and their evolutionary background An excellent presentation of developmental findings about children's mental capacities is *The Scientist in the Crib* (1999), by Alison Gopnik, Patricia Kuhl and Andrew Meltzoff, three specialists of infant cognition. See Michael Gazzaniga's *Conversations in the Neurosciences* (1997) for a good presentation of how specialised brain structures support specialised function. The essays gathered in *The Adapted Mind* present the main points of an evolutionary view of cognition (Barkow, Cosmides and Tooby, 1992), also presented in a more reader-friendly way in Robert Wright's *Moral Animal* (1994). The best introduction to social life as an evolutionary problem is Matt Ridley's *The Origins of Virtue* (1996).

4. Why gods and spirits?

Stewart Guthrie's *Faces in the Clouds* (1993) is a great compendium of anthropomorphic representation in art and religion. It also presents very good arguments for a psychological interpretation of religious agency. On the evolutionary origins of gods as predators and protectors, see Walter Burkert's *Creation of the Sacred* (1996).

5. *Why do gods and spirits matter?*

J. Q. Wilson's *Moral Sense* (1993) illustrates the notion that moral judgements are primarily based on intuitions about the intrinsic qualities of actions, rather than deductions from principles. Robert Frank's *Passions Within Reason* (1988) is a very entertaining presentation of commitment gadgets, passions as useful devices and moral feelings in general. As regards misfortune and witchcraft, Jeanne Favret-Saada's *Deadly Words* (1980) is among the best modern studies of the phenomenon.

6. *Why death in religion?*

For an excellent survey and explanation of diverse funerary rituals, see the articles in *Death and the Regeneration of Life* (Bloch and Parry, 1982). Walter Burkert's *Homo Necans* (1983) is a fascinating case-study of funerary ritual in Antiquity. The psychology of death-related and other rituals is also the main topic of Maurice Bloch's *Prey into Hunter* (1992).

7. *Why rituals?*

Anyone interested in what it feels like to perform rituals (and in how anthropology makes sense of such feelings) should read Caroline Humphrey and James Laidlaw's *Archetypal Actions: A Theory of Ritual* (1993), which follows a particular case (devotional puja among Jains) but extends the explanation to ritual in general. Lawson and McCauley's *Rethinking Religion* (1990) presents not only the view of ritual action discussed here but also a more general view of how psychology can make sense of religious practices.

8. *Why doctrines, exclusion and violence?*

The history of literacy and religious guilds is presented with great wit in Ernest Gellner's *Plough, Sword and Book* (1989). On the effects of literacy, the most important source is Jack Goody's *Domestication of the Savage Mind* (1977) as well as his *Logic of Writing and the Organisation of Society* (1986). Harvey Whitehouse's *Arguments and Icons* (2000) is a vast survey of the differences between doctrines and rituals, in terms of psychological and political effects. On fundamentalism, an indispensable source is the series of volumes put together by the Fundamentalism Project (Marty & Appleby, 1991; Marty & Appleby, 1993a; Marty & Appleby, 1993b; Marty & Appleby, 1994).

9. Why belief?

Michael Shermer's books *Why People Believe Weird Things* (1997) and *How We Believe* (1999) present a strong case for the idea of belief as mental negligence. A psychological interpretation of why people believe in particular kinds of spiritualistic or religious concepts is found in Nicholas Humphrey's *Leaps of Faith* (1996). Tanya Luhrmann's *Persuasions of the Witch's Craft* (1989) is a fascinating monograph that explains in great detail how people gradually make sense of and accept what they considered ludicrous beliefs. This is based on a thorough study of modern-day witches in London. On science versus religion, see Lewis Wolpert's *Unnatural Nature of Science* (1992), an excellent survey of the psychological obstacles to scientific thinking. For a more caustic approach to the debate, Richard Dawkins's wit makes for great reading – but the arguments are quite serious (Dawkins 1995 and 1998). Anyone interested in the prehistory of religious concepts should consult Steven Mithen's brilliant *Prehistory of the Mind* (1996), a survey of how minds evolved over the last four million years.

Notes

Chapter One

1 Problems with translating belief: Needham, 1972; discussion in Luhrmann, 1989, pp. 311ff.

2 Kwaio myths: Keesing, 1982, p. 102.

3 Kuna shamanism: Severi, 1993.

4 Relevant mysteries: (Sperber, 1996). Theories of religion as the 'explanation' of unexplained events: Tylor, 1871; Snow, 1922.

5 Reason and metaphysics: Kant, 1781; Kant and Schmidt, 1990. Intellectualism: Frazer, 1911; Stocking, 1987; Tylor, 1871.

6 Cartesian theatre of consciousness: Dennett and Weiner, 1991.

7 Emotions as programmes: Rolls, 2000; Lane and Nadel, 2000.

8 Anthropological functionalism: Stocking, 1984.

9 Accounts of culture as differential transmission of memes: Cavalli-Sforza and Feldman, 1981; Lumsden and Wilson, 1981; Durham, 1991; Dawkins, 1976.

10 Uncertainties in anthropological concept of culture: Cronk, 1999.

11   Problems with memes: Sperber, 1996.

12 Culture as epidemics of representations: Sperber, 1985; Sperber, 1996.

Chapter Two

1 Religion and the 'sacred' or 'numinous': see e.g. Otto, 1959; Eliade, 1959.
2 Imagined animals: Ward, 1994. Faculty of imagination: Kant and Vorländer, 1963.
3 Live mountain: Bastien, 1978.
4 Metamorphoses and ontological categories: Kelly and Keil, 1985. In mythology: Forth, 1998.
5 Listening ebony: James, 1988, pp.10, 303.
6 Spirits and cologne: Lambek, 1981.
7 Belief in the paranormal: Humphrey, 1996.
8 Devils in modern Greece: Stewart, 1991, pp. 251–3.
9 Ritual transformations and Yoruba biological beliefs: Walker, 1992.
10 God concept and story recall: Barrett, 1996.
11 Serious supernatural agents different from other supernatural themes: Burkert, 1996. God different from Mickey Mouse: Atran, 1998; see also comments in Barrett, 2000.

Chapter Three

1 English households: Hartcup, 1980.
2 Intuitive physics: see e.g. Kaiser, Jonides and Alexander, 1986.
3 Causal illusion: Michotte, 1963.
4 Differential activation with tools and animal-like stimuli: Martin et al., 1996.
5 Patients' understanding of stories requiring theory of mind inferences: Frith and Corcoran, 1996; Fletcher et al., 1995.
6 Autism and failure to meta-represent mental states: Baron-Cohen, Leslie and Frith, 1985; see also Baron-Cohen, 1995. False-belief tasks: Wimmer and Perner, 1983.
7 Autism as mind-blindness, description of systems involved: Baron-Cohen, 1995.
8 Systems involved in motor imagery: Jeannerod, 1994; Decety, 1996. Perceiving actions triggers imagined action: Decety and Grezes, 1999. Areas specialised in different kinds of pain: Hutchison et al., 1999.
9 Developmental questions are philosophical questions: Gopnik and Meltzoff, 1997.
10 Innards: Gelman and Wellmann, 1991; Simons and Keil, 1995.
11 Essentialism: Hirschfeld and Gelman, 1999.

12 All living species in taxonomic structure: Atran, 1990; Atran, 1994; Atran, 1996.

13 Causation in infants: Leslie, 1987; Rochat, Morgan and Carpenter, 1997. Children's inferences about self-initiated motion: Gelman, Spelke and Meck, 1983.

14 Infants' reactions to faces: Morton and Johnson, 1991; Pascalis et al., 1995.

15 Person identification and imitation in infants: Meltzoff, 1994; Meltzoff and Moore, 1983.

16 Infant counting: Wynn, 1990.

17 Uncertainties of 'innateness' claims: Elman et al., 1996. Concepts as skills: Millikan, 1998.

18 Evolution and specialization: Rozin, 1976.

19 General surveys of evolutionary psychology: Barkow, Cosmides and Tooby, 1992; Buss, 1999; Crawford and Krebs, 1998. Comparative cognitive development: Parker and McKinney, 1999.

20 Mate selection: Buss, 1989; Symons, 1979. Jealousy: Buss, 2000. Homicide and evolutionary explanations: Daly and Wilson, 1988. Survey of evolutionary perspectives: LeCroy and Moller, 2000.

21 Morning-sickness: Profet, 1993. Specialised food-related avoidance: Garcia and Koelling, 1966.

22 Disgust and associations: Rozin, 1976; Rozin, Haidt and McCauley, 1993.

23 Cognitive niche: Tooby and DeVore, 1987.

24 Information-processing in foraging: Mithen, 1990; Krebs and Inman, 1994. Foraging and complex social environments: Barton, 2000. General dependence on information: Tomasello, 2000. Cultural transmission and adaptability to novel environments: Boyd and Richerson, 1995.

25 Social intelligence: Byrne and Whiten, 1988. Evolutionary background of 'theory of mind': Povinelli and Preuss, 1995. Gaze-following in chimps: Povinelli and Eddy, 1996. Predation and rudimentary theory of mind: van Schaik and van Hooff, 1983; Barrett 1999.

26 Gossip: Gambetta, 1994; Haviland, 1977.

27 Requirements for co-operation: Boyd and Richerson, 1990. Social-exchange problems produce better logical performance: Cosmides and Tooby, 1989; Cosmides and Tooby, 1992. Replication in different cultures: Sugiyama, 1996. Selective impairment of social-exchange performance: Stone, 1997.

28 Signals: Bradbury and Vehrencamp, 2000; Hauser, 2000; Rowe, 1999. Utility of sender and receiver: Silk, Kaldor and Boyd, 2000.

29 Cues for trust: Bacharach and Gambetta, 1999. Cost of faking moral

dispositions: Frank, 1988.

30   Coalitions and groupishness: Ridley, 1996.

31   Comparative study of coalitions in different species: Harcourt and de Waal, 1992.

32   Features of coalitional psychology: Kurzban, 1999.

33   Episodic memory: Tulving, 1983; Tulving and Lepage, 2000.

34   Pretence, decoupling and meta-representation: Leslie, 1987; Leslie, 1994.

35   Intentions as crucial to identification of drawings: Bloom, 1998; Gelman and Bloom, 2000; Matan and Carey, 2000.

36   'What' and 'where' in auditory perception: Kaas and Hackett, 1999; Romanski et al., 1999. Motion detected by auditory cortex: Baumgart et al., 1999. Separation between noise and speech: Liegeois-Chauvel et al., 1999. Separation of pure tones: Kaas, Hackett and Tramo, 1999. Localisation of cortical areas involved in recalling tunes: Halpern and Zatorre, 1999. Evolution of capacities for music: Jerison, 2000.

37   Ochre in prehistory: Watts, 1999. Cognitive foundations of visual art: Dissanayake, 1992. Palaeolithic art as representing mental images: Halverson, 1992. Cognitive aspects of artistic imagination in Prehistory: Mithen, 1996.

Chapter Four

1   Quotations from Keesing, 1982, pp. 33, 40, 115.

2   Anthropomorphism: Guthrie, 1993.

3   Hyperactive agent detection and religious concepts: Barrett, 1996; Barrett, 2000.

4   Intuitive psychology based on predation: Barrett, 1999. Archaeological arguments for mind-reading in hunting: Mithen, 1996.

5   Shamanism as hunting: Hamayon, 1990. Traces of a biological past in religious themes: Burkert, 1996.

6   Imaginary companions: Taylor, 1999; quotation: p. 89.

7   Keesing, 1982, p. 42.

8   Spirits and shamans eavesdrop on people: Endicott, 1979, p. 132.

9   Inference on animal categories: Coley et al., 1999; Lopez, Atran et al., 1997.

10   Different domains of culture and their transmission: Boyer, 1998.

11   Alien beliefs and the Roswell myth: Saler, Ziegler and Moore, 1997. Serious alien cults: Lewis, 1995.

Chapter Five

1   Tamil karma: Daniel, 1983, p. 42.

2   Experimental study of reasoning: Krebs and Rosenwald, 1994.

3   Moral judgements as derived from moral feelings: Wilson, 1993.

4   Compare for instance Botswana: Maqsud and Rouhani, 1990, and Iceland: Keller, Eckensberger and von Rosen, 1989.

5   On moral development in a constructivist perspective: Nemes, 1984. On Kohlberg's theory of moral development (refining principles) and Hoffmann's account (internalising other people's emotions): Gibbs, 1991. Comparison of stage theories: Krebs and van Hesteren, 1994.

6   Lying as a concept and 'lie' as word-meaning: Wimmer, Gruber and Perner, 1984.

7   Moral rules vs. social conventions in children: Turiel, 1983; Turiel, 1994; Turiel, 1998. Moral rules vs. precautionary rules: Tisak and Turiel, 1984.

8   Studies in Korea: Song, Smetana, and Kim, 1987. Comparing newcomers and old-timers: Siegal and Storey, 1985; Tisak and Turiel, 1988. Moral intuitions of abused children: Smetana, Kelly and Twentyman, 1984; of neglected children: Sanderson and Siegal, 1988.

9   Problems of group-selection: Williams, 1966.

10 Kin-selection: Hamilton, 1964; see also Dawkins, 1976.

11 Reciprocal altruism: Trivers, 1971; Boyd, 1988; Krebs and van Hesteren, 1994.

12 Limiting your freedom of movement as a solution to commitment problems: Schelling, 1960. Relevance to co-operation and exchange: Frank, 1988.

13 Evolution of co-operation and urge to punish non-cooperators: Boyd and Richerson, 1992. General survey of morality and evolution: Katz, 2000.

14 Witchcraft in the French Bocage: Favret-Saada, 1980.

15 Evil eye: Pocock, 1973, p. 28.

16 Kwaio notions of misfortune: Keesing, 1982, p. 33.

17 Pocock, p. 28.

Chapter Six

1   Palaeolithic burials: see Davidson and Noble, 1989. Neanderthal: Stringer and Gamble, 1993; Hayden, 1993; Trinkhaus, 1989; Trinkhaus and Shipman, 1993. Taphonomic interpretation as accidental deposits: Gargett, 1999.

2   Literary mind: Fauconnier and Turner, 1998; Turner, 1996; Turner and Fauconnier, 1995.

3   Effect of mortality salience on punishing attitudes: Rosenblatt et al., 1989. Disapproval of dissent: McGregor et al., 1998. Effect on stereotyping: Schimel et al., 1999. On finding illusory group correlations: Lieberman, 1999. Similar effects in children: Florian and Mikulincer, 1998.

4   Terror-management, general points: Pyszczynski, Greenberg and Solomon, 1997. Limits of the effects: Florian and Mikulincer, 1997. Evolutionary critique: Buss, 1997. Other criticisms: Leary and Schreindorfer, 1997.

5   General features of death-rituals: Cederroth, Corlin and Linstrom, 1988; Lambrecht, 1938; Metcalf and Huntington, 1991; Bloch and Parry, 1982.

6   Batek funerals: Endicott, 1979, pp. 115–18.

7   Berawan double-funerals: Metcalf and Huntington, 1991, pp. 64–73.

8   Double-funerals as rites of passage: Hertz, 1960.

9   Arawete souls: Viveiros de Castro, 1992, p. 236. Tallensi ancestors; Fortes, 1987, p. 77. Ancestors and property: Goody, 1962.

10 Keesing, 1982, p. 33; Pocock, 1973, p. 37.

11 Sunflower in dead man's head: Ruskin, 1871.

12 Zoroastrian texts, pollution of corpses: Davies, 1999, p. 43.

13 China: Watson, 1982, p. 157. Madagascar: Bloch, 1982, p. 215.

14 Nepali kings: Leuchstag, 1958, p. 236.

15 Extant work *Onirocritica* of Artemidorus of Daldis.

16 Testing children's tacit assumptions about components of death: Orbach et al., 1987. Children's death concepts and predation: Barrett, 1999.

17 Kwaio concepts of the person: Keesing, 1982. Batek concepts: Endicott, 1979.

18 Special system for face-recognition: Henke et al., 1998; Nachson, 1995. Specific neural stream for face-identification: Bentin, Deouell and Soroker, 1999. Prosopagnosia and covert recognition: Renault et al., 1989; Wallace and Farah, 1992. Voice recognition not affected: Habib, 1986. Problem lies in assembling not identifying features: Bliem and Danek, 1999. Recognising inverted faces, general interpretation of prosopagnosia: Farah et al., 1995, De Renzi and di Pellegrino, 1998. Good learning of sheep faces: McNeil and Warrington, 1993.

19 Capgras delusion: Edelstyn and Oyebode, 1999; Wacholtz, 1996. Pets kidnapped and replaced with replicas: Somerfield, 1999; similar delusion with familiar objects: Anderson, 1988. Cotard delusion of own death: Leafhead and Kopelman, 1997.

20 Grief and reproductive potential: Crawford, Salter and Jang, 1989.

Chapter Seven

1 Spirit relics in Java: Beatty, 1999.
2 Sacrifice to the goddess Chandli: Preston, 1980; also cited in Fuller, 1992, p. 83.
3 Shaman induction among Kham Magar, Nepal: Sales, 1991.
4 Initiation of Gbaya boys, Central Africa: Vidal, 1976.
5 Clockwise movement as centrifugal: Bowen, 1997, p. 135.
6 Bloch on ritual: Bloch, 1974. Symbolism is not meaning: Sperber, 1975.
7 Obvious aspects of ritual: Rappaport, 1979.
8 Ritual as mode of action: Humphrey and Laidlaw, 1993. Evolutionary scenarios for first rituals: Knight, 1999.
9 Inferences from precautionary rules: Fiddick, Cosmides and Tooby, 2000.
10 Features of ritual: Fiske, 2000a.
11 Sacred and limits: Anttonen, 2000. Javanese ritual: Beatty, 1999, p. 94.
12 Accounts of living with compulsive obsession: Colas, 1998; Rapoport, 1997.
13 Ritual actions and OCD routines compared: Dulaney and Fiske, 1994; Fiske and Haslam, 1997.
14 Phenomenology of OCD: Eisen, Phillips and Rasmussen, 1999.
15 Baktaman initiation: Barth, 1975.
16 Deception and interaction in male initiation: Houseman, 1993, Houseman and Severi, 1998.
17 Kinship categories: Hirschfeld, 1986.
18 Acquisition of racial and ethnic concepts: Hirschfeld, 1993; Hirschfeld, 1996.
19 Social groups as transcendent: Bloch, 1992, p. 75.
20 Ritual structure: Lawson & McCauley, 1990.

Chapter Eight

1 Buid mediumship: Gibson, 1986.
2 Javanist ritual, *slamentan*: Beatty, 1999, p. 28.
3 Indonesia, religious identity: Beatty, 1999, p. 221.
4 Fang *evur*: Fernandez, 1982; Boyer, 1994.
5 Rapacious priests in Benares: Parry, 1995, pp. 119–20.
6 Invention and diffusion of literacy: DeFrancis, 1989. Cognitive consequences: Goody, 1977; Goody, 1986.

7   Paradoxes of religion and philosophy, connection with mysticism: Pyysiäinen, 1996.

8   Hindu distinction between general and local. Parry, 1985, p. 204.

9   Local and Sanskrit gods: Fuller, 1992 p. 256.

10 Original debates about the 'great' and 'small' traditions: Marriott, 1955, Dumont, 1959.

11 Imagistic and doctrinal modes of religiosity: Whitehouse, 1995; Whitehouse, 2000.

12 Social groups as essence-based: Atran, 1990; Boyer, 1990; Rothbart and Taylor, 1990; more thorough treatment and more evidence: Gil-White, 2001.

13 Discrimination based on arbitrary groups in the lab: Tajfel, 1970.

14 Groupishness: Ridley, 1996.

15 Studies of prejudice in social psychology: Fiske, 2000b. Domination and coalitions: Sidanius and Pratto, 1999.

16 General coalitional reasoning: Kurzban, 1999; in clandestine warfare: Bell, 1999.

Chapter Nine

1   Nozick, 1974.

2   Consensus effect, princeps article: Asch, 1955. False consensus: Ross, Greene and House, 1977; its development in children: Wetzel and Walton, 1985. Survey of generation effect: Burns, 1990; illustration in Peynircioglu and Mungan, 1993. Memory illusions in general: Roediger and McDermott, 1995; Roediger, 1996. Effect of imaginings on illusory memory: Goff and Roediger, 1998. Source monitoring problems: Mitchell and Johnson, 2000. Illustration with cross-modality illusory memory: Henkel, Franklin and Johnson, 2000. Confirmation bias: Wason and Johnson-Laird, 1972; in scientists Mynatt, Doherty and Tweney, 1977. Cognitive dissonance: Festinger, Riecken and Schachter, 1956.

3   Religious experience: James, 1972; on persistence of this stance: Taves, 1999.

4   Survey of psychology of religious experience: Argyle, 1990. On some variants of Buddhism as influenced by Western preoccupation with experience: Sharf, 1998.

5   Survey of special experience and religion: Bourguigon, 1973. Of neuro-psychological evidence: Newberg and D'Aquili, 1998. Self-awareness and religious feelings: Craik et al., 1999. Neuro-physiology of near-death and

out of body experience: Persinger, 1995; Persinger, 1999.

6   Factors relevant to individual belief: Batson, Shoenrade and Ventis, 1993, pp. 81–115.

7   Modern conditions do not require more rational or scientific outlook: Gellner, 1992. Science as unnatural: Wolpert, 1992. 'Naturalness' of religion and 'unnaturalness' of science: McCauley, 2000.

8   Liberation scenarios: Donald, 1991. Perspective-taking as crucial: Tomasello, Kruger and Ratner, 1993. Flexibility of modular architecture: Mithen, 1996; general discussion: Boyer, 1998.

Bibliographical References

Anderson, D. N. (1988) 'The delusion of inanimate doubles: Implications for understanding the Capgras phenomenon', *British Journal of Psychiatry*, 153, pp. 694–9.

Anttonen, V. (2000) 'Sacred', in W. Braun and R. McCutcheon (eds.), *Guide to the Study of Religion* (London and NY: Cassell), pp. 271–82.

Argyle, M. (1990) 'The psychological explanation of religious experience', *Psyke and Logos*, 11(2), pp. 267–74.

Asch, S. E. (1955) 'Opinions and social pressure', *Scientific American*, 193(5), pp. 31–5.

Atran, S. (1990) *Cognitive Foundations of Natural History. Towards an Anthropology of Science* (Cambridge: Cambridge University Press).

—— (1994) 'Core domains versus scientific theories: Evidence from systematics and Itza-Maya folkbiology', in L. A. Hirschfeld, S. A. Gelman et al. (eds.), *Mapping the Mind: Domain Specificity in Cognition and Culture* (NY: Cambridge University Press), pp. 316–40.

— (1996) 'From folk biology to scientific biology', in D. R. Olson, N. Torrance et al. (eds.), *The Handbook of Education and Human Development· New Models of Learning, Teaching and Schooling* (Oxford: Blackwells), pp. 646–82.

— (1998) 'Folk biology and the anthropology of science: Cognitive universals and cultural particulars. *Behavioral and Brain Sciences*, 21(4), pp. 547–609.

Bacharach, M. and Gambetta, D. (1999) 'Trust in signs', in K. Cook (ed.), *Trust and Social Structure* (NY: Russell Sage Foundation).

Barkow, J., Cosmides, L. and Tooby, J. (eds.) (1992) *The Adapted Mind: Evolutionary Psychology and the Generation of Culture* (NY: Oxford University Press).

Baron-Cohen, S. (1995) *Mindblindness: An Essay on Autism and Theory of Mind* (Cambridge, MA: MIT Press).

Baron-Cohen, S., Leslie, A. and Frith, U. (1985) 'Does the autistic child have a "theory of mind"?', *Cognition*, pp. 21, 37–46.

Barrett, H. C. (1999) 'Human cognitive adaptations to predators and prey', doctoral dissertation (Santa Barbara: University of California).

Barrett, J. L. (1996) 'Anthropomorphism, intentional agents, and conceptualizing God', unpublished PhD dissertation (Ithaca, NY: Cornell University).

— (2000) 'Exploring the natural foundations of religion', *Trends in Cognitive Science*, 4(1), pp. 29–34.

Barth, F. (1975) *Ritual and Knowledge Among the Baktaman of New Guinea* (Oslo and New Haven, Conn.: Universitetsforlaget and Yale University Press).

Barton, R. A. (2000) 'Primate brain evolution: Cognitive demands of foraging or of social life?', in S. Boinski, P. A. Garber et al. (eds.), *On the Move: How and Why Animals Travel in Groups* (Chicago: University of Chicago Press), pp. 204–37.

Bastien, J. W. (1978) *Mountain of the Condor. Metaphor and Ritual in an Andean Ayllu* (St Paul: West Publishing Co.).

Batson, C. D., Shoenrade, P. and Ventis, W. L. (1993) *Religion and* the Individual. A Socio-Psychological Perspective (NY: Oxford University Press).

Baumgart, F., Gaschler-Markefski, B., Woldorff, M. G., Heinze, H.-J. and Scheich, H. (1999) 'A movement-sensitive area in auditory cortex', *Nature*, 400(6746), pp. 724–6.

Beatty, A. (1999) *Varieties of Javanese Religion* (Cambridge: Cambridge University Press).

Bell, J. B. (1999) *The Dynamics of the Armed Struggle* (London: Frank Cass).

Bentin, S., Deouell, L. Y. and Soroker, N. (1999) 'Selective visual streaming in face recognition: Evidence from developmental prosopagnosia', *Neuroreport*, 10, pp. 823–7.

Bliem, H. and Danek, A. (1999) 'Direct evidence for a consistent dissociation between structural facial discrimination and facial individuation in prosopagnosia', *Brain and Cognition*, 40, pp. 48–52.

Bloch, M. (1974) 'Symbols, song, dance, and features of articulation: Is religion an extreme form of traditional authority?', *European Journal of Sociology*, 15, pp. 56–81.

—— (1982) 'Death, women and power', in M. Bloch and J. Parry (eds.), *Death and the Regeneration of Life* (Cambridge: Cambridge University Press), pp. 211–30.

—— (1992) *Prey into Hunter. The Politics of Religious Experience* (Cambridge: Cambridge University Press).

Bloch, M. and Parry, J. (eds.) (1982) *Death and the Regeneration of Life* (Cambridge: Cambridge University Press).

Bloom, P. (1998) 'Theories of artefact categorization', *Cognition*, 66, pp. 87–93.

Bourguigon, E. (ed.) (1973) *Religion, Altered States of Consciousness and Social Change* (Columbus, OH: Ohio State University Press).

Bowen, J. R. (1997) *Religions in Practice: An Approach to the Anthropology of Religion* (NY: Prentice Hall).

Boyd, R. (1988) 'Is the repeated prisoner's dilemma a good model of reciprocal altruism?', *Ethology and Sociobiology*, 9(2–4), pp. 211–22.

Boyd, R. and Richerson, P. J. (1990) 'Culture and cooperation', in J. J. Mansbridge et al. (eds.), *Beyond Self-Interest* (Chicago: University of Chicago Press), pp. 111–32.

— (1992) 'Punishment allows the evolution of cooperation (or anything else) in sizable groups', *Ethology and Sociobiology*, 13(3), pp. 171–95.

— (1995) 'Why does culture increase adaptability?', *Ethology and Sociobiology*, 16(2), pp. 126–43.

Boyer, P. (1994) 'Cognitive constraints on cultural representations: Natural ontologies and religious ideas', in L. A. Hirschfeld and S. Gelman (eds.), *Mapping the Mind: Domain-specificity in Culture and Cognition* (NY: Cambridge University Press).

— (1998) 'Cognitive tracks of cultural inheritance: How evolved intuitive ontology governs cultural transmission', *American Anthropologist*, 100, pp. 876–89.

Bradbury, J. W. and Vehrencamp, S. L. (2000) 'Economic models of animal communication', *Animal Behaviour*, 59(2), pp. 259–68.

Buchowski, M. (1997) *The Rational Other* (Poznan, Poland: Wydawnitcwo Fundacji Humaniora).

Burkert, W. (1996) *Creation of the Sacred: Tracks of Biology in Early Religions* (Cambridge, MA.: Harvard University Press).

Burns, D. J. (1990) 'The generation effect: A test between single- and multifactor theories', *Journal of Experimental Psychology: Learning, Memory, and Cognition*, 16(6), pp. 1060–67.

Buss, D. (1989) 'Sex differences in human mate preferences: Evolutionary hypotheses tested in 37 cultures', *Behavioral and Brain Sciences*, 12, pp. 1–49.

— (1997) 'Human social motivation in evolutionary perspective: Grounding terror management theory', *Psychological Inquiry*, 8(1), pp. 22–6.

— (1999) *Evolutionary Psychology: The New Science of the Mind* (Boston, MA: Allyn and Bacon, Inc.).

— (2000) *The Dangerous Passion: Why Jealousy is as necessary as Love and Sex* (NY: Free Press).

Byrne, R. W. and Whiten, A. (eds.) (1988) *Machiavellian Intelligence: Social Expertise and the Evolution of Intellect in Monkeys, Apes, and Humans* (Oxford: Clarendon Press/Oxford University Press).

Cavalli-Sforza, L. L. and Feldman, M. W. (1981) *Cultural Transmission and Evolution: A Quantitative Approach* (Princeton, NJ: Princeton University Press).

Cederroth, S., Corlin, C. and Linstrom, J. (eds.) (1988) *On the Meaning of Death. Essays on Mortuary Rituals and Eschatological Beliefs* (Uppsala: Almqvist and Wiksell).

Colas, E. (1998) *Just Checking. Scenes from the Life of an Obsessive-Compulsive* (NY: Pocket Books).

Coley, J. D., Medin, D. L., Proffitt, J. B., Lynch, E. and Atran, S. (1999) 'Inductive reasoning in folkbiological thought', in D. L. Medin, S. Atran et al. (eds.), *Folkbiology* (Cambridge, MA: MIT Press), pp. 206–32.

Cosmides, L. and Tooby, J. (1989) 'Evolutionary psychology and the generation of culture: II. Case study: A computational theory of social exchange', *Ethology and Sociobiology*, 10(1–3), pp. 51–97.

— (1992) 'Cognitive adaptations for social exchange', in J. H. Barkow, L. Cosmides and J. Tooby (eds.), *The Adapted Mind: Evolutionary Psychology and the Generation of Culture* (NY: Oxford University Press), pp. 163–228.

Craik, F. I. M., Moroz, T. M., Moscovitch, M., Stuss, D. T., Winocur, G., Tulving, E. and Kapur, S. (1999) 'In search of the self: A PET study', *Psychological Science*, 10, pp. 26–34.

Crawford, C. B. and Krebs, D. L. (eds.) (1998) *Handbook of Evolutionary Psychology: Ideas, Issues, and Applications* (Mahwah, NJ: Lawrence Erlbaum Associates, Inc.).

Crawford, C. B., Salter, B. E. and Jang, K. L. (1989) 'Human grief: Is its intensity related to the reproductive value of the deceased?', *Ethology and Sociobiology*, 10(4), pp. 297–307.

Cronk, L. (1999) *That Complex Whole. Culture and the Evolution of Behavior* (Boulder, CO: Westview Press).

Daly, M. and Wilson, M. (1988) *Homicide* (NY: Aldine).

Daniel, S. B. (1983) 'Tool box approach of the Tamil to the issues of moral responsibility and human destiny', in C. F. Keyes and E. V. Daniel (eds), *Karma. An Anthropological Inquiry* (Berkeley and Los Angeles: University of California Press), pp. 28–62.

Davidson, I. and Noble, W. (1989) 'The archaeology of perception: traces of depiction and language', *Current Anthropology*, 30, pp. 126–55.

Davies, J. (1999) *Death, Burial and Rebirth in the Religions of Antiquity* (Religion in the First Christian Centuries) (London: Routledge).

Dawkins, R. (1976) *The Selfish Gene* (NY: Oxford University Press).

— (1998) *Unweaving the Rainbow: Science, Delusion, and the Appetite for Wonder* (Boston: Houghton Mifflin).

De Renzi, E. and di Pellegrino, G. (1998) 'Prosopagnosia and alexia without object agnosia', *Cortex*, 34, pp. 403–15.

Decety, J. (1996) 'The neurophysiological basis of motor imagery', *Behavioural Brain Research*, 77(1–2), pp. 46–52.

Decety, J. and Grezes, J. (1999) 'Neural mechanisms subserving the perception of human actions', *Trends in Cognitive Sciences*, 3, pp. 172–8.

DeFrancis, J. (1989) *Visible Speech. The Diverse Oneness of Writing Systems* (Honolulu: University of Hawaii Press).

Dennett, D. C. and Weiner, P. (1991) *Consciousness Explained* (Boston, MA: Little, Brown and Co.).

Dissanayake, E. (1992) *Homo Aestheticus. Where Art Comes From and Why* (NY: Free Press).

Donald, M. (1991) *Origins of the Modern Mind* (Cambridge, MA: Harvard University Press).

Dulaney, S. and Fiske, A. P. (1994) 'Cultural rituals and obsessive-compulsive disorder: Is there a common psychological mechanism?', *Ethos*, 22(3), pp. 243–83.

Dumont, L. (1959) 'On the different aspects or levels of Hinduism', *Contributions to Indian Sociology*, 3, pp. 40–54.

Durham, W. H. (1991) *Coevolution. Genes, Cultures and Human Diversity* (Stanford, CA: Stanford University Press).

Edelstyn, N. M. J. and Oyebode, F. (1999) 'A review of the phenomenology and cognitive neuropsychological origins of the Capgras syndrome', *International Journal of Geriatric Psychiatry*, 14(1), pp. 48–59.

Eisen, J. L., Phillips, K. and Rasmussen, S. A. (1999) 'Obsessions and delusions: The relationship between obsessive-compulsive disorder and the psychotic disorders', *Psychiatric Annals*, 29, pp. 516–22.

Eliade, M. (1959) *The Sacred and the Profane. The Nature of Religion* (NY: Harcourt Brace Jovanovich).

Elman, J. L., Bates, E. A., Johnson, M. H. and Karmiloff-Smith, A. (1996) *Rethinking Innateness: A Connectionist Perspective on Development* (Cambridge, MA: MIT Press).

Endicott, K. (1979) *Batek Negrito Religion* (Oxford: Clarendon Press).

Farah, M. J., Wilson, K. D., Drain, H. M. and Tanaka, J. R. (1995) 'The inverted face inversion effect in prosopagnosia: Evidence for mandatory, face-specific perceptual mechanisms', *Vision Research*, 35, pp. 2089–93.

Fauconnier, G. and Turner, M. (1998) 'Conceptual integration networks', *Cognitive Science*, 22(2), pp. 133–87.

Favret-Saada, J. (1980) *Deadly Words: Witchcraft in the Bocage* (Cambridge: Cambridge University Press).

Fernandez, J. (1982) *Bwiti. An Ethnography of the Religious Imagination in Africa* (Princeton, NJ: Princeton University Press).

Festinger, L., Riecken, H. W. and Schachter, S. (1956) *When Prophecy Fails* (Minneapolis: University of Minnesota Press).

Fiddick, L., Cosmides, L. and Tooby, J. (2000) 'No interpretation without representation: The role of domain-specific representations and inferences in the Wason selection task', *Cognition*, 77(1), pp. 1–79.

Fiske, A. P. (2000a) 'Complementarity theory: Why human social capacities evolved to require cultural complements', *Personality and Social Psychology Review*, 4(1), pp. 76–94.

Fiske, A. P. and Haslam, N. (1997) 'Is obsessive-compulsive disorder a pathology of the human disposition to perform socially meaningful rituals? Evidence of similar content', *Journal of Nervous and Mental Disease*, 185(4), pp. 211–22.

Fiske, S. T. (2000b) 'Stereotyping, prejudice, and discrimination at the seam between the centuries: Evolution, culture, mind, and brain', *European Journal of Social Psychology*, 30(3), pp. 299–322.

Fletcher, P. C., Happe, F., Frith, U. and Baker, S. C. (1995) 'Other minds in the brain: A functional imaging study of "theory of mind" in story comprehension', *Cognition*, 57(2), pp. 109–28.

Florian, V. and Mikulincer, M. (1997) 'Fear of death and the judgment of social transgressions: A multidimensional test of terror management theory', *Journal of Personality and Social Psychology*, 73(2), pp. 369–80.

— (1998) 'Terror management in childhood: Does death conceptualization moderate the effects of mortality salience on acceptance of similar and different others?', *Personality and Social Psychology Bulletin*, 24(10), pp. 1104–12.

Fortes, M. (1987) *Religion, Morality and the Person. Essays on Tallensi Religion* (Cambridge: Cambridge University Press).

Forth, G. (1998) 'On deer and dolphin: Nage ideas regarding animal transformation', *Oceania*, 68, pp. 271–93.

Frank, R. (1988) *Passions within Reason. The Strategic Role of the Emotions* (NY: Norton).

Frazer, J. G. (1911) *The Golden Bough; A Study in Magic and Religion* (3rd edn; London: Macmillan).

Frith, C. D. and Corcoran, R. (1996) 'Exploring "theory of mind" in people with schizophrenia', *Psychological Medicine*, 26, pp. 521–30.

Fuller, C. J. (1992) *The Camphor Flame. Popular Hinduism and Society in India* (Princeton, NJ: Princeton University Press).

Gambetta, D. (1994) 'Godfather's gossip', *Archives Européennes de Sociologie*, 35, pp. 199–223.

Garcia, J. and Koelling, R. (1966) 'Relations of cue to consequence in avoidance learning', *Psychonomic Science*, 4, pp. 123–4.

Gargett, R. H. (1999) 'Middle Paleolithic burial is not a dead issue: The view from Qafzeh, Saint-Cesaire, Kebara, Amud and Dedriyeh', *Journal of Human Evolution*, 37, pp. 27–90.

Gellner, E. (1992) *Postmodernism, Reason and Religion* (London and NY: Routledge).

Gelman, R., Spelke, E. and Meck, E. (1983) 'What preschoolers know about animate and inanimate objects', in D. Rogers and J. A. Sloboda (eds.), *The Acquisition of Symbolic Skills* (London: Plenum).

Gelman, S. A. and Bloom, P. (2000) 'Young children are sensitive to how an object was created when deciding what to name it', *Cognition*, 76(2), pp. 91–103.

Gelman, S. A. and Wellmann, H. M. (1991) 'Insides and essence: Early understandings of the non-obvious', *Cognition*, 38(3), pp. 213–44.

Gibbs, J. C. (1991) 'Toward an integration of Kohlberg's and Hoffman's moral development theories. Special Section: Intersecting conceptions of morality and moral development', *Human Development*, 34(2), pp. 88–104.

Gibson, T. (1986) *Sacrifice and Sharing in the Philippine Highlands* (London: Athlone).

Gil-White, F. (2001) 'Are ethnic groups "species" to the human brain? Essentialism in our cognition of some social categories', *Current Anthropology*, forthcoming.

Goff, L. and Roediger, H. L. I. (1998) 'Imagination inflation for action events: Repeated imaginings lead to illusory recollections', *Memory and Cognition*, 26, pp. 20–33.

Goody, J. (1962) *Death, Property and the Ancestors; a Study of the Mortuary Customs of the LoDagaa of West Africa* (Stanford, CA: Stanford University Press).

Goody, J. R. (1977) *The Domestication of the Savage Mind* (Cambridge: Cambridge University Press).

— (1986) *The Logic of Writing and the Organization of Society*

(Cambridge: Cambridge University Press).

Gopnik, A. and Meltzoff, A. N. (1997) *Words, Thoughts and Theories* (Cambridge, MA: MIT Press).

Gopnik, A., Meltzoff, A. N. and Kuhl, P. K. (1999) *The Scientist in the Crib: Minds, Brains, and How Children Learn* (1st edn; NY: William Morrow and Co.).

Guthrie, S. E. (1993) *Faces in the Clouds. A New Theory of Religion* (NY: Oxford University Press).

Habib, M. (1986) 'Visual hypoemotionality and prosopagnosia associated with right temporal lobe isolation', *Neuropsychologia*, 24(4), pp. 577–82.

Halpern, A. R. and Zatorre, R. J. (1999) 'When that tune runs through your head: A PET investigation of auditory imagery for familiar melodies', *Cerebral Cortex*, 9(7), pp. 697–704.

Halverson, J. (1992) 'Paleolithic art and cognition', *Journal of Psychology*, 126(3), pp. 221–36.

Hamayon, R. (1990) *La Chasse à l'âme: esquisse d'une théorie du chamanisme sibérien* (Nanterre: Société d'Ethnologie).

Hamilton, W. D. (1964) 'The general evolution of social behavior (I and II)', *Journal of Theoretical Biology*, 7, pp. 1–52.

Harcourt, A. H. and de Waal, F. B. (eds.) (1992) *Coalitions and Alliances in Humans and Other Animals* (Oxford: Oxford University Press).

Hartcup, A. (1980) *Below Stairs in the Great Country Houses* (London: Sidgwick and Jackson).

Hauser, M. D. (2000) 'The sound and the fury: Primate vocalizations as reflections of emotion and thought', in N. L. Wallin, B. Merker et al. (eds.), *The Origins of Music* (Cambridge, MA: MIT Press), pp. 77–102.

Haviland, J. B. (1977) *Gossip, Reputation, and Knowledge in Zinacantan* (Chicago: University of Chicago Press).

Hayden, B. (1993) 'The cultural capacities of Neanderthals: A review and re-evaluation', *Journal of Human Evolution*, 24, pp. 113–46.

Henke, K., Schweinberger, S. R., Grigo, A., Klos, T. and Sommer, W. (1998) 'Specificity of face recognition: Recognition of exemplars of non-face objects in prosopagnosia', *Cortex*, 34, pp. 289–96.

Henkel, L. A., Franklin, N. and Johnson, M. K. (2000) 'Cross-modal source monitoring confusions between perceived and imagined events', *Journal of Experimental Psychology: Learning, Memory, and Cognition*, 26(2), pp. 321–35.

Hertz, R. (1960) *A Contribution to the Study of the Collective Representation of Death* (London: Cohen and West).

Hirschfeld, L. A. (1986) 'Kinship and cognition. Genealogy and the meaning of kinship terms', *Current Anthropology*, 27, p. 235.

— (1993) 'Discovering social difference: The role of appearance in the development of racial awareness', *Cognitive Psychology*, 25, pp. 317–50.

— (1996) *Race in the Making: Cognition, Culture and the Child's Construction of Human Kinds* (Cambridge, MA: MIT Press).

Hirschfeld, L. A. and Gelman, S. A. (1999) 'How biological is essentialism?', in S. Atran and D. L. Medin (eds.), *Folkbiology* (Cambridge, MA: MIT Press).

Houseman, M. (1993) 'The interactive basis of ritual effectiveness in male initiation rite', in P. Boyer (ed.), *Cognitive Aspects of Religious Symbolism* (Cambridge: Cambridge University Press), pp. 207–24.

Houseman, M. and Severi, C. (1998) *Naven and Ritual* (Leiden: Brill).

Humphrey, C. and Laidlaw, J. (1993) *Archetypal Actions. A Theory of Ritual as a Mode of Action and the Case of the Jain Puja* (Oxford: Clarendon Press).

Humphrey, N. (1996) *Leaps of Faith: Science, Miracles, and the Search for Supernatural Consolation* (NY: BasicBooks).

Hutchison, W. D., Davis, K. D., Lozano, A. M., Tasker, R. R. and Dostrovsky, J. O. (1999) 'Pain-related neurons in the human cingulate cortex', *Nature Neuroscience*, 2(5), pp. 403–5.

James, W. (1972 [1902]) *Varieties of Religious Experience* (London: Fontana).

— (1988) *The Listening Ebony: Moral Knowledge, Religion, and Power Among the Uduk of Sudan* (Oxford and NY: Clarendon Press/Oxford University Press).

Jeannerod, M. (1994) 'The representing brain: Neural correlates of motor intention and imagery', *Behavioral and Brain Sciences*, 17(2), pp. 187–245.

Jerison, H. (2000) 'Paleoneurology and the biology of music', in N. L. Wallin, B. Merker et al. (eds.), *The Origins of Music* (Cambridge, MA: MIT Press), pp. 176–96.

Kaas, J. H. and Hackett, T. A. (1999) '"What" and "where" processing in auditory cortex', *Nature Neuroscience*, 2(12), pp. 1046–7.

Kaas, J. H., Hackett, T. A. and Tramo, M. J. (1999) 'Auditory processing in primate cerebral cortex', *Current Opinion in Neurobiology*, 9(2), pp. 164–70.

Kaiser, M. K., Jonides, J. and Alexander, J. (1986) 'Intuitive reasoning about abstract and familiar physics problems', *Memory and Cognition*, 14, pp. 308–12.

Kant, I. (1781) *Critik der reinen Vernunft* (Riga: Verlegts Johann Friedrich Hartknoch).

Kant, I. and Schmidt, R. (1990) *Kritik der Reinen Vernunft* (3rd edn; Hamburg: F. Meiner).

Kant, I. and Vorländer, K. (1963) *Kritik der Urteilskraft* (Hamburg: F. Meiner).

Katz, L. D. (ed.) (2000) *Evolutionary Origins of Morality: Cross-Disciplinary Perspectives* (Thorverton, UK: Imprint Academic).

Keesing, R. (1982) *Kwaio Religion. The Living and the Dead in a Solomon Island Society* (NY: Columbia University Press).

Keller, M., Eckensberger, L. H. and von Rosen, K. (1989) 'A critical note on the conception of preconventional morality: The case of stage 2 in Kohlberg's theory', *International Journal of Behavioral Development*, 12(1), pp. 57–69.

Kelly, M. and Keil, F. C. (1985) 'The more things change . . . Meta-morphoses and conceptual structure', *Cognitive Science*, 9, pp. 403–6.

Knight, C. (1999) 'Sex and language as pretend-play', in R. Dunbar, C. Knight and C. Power (eds.), *The Evolution of Culture* (New Brunswick, NJ: Rutgers University Press), pp. 228–50.

Krebs, D. and Rosenwald, A. (1994) 'Moral reasoning and moral behavior in conventional adults', in B. Puka et al. (eds.), *Fundamental Research in Moral Development* (NY: Garland Publishing, Inc.), pp. 111–21.

Krebs, D. L. and Van Hesteren, F. (1994) 'The development of altruism: Toward an integrative model', *Developmental Review*, 14(2), pp. 103–58.

Krebs, J. R. and Inman, A. J. (1994) 'Learning and foraging: Individuals, groups, and populations', in L. A. Real et al. (eds.), *Behavioral Mechanisms in Evolutionary Ecology* (Chicago: University of Chicago Press), pp. 46–65.

Kurzban, R. O. (1999) 'The social psychophysics of cooperation in groups', PhD dissertation (Santa Barbara: University of California).

Lambek, M. (1981) *Human Spirits: A Cultural Account of Trance in Mayotte* (Cambridge and NY: Cambridge University Press).

Lambrecht, F. (1938) *Death and Death Ritual* (Washington, DC: Catholic Anthropological Conference).

Lane, R. D. and Nadel, L. (eds.) (2000) *Cognitive Neuroscience of Emotion* (NY: Oxford University Press).

Lawson, E. T. and McCauley, R. (1990) *Rethinking Religion: Connecting Culture and Cognition* (Cambridge: Cambridge University Press).

Leafhead, K. M. and Kopelman, M. D. (1997) 'Face memory impairment in the Cotard delusion', in A. J. Parkin et al. (eds.), *Case Studies in the Neuropsychology of Memory* (Hove, UK: Psychology Press/Erlbaum (UK) Taylor and Francis), pp. 166–77.

Leary, M. R. and Schreindorfer, L. S. (1997) 'Unresolved issues with terror management theory', *Psychological Inquiry*, 8(1), pp. 26–9.

LeCroy, D. and Müller, P. (eds.) (2000) *Evolutionary Perspectives on Human Reproductive Behavior* (NY: New York Academy of Sciences).

Leslie, A. (1987) 'Pretense and representation: the origins of "Theory of Mind"', *Psychological Review*, 94, pp. 412–26.

— (1994) 'Pretending and believing: Issues in the theory of ToMM', *Cognition*, 50(1–3), pp. 211–38.

Leuchstag, E. (1958) *With a King in the Clouds* (London: Hutchinson).

Lewis, J. R. (ed.) (1995) *The Gods have Landed. New Religions from Other Worlds* (Albany, NY: State University of New York Press).

Lieberman, J. D. (1999) 'Terror management, illusory correlation, and perceptions of minority groups', *Basic and Applied Social Psychology*, 21(1), pp. 13–23.

Liegeois-Chauvel, C., de Graaf, J. B., Laguitton, V. and Chauvel, P. (1999) 'Specialization of left auditory cortex for speech perception in man depends on temporal coding', *Cerebral Cortex*, 9(5), pp. 484–96.

Lopez, A., Atran, S., Coley, J. D. and Medin, D. L. (1997) 'The tree of life: Universal and cultural features of folkbiological taxonomies and inductions', *Cognitive Psychology*, 32(3), pp. 251–95.

Luhrmann, T. (1989) *Persuasions of the Witch's Craft* (Oxford: Blackwell).

Lumsden, C. J. and Wilson, E. O. (1981) *Genes, Minds and Culture* (Cambridge, MA: Harvard University Press).

McCauley, R. N. (2000) 'The naturalness of religion and the unnaturalness of science', in F. Keil and R. Wilson (eds.), *Explanation and Cognition* (Cambridge, MA: MIT Press), pp. 61–85.

McGregor, H. A., Lieberman, J. D., Greenberg, J., Solomon, S., Arndt, J., Simon, L. and Pyszczynski, T. (1998) 'Terror management and aggression: Evidence that mortality salience motivates aggression against worldview-threatening others', *Journal of Personality and Social Psychology*, 74(3), pp. 590–605.

McNeil, J. E. and Warrington, E. K. (1993) 'Prosopagnosia: A face-specific disorder', *Quarterly Journal of Experimental Psychology, A Human Experimental Psychology*, vol. 46(A), pp. 1–10.

Maqsud, M. and Rouhani, S. (1990) 'Self-concept and moral reasoning among Batswana adolescents', *Journal of Social Psychology*, 130(6), pp. 829–30.

Marriott, M. (1955) 'Little communities in an Indegenous Civilization', in M. Marriott (ed.), *Studies in Socio-cultural Aspects of the Mediterranean Islands* (Chicago: University of Chicago Press), pp. 29–47.

Martin, A., Wiggs, C. L., Ungerleider, L. G. and Haxby, J. V. (1996) 'Neural correlates of category-specific knowledge', *Nature*, 379, pp. 649–52.

Matan, A. and Carey, S. (2000) 'Developmental changes within the core of artefact concepts', *Cognition* 78, pp. 1–26.

Meltzoff, A. (1994) 'Imitation, memory, and the representation of persons', *Infant Behavior and Development*, 17, pp. 83–99.

Meltzoff, A. and Moore, M. K. (1983) 'Newborn infants imitate adult facial gestures', *Child Development*, 54, pp. 702–9.

Metcalf, P. and Huntington, R. (1991) *Celebrations of Death. The Anthropology of Mortuary Ritual* (2nd edn; Cambridge: Cambridge University Press).

Michotte, A. (1963) *The Perception of Causality* (London: Methuen).

Millikan, R. G. (1998) 'A common structure for concepts of individuals, stuffs and real kinds: More Mama, more milk, more mouse', *Behavioral and Brain Sciences*, 21, pp. 56–100.

Mitchell, K. J. and Johnson, M. K. (2000) 'Source monitoring: Attributing mental experiences', in E. Tulving, F. I. M. Craik et al. (eds.), *The Oxford Handbook of Memory* (NY: Oxford University Press), pp. 179–95.

Mithen, S. (1996) *The Prehistory of the Mind* (London: Thames and Hudson).

— (1990) *Thoughtful Foragers. A Study of Prehistoric Decision-Making* (Cambridge: Cambridge University Press).

Morton, J. and Johnson, M. (1991) 'CONSPEC and CONLERN: A two-process theory of infant face-recognition', *Psychological Review*, 98, pp. 164–81.

Mynatt, C. R., Doherty, M. E. and Tweney, R. D. (1977) 'Confirmation bias in a simulated research environment: An experimental study of scientific inference', *Quarterly Journal of Experimental Psychology*, 29(1), pp. 86–95.

Nachson, I. (1995) 'On the modularity of face recognition: The riddle of domain specificity', Institute for Advanced Studies Workshop on Modularity and the Brain (1993, Jerusalem, Israel) *Journal of Clinical and Experimental Neuropsychology*, 17(2), pp. 256–75.

Needham, R. (1972) *Belief, Language and Experience* (Chicago: Chicago University Press).

Nemes, L. (1984) 'The development of the child's morality according to Jean Piaget's concept and in psychoanalytic theory', *Psyche: Zeitschrift fur Psychoanalyse und Ihre Anwendungen*, 38(4), pp. 344–59.

Newberg, A. B. and D'Aquili, E. G. (1998) 'The neuropsychology of spiritual experience', in H. G. Koenig et al. (eds.), *Handbook of Religion and Mental Health* (San Diego, CA: Academic Press, Inc.), pp. 76–94.

Nozick, R. (1974) *Anarchy, State, and Utopia* (NY: Basic Books).

Orbach, I., Talmon, O., Kedem, P. and Har-Even, D. (1987) 'Sequential patterns of five subconcepts of human and animal death in children', *Journal of the American Academy of Child and Adolescent Psychiatry*, 26(4), pp. 578–82.

Otto, R. (1959) *The Idea of the Holy* (London: Oxford University Press).

Parker, S. T. and McKinney, M. L. (1999) *Origins of Intelligence: The Evolution of Cognitive Development in Monkeys, Apes, and Humans* (Baltimore, MD: Johns Hopkins University Press).

Parry, J. (1985) 'The Brahmanical tradition and the technology of the intellect', in J. Overing (ed.), *Reason and Morality* (London: Tavistock).

—— (1995) *Death in Banaras* (Cambridge: Cambridge University Press).

Pascalis, O., de Schonen, S., Morton, J., Deruelle, C. et al. (1995) 'Mother's face recognition by neonates: A replication and an extension', *Infant Behavior and Development*, 18(1), pp. 79–85.

Persinger, M. A. (1995) 'Out-of-body-like experiences are more probable in people with elevated complex partial epileptic-like signs during periods of enhanced geomagnetic activity: A nonlinear effect', *Perceptual and Motor Skills*, 80(2), pp. 563–9.

—— (1999) 'Near-death experiences and ecstasy: A product of the organization of the human brain', in S. D. Sala et al. (eds.), *Mind Myths: Exploring Popular Assumptions About the Mind and Brain* (Chichester, UK: John Wiley and Sons Ltd), pp. 86–99.

Peynircioglu, Z. F. and Mungan, E. (1993) 'Familiarity, relative distinctiveness, and the generation effect', *Memory and Cognition*, 21(3), pp. 367–74.

Pocock, D. F. (1973) *Mind, Body and Wealth* (Oxford: Blackwell).

Povinelli, D. J. and Eddy, T. J. (1996) 'Chimpanzees: Joint visual attention', *Psychological Science*, 7(3), pp. 129–35.

Povinelli, D. J. and Preuss, T. M. (1995) 'Theory of mind: Evolutionary history of a cognitive specialization', *Trends in Neurosciences*, 18(9), pp. 418–24.

Preston, J. J. (1980) *Cult of the Goddess. Social and Religious Change in a Hindu Temple* (New Dehli: Vikas).

Profet, M. (1993) 'Pregnancy sickness as adaptation: A deterrent to maternal ingestion of teratogens', in J. Barkow, L. Cosmides and J. Tooby (eds.), *The Adapted Mind. Evolutionary Psychology and the Generation of Culture* (NY: Oxford University Press).

Pyszczynski, T., Greenberg, J. and Solomon, S. (1997) 'Why do we need what we need? A terror management perspective on the roots of human social motivation', *Psychological Inquiry*, 8(1), pp. 1–20.

Pyysiäinen, I. (1996) 'Jnanagarbha and the "God's-eye view"', *Asian Philosophy*, 6, pp. 197–206.

Rapoport, J. (1997) *The Boy Who Couldn't Stop Washing: The Experience and Treatment of Obsessive Compulsive Disorder* (NY: New American Library).

Rappaport, R. A. (1979) *Ecology, Meaning and Religion* (Berkeley, CA: North Atlantic Books).

Renault, B., Signoret, J.-L., Debruille, B., Breton, F. et al. (1989) 'Brain potentials reveal covert facial recognition in prosopagnosia', *Neuropsychologia*, 27(7), pp. 906–12.

Ridley, M. (1996) *The Origins of Virtue. Human Instincts and the Evolution of Cooperation* (NY: Penguin Books).

Rochat, P., Morgan, R. and Carpenter, M. (1997) 'Young infants' sensitivity to movement information specifying social causality', *Cognitive Development*, 12(4), pp. 441–65.

Roediger, H. L. I. (1996) 'Memory illusions', *Journal of Memory and Language*, 35, pp. 76–100.

Roediger, H. L. I. and McDermott, K. B. (1995) 'Creating false memories: Remembering words not presented in lists', *Journal of Experimental Psychology: Learning, Memory, and Cognition*, 21(4), pp. 803–14.

Rolls, E. T. (2000) 'Precis of "The Brain and Emotion"', *Behavioral and Brain Sciences*, 23, pp. 177–233.

Romanski, L. M., Tian, B., Fritz, J., Mishkin, M., Goldman-Rakic, P. S. and Rauschecker, J. P. (1999) 'Dual streams of auditory afferents target multiple domains in the primate prefrontal cortex', *Nature Neuroscience*, 2(12), pp. 1131–6.

Rosenblatt, A., Greenberg, J., Solomon, S. and Pyszczynski, T. (1989) 'Evidence for terror management theory: I. The effects of mortality salience on reactions to those who violate or uphold cultural values', *Journal of Personality and Social Psychology*, 57(4), pp. 681–90.

Ross, L., Greene, D. and House, P. (1977) 'The false consensus effect: An egocentric bias in social perception and attribution processes', *Journal of Experimental Social Psychology*, 13(3), pp. 279–301.

Rothbart, M. and Taylor, M. (1990) 'Category labels and social reality: Do we view social categories as natural kinds?', in K. F. G. Semin (ed.), *Language and Social Cognition* (London: Sage Publications).

Rowe, C. (1999) 'Receiver psychology and the evolution of multicomponent signals', *Animal Behaviour*, 58(5), pp. 921–31.

Rozin, P. (1976) 'The evolution of intelligence and access to the cognitive unconscious', in J. M. Sprague and A. N. Epstein (eds.), *Progress in Psychobiology and Physiological Psychology* (NY: Academic Press).

Rozin, P., Haidt, J. and McCauley, C. R. (1993) 'Disgust', in M. Lewis and J. M. Haviland (eds.), *Handbook of Emotions* (NY: Guildford Press).

Ruskin, J. (1871) *Fors clavigera. Letters to the Workmen and Labourers of Great Britain* (Orpington, UK: G. Allen).

Saler, B., Ziegler, C. A. and Moore, C. B. (1997) *UFO Crash at Roswell. The Genesis of a Modern Myth* (Washington DC: Smithsonian Institution).

Sales, A. de (1991) *Je suis ne de vos jeux de tambours. La religion chamanique des Magar du nord* (Nanterre: Société d'Ethnologie).

Sanderson, J. A. and Siegal, M. (1988) 'Conceptions of moral and social rules in rejected and nonrejected preschoolers', *Journal of Clinical Child Psychology*, 17(1), pp. 66–72.

Schelling, T. (1960) *The Strategy of Conflict* (Cambridge, MA: Harvard University Press).

Schimel, J., Simon, L., Greenberg, J., Pyszczynski, T., Solomon, S., Waxmonsky, J. and Arndt, J. (1999) 'Stereotypes and terror management: Evidence that mortality salience enhances stereotypic thinking and preferences', *Journal of Personality and Social Psychology*, 77(5), pp. 906–26.

Severi, C. (1993) 'Talking about souls', in P. Boyer (ed.), *Cognitive Aspects of Religious Symbolism* (Cambridge: Cambridge University

Press), pp. 166–81.

Sharf, R. H. (1998) 'Experience', in M. C. Taylor (ed.), *Critical Terms in Religious Studies* (Chicago: University of Chicago Press), pp. 94–116.

Sidanius, J. and Pratto, F. (1999) *Social Dominance. An Intergroup Theory of Social Oppression and Hierarchy* (Cambridge: Cambridge University Press).

Siegal, M. and Storey, R. M. (1985) 'Day care and children's conceptions of moral and social rules', *Child Development*, 56(4), pp. 1001–8.

Silk, J. B., Kaldor, E. and Boyd, R. (2000) 'Cheap talk when interests conflict', *Animal Behaviour*, 59(2), pp. 423–32.

Simons, D. J. and Keil, F. C. (1995) 'An abstract to concrete shift in the development of biological thought: The insides story', *Cognition*, 56(2), pp. 129–63.

Smetana, J. G., Kelly, M. and Twentyman, C. T. (1984) 'Abused, neglected, and nonmaltreated children's conceptions of moral and social-conventional transgressions', *Child Development*, 55(1), pp. 277–87.

Snow, A. J. (1922) 'A psychological basis for the origin of religion', *Journal of Abnormal Psychology and Social Psychology*, 17, pp. 254–60.

Somerfield, D. (1999) 'Capgras syndrome and animals', *International Journal of Geriatric Psychiatry*, 14(10), pp. 893–4.

Song, M.-J., Smetana, J. G. and Kim, S. Y. (1987) 'Korean children's conceptions of moral and conventional transgressions', *Developmental Psychology*, 23(4), pp. 577–82.

Sperber, D. (1975) *Rethinking Symbolism* (Cambridge: Cambridge University Press).

— (1985) 'Anthropology and psychology. Towards an epidemiology of representations', *Man*, 20, pp. 73–89.

— (1996) *Explaining Culture: A Naturalistic Approach* (Oxford: Blackwell).

Stewart, C. (1991) *Demons and the Devil: Moral Imagination in Modern*

Greek Culture (Princeton, NJ: Princeton University Press).

Stocking, G. W. (1984) *Functionalism Historicized: Essays on British Social Anthropology* (Madison, WI: University of Wisconsin Press).

— (1987) *Victorian Anthropology* (NY and London: Free Press and Collier Macmillan).

Stone, V. E., Baron-Cohen, S., Cosmides, L., Tooby, J. and Knight, R. T. (1997) 'Selective impairment of social inferences following orbitofrontal cortex damage', Paper presented at the Cognitive Science Society (US) Conference (19th): Stanford, CA.

Stringer, C. and Gamble, C. (1993) *In Search of the Neanderthals: Solving the Puzzle of Human Origins* (London: Thames and Hudson).

Sugiyama, L. (1996), 'In search of the adapted mind: Cross-cultural evidence for human cognitive adaptations among the Shiwiar of Ecuador and the Yora of Peru', unpublished PhD dissertation (Santa Barbara, CA: University of California).

Symons, D. (1979) *The Evolution of Human Sexuality* (NY: Oxford University Press).

Tajfel, H. (1970) 'Experiments in inter-group discrimination', *Scientific American*, 223, pp. 96–102.

Taves, A. (1999) *Fits, Trances, and Visions: Experiencing Religion and Explaning Experience from Wesley to James* (Princeton, NJ: Princeton University Press).

Taylor, M. (1999) *Imaginary Companions and the Children who Create Them* (NY: Oxford University Press).

Tisak, M. S. and Turiel, E. (1984) 'Children's conceptions of moral and prudential rules', *Child Development*, 55(3), pp. 1030–39.

— (1988) 'Variation in seriousness of transgressions and children's moral and conventional concepts', *Developmental Psychology*, 24(3), pp. 352–7.

Tomasello, M. (2000) *The Cultural Origins of Human Cognition* (Cambridge, MA: Harvard University Press).

Tomasello, M., Kruger, A. C. and Ratner, H. H. (1993) 'Cultural learning', *Behavioral and Brain Sciences*, 16, pp. 496–510.

Tooby, J. and DeVore, I. (1987) 'The reconstruction of hominid behavioral evolution through strategic modeling', in W. Kinzey (ed.), *Primate Models of Hominid Behavior* (NY: SUNY Press).

Trinkhaus, E. (1989) 'Comments on "Grave shortcomings; the evidence for Neanderthal burial" by R. H. Gargett', *Current Anthropology*, 30, pp. 183–5.

Trinkhaus, E. and Shipman, P. (1993) *The Neanderthals: Changing the Image of Mankind* (NY: Knopf).

Trivers, R. (1971) 'The evolution of reciprocal altruism', *Quarterly Review of Biology*, 46, pp. 36–57.

Tulving, E. (1983) *Elements of Episodic Memory* (Oxford: Oxford University Press).

Tulving, E. and Lepage, M. (2000) 'Where in the brain is the awareness of one's past?', in D. L. Schacter, E. Scarry et al. (eds.), *Memory, Brain, and Belief* (Cambridge, MA: Harvard University Press), pp. 208–28.

Turiel, E. (1983) *The Development of Social Knowledge. Morality and Convention* (Cambridge: Cambridge University Press).

— (1994) 'The development of social-conventional and moral concepts', in P. Bill (ed.), *Fundamental Research in Moral Development* [Moral development: A compendium, vol. 2] (NY: Garland Publishing, Inc.), pp. 256–92.

— (1998) 'The development of morality', in W. Damon (ed.), *Handbook of Child Psychology* [5th edn, vol. 3] (NY: Wiley), pp. 863–932.

Turner, M. (1996) *The Literary Mind* (NY: Oxford University Press).

Turner, M. and Fauconnier, G. (1995) 'Conceptual integration and formal expression', *Metaphor and Symbolic Activity*, 10(3), pp. 183–204.

Tylor, E. B. (1871) *Primitive Culture* (London: Murray).

van Schaik, C. P. and van Hooff, J. A. (1983) 'On the ultimate causes of primate social systems', *Behaviour*, 85(1–2), pp. 91–117.

Vidal, D. (1976) *Garcons et filles. Le passage a l'age d'homme chez les Gbaya Kara* (Nanterre, France: Laboratoire d'Ethnologie et de Sociologie Comparative).

Viveiros de Castro, E. (1992) *From the Enemy's Point of View. Humanity and Divinity in an Amazonian Society* (Chicago: University of Chicago Press).

Wacholtz, E. (1996) 'Can we learn from the clinically significant face processing deficits, prosopagnosia and Capgras delusion?', *Neuropsychology Review*, 6, pp. 203–57.

Walker, S. J. (1992) 'Supernatural beliefs, natural kinds, and conceptual structure', *Memory and Cognition*, 20(6), pp. 656–62.

Wallace, M. A. and Farah, M. J. (1992) 'Savings in relearning face-name associations as evidence for "covert recognition" in prosopagnosia', *Journal of Cognitive Neuroscience*, 4(2), pp. 150–54.

Ward, T. B. (1994) 'Structured imagination: The role of category structure in exemplar generation', *Cognitive Psychology*, 27(1), pp. 1–40.

Wason, P. C. and Johnson-Laird, P. N. (1972) *The Psychology of Reasoning: Structure and Content* (London: Batsford).

Watson, J. (1982) 'Of flesh and bones: The management of death pollution in Cantonese society', in M. Bloch and J. Parry (eds.), *Death and the Regeneration of Life* (Cambridge: Cambridge University Press), pp. 156–86.

Watts, I. (1999) 'The origin of symbolic culture', in R. Dunbar, C. Knight and C. Power (eds.), *The Evolution of Culture* (New Brunswick, NJ: Rutgers University Press), pp. 113–46.

Wetzel, C. G. and Walton, M. D. (1985) 'Developing biased social judgments: The false-consensus effect', *Journal of Personality and Social Psychology*, 49(5), pp. 1352–9.

Whitehouse, H. (1995) *Inside the Cult: Religious Innovation and Transmission in Papua New Guinea* (Oxford: Oxford University Press).

— (2000) *Arguments and icons. Divergent Modes of Religiosity* (Oxford: Oxford University Press).

Williams, G. (1966) *Adaptation and Natural Selection. A Critique of Some Current Evolutionary Thought* (Princeton, NJ: Princeton University Press).

Wilson, J. Q. (1993) *The Moral Sense* (NY: Free Press).

Wimmer, H., Gruber, S. and Perner, J. (1984) 'Young children's conception of lying: Lexical realism – moral subjectivism', *Journal of Experimental Child Psychology*, 37(1), pp. 1–30.

Wimmer, H. and Perner, J. (1983) 'Beliefs about beliefs: Representation and constraining function of wrong beliefs in young children's understanding of deception', *Cognition*, 13, pp. 103–28.

Wolpert, L. (1992) *The Unnatural Nature of Science* (London: Faber and Faber).

Wynn, K. (1990) 'Children's understanding of counting', *Cognition*, 36, pp. 156–93.

Index